William Stanley Jevons

Methods of Social Reform and Other Papers

William Stanley Jevons

Methods of Social Reform and Other Papers

ISBN/EAN: 9783337295578

Printed in Europe, USA, Canada, Australia, Japan

Cover: Foto ©Suzi / pixelio.de

More available books at **www.hansebooks.com**

METHODS

OF

SOCIAL REFORM

AND OTHER PAPERS

BY

W. STANLEY JEVONS, M.A., LL.D., F.R.S.

London
MACMILLAN AND CO.
1883

[All rights reserved.]

PREFACE.

A FEW words will explain that this volume is a collection of the Essays published under the title of "Methods of Social Reform" in *The Contemporary Review*, and of other papers and addresses on kindred subjects. They extend over a period of fifteen years, and I have given at the commencement of each paper the date at which it was written, as I have thought it better to arrange them as far as I could according to subjects rather than by date. It was my husband's intention to have republished these Essays himself, and with this view he had already revised two of them—"Experimental Legislation and the Drink Traffic," and "Amusements of the People;" to the latter he had added several new paragraphs. He would, I am sure, have carefully edited and revised the others in the same way, but they are now republished just as they were originally written. The Essay on "The Use and Abuse of Museums" has not before been published. It was chiefly written in 1881, for *The Contemporary Review*, but was laid aside from the pressure of other work, and I am unable to say the exact time at which it was finished. It still needs the final revision which he would have given before sending it to Press. The Lecture on "Industrial Partnerships" is referred to by Mr. Jevons in his book on "The State in Relation to Labour," * p. 144, where he says that he sees no reason to alter the opinions expressed in the Lecture in favour of Industrial Partnerships, in spite of the failure of the experimental trials of the system by Messrs. Henry Briggs & Co., Messrs. Fox, Head & Co., and others.

HARRIET A. JEVONS.

2, THE CHESTNUTS, HAMPSTEAD.
    April, 1883.

---

* English Citizen Series. Macmillan & Co. 1882.

CONTENTS.

	PAGE
AMUSEMENTS OF THE PEOPLE	1
THE RATIONALE OF FREE PUBLIC LIBRARIES	28
THE USE AND ABUSE OF MUSEUMS	53
"CRAM"	82
TRADES SOCIETIES: THEIR OBJECTS AND POLICY	101
ON INDUSTRIAL PARTNERSHIPS	122
MARRIED WOMEN IN FACTORIES	156
MANCHESTER STATISTICAL SOCIETY—INAUGURAL ADDRESS	180
BRITISH ASSOCIATION — OPENING ADDRESS AS PRESIDENT OF SECTION F (ECONOMIC SCIENCE AND STATISTICS)	194
CRUELTY TO ANIMALS—A STUDY IN SOCIOLOGY	217
ON THE UNITED KINGDOM ALLIANCE AND ITS PROSPECTS OF SUCCESS	236
EXPERIMENTAL LEGISLATION AND THE DRINK TRAFFIC	253

		PAGE
ON THE ANALOGY BETWEEN THE POST OFFICE, TELEGRAPHS, AND OTHER SYSTEMS OF CONVEYANCE OF THE UNITED KINGDOM, AS REGARDS GOVERNMENT CONTROL	. . . .	277
THE POST OFFICE TELEGRAPHS AND THEIR FINANCIAL RESULTS	.	293
POSTAL NOTES, MONEY ORDERS, AND BANK CHEQUES	. .	307
A STATE PARCEL POST	. . . .	324
THE RAILWAYS AND THE STATE	. .	353

METHODS OF SOCIAL REFORM.

AMUSEMENTS OF THE PEOPLE.*

The possible Methods by which we may hope to accomplish Social Reform are almost infinite in number and variety. As society becomes more complex and the forms of human activity multiply, so must multiply also the points at which careful legislation and continuous social effort are required to prevent abuse, and secure the best utilisation of resources. Nor are these Methods of Social Reform to be regarded as alternatives, one or other or a few of which are to be considered sufficient. They are to be advocated and adopted conjunctively, not disjunctively. Each and all must be brought into simultaneous play, if any considerable effect is to be produced. It is common to hear social reformers express disappointment that their efforts seem to bear such slight results. Schools have been built, penny readings started, penny banks, libraries, and various useful institutions established, and yet crime and ignorance and drunkenness show no apparent diminution—nay, sometimes they show an increase.

But it is altogether a mistake to suppose that a few Methods of Social Reform, almost casually adopted according to the crotchets of the reformer, can be expected to make any serious impression upon the bad habits of a population—habits

---

* "Contemporary Review," October, 1878, vol. xxxiii., pp. 498–513.

which have become confirmed during centuries of ignorance and mistaken legislation. Time must be a great element in social reform, and it is hardly to be expected that any great change can become manifest in less than the thirty years during which a new generation displaces the older one. But in addition to this consideration, we must remember that it is of comparatively little good to close some flood-gates, while others are left wide open. If from ignorance or neglect, or, it may be, from sinister motives, we leave many of the more important causes of social mischief in full operation, it is quite likely that our efforts in other directions, however meritorious in themselves, will be neutralised. What is needed among social reformers is a long pull, and a strong pull, and especially a pull all together. Each individual may, according to his tastes and prejudices, choose his own strand of the rope, and exert his own force entirely upon that, if he likes; but he must not suppose that he alone can do any appreciable part of the work. He must be tolerant then of the different, or, it may sometimes appear, the inconsistent efforts of others. And it would be well that he should keep his mind open to conviction, that there are other directions in which his efforts might be much more advantageously devoted. If the citadel of poverty and ignorance and vice is to be taken at all, it must be besieged from every point of the compass—from below, from above, from within; and no kind of arm must be neglected which will tend to secure the ultimate victory of morality and culture.

It is obvious, of course, that in any single article it is impossible to treat of more than one Method of Social Reform. In selecting, for the subject of the present article, Public Amusements, I must not be supposed to attribute to it any exclusive or disproportionate weight. Nevertheless, there is hardly any other Method, taken separately, to which greater importance should be attributed than to the providing of good moral public amusements, especially musical entertainments. Up to quite recent years, the English people have, in this respect, been wofully backward, as compared with the more cultured Continental nations. There are still large parts of the manufacturing and more thickly populated districts of the kingdom where pure and rational recreation for the poorer classes can hardly be said to exist at all. The richer classes do not suffer much from this lack of local amusement. They take care to enjoy themselves in periodic visits to London, in tours abroad, or in residence at watering-places, where entertainments are provided. Their amusements on their own estates chiefly consist in shooting, and other forms of sport, in the prosecution of which they are led to exclude the mass of the people, even from the natural enjoyments of the air and the sun. It is hardly too much to say that the right to dwell freely in a grimy street, to drink freely in the neighbouring public-house, and to walk freely between the high-walled parks and the jealously preserved estates of our landowners, is all that the just and equal laws of England secure to the mass of the population.

England is traditionally called "Merrie England;" but there has always seemed to me to be something absurdly incongruous in the name at present. It is a case of anachronism, if not of sarcasm. England may have been merry in the days when the village green and the neighbouring common were still unenclosed; when the Maypole was set up, and the village fiddler and the old English sports were really existing institutions. But all that sort of thing is a matter of history. Popular festivals, fairs, wakes, and the like, have fallen into disuse or disrepute, and have to a great extent been suppressed by the magistrates, on the ground of the riotous and vicious assemblages which they occasioned.* There is no difficulty in seeing that there is a tendency, in England at least, to the progressive degradation of popular amusements.

* The fairs of London were for centuries places of popular enjoyment such as it was, but have been all long suppressed, on account of the riotous and dissolute proceedings which they occasioned. May Fair, now known only by the name of the fashionable spot where it existed, was suppressed in 1708; Bartholomew Fair, in spite of being occasionally presented by the grand jury as a nuisance, "next only to that of the playhouses," lingered on until it died out about fifty years ago, being gradually suppressed by the Corporation, who bought up the property.

Many opportunities of recreation have gone, for the same reason that May Fair, and Bartholomew Fair, and, within the last few years, Knott Mill Fair at Manchester, have gone. Horse-racing, indeed, still survives as a national sport, but it cannot long be tolerated, unless it be conducted with more regard to decency and morality. Already the so-called "gate-meetings" in the neighbourhood of the metropolis are denounced as "an intolerable nuisance," gathering together, as they do, the scum of the blackguardism and crime of London.*

But, if old amusements are by degrees to be suppressed, and no new ones originated, England must indeed be a dull England. Such it has, in fact, been for a length of time. Taking it on the average, England is as devoid of amusements as a country of such wealth can be. The people seem actually to have forgotten how to amuse themselves, so that when they do escape by an excursion train from their depressing alleys, there is no provision of music, no harmless games, nor other occupation for the vacant time. The unusual elevation of spirits which the fresh air occasions vents itself in horse-play and senseless vulgarity; and, in the absence of any counter-attraction, it is not surprising that the refreshment-bar and the nearest tap-room are the chief objects of attention.

I quite allow that when our English masses try to amuse themselves, they do it in such a clumsy and vulgar way as to disgust one with the very name of amusement. Witness the Bank Holidays on Hampstead Heath, where the best fun of the young men and women consists in squirting at each other with those detestable metal pipes which some base genius has invented. Then, again, what can be worse than the common run of London music-halls, where we have a nightly exhibition of all that is degraded in taste? Would that these halls were really music-halls! But the sacred name of music is defiled in its application to them. It passes the art of language to describe the mixture of inane songs, of senseless burlesques,

---

* Since the above was written these races have been either suppressed or regulated.

and of sensational acrobatic tricks, which make the staple of a music-hall entertainment. Under the present state of things, the most vulgar and vicious lead the taste, and the conductors of such establishments passively follow.

We value ourselves much upon our imagined superiority to other nations, and in some respects we really are superior. But my self-complacent feelings of national pride are always mortified when I go abroad, and am enabled to make direct comparison between English manners and Continental manners. And when I come back I feel still more mortified. For several years in succession it happened that I returned home from a tour in Norway or Sweden, so as to reach home by a Monday evening train travelling from Hull to Manchester. Perhaps Monday evening was an exceptionally bad time to enter the manufacturing districts, but certainly the contrast between the poor gentleman peasants of Scandinavia, and the rich, rowdy, drunken artisans of England, was something extremely painful. Of course, it is only a small percentage of the artisans, after all, who are really rowdy and drunken; but this percentage governs far too much the tone of public amusements. If, as is usually the case, we find foreign manners superior to English, it behoves us to inquire why. There is no wisdom in hiding our heads in our insular home, and pretending that we do not see the backward and uncultured character of that part of the population, at any rate, which obtrudes itself upon our notice. It is said that the term "gentleman" is a peculiarly English one, and that Continental nations have taken the name and the idea of the character from our nobility, who travel much abroad, and who often present, it must be allowed, excellent specimens of the gentleman. Fortunately our Continental neighbours do not travel in England so much as we travel abroad; and this accounts for the fact that they have not taken the name of "blackguard" from us. For I must confess that, in travels over several parts of the world, I have never met anything quite equal to the English blackguard. The American rowdy may be a more dangerous character in respect of his revolver and bowie knife, but he is, comparatively speaking, a man of refinement. Reform must begin with a true appreciation of the need of reform, and I do not think that those who will take the trouble personally to compare our popular amusements and assemblages, such as race-meetings, cheap trips, music-hall audiences, and the like, with the nearest corresponding manifestations in France, or Italy, or Denmark, or Sweden, or Germany, will think that I have used undue literary license in describing the difference.

Now I believe that this want of culture greatly arises from the fact that the amusements of the masses, instead of being cultivated, and multiplied, and refined, have been frowned upon and condemned, and eventually suppressed, by a dominant aristocracy. Amusement has been regarded as in itself almost sinful, and at the best as a necessary evil. Accordingly, villages and towns have grown up in the more populous parts of the kingdom absolutely devoid of any provision whatever for recreation. It seems to be thought that the end of life is accomplished if there be bread and beef to eat, beer to drink, beds to sleep in, and chapels and churches to attend on Sundays. The idea that the mass of the people might have their refined, and yet popular amusements, is only just dawning.* Strenuous workers no doubt the English people are; but all the more need there is in consequence that they should spend their surplus earnings wisely. As things are, they earn well, but they spend badly. The *fortiter in re* is theirs; but where is the *suaviter in modo* ? Too often the least tendency towards culture is condemned. If a factory-girl or a housemaid appears in a smart bonnet and a well-made dress, our high-class moralists object at once that

* The following abstract from a good legal authority of the last century puts this view of the matter in the most candid way, so as to need no comment. "Thus it appears by the common law, that a property in those living creatures, which, by reason of their swiftness or fierceness, were not naturally under the power of man, was gained by the mere caption or seizure of them, and that all men had an equal right to hunt and kill them. But, as by this toleration, persons of quality and distinction were deprived of their recreations and amusements, and idle and indigent people by their loss of time and pains in such pursuits were mightily injured, it was thought necessary to make laws for preserving game from the latter, and for the preservation of fish."— "Bacon's Abridgment," Art. *Game.* Gwillim's Edition.

she is aping her betters. How can good earnings be better spent than in aping your betters? How is real civilisation to be attained if the mere necessaries of life are to be good enough for the bulk of the people?

Among the means towards a higher civilisation, I unhesitatingly assert that the deliberate cultivation of public amusement is a principal one. Surely we may accept as an axiom that the average man or woman requires an average amount of recreation. At least it is not for our richer classes to say nay. The life of a young man or a young woman in aristocratic circles is one continuous round of varied amusements. Are we to allow that what is to them the perfection of existence is to have no counterpart whatever among the poor drudges of the farm or factory? Is it not all the more requisite that when there are few hours in the week to spare for recreation, those hours should be sweetened in the most wholesome and agreeable way? And as, by the progress of science and invention, those vacant hours are gradually prolonged, it becomes more and more requisite that provision should be made for their harmless occupation. The old idea of keeping people moral by keeping their noses to the grindstone must be abandoned. As things are going, people will, and, what is more, they ought to have all possible means of healthy recreation. The question is, the Free Library and the Newsroom *versus* the Public-house; and, as my more immediate subject, the well-conducted Concert-room *versus* the inane and vulgar Music-hall.

There is, indeed, a brighter side to this question than I have yet mentioned. All that I have been saying was more true of our population twenty or thirty years ago than it is now. What I shall advocate is mainly suggested by things already accomplished in one part of the country or another. I claim no originality for my remarks, unless perhaps it be that of treating the subject more seriously than is usual, and of insisting that popular amusements are no trivial matter, but rather one that has great influence on national manners and character.

The erection of the Crystal Palace forms an epoch in this

subject. That palace is, I might venture to say, the most admirable institution in the country. It has been of infinite service in showing what a rich nation might do in uniting Science, and Art, and Nature, for the entertainment and civilisation of the people. It has proved, once for all, that with noble surroundings, with beautiful objects of attraction, and with abundance of good music, the largest masses of people may recreate themselves, even in the neighbourhood of London, with propriety and freedom from moral harm. The fact, so properly insisted upon by Mr. Fuller, that not one person in a million among visitors to the Crystal Palace is charged with drunken and disorderly conduct, is worth a volume in itself. The Crystal Palace, as is well known, has already been imitated by the Alexandra Palace, and, on a smaller scale, by Aquariums, Winter Gardens, or somewhat similar institutions under various names which have been lately built in the principal watering-places. These watering-places are, in fact, running a race as to which shall present hesitating visitors with the best places of entertainment. The Pump-room and the Assembly-room are antiquated: but now Brighton has its Aquarium; Buxton its Public Gardens and Music Pavilion; Southport, Cheltenham, Blackpool, and Tynemouth have opened their Winter Gardens; Southend is erecting a Marine Palace; Eastbourne has got its Devonshire Park, where cricket, lawn tennis, croquet, rinking, and music are happily combined, and Scarborough has both the Spa Gardens and an Aquarium. Such institutions are, indeed, chiefly designed for the richer classes, and their great cost necessitates a somewhat high entrance-fee. They have, as yet, been undertaken only by professed pleasure towns, which can at the best be visited by the mass of the working classes by occasional excursion trains. But it is to be hoped that, as the practicability of erecting such institutions begins to be better understood, they may be gradually introduced into all towns, both great and small, gay and dull. Already it has dawned upon people that a town is incomplete without its public park, and a few wealthy men have made the noble present of a park to the borough with which they are connected. Manchester has been foremost in providing a series of parks at the cost of the ratepayers. But I hold that a public park should be considered incomplete without its winter garden and music pavilion, and naturally the music pavilion is incomplete without the music. It is well to have places where people may take the air; but it is better still to attract them every summer evening into the healthy, airy park by the strains of music.

There are many modes by which recreation and culture may be brought within the reach of the multitude; but it is my present purpose to point out that the most practicable and immediately efficacious mode is the cultivation of pure music. I have no wish to disparage Theatres, Art Galleries, Museums, Public Libraries, Science Lectures, and various other social institutions, the value and true uses of which I may perhaps attempt to estimate on some other occasions; but I am certain that music is the best means of popular recreation. It fulfils all the requirements. In the first place, it involves no bodily fatigue, since it can best be enjoyed sitting down. To inspect a picture gallery or a museum is always a tiring work, neither exercise nor repose; the standing or stooping posture, the twisting of the neck, and the straining of the eyes, tend to produce, after a few hours, a state approaching nervous and muscular exhaustion. This is not the way to recreate the wearied mechanic, or the overworked clerk or man of business. It may be a very improving occupation of time for those who are holiday-making, and can start in the morning with a good store of superfluous energy.

With musical entertainments it is altogether different. A comfortable seat, a supply of fresh air, and a quiet audience, are requisite physical conditions for the enjoyment of music, but these being secured, a good musical performance, at least for those who have any appreciation of harmony and melody, is perfect repose. There is no straining of the nerves or muscles, no effort of any kind, but mere passive abandonment of the mind to the train of ideas and emotions suggested by the strains. And there is this peculiar advantage about melody, that, *per se*, it is absolutely pure and remote from trivial ideas. The song and the dance may have their associations, good or evil; but the pure melody in itself is pure indeed; it is gay, or pathetic, or stately, or sublime, but in any case there is something in the thrill of a choice chord, and the progression of a perfect melody, which seems to raise the hearer above the trifling affairs of life. At times it "brings all Heaven before our eyes." And there is this further advantage about the exhilaration and elevation of mind produced by true music in the musical, that it is, more than any other form of excitement, devoid of reaction, and of injurious effects of any kind. What some seek at the cost of health, and life, and reputation, from alcohol, and from opium, that they might obtain innocuously from music, if they could cultivate true musical taste. Of course there is some nervous waste even in the enjoyment of music, and it is greater as the attention is more excited. Tedium must usually follow an entertainment of two or three hours; but so soon as tedium approaches, the attentive attitude of mind is destroyed, and the corresponding nervous waste ceases. The music, in short, holds the mind enchained just so long as there is energy of thought to spare; in the meantime the body remains in a perfect state of repose.

The theatre, no doubt, might, almost equally with the concert hall, become the means of pure and frequent relaxation, and for those not much blessed with musical susceptibility it has obvious superiority. But, as I shall perhaps attempt to show more fully on some future opportunity, the reform and purification of the drama is a far more difficult task than the promotion of musical entertainments. In the first place, the cost of theatrical performances is vastly greater than that of a simple musical concert. Not only is a specially constructed and expensive building required, with all kinds of property and machinery, but a large and costly staff of actors of all ranks, managers, scene-painters, carpenters, scene-shifters, etc., has to be constantly maintained. Moreover, a fair orchestra of musicians has to be provided as well, it being a curious but very well established fact that an audience must be put under the spell of music before they can thoroughly enjoy the drama. The crudeness and staginess of the play need to be subdued by the veil of melodic fancy. Thus the theatre is really music *plus* the drama, and any experiment in theatrical reform must involve the hazardous expenditure of great sums of money.

A second difficulty is, that music is naturally more pure and removed from the concrete and sensuous ideas of ordinary life than a drama can usually be. No doubt music is prostituted in many a lascivious song, but the question might well arise whether the impurity is not wholly in the words, not in the music. In any case the difficulty of purifying an already impure theatre must be far greater than of promoting orchestral performances where, with the simplest police regulations, there would arise no question of purity at all.

For these, and various secondary reasons which might be urged, I hold that musical cultivation is the safest and surest Method of popular culture; and it is greatly to the low state of musical education among the masses of English population that I attribute their helpless state when seeking recreation. In the majority of the Continental towns it is quite the rule to find a fair orchestra giving daily open-air concerts in the public square or park. The merchant and the shopkeeper, and the mechanic, as a matter of course, stroll down on a fine evening, and spend a tranquil hour or two with their families and neighbours. The husband perhaps takes his glass of thin beer, and the wife and family share a bottle or two of lemonade. A more harmless, wholesome, and recreative mode of spending the evening cannot be invented; but where is it possible to do the like in England, except at a few select watering-places?

Not to go further afield for the present, where, I want to know, can a young man or a family in London enjoy a few hours of inexpensive out-of-door popular music in the summer evenings? The parks are open, and it is possible to walk, and sometimes to sit down and repose in them; but where is the music? I suppose a military band still plays every morning at the change of guard at St. James's Palace, as I remember it used to do many years ago. A police band once started afternoon performances at the end of the Mall in St. James's Park, and there was the hotly-contested Sunday afternoon band in Regent's Park. Once or twice I heard one of the Guards' bands play near the Knightsbridge Barracks. With these trifling exceptions, I remember no open-air music in the whole of London of the kind which I advocate. With all our vast expenditure on the army, cannot they spare us a band?* With all the vast wealth of the empire, cannot the metropolis do what some third-rate town in France, or Germany, or Sweden does? Of course it cannot be really the want of funds, but because those who could so easily raise the funds in one way or another disapprove the object, or think it impracticable. To suggest an evening military concert in St. James's Park, the gardens of the Thames Embankment, or even Trafalgar Square, at once suggests the idea of a horrid crowd of roughs and pickpockets. All that is vulgar and disagreeable would be brought to the surface. The member of Parliament who was so shocked at seeing dirty little children in St. James's Park would be altogether scandalised at the vulgar throng which might be attracted by music. But are we really in such a hopelessly uncultured and brutal condition that we cannot venture even to try the means of improvement? What makes the people vulgar but the total want of means to render them refined?

So novel a thing as popular outdoor concerts in London might draw together surprised and somewhat disagreeable crowds at first. But when, by degrees, the novelty of the thing had worn off; when the roughs and pickpockets and disorderly boys found that the police were present also; when the shopkeeper found that he could safely bring out his wife and family, and, for a few pence, obtain seats and spend a cheerful cool hour or two, then the thing would be discovered to be just as practicable and enjoyable as it is in the Palais Royal, or in the capitals, and even the minor towns, of most Continental countries. Not long since it was thought to be impossible to open a public garden in the centre of London, so

---

* Of course I am aware that the bands of the regiments of the British Army are maintained at the cost of the officers of each regiment. The English people pay £15,000,000 a year to maintain their army, and yet they are told that the very military bands of that army are not their own.

great was the fear of collecting the residuum there. But, so far as I have observed, or heard, or read, absolutely no harm arises from the Thames Embankment Gardens, or from the admirable oasis in Leicester Square. The deserted churchyards are now being utilised as recreation-grounds; and in the long course of time perhaps Lincoln's Inn Fields, and other available spaces, will be put to their proper use. The introduction of the band on summer week-day evenings seems to me the natural corollary. The question, I may here remark, whether music is proper on Sunday afternoons is a totally different one, with which the matter ought not to be complicated.

What I have advocated for London should also be carried out proportionally in every town and village. Eventually each considerable town should have, as I have said, its park and music pavilion where the open-air concerts would take place. But for the present, it would be sufficient if a rifle corps band, or some amateur band, obtained permission to utilise any available open space, collecting the small sum necessary for expenses either by a trifling charge for reserved chairs, or by a subscription list among the shopkeepers and residents. This is already done at Hampstead, where the Hampstead Rosslyn Hill brass band, assisted by a local subscription list, plays every Saturday evening, during the summer months, on the Upper Terrace, Hampstead Heath.* Their successful performances have stirred up the zeal of the local Volunteer Corps band, which has recently added a performance on Thursday evenings. It cannot be said that the attendance at these out-of-door concerts is very extensive or very select, but no harm or nuisance whatever arises. As the value of such a harmless entertainment becomes understood, I should hope that the

---

* This band has now for fourteen or fifteen years furnished gratuitous entertainment for the people of Hampstead and north-western London. The services of the performers are honorary, as are also the zealous exertions of the Honorary Secretary, Mr. Alexander H. B. Ellis. The necessary expenses of bandmaster and instructor, of the printed music, attendants, stationery, postage, rent of practice room, etc., amount to about £75 or £80 a year, mostly defrayed by the contribution of about one hundred subscribers.

Metropolitan Board of Works would authorise the erection of a suitable music pavilion on some convenient part of the Heath, where these and other bands might perform under better acoustic conditions.

There is absolutely nothing but apathy to prevent the same thing being done in every considerable village in the country. A small subscription to buy the instruments, to construct a small orchestra, and to pay the incidental expenses, and a zealous volunteer bandmaster to get together the musical amateurs of the neighbourhood, and to give them a little training, is all that is needed. In many places the local volunteer corps already has an organised band, and it will not require much pressure to induce them to air their uniforms and display their skill. There is no doubt a certain number of places where this is already done; a few weeks since I happened to hear a band which had commenced performances on "The Vine," or public green of Sevenoaks. In the winter the same bands might give weekly cheap concerts in the drill-shed, the skating-rink, the assembly room, the village school-room, or any available chamber. Whenever practicable, it would be desirable at the same time to provide cheap non-intoxicating refreshments. Only in some such a way is it possible to countermine the increasing influence of the noxious music-hall. The people will have amusement and excitement of one kind or other, and the only question is, whether the business of recreation shall fall entirely into the hands of publicans, or whether local movements of no serious difficulty will not provide suitable counter-attractions.

It is a great question again whether the English church might not take a great part in affording, not amusement, but the occupation of thought, and the elevation of feeling which attaches to the performance of sacred music. Already it is common to give occasional performances of appropriate music at Christmas, or Easter, or during Lent. During one Easter I happened to be at Ely, and a selection from the music of the "Messiah" was performed one evening in the cathedral. A local amateur musical society had formed a small orchestra, and practised up the score. With the assistance of part of the militia band, especially the drummers, with the ordinary singers of the cathedral staff, some of whom took the solo parts, and with a volunteer chorus of young men and women, a very pleasing and impressive performance of the greatest of oratorios was given. What was wanting in the skill of the singers, or power and technical correctness of the orchestra and chorus, was far more than made up by the loveliness of the octagon dome beneath which it took place. The performance was preceded by a short service, the congregation joining in the hymns and responses, and by a brief address. Many hundreds of people attended, including palpable dusty labourers, railway porters, engine drivers, militiamen, and people of all ranks. It is not my purpose in this book to enter upon theological nor even religious topics, so that I can only speak of such performances from a layman's point of view. But in any case I find it difficult to imagine how the House of God can be desecrated by pure and sacred music, the deepest products of feeling of the mind. The cathedral churches of England have long been in a way the national schools of music, but I trust that they will do more and more in this way for the future. And I do not see why every considerable parish in the kingdom should not have its musical society, for the cultivation of high class and principally sacred music.

There is no place which needs the means of pure recreation more than the East End of London, and I may venture to suggest that an admirable opportunity for making the first experiment there exists ready at hand in the Columbia Market. It is sad to pass through the beautiful but deserted arcades of this intended market, and then discover a magnificent Gothic hall, occupied only by a few old chairs and tables, which seem as if they were forgotten alike by dealers and purchasers. The Baroness Burdett Coutts would amply retrieve her one great failure if she could be persuaded to make this noble building into a model place of recreation for the East of London. Slight alterations would convert the market hall into an excellent music gallery, where some of our social reformers should be allowed to provide good but simple concerts in the winter.* The performers need not be of the first rank, and amateur aid would do a good deal, though not all. I have heard of a West End choral society which makes a point of visiting the East End to give free concerts there, with the view of elevating the taste of the poorer classes. Were the Columbia Hall available for the purpose, abundant aid of the kind could no doubt be obtained by a vigorous committee; but it would be a mistake to depend wholly on volunteer performers. The mass of the people should be admitted at a charge of a penny or twopence, and a certain number of seats might be reserved at sixpence or a shilling each. Good tea, coffee, cocoa, with light refreshments, and all kinds of non-intoxicating drinks, should be provided at the back of the hall, if there were room, or, if not, in the adjoining buildings. The music should consist of the better class of dance music, old English melodies, popular classical songs; but there should be a careful intermixture of the higher order of music. My own observations lead to the conclusion that there is hardly any audience which will not be touched by a really beautiful melody, such, for instance, as that of Bach's Prelude as arranged by Gounod. It is only the great musical structures such as the Symphonies, with their elaborate introductions and complicated developments, which demand long musical training for their appreciation.

While I am speaking of Columbia Market I may go a step further, and suggest that the fine central area of the market could not possibly be better utilised than by converting it similarly into a recreation ground. A soft floor, and a good supply of swings, merry-go-rounds, and the like, would soon make it the happiest spot in the kingdom. At another time I shall argue that in a sound sensible state of things, every group of houses should as a matter of course have its play-grounds for children, five per cent. of all building land, for example, being com-

* Since the above was written, Columbia Market, having been previously offered to the parish authorities for the purpose of a hay market, has been converted into a tobacco and cigar manufactory. *The Times* of January 5th, 1881, p. 10 c, which announces this change, remarks apologetically, that the lighter part of the business will afford employment for the redundant female population of this district.

pulsorily set apart by law for recreative purposes. But, as such an idea never entered into the heads of our ancestors, the dangerous streets and the reeking alleys are the play-grounds of the mass of English children. Columbia Market offers the best possible opportunity for showing what might be done to remedy this state of things. Free gymnasia already exist at Primrose Hill, the Victoria and Battersea Parks, in the Alexandra Park at Manchester, and a good many other places, but they are far from the classes which use them; and a well-regulated place of recreation in the centre of such a dense poor population as that of Bethnal Green, would be a novelty indeed. In summer evenings the area of the market might be employed for open-air concerts by a brass band. To supply the poor with cheap good food was an excellent idea of the munificent founder of these buildings; but there are countless good shops in Shoreditch, and in the surrounding principal streets. There is no such thing as the institution for the supply of pure, wholesome, popular recreation which might be provided by the Columbia Play-ground and the Columbia Concert Hall.

The question arises whether any measures could be suggested for raising the tone of the numerous existing music-halls, which must long have a hold on a large part of the population. I will presently refer to one legislative and police measure, which is as indispensable as it is practicable. But, apart from this, it is difficult to see what direct means there are of influencing private competing owners. The magistrates can hardly exact a certain portion of Beethoven or Schumann as a condition of the license. It is the audience which must demand better entertainment, if the common run of music-halls are to be made to supply it. But it is to be earnestly hoped that the great public places of recreation, the Crystal and Alexandra Palaces and the Westminster Aquarium, will always carefully maintain the high tone and the perfect respectability by which alone they can fulfil their *raison d'être*. Already, indeed, it is a matter of regret to notice that Zazel draws better than the Pastoral Symphony, and that Negro minstrels must be enlisted to keep up the force of attraction. Our hopes of elevating public taste would be sadly dashed to the ground, were vulgarism to invade our highest places of entertainment. Nor do I believe that there would be any gain in the end. Long may the time be distant; but if once such a place be deserted by the middle and upper classes and set down as vulgar, the course of its decline can be foreseen. Whatever our great caterers do, they must make a point of mingling all classes together, and retaining a reputation as places of fashionable resort.

Nor is it only in open-air and purely popular musical entertainments that much good might be done in London. It has often been a matter of wonder to me that in the vast social world of London there is no really great hall, and no series of concerts such as Mr. Hallé conducts with pre-eminent success at the Free Trade Hall in Manchester. Excepting, perhaps, Exeter Hall, I do not happen to know any London hall where such performances could be successfully attempted. Of course there is the Albert Hall; but that is too large, and is hardly in London at all. I suppose that even its promoters will now allow that it is, in spite of its magnificent *coup d'œil* and its noble organ, an irretrievable blunder. Its position is essentially bad, and never can be much better. How strange it is that those whose purpose was the elevation of the public taste, the taste surely of the masses, should have placed their instruments of elevation as far as possible from the masses they were to elevate! The fashionable residents of Kensington, Belgravia, Tyburnia, are just the classes which cannot be supposed to need culture;* and even as regards some of those districts, it seems to have been forgotten that Hyde Park occupies one-half of the horizon of the Albert Hall, and thus for ever places a needless

---

* Yet read with what unconscious irony a reporter, writing of the Royal Albert Hall Amateur Orchestral Society, in *The Times* of the 14th May, 1879 (p. 12 *f*), says: "The Duke of Edinburgh, the president and founder of the Society, has resumed his seat in the orchestra, and consequently these concerts are again attracting the attention of the public."

physical obstacle of a mile or more in the way of those who seek recreation. Even when one reaches the hall, it strikes the spectator as quite unsuited to musical, and indeed almost all other purposes. The sound of the largest orchestra is swallowed up and dissipated in the vast expanse. The audience are so far removed from each other and from the orchestra, that they cease to act as a united audience. The warmth of sympathetic feeling, which is no small part of any public entertainment, is converted into a chilly attempt to discover, through the field-glass, what is going on in other parts of the house. The lesson we learn is not to wait for social reforms to be accomplished through mysteriously-moved bodies of Royal Commissioners.

What all the powers of South Kensington could never do has been to a great extent accomplished by the conductors of the Popular Concerts at St. James's Hall. They have made that hall the centre of the truest musical culture, and lasting honour is due to them for it. Yet we can hardly call the St. James's Hall Concerts really popular. They are only popular as contrasted with the great number of small, exclusive fashionable concerts which continually go on in the West End during the season, and which have no popular influence whatever. Even to the musical devotee a perpetual succession of stringed quartets and trios, and the like, is rather thin diet. One craves sometimes the stirring clang of the trombones, the roll of the drums, the solemn boom of the diapason, and the exciting crescendo of a great orchestra.* What London so unfortunately lacks, Manchester as fortunately enjoys. The existence in Manchester of a large resident, well-cultured German middle-class population, and the erection of the Free Trade Hall, have given Mr. Charles Hallé the means of educating the middle classes of Lancashire in musical taste, as they are educated in no other province of the United Kingdom. Mr. Hallé has explained his views about the progress of musical

---

* Since the above was written a great change seems to have come over St. James's Hall, and many series of admirable orchestral concerts have been given in the last few years, including those of Richter, Hallé, Lamoureux, and other conductors.

taste in England during thirty years past, in a paper read to the Social Science Association in 1879, Report, p. 768. But even Mr. Hallé's admirable concerts are not popular in the sense in which I should wish to see musical entertainments popular. Only about twenty such concerts are given in Manchester in the year,* and the expenses are such that the average charge of admission is decidedly high. But if a hall at least equal in size and acoustic excellence to the Free Trade Hall were erected in the centre of London, with its enormous resident population, and its ever-increasing streams of tourists and provincial visitors, it might be possible to maintain a varied but unceasing series of musical entertainments from one end of the year to the other. Why this should be impossible I am unable to understand, seeing that, in the very dullest season, the Messrs. Gatti are able, night after night, to give admirable Promenade Concerts at Covent Garden. These concerts, as they are so wisely conducted by Mr. Sullivan and Mr. Alfred Collier, fulfil in all respects (except one or two) my idea of what every great town should have nightly in the way of musical recreation. Those who have noticed the manner in which a confessedly popular and casual audience receive the Symphonies of Beethoven, and the remarkable impression produced by the truly pathetic singing of Madame Antoinette Sterling, will not despair of musical taste in England.

I wish that those who manage our English pleasure-places could be induced to take a trip to Copenhagen, and learn how much better they manage things there. The Tivoli pleasure-gardens there form the best possible model of popular recreation. Englishmen think of Denmark only as a very little nation, which they patronised, and advised, and lectured, and then coolly deserted in the hour of need. But though small in quantity, Denmark shames us in quality. We are not surprised when a Frenchman surpasses us in politeness, and a

---

* In addition to Mr. Hallé's more classical series should be mentioned a series of ten concerts given yearly by Mr. De Jong, in the same hall. I do not happen to have attended them, but believe that they fulfil, to a certain extent, the need of popular musical recreation.

German in profundity, and an American in ingenuity and affability; but it is truly mortifying to an English traveller in Scandinavia to discover that those who are as nearly as possible of our own flesh and blood far surpass us as regards the good-breeding and the general culture of the mass of the people. In Norway this might be attributed to the effects of peasant proprietorship, or to the retired country life of the peasants; but when we get to a large port like Copenhagen, placed under no favourable circumstances, and still find that the poorer classes are, comparatively speaking, ladies and gentlemen, one begins to realise the fact that there must be some methods of social reform which are unknown to our legislators.

The social superiority is of course greatly due to the good system of popular education which has long existed in Denmark. But my Danish friends, when questioned on the subject, attributed a high civilising influence to the Thorwaldsen Museum, and to the Tivoli Gardens, at Copenhagen. The museum in question contains a nearly complete collection of the works of the great Danish sculptor, and it is continually visited by all classes of Danish society, including Danish and Swedish peasants, who come from considerable distances by excursion trains and steamers, but are as unlike our cheap-trippers in manners as can be conceived. But Tivoli is my more immediate topic. Tivoli is simply a pleasure-garden, close to the town of Copenhagen, and of no great extent. It is, no doubt, the lineal descendant of Belsize, of Ranelagh, of Vauxhall. I fancy that the English have been in no way backward in originating places of recreation. From the beginning of last century a succession of such pleasure-gardens have been instituted in London; but, owing to the fatal folly of our legislators, they have fallen successively under the ban of public opinion. With Tivoli it is very different. The Royal Family of Denmark and the upper classes patronised and frequented it from the very first, and by good management the gardens are still thronged by equal proportions of all classes of the population. The principal attraction in the gardens is a fine string orchestra, which, under a large partially open pavilion, gives semi-classical concerts every evening throughout the summer. The programmes are chosen from the works of all the best musicians, including Bach, Beethoven, Wagner, Rossini, Gung'l, Mendelssohn, Weber, Gade, Strauss, Meyerbeer, Reinecke and others. In the intervals of the principal concert the Harmoniorkestre, or brass band, strikes up more popular tunes in other parts of the grounds. In a closed hall, with a small extra charge, conjuring performances go on, with various minor entertainments. On festival nights there is a small display of fireworks, in addition to an illumination of the grounds. More remarkable, however, are the performances on a kind of open-air stage employed for ballet-dancing and pantomimes, somewhat in the manner of the open-air theatres of the Champs Elysées. Of course our magistrates would not permit so demoralising a spectacle as ballet-dancing in the open air; but I wish they could see Froeken Leontine and Fanny Carey dance their *pas de deux*. They would then learn that among a truly cultured and a well-governed people, dancing may be as chaste as it is a beautiful performance. Dancing, *per se*—the exhibition of a graceful figure in graceful motions and attitudes—may be as chaste as a statue; indeed a good deal more chaste than many statues. But we are so accustomed to see ballet girls in evanescent skirts, in ambiguous attitudes, or dressed up as wasps or cupids, or something extravagant and low in taste, that we have established an inseparable association of ideas between dancing and immorality. I retain a grateful recollection of the Froeken Carey, who opened my eyes more than anything else to the degradation of public taste in England. I afterwards learned that Copenhagen is considered a great school for graceful and chaste dancing.

At other times the same stage is used for pantomime—not your absurd English pantomime, all grotesque, extravagant, full of tinsel, depending for effect upon numbers and magnitude, and the introduction of real donkeys, hansom-cabs, and the like—as if there were no real humour and fun left in the nation—but the real pantomime—all gesture and incident, no speech. I need not attempt to describe the remarkable series of comical adventures which befell the clown, and the invariable success which ultimately attended the machinations of harlequin; I need only say that it was a performance as amusing to the spectators as it was harmless, and totally devoid of coarseness or vulgarity. With this fact I was all the more struck when I happened subsequently to see a party of English clowns performing in the public gardens of a provincial Swedish town. This was a painful exhibition, especially to an English spectator, and culminated in the clown spitting copiously at his wife. Compared with our Crystal or Alexandra Palace, Tivoli is a very minor affair; but civilisation is not a question of magnitude, and, in spite of its comparatively small size, Tivoli is a model of good taste and decency, and of the way in which, under good regulation, all classes may be induced to mingle.

The cultivation of musical recreation is by no means confined to the larger towns of Scandinavia, but is to be found in towns of a size which in England would never entertain the idea of supporting anything of the sort. I was much struck with the fact, when, on one Sunday evening, I arrived at the very small seaport of Stavanger in Norway, and found the larger part of the population of the town, apparently after attendance of the evening service in the church, promenading in a small public garden adjoining the churchyard, where a very fair band was playing in a permanent raised orchestra.

I give below the programme of one of the similar kind of performances held at Bergen on Sunday afternoons in a small public garden, a trifling charge being here made for admission within an enclosure.

PARK-CONCERT.

PROGRAM:

1ste Afdeling.

1. Marsch af Op. "Carmen" . . . . Bizet.
2. Meditation & Preludium (Bach) . . . Gounod.
3. "An der schönen, blauen Donau" . . . Strauss.
4. Stabat-Mater . . . . Rossini.
5. Le Chant d'Amour Vals . . . . . Albert.
6. Bas-Arie af "Barberen" . . . . . Rossini.

2DEN AFDELING.

7. Overture til Op. "Den hvide Dame" . . Boieldieu.
8. Schaarwache-Marsch af Michaelis . . .
9. Pilegrimes—Chor af "Tannhäuser". . . Wagner.
10. Duet af Op. "Martha" . . . . . Flotow.
11. Preludium, Chor & Cavatine af Op. "Il Giuramento". . . . . . Mercadante.

One great cause of the degradation of English amusements is the exclusive and pseudo-aristocratic feeling of the middle and upper classes, which makes them fly the *profanum vulgus*. The shopkeeper apes the merchant; the merchant wants to be thought a squire; the squire is happy only among baronets and lords; finally, the lords love to bask in the sunshine of royalty. Thus it comes to pass, that to make an entertainment really fashionable and popular, a royal duke or a princess must be exhibited. There is no method of social reform by which we can hope to bring about a more rational state of things within the intervals of time with which we have to deal, and therefore the problem is to make the best of social matters as they exist. Under these circumstances it is, as it seems to me, a positive duty on the part of the middle and upper classes to frequent the well-conducted places of popular recreation, and help to raise their tone. If, to induce them to do so, they must have royal or titled leaders to flock after, then I hope that those who enjoy the wealth and the privileges of this kingdom will bear in mind that they have duties also, which duties they will not fulfil by fencing themselves round in their castles, and their opera boxes, and their own private entertainments.

But there is one other potent cause which at present almost necessitates exclusiveness in open-air recreation; and which tends more than anything else to degrade popular taste. For obvious reasons I can touch it but slightly here. I allude to the intrusion into English popular gatherings of what is euphemistically and comprehensively called the *demi-monde*. The evil is hardly felt in concerts and meetings where all are seated, and only in a minor degree in theatres, where the several ranks of people are separated from each other by the divisions of the house and the differences of charge. But the mingling of people in any form of English outdoor recreation is subject to the danger that a lady may find herself in company which she cannot tolerate. Hence, to make a long story short, the successive fall of our public gardens from the time of Belsize down to that of Cremorne.* It is needless to say, that things are very differently managed at Copenhagen, and in most Continental cities. Much of the delight which English families, and especially English ladies, find in residence abroad, arises from the freedom of public intercourse which rational police regulations allow. Why should we continue the perverse and legislatively insane practice of allowing our most public places to be turned into the markets of vice? Why do we tolerate a state of things under which a young man cannot seek an hour's recreation without meeting an evil magnet at every turn? With ever-vigilant ingenuity the *demi-monde* finds out each new opportunity, and, one after another, places of innocent recreation lose their repute, and pursue a course of gradual degradation ending in suppression. But this is not the place to pursue the subject, and I will only insist that it is impossible to estimate the insidious injury thus occasioned to the morals and culture of the people.

There are none so blind as they who will not see, and this is the kind of blindness which prevents us from seeing that the vulgarity of the cheap trip, the inanity of the music-hall, and the general low tone of popular manners, are no necessary characteristics of hard hands and short purses, but are due to

---

* The history of the places of popular amusement in London would make a good subject for a volume; it has however been partially written in Knight's "Pictorial History of London," or Professor Morley's "Bartholomew Fair."

The end of all the open-air places of recreation was usually ignominious if not disgraceful. Marylebone Gardens were opened in 1735. Dr. Arne, the celebrated musician, was leader of the orchestra, and produced much of Handel's music; the place was suppressed in 1778. Vauxhall, first known as New Spring Gardens, had a very long career; it was visited by Evelyn in 1661; it continued to exist as a place of amusement until July 25, 1859. A view of the Gardens as they existed during last century will be found in Stowe's "Survey of London," vol. ii., p. 774.

the way in which for so long a time popular education and popular recreation have been discountenanced. Of course the question of recreation is subordinate to that of education; now as—thanks especially to the sense and integrity, and firmness, and high statesmanship of Mr. Forster—the education question was put in a fair way of solution at the critical moment when it became possible, then I say that there are few subordinate methods of Social Reform which need more careful study and regulation than that of Public Amusements.*

APPENDIX.

It is a curious fact that the eighth book of Aristotle's "Politics" contains a careful and express inquiry into the subject of popular recreation, leading to the result upheld in the preceding article, that music is the best means for providing such recreation. The argument is, as usual with Aristotle, rather tedious and confused, and there is a good deal of repetition between the seven chapters of the book; but it is impossible not to be struck with the profundity of the treatment and with its lasting truth, as applied to a state of society two thousand years after the book was written. I give a very brief abstract of some parts of the book, as translated by Mr. Edward Walford, in Bohn's edition of the "Politics and Economics," 1853, pp. 270 to 286.

There are as nearly as possible four things which it is usual to teach children—reading, gymnastic exercises, and music, to which (in the fourth place) some add painting. As to music some persons may entertain a doubt, since most persons now use it for the sake of pleasure. But though both labour and rest are necessary, yet the latter is preferable, and by all means we ought to learn what to do when at rest. Play is more necessary for those who labour than for those who are

* Since writing the above I have learnt a good deal both about popular entertainments which were previously in existence, and many attempts which have since been made.

idle; for he who labours requires relaxation, and this play will supply. For this reason the ancients made music a part of education. They thought it a proper employment for freemen, and to them they allotted it; as Homer sings: "How right to call Thalia to the feast!" and, addressing some others, he says: "The band was called, to ravish every ear;" and, in another place, he makes Ulysses say, that the happiest part of man's life is

> When at the festal board in order placed,
> They listen to the song.

It is no easy matter distinctly to point out what power it has, nor on what accounts one should apply it, whether as an amusement and refreshment, like sleep or wine. Or shall we rather suppose that music has a tendency to produce virtue, having a power, as the gymnastic exercises have, to form the body in a certain way, and to influence the manners, so as to accustom its professors to rejoice rightly? And we all agree that music is one of the most pleasing things, whether alone or accompanied with a voice, as Musæus says:

> Music, man's sweetest joy,

for which reason it is justly admitted into every company and every happy life. From this anyone may suppose that it is fitting to instruct young persons in it. For all those pleasures which are harmless are not only conducive to the final end of life, but serve also as relaxations.

THE
RATIONALE OF FREE PUBLIC LIBRARIES.*

AMONG the methods of social reform which are comparatively easy of accomplishment and sure in action, may be placed the establishment of Free Public Libraries. Already, indeed, this work has been carried into effect in a considerable number of towns, and has passed quite beyond the experimental stage. In Manchester, Birmingham, Liverpool, and some other great towns, where such libraries have already existed for many years, there is but one opinion about them. Perhaps it might better be said that they are ceasing to be matter of opinion at all, and are classed with town-halls, police-courts, prisons, and poor-houses as necessary adjuncts of our stage of civilisation. Several great towns, including the greatest of all towns, great London itself, are yet nearly, if not quite, devoid of rate-supported libraries. As to towns of medium and minor magnitude, it is the exception to find them provided with such an obvious requisite. Under these circumstances it will not be superfluous to review the results which have already been achieved under William Ewart's Free Libraries Act, and to form some estimate of the reasons which may be urged in favour of or against the system of providing literature at the public cost.

The main *raison d'être* of Free Public Libraries, as indeed of public museums, art-galleries, parks, halls, public clocks, and many other kinds of public works, is the enormous increase

* "Contemporary Review," March, 1881, vol. xxxix., pp. 385–402.

of utility which is thereby acquired for the community at a trifling cost. If a beautiful picture be hung in the dining-room of a private house, it may perhaps be gazed at by a few guests a score or two of times in the year. Its real utility is too often that of ministering to the selfish pride of its owner. If it be hung in the National Gallery, it will be enjoyed by hundreds of thousands of persons, whose glances, it need hardly be said, do not tend to wear out the canvas. The same principle applies to books in common ownership. If a man possesses a library of a few thousand volumes, by far the greater part of them must lie for years untouched upon the shelves; he cannot possibly use more than a fraction of the whole in any one year. But a library of five or ten thousand volumes opened free to the population of a town may be used a thousand times as much. It is a striking case of what I propose to call *the principle of the multiplication of utility*, a principle which lies at the base of some of the most important processes of political economy, including the division of labour.

The extent to which this multiplication of utility is carried in the case of free lending libraries is quite remarkable. During the first year that the Birmingham Free Library was in operation every book in the library was issued on an average seventeen times, and the periodical literature was actually turned over about fifty times.* In the "Transactions of the First Annual Meeting of the Library Association" (p. 77), Mr. Yates, of the Leeds Public Library, has given an account of the stock and issues of his libraries. In the Central Library the average turn-over—that is to say, the average number of times that each book was used—was about eighteen times in 1873, gradually falling to about twelve times. In the branch libraries it was eight in 1873, falling to four-and-a-half. This fall in the turn-over is, however, entirely due to the increase in the stock of books, the total number of issues having largely increased. The general account of all the free libraries, as

* The Free Library of Birmingham. By Edward C. Osborne: "Transactions of the Social Science Association. London Meeting, 1862, p. 786.

given in a Parliamentary Paper—namely, a "Further Return concerning the Free Libraries Acts" (No. 277, 1877)—shows that each volume in the lending libraries of corporate towns is used on an average 6·55 in the year, and in the reference libraries 2·65 times; in other than corporate places the numbers are 5·92 and 3·81. In Scotland there is a curious inversion; the books of the lending libraries being used on an average 5·58 times, and those of the reference libraries as much as 9·22 times. The numbers of volumes issued to each borrower in the year are from sixteen to eighteen in England and Wales, and more than forty-four in Scotland.

Of course, books suffer more or less damage from incessant reading, and no small numbers of books in Free Libraries are sooner or later actually worn out by steady utilisation. Such books, however, can almost invariably be replaced with ease; in any case, how infinitely better it is that they should perish in the full accomplishment of their mission, instead of falling a prey to the butter-man, the waste-dealer, the entomological book-worm, the chamber-maid, or the other enemies of books which Mr. Blades has so well described and anathematised.

One natural result of the extensive circulation of public books is the very low cost at which the people is thus supplied with literature. Dividing the total expenditure of some of the principal Free Libraries by their total issues, we find that the average cost of each issue is: at Birmingham, 1·8d. per volume; at Rochdale, 1·92d.; at Manchester, 2·7d.; at Wolverhampton, the same. At Liverpool the cost was still lower, being only 1·55d.; and at Tynemouth it was no more than 1·33d. In the smaller libraries, indeed, the average cost is, as we might reasonably expect, somewhat larger; but, taking the total returns of issues and expenditure as given in Mr. Charles W. Sutton's most valuable "Statistical Report on the Free Libraries of the United Kingdom,"* we find the average cost per volume issued to be 2·31d. This is by no means a fair mode of estimating what the public get for their money.

---

* "Transactions of the Second Annual Meeting of the Library Association," Manchester, 1879, Appendix II. See also "Proceedings," pp. 92, 93.

We must remember that, in addition to the borrowing and consulting of books, the readers have in most cases a cheerful, well-warmed, and well-lighted sitting-room, supplied with newspapers and magazine tables. To many a moneyless weary man the Free Library is a literary club; an unexceptionable refuge from the strife and dangers of life. It is not usual to keep any record of the numbers of persons who visit Free Libraries for other purposes than to apply for books; but at the Manchester libraries in 1868–69 an attempt was made to count the numbers of persons making use of the institutions in one way or other.* It was found that there had been altogether 2,172,046 readers, of whom 398,840 were borrowers of books for home reading; 74,367, including 228 ladies, were readers in the reference library; 91,201 were readers to whom books were issued on their signature in the branch reading-rooms; and 1,607,638 made use of the current periodicals, books, pamphlets, and other publications, in the news-room, in regard to which no formality is required. Taking the population of Manchester at 338,722, we might say that every man, woman, and child visited the libraries on an average six-and-a-half times in the year; or, putting it in a more sensible manner, we might say, perhaps, that every person of adequate age visited the libraries on an average about thirteen times in the year.

The figures already given seem to show that there is probably no mode of expending public money which gives a more extraordinary and immediate return in utility and innocent enjoyment. It would, nevertheless, be a mistake to rest the claims of the Free Library simply on the ground of economy. Even if they were very costly, Free Libraries would be less expensive establishments than prisons, courts of justice, poor-houses, and other institutions maintained by public money; or the gin-palaces, music-halls, and theatres maintained by private expenditure. Nobody can doubt that there is plenty of money in this kingdom to spend for worse or for better. The whole annual cost of Free Libraries does

---

* "Seventeenth Annual Report to the Council of the City of Manchester on the Working of the Public Free Libraries," 1869, p. 5.

not amount to more than about one hundred thousand pounds per annum; say, one-fifth part of the cost of a single first-class iron-clad. Now, this small cost is not only repaid many times over by the multiplication of utility of the books, newspapers, and magazines on which it is expended, but it is likely, after the lapse of years, to come back fully in the reduction of poor-rates and Government expenditure on crime. We are fully warranted in looking upon Free Libraries as an engine for operating upon the poorer portions of the population. In many other cases we do likewise. Mr. Fawcett's new measure for attracting small deposits to the Post Office Savings Banks by postage stamps cannot possibly be approved from a direct financial point of view. Each shilling deposit occasions a very considerable loss to the department in expenses, and it is only the hope and fact that those who begin with shillings will end with pounds, or even tens and hundreds of pounds, which can possibly justify the measure. The Post Office Savings Banks are clearly an engine for teaching thrift—in reality an expensive one; so Free Libraries are engines for creating the habit and power of enjoying high-class literature, and thus carrying forward the work of civilisation which is commenced in the primary school.

Some persons who are evidently quite unable to deny the efficient working of the Free Library system, oppose arguments somewhat in the nature of the "previous question." They would say, for instance, that if there is so wonderful a demand for popular books, why do not the publishers issue cheap editions which anybody can purchase and read at home? Some astonishing things have no doubt been done in this way, as in the issue of the "Waverley Novels" at sixpence each. Even this price, it will be observed, is three, four, or more times the average cost of the issue of all kinds of literature from the larger Free Libraries. Any one, moreover, in the least acquainted with the publishing business must know that such cheap publication is quite impracticable except in the case of the most popular kinds of works. Quite recently, indeed, a "Pictorial New Testament" has been issued for a penny per copy, and Bunyan's "Pilgrim's Progress" in like manner. But the copies of these issues which I have met with are devoid of anything to call binding, and I presume it is understood that such publications could not have been undertaken from pecuniary motives. In the same way, the Bible Society, of course, can issue Bibles at whatever price they like, so long as their subscription list is sufficient.

Every now and then, when the papers are in want of padding, there springs up a crowd of correspondents who advocate cheap literature. A new novel, instead of costing 31s. 6d., ought not to cost more than 5s., or even 1s. Cheapness, we are assured, is the secret of profit, and, as the Post Office raises a vast revenue by penny stamps, so we have only to issue books at very low prices in order to secure a vast circulation and great profits. The superficiality of such kinds of argument ought to be apparent without elaborate exposure. It ought to be evident that the possibility of cheap publication depends entirely on the character of the publication. There are some books which sell by the hundred thousand, or even the million; there are others of which five hundred copies, or even one hundred, are ample to supply the market. Now, the class of publications which can be profitably multiplied, almost to the limits of power of the printing press, are those always vapid and not unfrequently vicious novelettes, gazettes, and penny dreadfuls of various name, whose evil influence it is the work of the Free Library to counteract.

Practically, the result of establishing Free Libraries is to bring the very best books within the reach of the poorest, while leaving the richer classes to pay the expenses of publication of such books. Any boy or beggar who can raise sixpence may enjoy from that "coign of vantage," the gallery, some excellent play or opera, which is really paid for by the stalls and boxes at 10s. 6d. or a guinea a head. A little observation will convince anyone that there are many social devices which carry the benefits of wealth to those who have no wealth. Public ownership is a most potent means of such vulgarisation of pleasures. A public park is open to everyone. Now, if the burgesses of a British borough are wise enough to open a Free Library, it is a free literary park, where the poorest may enjoy as a right what it is well, both for them and everybody else, that they should enjoy. Judging from the ample statements of the occupations of book borrowers given in the annual reports of various libraries, or the summary of such reports printed as a Blue Book,* it is quite plain that the borrowers are, for the most part, persons of no wealth, few probably having an income of more than £100 a year. Too many science lectures, cheap entertainments, and free openings of exhibitions, intended for the genuine working men, are taken advantage of chiefly by people who could well afford to pay; but in the Free Library the working man and the members of his family put in an unquestionable appearance. Thus, we find that at the Birmingham Library, out of 7,688 readers in the reference library, 56 are accountants, 17 actors, 115 agents, 27 apprentices, 80 architects, 153 artists, 31 bakers, 7 bedstead-makers, 25 bookbinders, 48 booksellers, 44 bootmakers, 141 brassworkers, 3 bricklayers, 17 brokers, 15 brushmakers, 26 builders, 18 burnishers, 7 butchers, 14 buttonmakers, 43 cabinetmakers, 90 carpenters, 14 carvers, 18 chainmakers, 85 chemists, 167 clergymen, 1,562 clerks, 19 coachmakers, 8 coal-dealers, 140 commercial travellers, 30 curriers, and so on to the end of the alphabet. Similar statistics are shown by all the libraries which record the occupations either of borrowers or reference library readers.

It must not be forgotten, too, that the cost of a book is not the only inconvenience which attaches to it. If a book is to be read only once, like a newspaper or penny dreadful, and then destroyed, the cost must be several, if not many, times as great as if furnished by a circulating library. If books are to be kept in the home, so that different members of the family may use them successively when of suitable age, there is the cost of the bookcase and the space taken up in a small house where it can ill be spared. No doubt a great deal of cheap literature is passed from hand to hand through the second-hand bookseller and thus multiplied in utility; but there is much inconvenience in this method, and the second-hand dealer likes to have a good percentage.

Mr. Sutton's valuable table of statistics enables us to form

* Return. Free Libraries Acts, No. 439, 1877.

THE RATIONALE OF FREE PUBLIC LIBRARIES.

a clear idea of the extent to which the Free Library movement is capable of further development. The number of rate-supported libraries, not counting branches, is now at least 86. Of these only 5 are found in boroughs having in 1871 a population less than 10,000; in 39 cases the population lay between 10,000 and 50,000; in 16 cases between 50,000 and 100,000; and in 15 cases the population exceeded 100,000. In the few remaining cases the population could not be stated. In almost all the towns in question, too, the new census will doubtless show greatly increased numbers of inhabitants. Opinions may differ as to the number of people which we may in the present day assign as adequate to the efficient support of a library; but, looking to the number of towns of about 20,000 inhabitants which already succeed with their libraries, we cannot doubt that every town of more than 20,000 inhabitants should possess its rate-supported library. In that case we can draw up from the census tables the following formidable list of English and Welsh towns which are clearly in default:

Aberdare.	Huddersfield.
Accrington.	Hull.
Ashton-under-Lyne.	Lincoln.
Barnsley.	London.
Bath.	Lower Sedgley.
Batley.	Merthyr Tydvil.
Burnley.	Oldham.
Burton-on-Trent.	Portsmouth.
Bury.	Rotherham.
Carlisle.	Rowley Regis.
Chatham.	Scarborough.
Cheltenham.	Shrewsbury.
Colchester.	Southampton.
Croydon.	Stalybridge.
Darlington.	Stockton.
Dewsbury.	Tipton.
Devonport.	Torquay.
Dover.	Tottenham.
Dudley.	Wakefield.
Gateshead.	West Derby.
Gorton.	West Ham.
Gravesend.	West Hartlepool.
Great Grimsby.	Yarmouth.
Halifax.	York.
Hastings.	

These cases of flagrant default vary much in blackness. Some of the towns, such as Gorton and Oldham, are near libraries supported by other larger towns, so that, somewhat meanly, they prefer to borrow books at other people's expense. Two or three towns, such as Southampton and Hastings, are perhaps, already provided with institutions partly serving in the place of Free Libraries. The remaining cases admit of little extenuation so far as my knowledge goes. Some cases are very bad. Bath appears to be the worst one of all. With a population numbering 52,557 in 1871, and which ought at least to make pretensions to intelligence and civilisation, the Bath ratepayers have four times rejected the Library Act. On the 8th of November, 1869, a public meeting was held in that town to consider the desirableness of adopting the Act, but a resolution in favour of the project was lost. The like result happened at a second meeting, on the 5th of November, 1872. In May, 1877, a common law poll of the burgesses was taken, with a negative result. Finally, as recently as October, 1880, a poll of the ratepayers was taken by means of voting-papers, but an ignorant majority again, for a fourth time, overruled an intelligent and public-spirited minority. On the last two occasions the trustees and owners of a considerable library, with the building in which it was deposited, offered the whole as a gift to the public if the Corporation were empowered to maintain it at the public expense, the library being, I believe, altogether suitable for the purpose. It is with regret that we must learn that the ratepayers have now lost their chance, the building having been sold and the books dispersed. With the exception of the metropolis, Hull appears to be the largest town in England which is still devoid of a rate-supported library, the population having been 121,892 in 1871, since probably increased in as high a ratio as in any other town in the kingdom. There is hardly any place which would derive more benefit from a Free Library, or which could more readily afford it. With some surprise, too, we find Burton-on-Trent in the list of defaulters; where there are many great breweries one might expect to meet one moderately-sized library.

It is quite an open question whether all towns of 10,000 inhabitants ought not to have libraries. The number of such towns, even in 1871, was 221, since greatly increased. This view of the matter would make a list of 135 defaulters, to be increased to at least 150 when the results of the new census are published. The question must soon arise, too, whether literature is to be confined to towns—whether rural parts may not share in the advantages of a library seated in the nearest market-town. Owing to the simple intervention of distance country people never can have the facilities of town dwellers; but on market-days almost every farmer's family could exchange books.

Thirteen or fourteen years ago, Mr. George Harris proposed the establishment of Parochial Libraries for working men, in small towns and rural districts.* The ground upon which he advocated his plan is very good as applying to Free Libraries generally—namely, that the country already spends a great deal of money in promoting education, and yet omits that small extra expenditure on a universal system of libraries which would enable young men and women to keep up the three R's and continue their education. We spend the £97, as Mr. Harris put it, and stingily decline the £3 per cent. really needed to make the rest of the £100 effective. But as applied to rural districts his scheme is weak in the fact that numbers and concentration are needed to make an efficient, attractive, and economical library. A small collection of a few hundred books is soon exhausted by an active reader, and fails ever afterwards to present the novelty which is the great incentive to reading. The fact is that there exists no legal impediment to the establishment of parochial libraries, because the Sixth Section of the Public Libraries Amendment Act, 1866 (29 & 30 Vic. cap. 114), provides that the Public Libraries Act of 1855, and the corresponding Scotch Act, "shall be applicable to any borough, district, or parish, or burgh, of whatever population." Moreover, the Fourth Section of the same Act enables any parish of whatever population to unite with the Town Council

* "Transactions of the Social Science Association," Manchester Meeting, 1866, p. 416.

of a neighbouring borough, or a Local Board, or other competent authority, and provide a Free Library at the joint expense. So far as I am aware these powers have hardly been put into operation at all.

According to Mr. Sutton's tables, there is only one Free Library district, that of Birkenhead, which has succeeded in incorporating the "out-townships." At Leamington, Newport, Northampton, Southport, Thurso, and Wigan, attempts have been made to get neighbouring districts to join, but without success. In several important boroughs, such as Liverpool, Salford, Manchester, even the lending libraries are open to residents of the country around, and in other places the librarians interpret their rules with great liberality. It goes without saying that the reference departments are freely open to all comers, any questions which are asked having a purely statistical purpose. The Manchester librarians printed in 1865 a table showing the residences of readers. While 62,597 belonged to Manchester and Salford, 5,666 came from other parts of Lancashire, 3 from Bedford, 849 from Cheshire, 124 from Derbyshire, 2 from Devonshire, 2 from Durham, 3 from Leicestershire, 83 from London, 139 from Yorkshire, 5 from Ireland, 8 from Scotland, 4 from Wales, and 6 from America. Although this liberality is wise and commendable in the case of such wealthy cities as Manchester and Liverpool, it is obviously unfair that small towns should provide books for half a county; and though the difficulty is surmounted in a few places, such as Dundalk and Rochdale, by allowing non-residents to pay a small subscription, the really satisfactory method would be for the parishes to adopt the Free Libraries Acts, and pay a small contribution to the funds of the nearest Free Library district.

If this were frequently done, there is little doubt that some arrangement could be devised for circulating the books of the lending department through the surrounding parishes, as proposed by Mr. J. D. Mullins. It would be rather too Utopian to suggest the adoption in this country of the method of book-lending which has long been in successful operation in the colony of Victoria. Thus, under the enlightened management of Sir Redmond Barry, whose recent death must be a serious loss to the colony, the duplicates of the Melbourne Public Library are placed in cases of oak, bound with brass clips, lined with green baize, and divided by shelves. Each case contains about fifty volumes, and is transmitted free of cost by railway or steamer to any Public Library, Mechanics' Institution, Athenæum, or corporate body which applies for a loan. When a series of lectures on any subject are about to be given in some remote part of the colony, a box of suitable books bearing on the subject will be made up at Melbourne upon application. The volumes may be retained for three months or more. The number of volumes thus circulated in 1876–7 was 8,000, and by the multiplication of utility, they were rendered equivalent to 32,000 volumes, in seventy-two towns of an aggregate population of 440,000. A full description of this method of circulation was given by Sir Redmond Barry at the London Conference of Librarians in 1877, in the Report of which important meeting it will be found (pp. 134–5, 194–9) duly printed. An account of an enterprising village library club in the New York county will be found in the American "Library Journal," vol. iii. No. 2, p. 67.

This method of circulating libraries is not, however, so novel as it might seem to the average Englishman. Not to speak of the extensive systems of country circulation maintained by Mudie, Smith, the London Library, and some other institutions, there has long existed in East Lothian a system of Itinerating Libraries, originally founded by Mr. Samuel Brown of Haddington. The operation of these libraries is fully described in a very able and interesting pamphlet upon "The Free Libraries of Scotland," written by an Assistant Librarian, and published by Messrs. John Smith and Son, of 129, West George Street, Glasgow. Samuel Brown's plan was to make up a collection of fifty books, to be stationed in a village for two years, and lent out gratuitously to all persons above the age of twelve years who would take proper care of them. At the end of the two years the books were called in and removed to another town or village, a fresh collection of fifty different works taking their place. The imperative need of novelty was thus fully provided for, and the utility of the books was multiplied in a very effective way. The scheme was for many years very successful, though hardly so much so as the more recent Free Libraries. The books appear to have been issued on an average about seven or eight times a year. At one period there were as many as fifty of these local libraries, all confined within the limits of East Lothian. The system is said to have been started about the year 1816, and it reached its climax about 1832. In that year a charge of one penny per volume was imposed during the first year of issue, Samuel Brown being of opinion that he had so far educated the population that they could bear this small impost. In this he was mistaken, and the number of readers began to fall off. The death of the originator in 1839 accelerated the decline of his admirable scheme, and at present but slight vestiges of his remarkable network of libraries remain.

It is interesting to find that this system of itinerating libraries attracted the special attention of Lord Brougham, and is described in his "Practical Observations upon the Education of the People" (London, 1825), a tract which marks an era in social reform, and contains the germs of much that has since been realised. Lord Brougham says of Samuel Brown's plan:

"It began with only a few volumes; but he now has nineteen *Itinerating Libraries* of fifty volumes each, which are sent round the different stations, remaining a certain time at each. For these there are nineteen divisions, and fifteen stations, four divisions being always in use at the chief town, and two at another town of some note. An individual at each station acts as librarian. There are 700 or 800 readers, and the expenses, under £60 a year, are defrayed by the produce of a sermon, the sale of some tracts, and subscriptions, in small sums averaging 5s. This plan is now adopted in Berwickshire, by Mr. Buchan, of Kelloe, with this very great improvement, that the current expenses are defrayed by the readers, who pay twopence a month, and, I hope, choose the books."

I cannot help thinking that this plan of itinerating libraries, or a cross between it and what we may call the Redmond Barry plan, as carried out at Melbourne, is just the thing needed to extend the benefits of the Free Library to the rural parts of England and Wales. Every three months, for instance, the central library in the market-town might despatch to each principal village in the neighbourhood a parcel of fifty books in a box like that used at Melbourne; after remaining twelve months in use there, the parcel should be returned to the principal library for examination and repair, and then reissued to some other village. A farthing or at the most a halfpenny rate would amply afford a sufficient contribution from the country parish to the market-town. The books might be housed and issued in the Board school-room, the parish school-room, the workman's club, or other public building, at little or no cost. Even the vestry of the parish church would not be desecrated by such a light-and-life-giving box of books. Should this plan of circulation be eventually carried into effect, we might expect that every town of 5,000 inhabitants would become the centre of a district. Estimating roughly, we ought to have some 500 Free Central Libraries and News-rooms, with a great many more, perhaps 3,000, village circulating libraries.

It ought to be added that even should the Free Library system assume in time the dimensions here contemplated there is no fear of injury to the interests of any respectable publishers, owners of circulating libraries, newspaper proprietors, or others. It is the unanimous opinion of those who observe the action of Free Libraries that they create rather than quench the thirst for literature. As Mr. Mullins says: "Booksellers, who feared that they would injure their trade, find that they create a taste for reading, and multiply their customers. Subscription Libraries find that the Free Libraries, so far from injuring them, serve as pioneers for them." At the same time, this plan would add considerably to the funds of the town libraries, and the country people when going to town would fairly acquire the right of using the news-rooms and reference library. No doubt it seems rather a grotesque idea to speak of a country bumpkin frequenting a reference library, but it is what we are gradually coming to. At any rate, it may most confidently be said that we must come to it, unless we are content to be left far behind in the race of intellectual, material, and moral progress. What we are too stupid and antiquated to do, the Colonies and the United States are doing. The eyes of the British landowner and the British farmer have been opened a little in the last few years, and the most conservative people will perhaps appreciate more than they would formerly have done the value of the warning —"Beware of the competition of your own educated offspring."

It is difficult, however, to find fault with minor towns, while the vast metropolis of London, in the wider sense of the name, remains practically devoid of rate-supported libraries. The fact itself is its own condemnation; no extenuation is possible; it is a case of mere ignorant impatience of taxation. It would not be correct to say there are no Free Libraries in London. There is in Westminster a real rate-supported library belonging to the united parishes of St. Margaret and St. John, started as long ago as 1857, with only three dissentient votes. It is a lending library possessing 11,700 volumes, with an annual issue of nearly 85,000 volumes, and it is supported by a halfpenny rate. To show the extent of the deficiency in London, it is enough to mention that the 86 provincial towns possessing Free Libraries have an aggregate population (in 1871) of not quite 6,000,000 persons; while London, with its one small rate-supported library, has a population of 3,620,000 persons.

Though there is only one library under the Public Libraries Act as yet, there are several Free Libraries of various importance and character. There is the admirable Guildhall Library, so well managed by Mr. Overall, and supported by the Corporation of the City. There is a small Free Library at Notting Hill, maintained entirely by the munificence of Mr. James Heywood, F.R.S. Several institutions, too, have of late thrown open small libraries to the public, as in the case of the Free Library of 1,000 volumes, with abundant periodicals, maintained entirely on voluntary contributions by the South

London Working Men's College at 143, Upper Kennington Lane. Bethnal Green practically possesses a fair library of 5,000 volumes, opened to the public by the trustees of "The Hall" in London Street. In St. Pancras an anonymous lady benefactress opened a small Free Library at 29, Camden Street, and after three years of successful operation it was placed in the hands of a committee of subscribers and residents of the parish, who are gradually increasing its usefulness.

There are, it is true, several other important libraries which are practically free to the public. The Lambeth Palace Library is open to the public on Mondays, Wednesdays, Thursdays, and Fridays, and Tuesday mornings; but the collection of books, though highly valuable to the scholar, is totally unsuited to popular use. The excellent library of the London Institution in Finsbury Circus is practically opened to the use of any suitable readers by the liberality of the managers of that institution and the public spirit of its principal librarian, Mr. E. B. Nicholson. The remarkable scientific library collected by Sir Francis Ronalds and bequeathed to the Society of Telegraph Engineers, is also available to the public. But such special libraries do not in the least fill the place occupied in Manchester, Birmingham, and other towns by the public libraries, with their numerous branches, news-rooms, &c.

It has been seriously argued that London does not want rate-supported libraries, because there is in the British Museum a vast library maintained at the cost of the State. To anyone in the least acquainted with the British Museum it is not necessary to give an answer to such an absurd argument. It would be in the highest degree wasteful and extravagant to open such a library to popular use. Panizzi's great reading-room is the national literary laboratory, whence no small part of the literature of the country directly or indirectly draws its material and inspiration. The cost may be considerable, but the work done there is essential. Already the privileges of the reading-room are to some extent abused by loungers, students reading the commonest text-books, or others who like the soft seats and rather warm atmosphere; but it is impossible to draw the line with perfect accuracy. If any change is to be made, more restriction rather than more freedom of entry to the Museum Library is desirable. In any case, the National Library is probably the most admirable and the most admirably managed institution belonging to the British nation; but it has nothing to do with the Free Library movement.

Not far from the Museum is another library which might well be converted into a Free Public Library. It is known as Dr. Williams's Library, and is placed in a very suitable building in Grafton Street, close to University College. It was founded by a Nonconformist minister, and contains a rather strong infusion of theological literature. In later years, however, the trustees have added the best books of general literature and science, and they admit any properly introduced person to read or even borrow the books. It can hardly be maintained, however, that the library renders the public services which it might readily do. In the close vicinity of University College and the Museum, it is not needed as a scholar's library, and therefore I think it should be converted into a people's library.

In spite of the existence of the above-mentioned and possibly several other practically Free Libraries, the fact is that there is no institution well adapted to give London ratepayers an idea of the advantages which are really within their reach under the Libraries Act, if they would once overcome the interested owners of cottage property and others, who from selfish motives oppose everything appearing to tend towards the slightest increase of the rates. If the populace of London could become personally acquainted with a well-constructed Free Library, with its open doors, its cheerful lights and bright fires, its inviting newspaper stands, its broad tables littered over with the best and most attractive periodical literature, with here and there a small table for chess and other quiet occupations, I feel sure they would demand a like institution in every division of that house-covered province called London. For some years past the Metropolitan Free Libraries Association, an offshoot of the Librarians' Conference, has been striving, under the able management of Mr. Edward B. Nicholson, to procure the adoption of the Acts in the metropolis, and it is to be hoped that we shall soon hear of some success.

In addition to their principal work of popularising the best literature of the country, public libraries have other functions to perform of no slight importance. The reference departments will naturally become, in the progress of time, the depositories of collections of local literature and records which would otherwise not improbably perish. The public librarian will consider it part of his duty to collect the ephemeral publications of the local press. Local pamphlets, municipal reports, companies' reports, fly-sheets of various kinds, local newspapers, minor magazines, election squibs; in fact, all the documents which register the life of the town and country, should be sedulously brought together, filed, and bound after due arrangement. It is sometimes supposed that the British Museum collects everything which issues from the press, but this applies at the best only to publications having copyright. Mr. W. E. A. Axon has urged that the Museum should not only collect all literature, but issue periodical indexes of all that is printed. I hardly see how it is possible for the Museum to cope with the ever-increasing mass of printed documents. Already the newspaper collections are increasing so much in bulk that it is difficult to find space for them. I know, as a positive fact, that there are immense numbers of statistical reports, police reports, country finance reports, and documents of all kinds, public, private, or semi-private, which seldom do and hardly can find their way to the Museum, or to any great metropolitan library; but where the Museum necessarily fails, the local library can easily succeed, so as to become in time the depository of invaluable materials for local history and statistical inquiry.

A good deal is already being done in this direction, as explained by Mr. W. H. K. Wright, of the Plymouth Free Library, in the Report of the first annual meeting of the Library Association (pp. 44-50). At Liverpool Mr. Cowell is collecting, arranging, and cataloguing a large number of books, plans, maps, and drawings of local interest. At Rochdale and Bristol like efforts are being made. In the Leicester

Library there is a distinct "Leicestershire Department." Birmingham has unfortunately lost its Shakespeare and Cervantes Libraries, and what is almost worse, its irreplaceable Staunton collection of Warwickshire literature has fallen a victim to the flames. But Mr. Mullins is doing all that can be done to recreate a valuable local library. At Plymouth Mr. Wright is himself forming the nucleus of a future Devon and Cornwall library.

Free Libraries will also become eventually the depositories of many special collections of books formed in the first place by enthusiastic collectors. At the London Conference of Librarians Mr. Cornelius Walford showed (Report, pp. 45–49) what important services may be done in this way; and in the Second Annual Report of the Library Association (pp. 54–60, Appendix, pp. 139–148) there is a really wonderful account by Mr. John H. Nodal of the special collections of books existing in the neighbourhood of Manchester. The best possible example of what may be done by a Free Library is furnished by the Wigan Free Public Library. The librarian at Wigan, Mr. Henry Tennyson Folkard, has formed a remarkable collection of works relating to mining, metallurgy, and manufactures, and has lately issued a first index catalogue. This forms a complete guide, or at least a first attempt at a complete guide, to the literature of the subject. It is to be hoped that in time other librarians will take up other special branches of literature, and prepare like bibliographical guides.

It is not well to ignore the fact that there may be a dark, or at least sombre and doubtful, side to the somewhat *couleur de rose* view which we have taken of Free Libraries. There are a few persons who assert that reading is capable of being carried to a vicious and enervating excess. At the Manchester meeting of the Library Association, Mr. J. Taylor Kay, the librarian of Owen's College, read a paper, much criticised at the time, on "The Provision of Novels in Rate-supported Libraries." In previous years Mr. Kay was one of the staff at the Manchester Free Library, and the following is the result of his observation of readers: "For many years a remarkable fact has been before my notice, and continually confirmed by a long experience in the Manchester Free Libraries, that schoolboys or students who took to novel reading to any great extent never made much progress in after-life. They neglected real practical life for a sensually imaginative one, and suffered accordingly from the enervating influence." This matter is far too debatable to be argued out in this place; and I would only answer to Mr. Kay that it is quite too late in the political day to think of restraining the reading of sensational literature. In this respect our boats were long since burnt behind us. Time was when the paper duty and various cunningly devised stamp duties were supposed to save the common people from the demoralising effects of literature. But the moralist has now only to notice some of the dingy shops crowded with cheap penny and halfpenny papers, in order to feel that restraint of literature is a thing of the past, as much as the parish stocks or the ducking-stool. There is a perfect deluge of low class and worthless periodical literature spreading over the country, and it can only be counteracted by offering gratuitous supplies of literature, which, whether it be fiction or not, may at any rate be pure and harmless, and often of great moral and intellectual excellence. What between the multiplying powers of the steam-press and the cheapness of straw and wood paper, fiction of the "penny dreadful" class can be issued *ad infinitum*. The only question is, whether the mass of the people are to read the most worthless and often immoral trash, or whether they are to have the best class of fiction—that of Dickens, of George Eliot, of Trollope, and the rest—placed within their reach.

Many attempts have been made and are being made by societies or by enlightened publishers to place constant supplies of pure and yet attractive literature within the reach of the mass of the people. But I venture to think that a wide extension of the Free Library system is a necessary complement to such efforts. It seems to me impossible to publish the best light literature at a price to compete with the inane penny or halfpenny novelettes, whereas the Free Library offers the best works of fiction or general literature free of charge to the borrowers, and at a cost to the public not exceeding a penny or twopence for a whole volume.

One point which it is worth while to notice about Free Libraries is, that they are likely to be most permanent and progressive institutions. I have pointed out in a former article ("Contemporary Review," Feb. 1880, vol. xxxvii., p. 181), how evanescent many kinds of social movements have proved to be. But an important collection of books, once formed and housed, is a solid nucleus, which attracts gifts and legacies, and often grows altogether beyond the conception of the first founders. It would be possible to mention many public libraries which had small beginnings, and are already great. With the increase of education and general intelligence, libraries will be far more esteemed institutions half a century hence than they are now. It is difficult to imagine, then, a wiser and better way in which a rich man or a rich woman may spend available wealth than in founding a Free Library in some town which has hitherto feared the first cost of the undertaking. Several Free Libraries have already been established more or less at the cost of individuals. The Liverpool Library was built at the expense of the late Sir William Brown, on a site given by the Corporation. The Paisley Library building was presented by Sir P. Coats. Mr. David Chadwick gave a building and books, all complete, to Macclesfield. Mr. Bass built the Derby Library. The Wigan Library building was erected by Mr. Thomas Taylor, while Mr. Winnard presented £12,000 for the purchase of books. The site of the Stoke-upon-Trent Library, together with a handsome sum of money, was given by Mr. C. M. Campbell, a local society presenting a library of books and a museum. At Reading the adoption of the Act was defeated seven years ago; but Mr. William Palmer, of the great biscuit firm, proceeded to open a library at his own expense, under the management of a lady-librarian. The library soon became so popular that when the ratepayers again voted there was only a single dissentient. Hereford, Coventry, and several other places, owe their libraries partly to benefactors, while in many cases valuable collections of books have been handed over to the public by individuals or societies. It is to be hoped that the list of benefactions will be largely increased in future years.

The economical working of Free Libraries has been much advanced by the invention of Indicators, which, like finger-posts at cross-roads, afford a great deal of information at the least possible cost. The one now most in use was invented by Mr. John Elliot, librarian to the Wolverhampton Public Library. It was preceded, indeed, by a rude kind of indicator-board with the numbers of the books painted upon it, and pegs which could be stuck into holes so as to show to the library attendants whether the book so numbered was in or out. Mr. Diall, of Liverpool, improved upon this board by using numbered blocks, so moving upon a slide that they would exhibit to the public the numbers of all books available for borrowing.

Mr. Elliot's indicator is a much more valuable instrument, for it not only shows at a glance whether any book is in or out, but it also affords a means of recording mechanically the names of borrowers, so as almost entirely to replace the use of book-ledgers or other written records. It is well described by Mr. W. J. Haggerston, of the South Shields Library, at a conference of the Northern Union of Mechanics' Institutions. Some account of it will also be found in the "Transactions" of the First Meeting of the Library Association, in the paper of Mr. James Yates (pp. 76–78) already referred to. The Indicator consists of upright square frames, each containing a thousand small shelves, in ten vertical divisions of one hundred shelves each. The two faces of the frame are identical, with the exception that the one exposed towards the public is covered with plate-glass so as to prevent meddling, while the librarians have access to the inner face. Each shelf is numbered on both faces with the number of the one book which it represents. When a borrower takes a book out he hands his library ticket to the librarian, who writes upon it the number of the book taken and the date of borrowing, and then places it on the shelf corresponding to the book, where it remains until the book is returned. If any other person comes intending to borrow the same book, he looks at the Indicator, and seeing the ticket of the borrower lying on the corresponding shelf, knows at once that the book is out. It is also possible to indicate, by appropriate marks placed on the shelves, that books are at the binder's, withdrawn from circulation, or missing. An immense deal of trouble in searching and inquiring is saved by this simple means. The Indicator, as thus constructed, has been in use at the Public Libraries of Paisley, Exeter, Coventry, Hereford, Bilston, Stockton-on-Tees, Leeds, South Shields, Wolverhampton, Cardiff, Leicester, Derby, Sheffield, Darlaston, and Southport, besides some private subscription libraries.

Efficient as Elliot's Indicator may seem, Mr. Cotgreave, formerly Librarian at Wednesbury, but now in charge of the beautiful little Library approaching completion at Richmond (Surrey), has succeeded in making improvements upon it. In this new Indicator the frames and shelves are much the same as in Elliot's, but each shelf bears a very small book or ledger, about three inches long and one inch wide. This is attached to a tin slide bearing the number of the library book on each end, but in different colours. When a borrower applies for any book, say 117D, the librarian, while delivering the book, takes out of the Indicator the corresponding slide and small ledger, records in spaces therein the number of the borrower's card and the date of issue, and then replaces the slide with the reverse end foremost—*i.e.*, towards the public. Any subsequent applicant will then see by the altered colour of the book number that the book is out. Mr. Cotgreave has also devised a simple system of date marks, which will show in which week, and, if required, on what day in each week, a book was borrowed. The chief advantage of this Indicator is the fact that it preserves in the small ledger a permanent record of the use of each book. There are various incidental advantages not easily to be appreciated, except by those frequently using these devices. It is almost impossible, for instance, to make mistakes with Cotgreave's Indicator by misplacing cards, because all the shelves are full except that which is being dealt with. The numbers of the books, again, can be rearranged, if required, without taking the framework of the Indicator to pieces.

The economy effected in the working of a large public

library by the use of these Indicators is very remarkable. Thus it is stated that in the Leeds Public Library books can be easily issued by the use of Elliot's Indicator at the rate of 76 per hour, at a cost of £1 3s. 3d. per 1,000 volumes. In the Leeds Mechanics' Institution books were issued *without* an Indicator at the rate of 11 per hour, at a cost of £5 6s. per 1,000. At South Shields as many as 169 volumes have been issued in one hour, being at the rate of nearly one volume per minute for each member of the staff! At Wolverhampton one librarian, assisted by two boys, effected a total issue in one year of 97,800 books. Technical details of this sort may seem trifling, but they are really of great importance in showing what ingenuity and systematisation can do in bringing the best classes of literature within the reach of the people.

Looking back over ten, fifteen, or twenty years, it is surprising to notice what an advance has been accomplished in our notions of library economy and etxension. This is greatly due, I believe, to the reflex effect of American activity. A glance through the Special Report on the Public Libraries in the United States of America, their history, condition, and management, issued at Washington in 1876, shows how wide are the American ideas of Library management. *The Library Journal*, edited by Mr. Melvil Dewey, and forming the official organ of the American and English Library Associations, supplies equally striking evidence of Library enterprise. The Library Association of the United Kingdom may have been inspired by the American spirit of associated labour, but it has soon become a thoroughly British body. I doubt whether any association could be named, which, in two short years, or, including the preliminary conference of librarians, in three years, has done more real and useful work. The two Annual Reports, together with the Conference Report, owe much to the editing which they have received from Mr. Henry R. Tedder and Mr. Ernest Thomas. The indexes prepared by Mr. Tedder are models of the indexing art, and must almost satisfy the requirements of the Index Society. These Reports, too, will probably be sought after by bibliophiles on account of their beautiful typographical execution, due to Messrs.

Whittingham & Co., of the Chiswick Press. A French critic, recently writing in *Le Livre*, the French Bibliographical Journal, has commented on the luxurious paper and printing of these remarkable Reports. But it is more pertinent to our immediate purpose to observe that the Reports are full of all kinds of information bearing upon the advantages, purposes, and management of Public Libraries. The Library Association has also recently commenced the issue, through Messrs. Trübner, of a monthly journal of proceedings which contains much additional information. Those who are unable to consult these more voluminous publications, but desire to know how a Free Public Library is started, should procure Mr. W. E. A. Axon's well-known little *brochure*, "Hints on the Formation of Small Libraries intended for Public Use." This tract was prepared for the Co-operative Congress of 1869, has been printed several times in a separate form at home and abroad, and is to be found reprinted in Mr. Axon's "Handbook of the Public Libraries of Manchester and Salford" (pp. 183-9). More detailed information, including the text of the Free Libraries Acts, is to be found in Mr. J. D. Mullins' tract on "Free Libraries and News-rooms; their Formation and Management," the third edition of which was lately on sale by Messrs. Henry Sotheran & Co., at 36, Piccadilly. The standard work upon the subject is, of course, Mr. Edward Edwards' "Memoirs of Libraries," published in two volumes in 1859, a work which has been of great service in promoting the cause of the Libraries Acts.

THE USE AND ABUSE OF MUSEUMS.*

It is a remarkable fact that, although public Museums have existed in this country for more than a century and a quarter, and there are now a very great number of Museums of one sort or another, hardly anything has been written about their general principles of management and economy. In the English language, at least, there is apparently not a single treatise analysing the purposes and kinds of Museums, or describing systematically the modes of arrangement. In the course of this article I shall have occasion to refer to a certain number of lectures, addresses, or papers which have touched more or less expressly upon this subject; but these are all of a slight and brief character. The only work at all pretending to a systematic form with which I am acquainted is that upon "The Administrative Economy of the Fine Arts in England," by Mr. Edward Edwards, of the British Museum. But this book was printed as long ago as 1840, and has long been forgotten, if indeed it could ever have been said to be known. Moreover it is mostly concerned with the principles of management of art galleries, schools of art, and the like. Many of the ideas put forward by Edwards have since been successfully fathered by better-known men, and some of his suggestions, such as that of multiplying facsimiles of the best works of art, are only now approaching realisation.

It is true, indeed, that a great deal of inquiry has taken

* Written in 1881-82.

place from time to time about the British Museum, which forms the Alpha, if not the Omega, of this subject. Whatever has been written about Museums centres upon the great national institution in Bloomsbury. The Blue Book literature is abundant, but naturally unknown to the public. The evidence taken before the recent Royal Commission on Scientific Instruction and the advancement of Science, contains a great deal of information bearing upon Museum economy, including the opinions of the chief officers of the British Museum; but little or nothing bearing on the subject was embodied in the reports of the Commission.

I do not propose in this article to boil down the voluminous contents of Blue Books, but, depending chiefly upon my own memory of many museums and exhibitions which I have visited from time to time, to endeavour to arrive at some conception of the purposes, or rather the many purposes, which should be set before us in creating public collections of the kind, and the means by which those purposes may be most readily attained. Although the subject has hardly received any attention as yet, I believe it is possible to show on psychological or other scientific grounds that much which has been done in the formation of Museums is fundamentally mistaken. In other cases it is more by good luck than good management that a favourable result has been attained. In any case a comparison of the purposes and achievements of Museums must be instructive.

According to its etymology the name Museum means a temple or haunt of the Muses, and any place appropriated to the cultivation of learning, music, pictorial art, or science might be appropriately called a Museum. On the Continent they still use *Musée* in a rather wider sense than we in England use Museum; but it is remarkable that, although the art of delighting by sound has long been called emphatically *Music*, we never apply the name Museum to a Concert Hall. In this country we have specialised the word so much that we usually distinguish Museums from libraries, picture galleries and music halls, reserving the name for collections and displays of scientific specimens, or concrete artistic objects and curiosities of various kinds. As a library contains books which speak from the printed page, or the ancient inscribed parchment, so the Museum contains the books of Nature, and the sermons which are in stones. About the use and abuse of printed books there cannot arise much question. It may be assumed as a general rule that when a person reads a book, he understands it and draws some good from it. The labour of reading is a kind of labour test, and gives statistics to the effect that certain classes of books are used so many times in the year on the average; there is little need to go behind these facts. But it is somewhat otherwise with public Museums, because the advantage which an individual gets from the visit may vary from *nil* up to something extremely great. The degree of instruction derived is quite incapable of statistical determination. Not only is there great difference in degree, but there is vast difference also in the kind of benefit derived. Many go to a public Museum just as they take a walk, without thought or care as to what they are going to see; others have a vague idea that they will be instructed and civilised by seeing a multitude of novel and beautiful objects; a very small fraction of the total public go because they really understand the things displayed, and have got ideas about them to be verified, corrected, or extended. Unfortunately it is difficult to keep the relative values of these uses of a Museum distinct. There seems to be a prevalent idea that if the populace can only be got to walk about a great building filled with tall glass-cases, full of beautiful objects, especially when illuminated by the electric light, they will become civilised. At the South Kensington Art Museum they make a great point of setting up turnstiles to record the precise numbers of visitors, and they can tell you to a unit the exact amount of civilising effect produced in any day, week, month, or year. But these turnstiles hardly take account of the fact that the neighbouring wealthy residents are in the habit, on a wet day, of packing their children off in a cab to the so-called Brompton Boilers, in order that they may have a good run through the galleries. To the far greater part of the people a large brilliantly lighted Museum is little or nothing more than a promenade, a bright kind of lounge, not nearly so instructive as the shops of Regent Street or Holborn. The well-known fact that the attendance at Museums is greatest on wet days is very instructive.

Not only is a very large collection of various objects ill-suited for educational purposes, but it is apt to create altogether erroneous ideas about the true method of education. The least consideration, indeed, ought to convince any sensible person that to comprehend the purpose, construction, mode of use, and history of a single novel object or machine, would usually require from (say) half-an-hour up to several hours or days of careful study. A good lecturer can always make a lecture of an hour's duration out of anything falling within his range of subject. How then is it possible that persons glancing over some thousands of unfamiliar specimens in the British Museum or the South Kensington Courts, can acquire, in the moment devoted to each, the slightest comprehension of what they witness? To children especially the glancing at a great multitude of diverse things is not only useless but actually pernicious, because it tends to destroy that habit of concentration of attention, which is the first condition of mental acquisition. It is no uncommon thing to see troops of little schoolboys filing through the long galleries of a Museum. No more senseless employment could be imagined. They would be far better employed in flattening their noses for an hour or two against the grocer's shop window where there is a steam mill grinding coffee, or watching the very active bootmaker who professes to sole your boots while you wait.

A great deal has been said and written about the unities of the drama, and "canons" are said to have been laid down on the subject. It does not seem, however, to have occurred to the creators and managers of Museums, that so far as education is aimed at, a certain unity of effect is essential. There may be many specimens exhibited, but they ought to have that degree of relation that they may conduce to the same general mental impression. It is in this way, I believe, that the Thorwaldsen Museum at Copenhagen exercises a peculiarly impressive effect upon the multitudes of all classes of Danes and Swedes who visit it. This Museum contains in a single building almost the whole works of this great sculptor, together with all the engravings and pictures having reference to the same. Very numerous though the statues and bas-reliefs are, there is naturally a unity of style in them, and the visitor as he progresses is gradually educated to an appreciation of the works. The only objects in the building tending towards incongruity of ideas are Thorwaldsen's own collection of antiquities and objects of art; but even these are placed apart, and if visited, they tend to elucidate the tastes and genius of the artist.

In somewhat the same way we may explain the ineffaceable effect which certain other foreign galleries produce upon the traveller, especially those of the Vatican. This is not due simply to the excellence of any particular works of art, for in the Louvre or the British Museum we may see antique sculpture of equal excellence. But in the principal Vatican galleries we are not distracted by objects belonging to every place and time. The genius of the classical age spreads around us, and we leave one manifestation of it but to drink in a deeper impression from the next.

I hardly know anything in this kingdom producing a like unity and depth of effect. No doubt the gallery in the British Museum appropriated to the Elgin and other Greek sculptures presents a striking unity of genius well calculated to impress the visitor, provided he can keep clear of the Assyrian bulls which are so close at hand, and the great variety of Egyptian and other antiquities which beset his path. It is in the Crystal Palace, however, that we find the most successful attempt to carry the spectator back to a former stage of art. The Pompeian House is the best possible Museum of Roman life and character. For a few minutes at least the visitor steps from the present; he shuts out the age of iron, and steam, and refreshment contractors, and the like, and learns to realise the past. As to the Alhambra Court, it is a matchless lesson in art and architecture.

Everybody must have felt again how pleasing and impressive is the Hampton Court Palace, with its gardens and appropriate collections of historical pictures. In the same way I would explain the peculiar charm attaching to the Museum of the Hôtel de Cluny, where the ancient buildings and traditions of the place harmonise entirely with its present contents and purposes.

In Museums, as a general rule, we see things torn from their natural surroundings and associated with incongruous objects. In a great cathedral church we find indeed architectural fragments of many ages, and monuments of the most diverse styles. But they are in their places nevertheless, and mark and register the course of time. In a modern art Museum, on the contrary, the collection of the articles is accidental, and to realise the true meaning and beauty of an object the spectator must possess a previous knowledge of its historical bearings and a rare power of imagination, enabling him to restore it ideally to its place. Who, for instance, that sees some of the reproductions of the mosaics of Ravenna hanging high up on the walls of the Museum at South Kensington, can acquire therefrom the faintest idea of the mysterious power of those long lines of figures in the Church of St. Apollinaris? Although it is, no doubt, better to have such reproductions available, it is not well to cherish delusion. The persistent system of self-glorification long maintained by the managers of the South Kensington Museum seems actually to have been successful in persuading people that the mere possession and casual inspection of the contents of the South Kensington courts and galleries has created æsthetic and artistic tastes in a previously unæsthetic people. Such a fallacy does not stand a moment's serious examination. It is dispersed, for instance, by the single fact that the fine arts are in a decidedly low state in Italy, although the Italians have had access to the choicest works of art since the time of the Medicis. It might also be easily pointed out that the revival of true æsthetic taste in England, especially in the direction of architecture, began long before South Kensington was heard of. It is to men of genius, such as Pugin, and Barry, and Gilbert Scott, and to no Government officials, that we owe the restoration of true taste in England, only prevented for a short time, as I hope, by the present craze about the bastard Queen Anne style.

The worst possible conception of the mode of arranging Museums is exemplified at South Kensington, especially in those interminable exhibition galleries which the late Captain Fowke erected around the Horticultural Society's unfortunate gardens. When I went, for instance, to see the admirable collection of early printed books, at the Caxton Loan Exhibition, I had to enter at the south-eastern entrance, and after successfully passing the turnstiles found myself in the midst of a perplexing multitude of blackboards, diagrams, abacuses, chairs and tables, models of all sorts of things, forming, I believe, the educational collections of the Science and Art Department. Having overcome tendencies to diverge into a dozen different lines of thought, I passed on only to find myself among certain ancient machines and complicated models which it was impossible not to pause at. Having torn myself away, however, I fell among an extensive series of naval models, with all kinds of diagrams and things relating to them. Here forgetfulness of the Caxton Exhibition seemed to fall upon all the visitors; a good quarter of an hour, and the best, because the freshest, quarter of an hour, was spent, if not wasted. But when at length it occurred to people that it was time to see that which they came to see, the only result was to fall from Scylla into Charybdis in the form of the late Mr. Frank Buckland's admirable Fishery Collection. Now at the Norwich Fisheries Exhibition, and under various other circumstances, nothing can be better and more appropriate and interesting than the collection of fish-culture apparatus, the models of big salmon and the like. But anything less congruous to old Caxton editions cannot be imagined. As a matter of fact, I observed that nearly all the visitors succumbed to these fish, and for a time at least forgot altogether what they were come about. When at length the Loan Exhibition was reached, the already distracted spectator was ill fitted to cope with the very extensive series of objects which he wished seriously to inspect. In returning, moreover, he had again to run the gauntlet of the big fish, the complicated naval machines, and the educational apparatus. An afternoon thus spent leaves no good mental effect. To those who come merely to pass the time, it carries out this purpose; but the mental impression is that of a nightmare of incomprehensible machines, interminable stairs, suspicious policemen, turnstiles, and staring fish.

But I must go a step further and question altogether the wisdom of forming vast collections for popular educational purposes. No doubt the very vastness of the Paris and other International Exhibitions was in itself impressive and instructive, but speaking from full experience of the Paris as well as the London exhibitions, I question whether it was possible for any mind to carry away useful impressions of a multitude of objects so practically infinite. A few of the larger or more unique objects may be distinctly remembered, or a few specimens connected with the previous studies and pursuits of the spectator may have been inspected in a way to produce real information; but I feel sure the general mental state produced by such vast displays is one of perplexity and vagueness, together with some impression of sore feet and aching heads.

As regards children, at any rate, there can be no doubt that a few striking objects are far better than any number of more monotonous ones. At the Zoological Gardens, for instance, the lions, the elephants, the polar bears and especially the sea lions, are worth all the rest of the splendid collection put together. After the ordinary visitor, whether young or old, has become well interested in these, it has an obviously depressing and confusing effect to proceed through the long series of antelopes.

In this, as in so many other cases, the half is better than the whole. Much inferior as the Hamburg Zoological Gardens may be in the variety of the collection to that in the Regent's Park, I am inclined to prefer it as regards the striking manner in which the principal animals are displayed.

The evil effect of multiplicity of objects used to be most strikingly displayed in that immensely long gallery at the British Museum which held the main part of the zoological collections. The ordinary visitor, thoroughly well distracted by the room previously passed through, here almost always collapsed, and sauntered listlessly along the closely-packed ranks of birds, monkeys, and animals of every possible shape and clime. If the attention could be stimulated anew, this was done by a few cases containing beautiful birds grouped about nests in the manner of life. These are, I presume, the experimental cases referred to by Dr. J. E. Gray in his remarks on Museums;* and I can positively assert that these few cases were, for popular purposes, actually superior to the whole of the other vast collections in the room. The fact of course is that the contents of the British Museum have been brought together for the highest scientific ends, and it is a merely incidental purpose which they serve in affording a show for young or old people who have nothing else to do but wander through the store-rooms. The delectation of loungers and youngsters is no more the purpose of a great national Museum than the *raison d'être* of the Royal Mint is to instruct visitors in mechanical processes, or the final end of the House of Commons is to interest the occupants of the galleries. I ought to add that, although the preceding remarks on the evil educational effect of vast collections are founded entirely on my own observation and experience, they are entirely borne out by the opinions of Dr. Gray, of Dr. Gunther, and of several witnesses who gave evidence before the Commission on Scientific Instruction.

I venture to submit that on psychological and educational grounds the arrangement of diverse collections in a long series of continuous galleries, worst exemplified at South Kensington, but also unfortunately to be found in the older galleries of the British Museum, is a complete mistake. Every collection ought to form a definite congruous whole, which can be visited, studied, and remembered with a certain unity of impression. If a great Museum like the British Museum contains many departments, there ought to be as many distinct buildings, each adapted to its special purpose, so as to exhibit a distinct and appropriate

* British Association, Bath Meeting, 1864; "Address to the Section of Botany and Zoology," *Trans. of Sections*, pp. 75-80.

coup d'œil. Were a skilful modern artist, for instance, to construct a special building for the Greek sculptures of the Museum, how vastly would it assist in displaying their beauties.

On the whole I am inclined to think that the Museum of Economic Geology in Jermyn Street is one of the best models, combining strictly scientific purposes and arrangement with good popular effect. The larger objects and more interesting groups and cases are brought forward in a conspicuous manner, and can be reached without passing through an interminable series of distracting specimens of less interest. The general disposal of the geological collections is such as to give some idea of their natural order and succession. At the same time the *coup d'œil* of the Museum is distinctly good, the light in the more essential parts is excellent, and the size and general approach to homogeneity of the collections is such as fully to occupy without exhausting the attention of the visitors.

After all, the best Museum is that which a person forms for himself. As with the books of a public library, so in the case of public Museums, the utility of each specimen is greatly multiplied with regard to the multitude of persons who may inspect it. But the utility of each inspection is vastly less than that which arises from the private possession of a suitable specimen which can be kept near at hand to be studied at any moment, handled, experimented and reflected upon. A few such specimens probed thoroughly, teach more than thousands glanced at through a glass-case. The whole British Museum accordingly will not teach a youth as much as he will learn by collecting a few fossils or a few minerals, *in situ* if possible, and taking them home to examine and read and think about. Where there is any aptitude for science, the beginning of such a collection is the beginning of a scientific education. The passion for collection runs into many extravagances and absurdities; but it is difficult to collect without gaining knowledge of more or less value, and with the young especially it is almost better to collect any kind of specimens than nothing. Even the postage-stamp collecting mania is not to be despised or wholly condemned. At any rate a stamp collector who arranges his specimens well and looks out their places of issue in an atlas, will learn more geography than all the dry text-books could teach him. But in the case of the natural sciences the habit of collecting is almost essential, and the private Museum is the key to the great public Museum. The youth who has a drawer full of a few score minerals at home which he has diligently conned, will be entranced with delight and interest when he can first visit the superb collection of the British Museum. He will naturally seek out the kinds of minerals previously known to him, and will be amazed at the variety, beauty, and size of the specimens displayed. His knowledge already having some little depth will be multiplied by the extent of the public collection. The same considerations will of course apply to palæontology, zoology, petrology, and all other branches of the classificatory sciences.

In all probability, indeed, botany is the best of all the natural sciences in the educational point of view, because the best Public Botanical Museum is in the fields and woods and mountains. In this case the specimens are available in every summer walk, and can be had without the slaughter attaching to zoology and entomology. Though the average Englishman of the present generation too often makes it the amusement and joy of his life to slaughter any living thing he comes across, surely our young ones should be brought up differently. Now botany affords in an easy and wholly unobjectionable way an unlimited variety of beautiful natural objects, the diagnosis and classification of which give a mental exercise of the most valuable possible kind. There can be no doubt whatever that the late Professor Henslow was perfectly right in advocating the general teaching of botany to children even in primary schools, and his efforts were the first step towards that general extension of real as opposed to verbal teaching, which we may hope to see ultimately prevail. Botany, however, is less related to the subject of public Museums than other natural sciences, because it is quite clear that every botanical student should form his own herbarium, and the great public herbaria of Kew and Bloomsbury can be of little use, except to facilitate the researches of scientific botanists. The glass-houses of Kew, of the Botanical Gardens at Liverpool, Manchester, Edinburgh, and elsewhere, must naturally delight a botanical student more than other people; but the great cost of maintaining an elaborate botanical garden renders it undesirable to attempt the work in many places. It is very desirable, however, that every local Museum should have an herbarium of the local plants, which, though kept under lock and key, should be rendered accessible to any person wishing to consult it for really botanical purposes. Such a public herbarium greatly encourages the private collector by the facility for verifying names and ascertaining deficiencies.

But whatever may be said against particular Museums and collections, there can be no doubt whatever that the increase in the number of Museums of some sort or other must be almost co-extensive with the progress of real popular education. The Museum represents that real instruction, that knowledge of things as they are which is obtained by the glance of the eye, and the touch of the fingers. The time ought to have arrived when the senseless verbal teaching formerly, and perhaps even yet, predominant in schools should be abandoned. A child should hardly be allowed to read about anything unless a specimen or model, or, at any rate, a picture of the thing can be placed before it. Words come thus to be, as they should be, the handles to ideas, instead of being empty sounds. The Kindergarten system is a reform entirely in the right direction, though it seems to run into some extravagances and absurdities, owing to the natural excess of zeal and ingenuity in reformers. But I hope the time is not far distant when it will be considered essential for every school to contain a small Museum, or, more simply speaking, a large cupboard to contain a few models of geometrical forms, mechanical powers, together with cheap specimens of the commoner kinds of rocks, minerals, and almost any kinds of objects interesting to children. Mr. Tito Pagliardini has recently advocated the attaching of a rural scholastic Museum to every village Board-school,* but he quite overshoots the mark in recommending that every school should have a separate wing of the building filled with

* "Transactions" of the Social Science Association, Cheltenham, 1878, pp. 721-728.

all the birds shot in the neighbourhood, or any miscellaneous objects which any people of the neighbourhood may present. Again, when he insists that "the walls of every school-room should be literally papered with maps, and the beautiful synoptic diagrams and tables of geology, natural history, botany, etc. . . . and copies of choice works of art to be found in that educational paradise, the South Kensington Museum," he just illustrates what ought *not* to be done. The papering of the walls of a school-room with all sorts of diverse and incongruous things is calculated only to confuse youthful minds and render them careless about the said diagrams, etc., when they become the subjects of a lesson. The walls of a school-room may well be rendered lively by a few good pictures or other pleasing objects, but it would be much better to stow away the diagrams and other things derived from "the Educational Paradise," until they are needed. A diagram thus brought out freshly and singly would be far more likely to attract the children's interest than if it had long been familiar and unheeded among a crowd of other incomprehensible diagrams. On the same ground I would rather have the small Museum enclosed in an opaque cupboard than constantly exposed to view.

Doubts may be entertained whether sufficient discrimination has always been observed as regards the classes of things exhibited in recently formed or recently proposed Museums. The so-called National Food Collection, originally formed at South Kensington in 1859, is a case in point. It arose out of an attempt to represent the chemical compositions of different kinds of food, by means of small heaps of the constituent substances. It was an experiment, and a very proper experiment, in "visual teaching," the idea being that the poorer classes who know nothing of chemistry might learn by direct observation what kinds of food yield most nutriment. But, as a general rule, novel experiments may be expected to fail. I fancy that the result of this experiment is to show that such "visual teaching" is a mistake. On a little consideration it will be understood that in such collections the specimens have a totally different function to perform from that of true specimens. They are indicators of quantity and proportion, relations which may be better learned from diagrams, printed books, or oral instruction; whereas the purpose of a true Museum is to enable the student to see the things and realise sensually the qualities described in lessons or lectures; in short, to learn what cannot be learnt by words. As to the actual food itself, and its constituents, they are either so familiar as not to need any exhibition, or at any rate they need not be repeated over and over again as they are in this teaching collection. There is not space to argue the matter out at full length here; but it seems to me that in these food collections, now relegated to the Bethnal Green Museum, the line is wrongly drawn between oral or printed and visual teaching. It is a further serious objection to such collections, if collections they can be called, that if developed to any great extent they would render Museums insufferably tedious. A well designed popular Museum should always attract and recreate and excite interest; the moral should be hidden, and the visitor should come and go with the least possible consciousness that he is being educated.

Another mistake which is made, or is likely to be made, is in forming vast collections of technical objects, the value and interest of which must rapidly pass away. We hear it frequently urged, for instance, that a great industrial country like England ought to have its great industrial Museum, where every phase of commercial and manufacturing processes should be visibly represented. There ought to be specimens of the new materials in all their qualities and kinds; the several stages of manufacture should be shown by corresponding samples; the machines being too large to be got into the Museum should be shown in the form of models or diagrams; the finished products, lastly, should be exhibited and their uses indicated. It is easy enough to sketch out vast collections of this sort, but it is a mere phantasm which, it is to be hoped, it will never be attempted to realise. Something of this kind was sketched out by Mr. C. J. Woodward, of the Midland Institute, in his paper on " A Sketch of a Museum suited to the wants of a manufacturing district, with a special reference to Birmingham and the neighbourhood." *

It is forgotten that if such a technical exhibition were to be so complete and minute as to afford every information to those engaged in each particular trade, it would be far vaster in aggregate extent than any Great International Exhibition yet held. If it were to be a permanent Museum, ten years would hardly elapse before its contents would become obsolete, owing to the progress of invention. Either, then, the Museum would have to be constantly expanded so as to contain the new alongside of the old, or else the new would have to push out the old. In the latter case the Museum would approximate to a shop, or at best to the periodic exhibitions of which we have so many, and which are of a different character and purpose from the permanent typical collections which we call Museums. The fact is, however, that the real technical exhibitions of the country are to be found in the shop windows and the factories; and when the newest phases of productive ingenuity may be readily examined in the reality of life, it is a waste of good money to establish great buildings and great staffs of officers to carry on what is, comparatively speaking, child's play. If anybody wants to see the newest notions of the day in the way of machinery, domestic utensils, tools, toys, and the infinite objects of ordinary use, he has only to saunter down Holborn from Bloomsbury to the Holborn Viaduct. He will there find an almost unbroken succession of remarkable shop-window exhibitions, with which no exhibition, even under the most distinguished patronage, can possibly compete.

From this point of view I think it is a happy thing that the Loan Exhibition of Scientific Instruments was dispersed and not converted into a permanent Museum, as some scientific men wished. The collection was indeed an admirable one, and every ten or fifteen years we might wish to see a like one. But the greater part of the contents could not have that finality and permanent interest demanding their perpetual exhibition,

* Social Science Association, Birmingham, 1868, p. 449.

Each chemical or physical research needs its own peculiar apparatus, which ought to be sufficiently described, if successful, in the scientific record of the experiments. Were all the apparatus used to be treasured up at South Kensington, it could only produce additional bewilderment in those whose brains have been already scattered by the educational and other numerous collections of that locality. As to the principal instruments, such as microscopes, telescopes, dividing engines, cathetometers, thermometers, hygrometers, anemometers, and the like, they undergo such frequent modification and improvement, that the best forms would never be sought in a Museum, but in the shops of the principal manufacturers. No doubt, however, there are a few standard instruments employed in researches of especial importance which it would be well to preserve for ever.

The same considerations hardly apply to the Parkes Museum of Hygiene now open to the inspection of the public during certain hours at University College, London. This may be regarded as the collection of samples of a most important kind of sanitary Institute. To allow such a Museum to grow to any great bulk, and to preserve all the obsolete forms of syphon traps, sinks and what not, would surely defeat its own purposes.

It is an interesting sign of the times that the holding of industrial exhibitions has of late years become itself a profitable branch of industry. Some years since the proprietors of the Pomona Gardens, a place of popular entertainment at Manchester, built a large exhibition hall and opened an exhibition of machinery, which quite eclipsed that shortly before brought together by a more public body. In the last few years the Agricultural Hall at Islington has been a scene of industrial exhibitions of a very interesting character, which, it is to be hoped, will dispel for ever the disgusting walking feats formerly carried on there. Each exhibition indeed is somewhat limited in extent, but it is quite as large and as various as a visitor can inspect during an afternoon, and the latest novelties of invention, but a few weeks old, may often be seen there.

Then, again, if anybody wants to learn how things are made, it can only be done by visiting the factories themselves and seeing the real work in progress. A busy factory is one of the very best kinds of educational Museums, and it is impossible to urge too strongly upon the proprietors of large works conveniently situated in or near large towns, the advantage which they confer upon the public by allowing inspection. I know several important works in Manchester and elsewhere where wise and liberal ideas have long prevailed in this way. The visitor, furnished with the least proper introduction, is handed over at once to an intelligent guide, and shown round the regular course of the manufacture. On leaving, the visitors deposit about sixpence per head in a box to be devoted to the workmen's benefit society. The expense and interruption to work produced by systematic visiting in this way must be very slight, and must usually be more than repaid (though this, I am sure, is not the motive) by the advertisement of the goods. Proprietors of factories generally close their works to the public under the plea that they have all sorts of secret processes and arrangements which they cannot allow strangers and foreigners to learn; but in most cases this is absurd. If there is any real secret to be learned, there are hundreds of workmen in a busy factory through whom it can be learned. Of course, what applies to private factories, may be said still more strongly of Government works of all kinds. Entrance is already obtained pretty easily to the Royal Mint, the Dockyards, Woolwich Arsenal, etc. So great is the educational and recreational value of admission to such establishments, that the Government ought to insist upon the utmost possible freedom of admission for visitors consistent with the work being carried on. The manner in which the public were until lately admitted, or rather not admitted, to the Tower Museum, for instance, was highly absurd and objectionable. The Tower is just one of those natural historical Museums which, from the unity and appropriateness of its contents and surroundings, is calculated most strongly to impress the visitor. It is an almost unique and priceless historical possession. But it is impossible to imagine why entrance should be barred on most days of the week by a charge of 6d., while the costly Museums in other parts of the town are free. Not even students have to be considered; and nothing but free opening on every day of the week can be considered a satisfactory settlement.

A good deal has been said about the cellars of the British Museum, where there are supposed to be great quantities of duplicates or other valuable objects stowed away uselessly. I cannot profess to say, from my own knowledge, what there may or may not be in those cellars; but I have no hesitation in asserting that a great national Museum of research like that at Bloomsbury ought to have great cellars or other store-rooms filled with articles which, though unfitted for public exhibition, may be invaluable evidence in putting together the history of the world, both social and physical. If the views advocated above are correct, it distinctly injures the effect, for popular educational purposes, of fine specimens of art and science to crowd them up with an infinite number of inferior or less interesting objects; accordingly a great number of imperfect remains, fragments of statues and monuments, inferior copies, or approximate duplicates, should be stowed away. This both saves expense, prevents weariness and confusion of ideas to the public, and facilitates the studies of the scholar. In the same way as Dr. Gunther shows, by far the largest part of the biological collections should be packed in drawers, and only the more distinct and typical specimens exposed to view. But then come a number of zealous, well-meaning men who urge that these drawers and cellars full of expensive articles ought to be offered to the provinces, so that fifty Museums might be filled out of what is unseen in one. Such suggestions, however, proceed upon an entire misapprehension of the purposes of a great collection, and of the way in which the mysteries of the past, the only key to the mysteries of the present, are being unfolded by the patient putting together of link and link.

Of course when two things are real duplicates, like two coins from the same dies, there will not usually be any motive for retaining both in a Museum; a curator will then, as a matter of course, arrange for an exchange of the duplicate with some other duplicate from another Museum. But there may be many things which might seem at first sight to be duplicates, but are not. In many cases the slighter the differences the more instructive these are. The great national herbarium, for instance, ought to contain the floras of all parts of the world, and a certain number of plants will appear to be identical, though coming from opposite sides of the globe. These coincident specimens are, however, the very clues to the former relations of floras, or to the currents, cataclysms, or other causes which can be supposed to explain otherwise inexplicable resemblances. The same is obviously true, *cœteris paribus,* of all the other biological collections.

It is also true, in a somewhat different manner, of historical objects. If, as the whole course of recent philosophy tends to prove, things grow in the social as in the physical world, then the causes of things can only be safely traced out by obtaining specimens of so many stages in the growth that there can be no doubt as to the relation of continuity. Some of the ancient British coins, for instance, bear designs which to all appearance are entirely inexplicable and meaningless. Careful study, however, consisting in the minute and skilful comparison of many series of specimens of coins, showed that these inexplicable designs were degraded copies of Byzantine or other earlier coinages. The point of the matter, however, is that no one would recognise the resemblance between the first original and the last degraded copy. We must have a series of intermediate copies, as necessary links in the induction. Now it is apparent that if these indispensable links being merely duplicates of each other, are dispersed to the provincial Museums of Manchester, Liverpool, Bristol, Newcastle and the rest, the study of their real import must be indefinitely retarded. Concentration and approximate reduplication of specimens is in fact the great method of biological and historical inquiry. This instance of the coins, too, is only a fair specimen of what holds of all the sciences referred to. The forms of architecture, the derivation of customs, the progress of inventions, the formation of languages, the establishment of institutions, all such branches of anthropological science can only be established by the comparison of chains of instances. A century ago etymology was a reproach to learning, being founded on mere guess-work as to the resemblance of words; now the etymology of a word is established by adducing the series of approximate duplicates which show, beyond the reach of doubt, how the world has come to be what it is. We can swear to its identity because we have followed it, so to say.

To distribute the supposed duplicates of the British Museum or of other great scientific collections would be simply to undo the work of a century's research, and to scatter to the points of the compass the groundwork of learning and history. Did we proceed in this country on autocratic principles, the opposite course would be that most beneficial to human progress, namely, to empower the Librarians and Curators of the British Museum to seize whatever books, specimens, or other things they could find in any of the provinces suitable for the completion of the National Collections.

It is quite possible that a good deal might be done in the way of concentration and completion of scientific collections, but of course it must be done either by the legitimate process of sale and purchase, or by some systematic arrangement between curators. It is a matter exclusively of scientific detail, in which the men specially acquainted with each collection can alone form any opinion.

It is naturally a point of the highest importance to ascertain if possible the best constitution for the control of a Museum, and the best mode of organisation of the staff. Without undertaking to argue the matter here as fully as it would deserve, I venture to express the opinion that a Museum ought to be regarded as a place of learning and science, and not as a mere office or shop for the display of so many samples. It ought therefore to be controlled in the manner of a college, by a neutral and mixed board of men of science and of business. Such a council or board will retain in their own hands most questions relating to finance, the structure of the Museum, and what does not touch the professional and scientific work of the curators. They will appoint a chief curator or librarian, and in a case of a large Museum, the chiefs of the separate branches; but will probably leave to the chief curator the minor appointments. If a happy and successful choice is made as regards the curators, especially the chief, it will probably be found that the whole direction of the institution will centre in the latter, who will form the medium of communication between his colleagues the branch curators, and the board. All important matters involving the scientific organisation of the Museum will be discussed among the curators and reported to the board before the latter pass any final decision upon them. The advantages of such a constitution for the purposes in view are manifold.

In the first place the fear of political influence and jobbery in the appointments is reduced to a minimum, the board consisting of men of such diverse character and interests that they are not as a body accessible to private influence. To secure this end, however, it is quite essential that the board should not be elected by themselves, or by any single power having both the means and the motive for one-sided appointments. The system of representative elections regularly adopted of late in the schemes of the Endowed Schools or Charities Commissions sufficiently secures this end. A second advantage is that the board, having no common opinions on scientific matters, practically leave the curators in the perfect freedom of thought and action which is requisite for the prosecution of learning and science. The officialism of a government office is absolutely incompatible with the labour of discovery. The tendency of an official is always to elevate himself at the expense of his subordinates. He serves the state or some branch of the state and they serve him; but any distinction which those subordinates attain, except through serving their chief, is sure to detract so far from the conspicuous merits of the latter.

Under the kind of board of control described, the action of affairs is very different. The different curators of branches being appointed directly by the board, their services, whether to the institute or to science in general, stand out separate from that of the chief curator, who being only *primus inter pares,* becomes rather elevated than depressed by their distinction. As he cannot appropriate their reputation and abilities for his own purposes, he can only magnify himself by magnifying them, and by cordially assisting in everything which seems likely to conduce to the success of the institution. The subject of the control of public institutions is one well worthy of careful treatment, and which would readily fill a volume, but it cannot be pursued here. I will add, however, that what is said above is no mere fiction of the imagination, but founded upon long continued and intimate acquaintance with the working of the constitution of Owens College, probably the best governed and most successful scientific institution of recent times.

The British Museum has from its first institution, in 1753, been under the government of a board of trustees including certain family trustees representing the benefactors of the Museum. The inestimable services to many branches of history, learning, and science, which the Museum has rendered throughout its career of little more than a century form a sufficient general justification of its mode of governance. But it may well be allowed at the same time that the repeated complaints as to the conservatism and inactivity of the trustees are not without ground. The fact that some of these trustees, to the number of nine, are irresponsible and irremovable family trustees, and that the remainder consist, for the most part, of the great officers and dignitaries of the State, such as the Archbishop of Canterbury, the Lord Chancellor, the Speaker, the Secretaries of State, while only one is nominated by the Queen, and fifteen others are co-optated by the rest, sufficiently shows that it must be an inert body. The only infusion of science among so very much dignity consists in the presidents of the Royal Society, the Royal College of Physicians, the Society of Antiquaries, and the Royal Academy. It would surely be an obvious reform, while retaining the family trustees in accordance with the national compact, to replace many of the present official trustees, who cannot possibly have time to attend to vertebrates and invertebrates, by the presidents or representatives of the great learned societies, such as the Linnæan, Geological, Zoological, Society of Antiquaries, etc. The co-optated trustees, too, instead of being the great dignitaries and aristocrats over again, might be chosen to a great extent from among the more distinguished historians, artists, or men of learning, as was once done in the case of Hallam. It would be a mistake, however, to make such a body preponderatingly scientific, and there should be an infusion of men of action, such as distinguished engineers and leading bankers.

It would be a difficult matter to classify the various kinds of Museums in a manner at all complete and natural. There are very many kinds of Museums, and the species shade into each other or overlap each other in the way most perplexing to the systematic classifier. Dr. Gunther divided Museums into three classes,* but I am inclined to add three others, and we then obtain the six following principal classes:

I. Standard National Museums.
II. Popular Museums.
III. Provincial Museums.
IV. Special Museums.
V. Educational Museums.
VI. Private Museums.

The Standard National Museum of Great Britain is, of course, the British Museum; and even in a very rich kingdom there can hardly be more than one really national collection. There may, indeed, be outlying portions of the national collection, such as the Museums and Herbarium at Kew, the Patent Office Museum, the India Museum, and other collections at South Kensington. The principal purpose of all such central collections must be the advancement of knowledge, and the preservation of specimens or works of art which hand down the history of the nation and the world. It can only be in a merely secondary way that such invaluable and costly Museums are opened for the amusement of casual sight-seers and strollers. Properly speaking, there ought to be a series of Museums both in London and the larger towns, which I have specified in the second place as Popular Museums. These are best represented in London by the

* British Association, Swansea, 1880; report, p. 592.

Bethnal Green Museum, and in the provinces by that admirable establishment, the Peel Park Museum at Salford. Practically, indeed, it is impossible to separate the popular from the Provincial Museums; the latter is not wholly designed for popular use, and may have important scientific and historical collections, ill-suited for recreative and educational purposes. For reasons of economy, however, the popular and the scientific Museums are generally merged together, as at Peel Park and many other places. Of Provincial Museums I will, however, speak more fully below.

Special Museums form a very numerous but varied group, and include any narrow collection formed by an institution for particular purposes. The Monetary Museum at the Paris Mint is a good instance, and it is pleasant to notice that the nucleus of a similar Museum already exists at our Mint on Tower Hill, and is being arranged and improved. The superb Museum of the Royal College of Surgeons is a special one, if, indeed, it does not more properly belong to the class of Standard National collections. Among other special collections may be mentioned the Architectural Museum in Tufton Street, Westminster, the Museums of the several learned societies, of the Royal United Service Institution, and the Parkes Museum of Hygiene.

Under the fifth class of Educational Museums we place those maintained by colleges and schools, for the illustration of lectures or the direct use of students. Every teaching institution ought to have some kind of Museum, and many already have extensive collections. University College has a large Museum of anatomical and pathological specimens in addition to other collections. Owens College has fortunately received the considerable Museum formerly maintained in Peter Street by the Natural History Society, but is in need of funds to erect a suitable building, so as to allow of the popular use of the Museum in accordance with the terms of the gift. The universities of Edinburgh and St. Andrews possess great natural history collections, which probably surpass the bounds of simply educational Museums, and assume an almost national importance. The same may be said of the Ashmolean Museum at Oxford and the Fitzwilliam Museum at Cambridge. Under the fifth class must also be placed the minor teaching Museum already formed at Harrow, Clifton, and some other public schools, and the indefinitely numerous small collections, which will, I hope, be eventually found, as already explained, in all schools.

Of the sixth class of private Museums it is not necessary to say much. They are usually formed for special scientific purposes, and often become by bequest or purchase the foundation of the corresponding branches of the national collection.

So far as I am aware no complete and systematic information is anywhere to be found as to the number, kind, purposes, and regulations of the local Museums of the United Kingdom. Those which were formed under the Museum Act (8th and 9th Vict. cap. 43) or under the Free Libraries Acts, may be found enumerated in the statistical tables mentioned in my previous article on Free Libraries. But there are undoubtedly great numbers of Museums owned by local learned societies, by royal institutions, or even by private persons which are more or less open to the public.

But when the Free Library and Museum Acts come fully into operation it is to be hoped that every county town, and every town of, say, 20,000 inhabitants and upwards, will have its public Museum in addition to, but in no case in place of, its public library. There ought to be a great many more libraries than Museums, and for pretty obvious reasons it would be better to concentrate the Museums than divide them up into a great number, which cannot maintain proper curators. Probably about one hundred efficiently maintained public Museums would suffice for the whole of England, and other local collections might often be usefully absorbed into the public Museums when established. It is very desirable, however, that in forming such county Museums, definite ideas should be entertained as to the purposes of the local collection and of the proper means to carry out such purposes.

Everybody knows what a heterogeneous and absurd jumble a local Museum too often is in the present day. Any awkward article which a person of the neighbourhood wanted to get rid of is handed over to the Museum and duly stuck up, labelled with the name of its donor. A Roman altar dug up in a neighbouring farm supports a helmet of one of Cromwell's soldiers; above hangs a glass-case full of butterflies, surmounted by poisoned arrows and javelins from the hill tribes of India. A large cork model of a Chinese temple blocks up one corner of the room, while other parts are obstructed by a brass gun of unknown history and no interest, a model of an old three-decker, an Egyptian mummy, and possibly the embalmed remains of some person who declined to be laid under the turf.* Elsewhere in the valuable collection will probably be found the cups which a great cricketer of the county won, a figure of a distinguished racehorse, the stuffed favourite pug-dog of a lady benefactor, and so forth. There is really no exaggeration in this fancy sketch of a county Museum, and it is far better to have such a Museum than none at all. Indeed, for children such a collection is not unsuitable, and is better than a large collection. But it is to be hoped that when local Museums are multiplied and improved, their contents may be so exchanged and selected and arranged, as to produce an orderly and sensible, if not a very scientific, result.

I venture to suggest that as a general rule a local Museum should consist of four principal departments; there may be one or two more, but there should not be many more nor many less. In the first place every local Museum should have its archæological department devoted to the preservation of any antique articles connected with the neighbourhood. Not only are valuable relics thus preserved, but they are preserved at the place where they have special significance, and may lead to special researches. Such relics will be of all ages, from the flint knives of the palæolithic age to the tinder-box which the town clerk's father used. We cannot help the mixture of times, which, after all, is not without its lessons. But then we must not mix up with such local relics those of other places and nations. These should be exchanged with some other collection to which they will be appropriate.

* As was formerly the case in the Natural History Museum, Peter Street, Manchester.

A second branch of the Museum should contain some representation of the local natural history, the rarer birds and insects, especially those which are likely to become extinct, the rocks and fossils of any formation for which the locality is celebrated, the local herbarium already referred to. It will not, however, be usually possible to attempt all the branches of the natural history, and the curator may properly develop disproportionately that branch in which he feels most interest and has most facilities, or which is less represented in neighbouring towns.

A third branch of the Museum may profitably contain almost any kind of collection which forms the special hobby or study of the curator, or of any local enthusiast who likes to make the public museum the depository of his treasures. Whether it be old china, or Japanese idols, or Australian boomerangs, or crystals of calcite, or old bank-notes, or church-door keys, or the fangs of serpents; it hardly matters what product of nature or industry be thus specially represented, provided that it be systematically, and, as far as possible, completely studied. Almost any such thorough collection will lead to new knowledge, and if the curator be an intelligent and scientific man he will be able to arrange and explain it so as to excite interest in his visitors. He will do this far more effectually if he be allowed liberty of choice in some portion of his collection, in respect to which he, so to speak, enjoys a certain endowment of research. In fact, unless the curator of a museum becomes an original student and collector in one or more branches, he is more a cabinet maker and head door-keeper to his institution than the man of science who should be a light to half the county.

The remaining fourth branch of the local Museum should be simply a blank space, available for the reception of occasional loan collections, either from the authorities of South Kensington, or from other local museums, from private collectors, or from the united loans of private owners. The idea of loan collections was perhaps not originated at South Kensington, but it has certainly been developed there in a degree previously unknown. It is doubtless capable of rendering the greatest possible services to Museum economy. The loan collection of Japanese art lately exhibited at Nottingham Castle, for instance, was beyond praise.

But surely this loan system can be worked without the intervention of Government officials. As soon as the curators of Museums become an organised body, *en rapport* with each other, it would be easy to arrange for exchanges of loan collections, and any very good and complete collection formed in one town as the special hobby of its curator, might be gradually circulated round the entire country, and thus vastly multiplied in utility. Thus the local Museum would practically operate as one vast divided Museum, although each curator with his superintending committee would maintain their perfect autonomy.

It is essential, however, to good Museum economy that wholly irrelevant and trifling articles, such as the local cricketers' cups, the stuffed pug-dogs, the models of three-deckers, etc., should be got rid of by exchange or donation. In a well-arranged Museum they serve only to produce distraction and ridicule.

There already exist some good models of what county or other local Museums may become. The Ipswich Museum, in which the late Professor Henslow had a leading part, is, I believe, a very good one, but I have not seen it. The Nottingham Castle Museum, due to a suggestion of Sir Henry Cole, is as yet rather dependent on South Kensington, but in any case it is a charming addition to the resources of the town, and must have very perceptibly brightened the lives of the Nottingham people. There are a good many old castles which might surely be utilised in the same way.

I venture to suggest, in conclusion, that the best possible step which could now be taken to improve the Museums of the United Kingdom would be the constitution of a Museum Association on the lines of the well-known Librarians' Association. If the curators of all the public Museums would follow the example of other professional bodies, and put their heads together in a conference, they might evolve out of the existing chaos some unity of ideas and action. At any rate they would take the first important step of asserting their own existence. There have been enough of blue-books and royal commissions, and we have heard too much of what "my Lords" of the Council have got to say. Let the curators themselves now speak and act, and let them especially adopt as their motto—"Union, not centralisation."

"CRAM."[*]

A HUMAN institution has, like man, its seven ages. In its infancy, unknown and unnoticed, it excites in youth some interest and surprise. Advancing towards manhood, everyone is forward in praising its usefulness. As it grows up and becomes established, the popular tone begins to change. Some people are unavoidably offended or actually injured by a new institution, and as it grows older and more powerful, these people become more numerous. In proportion to the success of an undertaking, will be the difficulties and jealousies which are encountered. It becomes the interest of certain persons to find out the weak points of the system, and turn them to their private advantage. Thus the institution reaches its critical age, which, safely surmounted, it progresses through a prosperous middle life to a venerable old age of infirmities and abuses, dying out in the form of a mere survival.

There is no difficulty in seeing what period of life the examination system has now reached. It is that critical age at which its progress is so marked as to raise wide-spread irritation. To abuse examinations is one of the most popular commonplaces of public speeches and after-dinner conversation. Everybody has something to say in dispraise, and the reason is pretty obvious. Many persons have been inconvenienced by examinations; some regret the loss of patronage; others the loss of patrons and appointments; schoolmasters do not

[*] "Mind," April, 1877; No. VI.

like having their work rudely tested: they feel the competition of more far-sighted teachers who have adapted themselves betimes to a new state of things. In these and other ways it arises that a formidable minority actually have good grounds for hating examinations. They make their feelings widely known, and the general public, ever ready to grumble at a novelty of which they hear too much, and do not precisely appreciate the advantages, take up the burden of the complaint.

Fortunately, too, for the opponents of examination, an admirable "cry" has been found. Examination, they say, leads to "Cram," and "Cram" is the destruction of true study. People who know nothing else about examination know well enough that it is "Cram." The word has all the attributes of a perfect *question-begging epithet*. It is short, emphatic, and happily derived from a disagreeable physical metaphor. Accordingly, there is not a respectable gentleman distributing prizes to a body of scholars at the end of the session, and at a loss for something to say, who does not think of this word "Cram," and proceed to expatiate on the evils of the examination system.

I intend in this article to take up the less popular view of the subject, and say what I can in favour of examinations. I wish to analyse the meaning of the word "Cram," and decide if possible, whether it is the baneful thing that so many people say. There is no difficulty in seeing at once that "Cram" means two different things, which I will call "good Cram" and "bad Cram." A candidate, preparing for an important competitive examination, may put himself under a tutor well skilled in preparing for that examination. This tutor looks for success by carefully directing the candidate's studies into the most "paying" lines, and restricting them rigorously to those lines. The training given may be of an arduous thorough character, so that the faculties of the pupil are stretched and exercised to their utmost in those lines. This would be called "Cram," because it involves exclusive devotion to the answering of certain examination-papers. I call it "good Cram."

"Bad Cram," on the other hand, consists in temporarily impressing upon the candidate's mind a collection of facts, dates, or formulæ, held in a wholly undigested state and ready to be disgorged in the examination-room by an act of mere memory. A candidate, unable to apprehend the bearing of Euclid's reasoning in the first book of his " Elements," may learn the propositions off by heart, diagrams, letters, and all, like a Sunday scholar learning the collects and gospels. Dates, rules of grammar, and the like, may be "crammed" by mnemonic lines, or by one of those wretched systems of artificial memory, teachers of which are always going about. In such ways it is, I believe, possible to give answers which simulate knowledge, and no more prove true knowledge than the chattering of a parrot proves intellect.

I am far from denying the existence of "bad Cram" of this character, but I hold that it can never be advantageously resorted to by those who are capable of "good Cram." To learn a proposition of Euclid by heart is far more laborious than for a student of moderate capacity to master the nature of the reasoning. It is obvious that all advantages, even in an examinational point of view, are on the side of real knowledge. The slightest lapse of memory in the bad "crammer," for instance, the putting of wrong letters in the diagram, will disclose the simulated character of his work, and the least change in the conditions of the proposition set will frustrate his mnemonic devices altogether. If papers be set which really can be answered by mere memory, the badness is in the examiners.

Thorough blockheads may be driven to the worst kind of "Cram," simply because they can do nothing better. Nor do the blockheads suffer harm; to exercise the memory is better than to leave the brain wholly at rest. Some qualities of endurance and resolution must be called into existence, before a youth can go through the dreary work of learning off by heart things of which he has no comprehension. Nor with examiners of the least intelligence is there any reason to fear that the best directed "bad Cram" will enable a really stupid candidate to carry off honours and appointments due to others

No examination-papers even for junior candidates should consist entirely of "book-work," such as to be answered by the simple reproduction of the words in a text-book. In every properly conducted examination, questions are, as a matter of course, set to test the candidate's power of applying his knowledge to cases more or less different from those described in the books. Moreover, good examiners always judge answers by their general style as well as by their contents. It is really impossible that a stupid, slovenly candidate can by any art of "cramming" be enabled to produce the neat, brief, pertinent essay, a page or two long, which wins marks from the admiring examiners.

If we may judge from experience, too, "bad Cram" does not pay from the tutor's point of view. That this is so we may learn from the fact that slow ignorant pupils are ruthlessly rejected by the great "coaches." Those who have their reputation and their living to make by the success of their candidates cannot afford to waste their labour upon bad material. Thus it is not the stupid who go to the "cramming" tutors to be forced over the heads of the clever, but it is the clever ones who go to secure the highest places. Long before the critical days of the official examination, the experienced "coach" selected his men almost as carefully as if he were making up the University boat. There is hardly a University or a College in the kingdom which imposes any selective process of the sort. An entrance or matriculation examination, if it exists at all, is little better than a sham. All comers are gladly received to give more fees and the appearance of prosperity. Thus it too often happens that the bulk of a college class consists of untutored youths through whose ears the learned instructions of the professor pass, harmlessly it may be, but uselessly. Parents and the public have little idea how close a resemblance there is between teaching and writing on the sands of the sea, unless either there is a distinct capacity for learning on the part of the pupil, or some system of examination and reward to force the pupil to apply.

For these and other reasons which might be urged, I do not consider it worth while to consider "bad Cram" any further. I pass on to inquire whether "good Cram" is an objectionable form of education. The good "cramming" tutor or lecturer is one whose object is to enable his pupils to take a high place in the list. With this object he carefully ascertains the scope of the examination, scrutinises past papers, and estimates in every possible way the probable character of future papers. He then trains his pupils in each branch of study with an intensity proportioned to the probability that questions will be asked in that branch. It is too much to assume that this training will be superficial. On the contrary, though narrow it will probably be intense and deep. It will usually consist to a considerable extent in preliminary examinations intended both to test and train the pupil in the art of writing answers. The great "coaches" at Cambridge in former days might be said to proceed by a constant system of examination, oral instruction or simple reading being subordinate to the solving of innumerable problems. The main question which I have to discuss, then, resolves itself into this: whether intense training directed to the passing of certain defined examinations constitutes real education. The popular opponents of "Cram" imply that it does not; I maintain that it does.

It happened that, just as I was about to write this article, the Home Secretary presided at the annual prize-distribution in the Liverpool College, on the 22nd December, 1876, and took occasion to make the usual remarks about "Cram." He expressed with admirable clearness the prevailing complaints against examinations, and I shall therefore take the liberty of making his speech in some degree my text. "Examination is not education," he said. "You require a great deal more than that. As well as being examined, you must be taught. . . . In the great scramble for life there is a notion at the present moment of getting hold of as much general superficial knowledge as you can. That to my mind is a fatal mistake. On the other hand, there is a great notion that if you can get through your examination and 'cram up' a subject very well, you are being educated. That, too, is a most fatal mistake. There is nothing which would delight me so much, if I were an examiner, as to baffle all the 'cramming' teachers whose pupils came before me." (Laughter.)

Let us consider what Mr. Cross really means. "Examination," he says, "is not education; we require a great deal more; we must be taught as well as be examined." With equal meaning I might say: "Beef is not dinner; we want a great deal more; we must have potatoes, bread, pudding, and the like." Nevertheless, beef is a principal part of dinner. Nobody, I should think, ever asserted or imagined that examination alone was education, but I nevertheless hold that it is one of the chief elements of an effective education. As Mr. Cross himself said, in an earlier part of his speech, "The examination is a touchstone and test which shows the broad distinction between good and bad. . . . You may manage to scramble through your lessons in the 'half,' but I will defy you to get through your examinations if you do not know the subjects."

Another remark of Mr. Cross leads me to the main point of the subject. He said: "It is quite necessary in the matter of teaching that whatever is taught must be taught well, and nothing that is taught well can be taught in a hurry. It must be taught, not simply for the examination, but it must sink into your minds, and stay there for life."

Both in this and his other remarks Mr. Cross commits himself to the popular but wholly erroneous notion that what boys learn at school and college should be useful knowledge indelibly impressed upon the mind, so as to stay there all their lives, and be ready at their fingers' ends. The real point of the objections to examination commonly is, that the candidate learns things for the examination only, which, when it is safely passed, he forgets again as speedily as possible. Mr. Cross would teach so deliberately and thoroughly that the very facts taught could not be forgotten, but must ever after crop up in the mind whatever we are doing.

I hold that remarks such as these proceed from a wholly false view of the nature and purposes of education. It is implied that the mind in early life is to be stored with the identical facts and bits of knowledge which are to be used in after-life. It is, in fact, Mr. Cross and those who think with him who advocate a kind of "Cram," enduring, it is true, but still "bad Cram." The true view of education, on the contrary, is to regard it as a course of training. The youth in a gymnasium practises upon the horizontal bar, in order to develop his muscular powers generally; he does not intend to go on posturing upon horizontal bars all through life. School is a place where the mental fibres are to be exercised, trained, expanded, developed, and strengthened, not "crammed" or loaded with "useful knowledge."

The whole of a youth's subsequent career is one long course of technical "cramming," in which any quantity of useful facts are supplied to him *nolens volens*. The merchant gets his technical knowledge at the clerk's desk, the barrister in the conveyancer's offices or the law courts; the engineer in the workshop and the field. It is the very purpose of a *liberal education*, as it is correctly called, to develop and train the plastic fibres of the youthful brain, so as to prevent them taking too early a definite "set," which will afterwards narrow and restrict the range of acquisition and judgment. I will even go so far as to say that it is hardly desirable for the actual things taught at school to stay in the mind for life. The source of error is the failure to distinguish between the *form* and the *matter* of knowledge, between the facts themselves and the manner in which the mental powers deal with facts.

It is wonderful that Mr. Cross and those who moralise in his strain do not perceive that the actual facts which a man deals with in life are infinite in number, and cannot be remembered in a finite brain. The psychologists, too, seem to me to be at fault in this matter, for they have not sufficiently drawn attention to the varying degrees of duration required in a well-organised memory. We commonly use the word memory so as to cover the faculties of Retention, Reproduction, and Representation, as described by Hamilton, and very little consideration will show that in different cases we need the powers of retention, of suggestion, and of imagination in very different degrees. In some cases we require to remember a thing only a few moments, or a few minutes; in other cases a few hours or days; in yet other cases a few weeks or months: it is an infinitesimally small part of all our mental impressions which can be profitably remembered for years. Memory may be too retentive, and facility of forgetting and of driving out one train of ideas by a new train is almost as essential to a well-trained intellect as facility of retention.

Take the case of a barrister in full practice, who deals with several cases in a day. His business is to acquire as rapidly as possible the facts of the case immediately before him. With the powers of representation of a well-trained mind, he holds these facts steadily before him, comparing them with each other, discovering their relations, applying to them the principles and rules of law more deeply graven on his memory, or bringing them into connection with a few of the more prominent facts of previous cases which he happens to remember. For the details of laws and precedents he trusts to his text-writers, the statute-book, and his law library. Even before the case is finished, his mind has probably sifted out the facts and rejected the unimportant ones by the law of obliviscence. One case done with, he takes up a wholly new series of facts, and so from day to day, and from month to month, the matter before him is constantly changing. The same remarks are even more true of a busy and able administrator like Mr. Cross. The points which come before him are infinite in variety. The facts of each case are rapidly brought to his notice by subordinates, by correspondence, by debates in the House, by deputations and interviews, or by newspaper reports. Applying well-trained powers of judgment to the matter in hand, he makes a rapid decision and passes to the next piece of business. It would be fatal to Mr. Cross if he were to allow things to sink deep into his mind and stay there. There would be no difficulty in showing that in like manner, but in varying degrees, the engineer, the physician, the merchant, even the tradesman or the intelligent artisan, deal every day with various combinations of facts which cannot all be stored up in the cerebral framework, and certainly need not be so.

The bearing of these considerations upon the subject of

examinations ought to be very evident. For what is "cram" but the rapid acquisition of a series of facts, the vigorous getting up of a case, in order to exhibit well-trained powers of comprehension, of judgment, and of retention before an examiner? The practised barrister "crams" up his "brief" (so-called because, as some suppose, made *brief* for the purpose) and stands an examination in it before a judge and jury. The candidate is not so hurried; he spends months, or it may be two or three years, in getting up his differential calculus or his inorganic chemistry. It is quite likely that when the ordeal is passed, and the favourable verdict delivered, he will dismiss the equations and the salts and compounds from his mind as rapidly as possible; but it does not follow that the useful effect of his training vanishes at the same time. If so, it follows that almost all the most able and successful men of the present day threw away their pains at school and college. I suppose that no one ever heard of a differential equation solving a nice point of law, nor is it common to hear Sophocles and Tacitus quoted by a leading counsel. Yet it can hardly be denied that our greatest barristers and judges were trained in the mathematical sciences, or if not, that their teachers thought the classics a better training ground. If things taught at school and college are to stay in the mind to serve us in the business of life, then almost all the higher education yet given in this kingdom has missed its mark.

I come to the conclusion, then, that well-ordered education is a severe system of well-sustained "Cram." Mr. Herbert Spencer holds that the child's play stimulates the actions and exercises of the man. So I would hold that the agony of the examination-room is an anticipation of the struggles of life. All life is a long series of competitive examinations. The barrister before the jury; the preacher in his pulpit; the merchant on the Exchange flags; the member in the House—all are going in for their "little-goes," and their "great-goes," and their "triposes." And I unhesitatingly assert that as far as experience can guide us, or any kind of reasoning enable us to infer, well-conducted competitive examinations before able examiners, are the best means of training, and the best method of selection for those who are to be foremost in the battle of life.

I will go a step further, and assert that examination in one form or another is not only an indispensable test of results, but it is a main element in training. It represents the active use of faculties as contrasted with that passive use which too often resolves itself into letting things come in at one ear and go out at the other. Those who discuss examinations in the public papers, seem to think that they are held occasionally and for the sole purpose of awarding prizes and appointments; but in every well-ordered course of instruction there ought to be, and there usually are, frequent less formal examinations of which outsiders hear nothing. The purposes of these examinations are manifold; they test the progress of the class, and enable the teacher to judge whether he is pursuing a right course at a right speed; they excite emulation in the active and able; they touch the pride even of those who do not love knowledge much, but still do not like to write themselves down absolute blockheads; and they are in themselves an exercise in English composition, in the control of the thoughts, and the useful employment of knowledge. In direct educational effect a written examination may be worth half-a-dozen lectures. Mr. Cross says that examination is not education; I say that it is. Of course you cannot examine upon nothing, just as you cannot grind flour in a mill unless you put the grain in. Nevertheless, examination in some form or other represents the really active grinding process in the pupil's mind.

It is not merely that which goes into the eyes and ears of a student which educates him; it is that which comes out. A student may sit on the lecture-room benches and hear every word the teacher utters; but he may carry away as much useful effect as the drowsy auditor of a curate's sermon. To instruct a youth in gymnastics, you do not merely explain orally that he is to climb up one pole, and come down another, and leap over a third. You make him do these motions over and over again, and the education is in the exertion. So intellectual education is measured, not by words heard or read, but by thoughts excited. In some subjects mental exertion in the pupil is called forth by the working of problems and exercises. These form a kind of continuous examination, which should accompany every lecture. Arithmetic is only to be learnt by sums upon the schoolboy's slate, and it is the infinite variety of mathematical tasks from common addition upwards which makes mathematical science the most powerful training-ground of the intellect. The late Professor De Morgan was probably the greatest teacher of mathematics who ever lived. He considered it requisite that students should attend his expository lectures for an hour and a quarter every day; but he always gave an abundance of exercises as well, which, if fully worked out, would take at least as long, and often twice as long a time. Exercises are the sheet-anchor of the teacher, and in this way only can we explain the extraordinary propensity of classical teachers towards Latin verses. As I have heard such teachers explain, verses, though useless in every other way, afford a definite measurable amount of exercise—a manageable classical treadmill. For many years past it was my duty to teach several subjects—Logic, Mental and Moral Philosophy, and Political Economy. Experience made me acutely aware of the very different educational values of these diverse subjects. Logic is by far the best, because when properly taught it admits of the same active training by exercises and problems that we find in mathematics. It is no doubt necessary that some instruction should also be given to senior students in philosophy and political economy; but it is difficult in these subjects to make the student think for himself. Examination, then, represents the active as opposed to the passive part of education, and in answer to Mr. Cross's statement that examination is not education, I venture to repeat that, in some form or other, examination is the most powerful and essential means of training the intellect.

I now pass on to the wholly different question whether open competitive examinations are the best means of selecting men for important appointments. In this view of examinations the educational results are merely incidental, and the main object is to find an impartial mode of putting the right man into the right place, and thus avoiding the nepotism and corruption which are almost inseparable from other methods of appointment. At first sight it might seem absurd to put a man in a position requiring judgment and tact and knowledge of the world because he answers rightly a few questions about mathematics and Greek. The head-master of a great school succeeds; not by the teaching of the higher forms, but by the general vigour and discretion of his management. He is an administrator, not a pedagogue; then why choose a high wrangler, because of his command over differential equations? Why make a young man a magistrate in Bengal, because of his creditable translations from the classics, or his knowledge of English history? Would it not be far better to select men directly for any success which they have shown in the management of business exactly analogous to that they will have to perform?

Experience must decide in such matters, and it seems to decide conclusively in favour of examinations. Public opinion and practice at any rate are in favour of this conclusion. For a long time back the honours' degrees of Oxford and Cambridge have been employed as a means of selection. It does not of course follow that a high wrangler, or a double first, will suit every important position; but it is almost always expected nowadays that a man applying for a high post shall have some high degree. Even those who are unfettered in their powers of appointment will seldom now appoint a young man to a conspicuous post unless his degree will justify the appointment in the eyes of the public. The President of the Council, for instance, is unrestricted in the choice of School Inspectors, but he practically makes a high degree a *sine quâ non*. Not only does he thus lessen his responsibility very greatly, and almost entirely avoid suspicion of undue influence, but the general success and ability of those appointed in this manner fully bear out the wisdom of the practice.

The fact seems to be that the powers which enable a man to take a conspicuous place in a fierce competitive examination are closely correlated, if they be not identical, with those leading to success in the battle of life. It might be expected that a high wrangler or a double first would generally be a weakly bookworm, prematurely exhausted by intense study, unable to expand his mind beyond his books, and deficient in all the tact and worldly knowledge to be acquired by mixing in the business of life. But experience seems to negative such ideas. The weakly men are weeded out before they get to the final struggle, or break down in the course of it. The true bookworm shows himself to be a bookworm, and does not fight his way to a high place. Success in a severe examination requires, as a general rule, a combination of robust physical health, good nerve, great general energy, and powers of endurance and perseverance, added to pure intellectual ability. There are of course exceptions in all matters of this sort, but, so far as we can lay down rules in human affairs, it is the *mens sana in corpore sano* which carries a candidate to the higher part of the list.

A man must not always be set down as a blockhead because he cannot stand the examination-room. Some men of extensive knowledge and much intelligence lose their presence of mind altogether when they see the dreadful paper. They cannot command their thoughts during the few hours when their success in life is at stake. The man who trembles at the sight of the paper is probably defective in the nerve and moral courage so often needed in the business of life. It by no means follows, again, that the man of real genius will take a conspicuous place in the list. His peculiar abilities will often lie in a narrow line and be correlated with weakness in other directions. His powers can only be rendered patent in the course of time. It is well known that some of the most original mathematicians were not senior wranglers. Public examinations must be looked upon as tests of general rather than special abilities; talent, strength, and soundness of constitution win the high place, powers which can be developed in any direction in after-life.

If evidence were needed to support this view of the matter it is amply afforded by the recent Parliamentary Report on the education and training of candidates for the Indian Civil Service. Whatever may be thought as to the details of the methods of training, which have been recently modified, there can be no doubt that this Report is conclusive as to the success of examinational selection. The ability of the statements furnished to this Report by officers appointed by open competition goes far to prove the success of the system. It is impossible to imagine a severer test than that system has passed through in the case of the Indian Civil Service. Young men selected for the amount of Latin, Greek, Mathematics, French, German, Logic, Political Economy, and so forth, which they could "cram up," have been sent out at twenty-one or twenty-three years of age, and thrown at once into a new world, where it is difficult to imagine that their "crammed" knowledge could be of the least direct use. There they have been brought into contact with a large body of older officers, appointed under a different system, and little prejudiced in favour of these "Competition Wallahs." Yet the evidence is overwhelming to the effect that these victims of "Cram" have been successful in governing India. A large number of the best appointments have already been secured by them, although the system has only been in existence for twenty-two years, and seniority is naturally of much account. The number who are failures is very small, certainly smaller than it would be under the patronage system. It is impossible that I should, within the limits of this article, present the evidence accumulated on this subject. I must refer the reader to the Blue Book itself, which is full of interest for all concerned in education.* I must also refer the reader to the remarkably able essays on the subject published by Mr. Alfred Cotterell Tupp, B.A., of the Bengal Civil Service,† to which essays I am indebted for some of my ideas on this subject. Mr. Tupp gives a powerful answer to the celebrated attack on the competitive system contained in the *Edinburgh Review* of April, 1874. He gives statistical tables and details concerning the careers of the men selected

* "The Selection and Training of Candidates for the Indian Civil Service" (C. 1446) 1876. Price 3s. 5d.

† "The Indian Civil Service and the Competitive System: a Discussion on the Examinations and the Training in England." London: R. W. Brydges, 137, Gower Street. 1876.

by competition, and a general account of the examinations and of the organisation in which the Civil servant takes his place. The evidence against selection by competition seems to come to this, that, after a most complete inquiry, the worst that can be made out against the "Competition Wallahs" is that some of them do not ride well, and that there is a doubt in some cases about the polish of their manners, or the sweetness of their culture.

Doubt, indeed, was thrown by some writers upon the physical suitability of selected candidates; but on this point a most remarkable fact was brought to light. All the candidates for the Indian Civil Service have to undergo two strict medical examinations before Sir William Gull, so that this eminent physician is able to speak with rare authority as to the physical health of the candidates. This is what he says (Report, p. 36) : "I still continue to be impressed with the fact that a sound physical constitution is a necessary element of success in these competitive examinations. The men who have been rejected have not failed from mere weakness of constitution, but (with only a solitary exception or two) from a mechanical defect in the valves of the heart in otherwise strong men, and for the most part traceable to over-muscular exercises. . . . There is a somewhat prevalent opinion, that the courses of study now required for the public service are calculated to weaken the physical strength of candidates. Experience does not only not confirm this, but abundantly proves that the course of life which conduces to sound intellectual training, is equally favourable to the physical health of the student."

Unless then we are prepared to reject the opinion of the physician who has had the best possible means of forming a sound conclusion, a competitive examination is actually a good mode of selecting men of good physical health, so closely are the mental and bodily powers correlated as a general rule.

It is impossible that I should in a single article treat of more than two or three of the principal arguments which may be urged in defence of the examination system. Did space admit I might go on to point out the great improvement which has taken place in education since effective examinations were established. The condition of Oxford and Cambridge as regards study in the present day may not be satisfactory, but it is certainly far better than at the close of the last century. The middle-class schools are yet far from what they ought to be, but the examination system set on foot by the old universities is doing immense good, giving vigorous and definite purpose where before a schoolmaster had hardly any other object than to get easily through the " half." Primary schools would for the most part be as bad as the old dame-schools, did not the visits of Her Majesty's Inspectors stir them up to something better. In one and all of the grades of English education, to the best of my belief, examination is the sheet-anchor to which we must look.

I will not conclude without adverting briefly to a few of the objections urged against the examination system. Some of these are quite illusory; others are real, though possibly exaggerated. No institution can be an unmixed good, and we must always strike a balance of advantage and disadvantage. One illusory objection, for instance, is urged by those who take the high moral ground and assert that knowledge should be pursued for its own sake, and not for the ulterior rewards connected with a high place in the examination list. The remarks of these people bring before the mind's eye the pleasing picture of a youth burning the midnight oil, after a successful search for his favourite authors. We have all of us heard how some young man became a great author, or a great philosopher, because, in the impressible time of boyhood, he was allowed to ransack the shelves of his ancestral library. I do not like to be cynical, but I cannot help asserting that these youths, full of the sacred love of knowledge, do not practically exist. Some no doubt there are, but so small is the number with which the school or college teacher will meet in the course of his labours, that it is impossible to take them into account in the general system. Every teacher knows that the bulk

H

of a junior class usually consists of intellects so blunt or so inactive that every kind of spur is useful to incite them to exertion.

Nor do I believe that the few who are by nature ardent students need suffer harm from a well-devised system of university examinations. It is very pleasant to think of a young man pursuing a free and open range of reading in his ancestral library, following his native bent, and so forth; but such study directed to no definite objects would generally be desultory and unproductive. He might obtain a good deal of elegant culture, but it is very doubtful whether he would acquire those powers of application and concentration of thought which are the basis of success in life. If a man really loves study and has genius in him, he will find opportunities in after-life for indulging his peculiar tastes, and will not regret the three or four years when his reading was severely restricted to the lines of examination. Of course it is not desirable to force all minds through exactly the same grooves, and the immense predominance formerly given to mathematics at Cambridge could not be defended. But the schemes of examination at all the principal universities now offer many different branches in which distinction may be gained.

The main difficulty which I see in the examination system is that it makes the examiner the director of education in place of the teacher, whose liberty of instruction is certainly very much curtailed. The teacher must teach with a constant eye to the questions likely to be asked, if he is to give his pupils a fair chance of success, compared with others who are being specially "crammed" for the purpose. It is true that the teacher may himself be the examiner, but this destroys the value of the examination as a test or means of public selection. Much discussion might be spent, were space available, upon the question whether the teacher or the examiner is the proper person to define the lines of study. No doubt a teacher will generally teach best, and with most satisfaction to himself, when he can teach what he likes, and, in the case of University professors or other teachers of great eminence, any restriction upon their freedom may be undesirable. But as a general rule examiners will be more able men than teachers, and the lines of examination are laid down either by the joint judgment of a board of eminent examiners, or by authorities who only decide after much consultation. The question therefore assumes this shape—Whether a single teacher, guided only by his own discretion, or whether a board of competent judges, is most to be trusted in selecting profitable courses of study?

Few have had better opportunity than I have enjoyed both as teacher and examiner in philosophical and economical subjects, of feeling the difficulties connected with a system of examination in these subjects. Some of these difficulties have been clearly expounded in the series of articles upon the state of philosophical study at the different Universities published in *Mind*. It is hardly needful to refer to the excellent discussion of the philosophical examination in the London University by the Editor in No. IV. I should not venture to defend University examinations against all the objections which may be brought against them. My purpose is accomplished in attempting to show that examination is the most effective way of enforcing a severe and definite training upon the intellect, and of selecting those for high position who show themselves best able to bear this severe test. It is the popular cry against " Cram " that I have answered, and I will conclude by expressing my belief that any mode of education which enables a candidate to take a leading place in a severe and well-conducted open examination, must be a good system of education. Name it what you like, but it is impossible to deny that it calls forth intellectual, moral, and even physical powers, which are proved by unquestionable experience to fit men for the business of life.

This is what I hold to be Education. We cannot consider it the work of teachers to make philosophers and scholars and geniuses of various sorts: these, like poets, are born not made. Nor, as I have shown, is it the business of the educator to impress indelibly upon the mind the useful knowledge which is to guide the pupil through life. This would be " Cram " indeed. It is the purpose of education so to exercise the faculties of mind that the infinitely various experience of after-life may be observed and reasoned upon to the best effect. What is popularly condemned as "Cram" is often the best-devised and best-conducted system of training towards this all-important end.

TRADES SOCIETIES
THEIR OBJECTS AND POLICY *

    i. Preface.
    ii. The Legal Position of Trades Societies.
    iii. The Different Objects they have in view.
    iv. Their Actions as Friendly Societies.
    v. Their Actions as Sanitary Associations.
    vi. Their Attempts to Regulate Wages.
    vii. How far are such attempts successful?
    viii. Opposition to the Introduction of Machinery.
    ix. On Co-operation and Conciliation.
    x. The Future of the Operative Classes.

I.

WHEN I received an invitation from the Trades Unionists' Political Association to address you on the present occasion, I felt it to be an honour and a pleasure to have an opportunity of putting before you my ideas upon a question which now occupies so much public attention, and is of such great importance to the prosperity of the country. I must, first of all, acknowledge warmly the liberal and candid spirit in which the association have offered to one whom they probably suppose to be an opponent, an opportunity of bringing forward his unwelcome views. It happens that rather more than a year ago, in a public lecture which it was my duty to give at Owens

---

* Delivered by request of the Trades Unionists' Political Association in the Co-operative Hall, Upper Medlock Street, Hulme, Manchester, March 31st, 1868.

College, I touched upon the subject of Trades Unions, and my words were strongly criticised by Mr. Macdonald, the president of this association, and by some others who seemed to think that my opinions were most unbecoming in the so-called "Cobden Lecturer." I have no doubt therefore that the association and the unionists of this city suppose me to be totally against their views, and I am glad to be able to-night to explain exactly how far it may be the case. At any rate I hope to convince you that I am not in any degree involved in the prejudices of the other party, the capitalists.

I can add most sincerely that my only reluctance in addressing you arose from my consciousness of the imperfect manner in which I may put my notions before you. Others who address you have every advantage of oratorical power and popularity in their favour. I labour under the double misfortune of feeling impelled to put forward some opinions which may not please you, and of putting them forward imperfectly.

It is impossible in my opinion wholly to praise or wholly to condemn a great and wide-spread institution like that of Trades Societies. The men who compose and who manage these societies differ so much in different places and in different trades, and the objects and actions which societies put before themselves are so diverse, that we must carefully discriminate in the award of praise or blame.

Public opinion seldom sufficiently discriminates, and is too apt to ascribe to the whole what it knows only of the part. But it seems to me that as we should certainly not condemn the whole aristocracy because a few of its members are convicted of crime, or misconduct, or folly, so we should still less assail the character of such a vast number of men as the united operatives of England, because some of their number have been concerned in deeds which we cannot approve.

So far am I from wishing that the workmen of England should cease to associate and unite together, that I believe some kind of association to be indispensable to the progress and amelioration of the largest and in some respects the most important class of our population. I believe that the capacity which British workmen exhibit in so high a degree for forming legitimate and orderly associations is one of the finest characteristics of our race, and one of the best proofs of the innate capacity for self-government which I believe we all possess. No one who looks upon the growing numbers and improving organisation of the Trades Societies can doubt that they will play a considerable part in the history of this kingdom. But the greater their extent and influence become, the more essential it is that they should be well advised and really liberal in their aims and actions. It is in their power to do almost incalculable good or harm to themselves and the country of which they form so considerable a part. It is therefore especially necessary that those who direct the policy of these societies should reflect and inquire thoroughly into the results of their rules and actions. They would then perceive that the objects which they set forth as their purpose cannot in some cases be properly achieved by the means they use, and that though the immediate results of their policy may seem to be beneficial, the ultimate results involve injury of a hidden but most extensive kind, which they would not easily have anticipated. There are certain ancient fallacies which have misled men since trades began to be carried on, and it is only within the last hundred years that economists have at all seen their way out of these fallacies, and discovered the true beneficence of the freedom of trade and the freedom of industry. It is the grand principle of freedom of industry, explained by Adam Smith and gradually brought into practice in the policy and laws of the kingdom, which has in great part secured to us our present prosperity. And it would be an inconceivable misfortune for this country and the world if the productive classes, whose numbers and powers increase with that prosperity, should thoughtlessly reverse the policy which gave them birth.

I cannot help quoting here what is said on this point by one of the most conscientious, liberal, and learned statesmen this country ever had—I mean Sir George Cornewall Lewis. He says:

"Some theories, indeed, are so alluring and attractive, especially on a superficial consideration, that nothing short of an actual experimental proof of their evil operation is sufficient to convince the world of their unsoundness. . . Such is the theory of commercial protection, and such too is the theory of protection of labour, which is now advancing into popular favour, and under which mankind seem destined to suffer before they have discovered its true tendencies."—*See his Treatise on the Methods of Observation and Reasoning in Politics.*

II.

I wish to speak in the first place of the legal position of Trades' Societies. A recent trial at the Manchester Law Courts has shown that these societies are in no way illegal, except that they have not the special facilities granted to Friendly Societies by the statute concerning them.

The members of a union are subject to no penalty or disability because they belong to a union, and can as individuals protect their property as before. They suffer under no grievance therefore, and are in no worse position than clubs, committees, or private societies, of which thousands exist or are created every year in other classes of society, but which are not incorporated or registered under the Friendly Societies Act.

But if unionists think that there is still something vexatious and hurtful in their exclusion from the advantages of the Friendly Societies Act, I for my part should be glad to see them brought under it.

I think that the change would probably tend to raise their character in the eyes of themselves and of the public—would make them open associations rather than close and secret clubs. I hope that the time is not far distant when all Trades Societies will stand upon an open and recognised basis—will have their accounts properly audited and published to all whom they may concern. It is with great pleasure that I occasionally notice the accounts and report of the Amalgamated Society of Carpenters and Joiners, published in the daily papers, and I look forward to the time when all Trades Societies may be thus open and above-board.

Again, I think it is very necessary that the reformed House

of Commons should endeavour to define the law of conspiracy as relating to Trades Societies—should distinguish as far as possible between legal persuasion and illegal intimidation, so that, while every unionist may aid his fellow-men in truly voluntary association, he will know accurately when he is infringing the liberty which is the most sacred possession of every one of us.

III.

Coming to the chief subject of my lecture, what I wish most strongly to point out is the fact that Trades Societies have usually *three distinct kinds of object in view*.

Neither the societies themselves, nor the public, sufficiently distinguish these very diverse objects. It is sufficiently apparent indeed that Unions usually combine the character of Benefit and Friendly Societies with those of strict Trades Societies; but I have not seen it sufficiently pointed out that, even in strikes and trade disputes there is often a twofold object in view, the one relating simply to the rate of wages, the other to the hours of labour, the health, safety, comfort, and moral condition of the operative. Now I must insist that the rate of wages is a question to be kept distinct from all others, and I proceed to consider the three separate objects which Unions fulfil.

IV.

The first and most obvious way in which Trades Societies strive to confer benefit upon their members is in acting as Benefit or Friendly Societies. So far as they relieve the necessitous and unfortunate at the expense of the prosperous they confer an unmitigated benefit, and act as insurance societies of most efficient character. Friendly Societies, such as the Odd Fellows, the Foresters, the Hearts of Oak, the Royal Liver Society, etc., are very excellent things in their way, but men of a trade have peculiar facilities for giving each other legitimate and judicious aid from the intimate knowledge which they naturally possess or can easily gain of each other's circumstances. Lord Elcho well observed in his speech at Dalkeith

(*Times*, January 29th, 1867), that Trades Societies are thus a great benefit to the country. "They are the means," he says, "by their sick funds, by their accident funds, by their death funds, by their funds for supporting men when out of employment, of keeping men off the poor rates." The advantages thus conferred are, however, so evident, they have been so well summed up by Messrs. Ludlow and Jones in their excellent little work on the "Progress of the Working-classes" (pp. 211–214), and they are so generally recognised, even by Lord Derby himself, that I need hardly dwell further on them.

At the same time, it is impossible to help seeing that men in a trade when acting together are always apt to become narrow and exclusive in their ideas, whether they be merchants, bankers, manufacturers, or operatives. It is in Trades Societies which combine many grades of workmen and several branches of industry, like the Amalgamated Society of Engineers, that we naturally find the most enlightened policy. It is, therefore, I am glad to notice every step which the societies take towards amalgamation or united action. This amalgamation must gradually destroy selfish or exclusive notions, and it will often render apparent to the men of one trade that they are pursuing objects inconsistent with the welfare of their fellow-men in another trade.

v.

A second and more distinctive function or duty of Unions consists in their efforts to shorten the hours of labour, to render factories more wholesome and safe, and generally to improve the condition of the workman. Under this head I do not refer to any attempt to raise the mere rate of wages, which is altogether a different matter, and will be considered a little later. Both workmen and employers seem to me too indiscriminating in this respect. The employer is too apt to resent and refuse every demand of his men as an infringement of his right of judgment and management. The workmen, on the other hand, are too much given to make a rise of wages the hidden if not the apparent result of every reform they demand. I suppose that no Union ever yet proposed a reduction of the hours of labour without wanting the same wages as before; thus really attempting somewhat by a side-wind to raise the rate per hour. But the rate of wages and the length of hours are two totally distinct things. Ten hours' labour are certainly not worth so much to an employer as twelve hours'; though, as the workman is fresher and more careful, they are probably worth as much as eleven hours on the old system. I think then that those who demand a reduction of one-sixth in the hours of labour should be willing to concede a reduction of at least one-twelfth in the wages. Not but that the workman is at liberty, if he like, to ask for an increase in the rate of wages too. What I want to say is, that it is not judicious for him to mix up in one demand two totally different objects; for if he does not discriminate between the objects he has in view, he can hardly expect the employer will. I say again, that I think the rate of wages is a matter which stands upon a totally different footing from any regulations which concern the health and safety of the workman.

Here I should probably find myself at variance with most of the class of employers who are too much accustomed by habit and prejudice to disregard a hundred little matters which are of vital importance to the workman. The man employed is too often regarded by the employer as a mere machine working for the benefit of the employer, who naturally endeavours to get the most out of him, regardless of moral and sanitary results. But in the eye of the economist and the statesman, in regard to the public interests, and before the face of God, the welfare of the working-man and the working-man's class is as much an object of care as that of the wealthiest capitalist; and, indeed, in proportion to the numbers concerned, vastly more so. The fact is, that property and capital are jealously guarded by the legislator, not so much for the benefit of a small exclusive class, but because capital can hardly be accumulated and employed without vivifying industry, and diffusing comfort and subsistence through the whole body of society. I am quite free to allow that the wealthy capitalist is but as the trustee who holds his capital rather for the good of others than himself. The man who employs a hundred thousand pounds in manufactures or trade diffuses almost infinitely more benefit to those he employs than any satisfaction he draws from it himself. No one, again, who in the least understands the mysterious working of society would think of interfering with the capitalist in the disposal of his capital. He must be allowed to put it into a trade or take it out with the most perfect freedom, otherwise property would cease to be property, and would soon cease to exist at all.

But, on the other hand, I must contend that the workman has a right to guard his own health, convenience, comfort, and safety, and this he cannot efficiently do while he remains an isolated individual. The reason is evident; the employers form a small class, between whom communication and concert are much more easy than between their men, and who have usually a strong disinclination to alter, for the benefit of their men, any custom or regulation which seems to be for their own advantage. The single workman, dependent for his living upon his week's wages, is utterly incompetent to enforce any concession from his wealthy employer. Union is the natural remedy. It is true that public opinion, the example of the more liberal employers, or the paternal care of the legislature, may effect and has effected many important improvements. But progress through these means is too slow for the nineteenth century, and for my part I doubly esteem any improvement or progress which a man obtains for himself. It is the noblest attribute of the Anglo-Saxon that, go where he may, he is able to take care of himself. It is the consciousness of that which renders us a self-governed and yet a most orderly people.

I am sure, therefore, that it is desirable for every class of workmen to combine and take care of their own interests; for unless they are very much wanting in sense and intelligence, they can do it better than anyone can do it for them. I like to see journeymen bakers reduce their hours of labour to a length approaching moderation. I only wish that shopmen, clerks, and others could more readily unite in obtaining a shortening of the hours of attendance, the length of which reduces their opportunities of improvement, rest, and relaxation without equivalent benefit to the public. I am perfectly ready to admit that as the power of machinery increases, as the industry of the country improves generally, and wealth becomes not only greater but more diffused, a general shortening of the hours of labour may be one of the best objects in view and one of the best means to further progress. An Eight Hours Bill has been attempted in America, and has been more than whispered here, and it is in no way an illegitimate object to keep in view. But it must be pursued with great moderation and deliberation, for many reasons. By reducing the productive powers of machinery one-fifth, it would place the manufacturers of this country at a great disadvantage compared with those on the Continent, who now possess the best English machinery, or other machinery equal to it, and who can even now occasionally send yarn into the Manchester market.

But what I wish especially to point out to you is that a man's duty to himself after all should give place to his duty to his children and his wife. It is right for a man or for anyone who works to desire to reduce his working hours from ten to eight, but I think he should abstain from doing so until his children are put to school, and kept there till they are well educated and likely to do better than their parents. It will be a happy day for England when the working-classes shall agitate thoroughly, not for an Eight Hours Bill, but for compulsory education and further restrictions in the employment of children. Our children first, ourselves after, is a policy I should like to see Unions adopt; and I am glad to see that the Trades Unionists' Association is not unmindful of the subject of education in their prospectus.

In a great many instances I think that workmen are not half careful enough of their safety and welfare. In the case of the coal-mines especially, I am sorry to see the complaints and agitation of unionists directed rather to raising the wages and regulating the mode of weighing the coal, etc., than to measures for securing the safety and wholesomeness of the mines. It is probable that coal-mines will never be properly looked after until the men take it upon themselves to do so; for they alone can have the most intimate knowledge of the condition of the mine, and they alone can efficiently restrain and detect the carelessness which every year leads to such deplorable disasters. I am well aware that the Coal-miners' Unions have already often demanded improved inspection of mines, and they aided in procuring a law for the compulsory sinking of a second shaft in every coal-mine. But I think that great good would result if they would bestow still more attention on the safety and wholesomeness of mines, and leave the rate of wages to the operation of natural laws. Mines will never be thoroughly safe until the men in each form a sort of vigilance committee, alive to every imperfection or carelessness in the management. Watchfulness on the part of the men will not at all tend to relax the care of the proprietors and viewers, but will rather tend to increase it. And if the managers of a mine will not listen to the complaints of their men, it is quite right that there should be some organised association of miners competent to bring forward any reasonable complaints in an efficient manner.

VI.

When I come to the third and usually the chief object which Unions have in view, namely, the regulation of the rate of wages, I feel I shall part company with the sympathies of most of you. The more I learn and think about the subject the more I am convinced that the attempt to regulate wages is injurious to the workmen immediately concerned in the majority of cases, and that in all cases it is thoroughly injurious to the welfare of the community. And if there is one conclusion we can draw from the history of past times, or from the uniform opinion of the best writers, it is that to interfere with the prices and rates at which men find it profitable to exchange with each other is hurtful and mistaken.

You may think it absurd that I should wish to see Union

assisting in regulating the hours of labour, and many other circumstances concerning their welfare, and yet should wish them to desist from any interference in the still more important point, their wages. But that is just the point I want to bring out clearly; whether a man shall work eight or ten to twelve hours a day is in his own power to determine; but whether, when he does work, he shall fairly earn four or six or eight shillings a day, it is not within his own power to determine. It depends upon a multitude of circumstances entirely beyond his control. If he attempts to secure more than the free course of trade, and the skill of his own hands give him, he either fails ignominiously, or he only succeeds by depriving others of their fair earnings.

That I may be the more clear and distinct I will put my notions in the form of the following propositions:

Firstly. The supposed struggle with capitalists in which many Unions engage, for the purpose of raising wages, is not really a struggle of labour against capital, but of labour against labour—that is, of certain classes or sections of labourers against other classes or sections.

Secondly. It is a struggle in which only a few peculiarly situated trades can succeed in benefiting themselves.

Thirdly. Unions which succeed in maintaining a high rate of wages only succeed by PROTECTION—that is, by levying contributions from other classes of labourers and from the population in general.

Fourthly. Unionism as at present conducted tends therefore to aggravate the differences of wages between the several classes of operatives; it is an effort of some sections to raise themselves at the expense of others.

I feel sure you will not at first believe my statement that the struggle of the Unions is not with capitalists but with their fellow-workmen. Probably you imagine that when certain workmen in a factory combine and get higher wages than before, the increase comes out of the excessive profits of the employer. But this is not the case. His loss, if any, will be very temporary, and he will indemnify himself by raising the price of his goods. It is the purchasers and consumers who will pay, and these comprehend the whole of the population.

Take the case of the building trades, and let us assume that their Unions obtain for them higher wages than they would otherwise gain, which from their peculiar circumstances is probably the case. Do you suppose the increase comes out of the pockets of master-builders and contractors? Certainly not. Before making a tender every contractor ascertains the cost of his materials and the amount of wages he will have to pay, and adds on the profit he thinks proper. Those pay the increase of wages who pay for the building; and, to make a long matter short, everyone who lives in a house pays a contribution in the form of increased rent to the class of operatives engaged in the building trades. The rich pay this tax in the building of their mansions. They can easily bear it; but it is the very poor who suffer, for they are to some extent compelled by it to live in unhealthy and degrading dwellings. You must know how much the condition of a family is influenced by the cleanliness and comfort of their dwelling. "As the home, so the people." Accordingly a multitude of schemes have been proposed and partly carried out in London, Liverpool, and elsewhere, for rebuilding the unhealthy dwellings of the poorest classes. To this excellent movement the high cost of building is a great, if not at present an insuperable, obstacle. It is found almost impossible to make the new houses comfortable and wholesome, and yet to pay the current rate of interest on house property, without which the undertaking cannot be carried on but from charitable motives. If then the operatives of the building trades gain, it is at the expense mainly of multitudes of their fellow-countrymen who are retained in wretched unhealthy dwellings unworthy of the nineteenth century.

What is true of this example is more or less true of others. If the Printers' and Compositors' Unions, for instance, keep their wages at a higher level, the excess is paid in every newspaper and book, hindering the diffusion of knowledge. We have removed the advertisement and newspaper stamp, and paper duty, because they hindered the diffusion of knowledge, the proceeds of which at any rate went to the general purposes of the country, and yet you continue to pay a small tax to a body not exceeding in all about 30,000 men.

In the case of some trades, such as the iron trade or the coal trade, the effect of increased prices is even more injurious. Not only do consumers pay in the increased cost of coal or of iron goods, but even wages are affected. Coal and iron are materials of such universal importance that they cannot rise in price without diminishing the prosperity of many other trades. It is the cheapness of these materials which has greatly contributed to render Lancashire and Staffordshire the workshops of the world, and so far as colliers raise their own wages by combination, they do it by obstructing the very source and fountain-head of the prosperity of all other classes.

Unionism, then, is simply PROTECTION. Every Union which, by limiting the number of apprentices, by prohibiting labour below a certain rate of wages, or by any similar device, keeps the rate above what it would otherwise be, levies a little protective revenue of its own.

Perhaps you will reply that combination is equally open and lawful for all. Let all trades combine, and then they will all be benefited, and the increased wages must come out of the pockets of the capitalists. Nothing however could be more unfounded.

In the first place all trades have not equal opportunities for combination. Small close trades like those of Sheffield, carried on in one spot only, have the greatest facilities and must have the advantage over those which are scattered about in every part of the country.

Those who require special skill and apprenticeship, like compositors, will be more successful than those whose work is readily learned. The hatters are said to be very successful in their combinations; the tailors are less so, for very obvious reasons; while the shoemakers, who carry on their work in every street and in every part of the country, are hardly organised at all, so far as I am aware.

There is again this important difference between trades: some work for home trade only, like the building trade, and do not meet any foreign competition; others work for foreign consumers, and cannot raise their wages and prices without losing their customers.

It is pretty obvious, then, that all trades cannot enjoy equally the supposed advantages of combination, and that some, therefore, must gain by the loss of others. But even if all were equally able to combine, we should only come to the result that each trade would be trying to improve its position at the expense of every other trade, and none would experience any real benefit, but, instead of benefit, a great deal of loss. Unionists overlook the fact that wages are only worth what they will buy. You cannot live upon the gold or silver you get at the week's end, and you must turn it into food and drink and clothing before it is of any use to you. How much you will get depends upon the price at which you can buy things as much as upon the amount of wages. Thus it is evident that if the prices of things are increased, the wages are so far of less benefit to the workman who receives them. And even supposing wages to be raised ten per cent., this would bring with it no advantage if prices were raised in the same degree.

One of the chief means by which the condition of the English people has been improved of late years has been the cheapening of manufactures and bread and a great variety of imported commodities. By taking off duties, by making trade free, and by increasing the productive powers of machinery, the comforts of life are placed within the reach of persons who could not before afford them. Even if wages in general were not much raised above what they were twenty or thirty years ago, more could be bought for the wages.

Unionists overlook all this. They look upon men as producers only, and imagine the dearer things are, the better people will be off. But we only produce that we may consume, and real prosperity consists in having a great abundance of cheap comforts which everyone can purchase. The cheaper things are the better we are off. You know and feel the advantages of cheap bread, and the hardship of dear bread. But you do not consider that every combination of workmen who can raise their own wages makes something dearer for other workmen, and that even if all could combine with equal ease they would only make all things dear, and hinder the production of the commodities upon which we live.

∠ I apprehend that the notion which lies at the bottom of Unionism is this: That a man is bound to think, not only of himself, but of his fellow-workmen. The principles of Unionism condemn a man who accepts work at a less rate than the current wages, because he may be leading the way to a reduction of wages affecting hundreds or thousands of fellow-workmen. There can be no doubt that in one point of view this principle of looking to the advantage of the many rather than the one, is noble and disinterested; and I do not doubt that if the history of strikes and trade disputes were fully written, it would disclose as many instances of fidelity and heroism and the fearless encounter of hardship and even death as many a war described in history.

But the Unionist overlooks the fact that the cause to which he is so faithful, is only the cause of a small exclusive class; his triumph is the injury of a vastly greater number of his fellow-workmen, and regarded in this point of view, his cause is a narrow and selfish one, rather than a broad and disinterested one. The more I admire the perseverance, the self-forgetfulness, the endurance, abstinence, and a hundred other good qualities which English workmen often display during the conduct of a great trade dispute, the more sincerely do I regret that so many good qualities should be thrown away, or rather misused, in a cause which is too often a hurtful one to their fellow-men.

VII.

I wish to say a few words on the question how far Trades Societies have succeeded in raising wages, for it is a very favourite and apparently strong argument with Union leaders to point to the improved condition of their men as a proof of the benefits conferred by the Union. I am far from denying that in some trades, especially the building trades, wages have been raised, because those trades have special opportunities for protecting themselves at the cost of the rest of the country.

But I believe there are no grounds for asserting that a general rise of wages has been secured by means of Trades Unions. Assuming such a general rise to have occurred, there are several other causes which would amply account for it. The liberation of industry and trade from many mistaken restrictions, the removal of Government protective duties, and the progress of free trade, in many countries, have thrown manufactures into a state of progress more rapid than was ever known before. Our exports and imports were doubled in the twelve years from 1854 to 1866. This could hardly fail to increase wages in many trades. A candid observer who inquired into the subject would soon, I believe, come to this conclusion, that it is only in progressive trades that strikes and combinations succeed at all in raising wages, and it is the progressive state of the trade that is the secret of their success. It is a little of the breeze of general prosperity which really fills the sails of the unions.

Continued and extensive emigration has further contributed to the rise of wages. It has gone so far that we have heard complaints, both from the United States and New South Wales, that you are swamping the labour market there, and infringing your own union principles.

Another cause that has contributed to the rise in money wages is the depreciation of gold following upon the greatly increased supplies from California and Australia. It seems now to be pretty generally received as true that the prices of materials and such articles as are not cheapened by the removal of duty or the improvement of manufactures, have tended to become seriously higher. It is doubtful whether the money cost of living has not advanced for this reason, in spite of the causes which would render it cheaper. Under these circumstances it was to be expected that wages and all salaries not invariably fixed would advance; otherwise the receivers would be worse off than before, instead of better. I ask you then how you can be sure, supposing you receive 20 or 40 per cent. higher wages now than fifteen years ago, that a good part of the increase is not due to the depreciation of gold, and the rest perhaps to the prosperity of trade.

I am confirmed in these opinions by the fact that, in a great many occupations in which combinations are quite unknown, considerable improvements in wages have been enjoyed, together with a reduction of the hours of labour in many cases. No one has ever heard of an Amalgamated Society of Cooks and Housemaids, and yet cooks and housemaids, as every housekeeper knows and feels, are able to ask higher wages now by 20 or 30 per cent. than they were ten or twenty years ago. Those who used to get £10 to £14 a year would now get between £12 and £18.

In the same way I believe there has been a general rise in the salaries of mercantile clerks; and it was on this ground that the clerks of the Bank of England not long since applied to the Directors for a general advance of salaries, which they readily obtained. In all Government offices there has been a rise of salaries, varying from 17 to 70 per cent., and the Custom House clerks are now urging a further advance of their salaries on the ground that they stand much lower in the scale of increase than the other Government establishments. Similarly it is found necessary by degrees to raise the wages of soldiers, policemen, and postmen. These are all facts which tend to show that increased money wages are not necessarily due to the beneficent action of Trades Unions. To the extent of 20 per cent., or more, the rise may be after all nominal, and due to the depreciation of the money in which the wages are paid. After we deduct this, the surplus is, in most cases, probably due to the natural prosperity of the trade; and it is liberty of trade and industry—not restriction—which favours industrial prosperity.

VIII.

To go to another point—that of the introduction of machinery—I really will not insult you by supposing that you are, generally speaking, opposed to the introduction of machinery. It must be apparent to you that it is by the use of machinery that the power and usefulness and prosperity of the artizans of this kingdom are created. Opposition to its introduction is purely suicidal. All the more enlightened

Trades Societies have, I believe, ceased any such opposition; and if they wish to advance the social and intellectual condition of their fellow-men they will urge upon them to favour machinery. Every step achieved in the use of machinery raises man above a mere labourer, and makes him an intellectual agent, capable of ruling the things about him. In America they view the use of machinery in a very different light, and all classes welcome the introduction of a labour-saving machine because it means the supply of more of the conveniences of life at diminished cost and trouble. There was a remarkable account in *The New York Tribune* lately of a new machine, which enables a single workman to make 60,000 fish-hooks in a day. It remarks, "That the fish-hooks are cheaper than any other need hardly be added. Hitherto the Americans have fished with British-made hooks, but that day is over. The European hooks have till now been made by hand—slowly, clumsily, expensively. We read recently an account in *The (British) Working-man* of the fish-hook manufacture in England, which seems, in the light of what we saw in Newhaven, the description of some antediluvian process invented by Tubal Cain. The aggregate cost must be ten times that of making by the automatic Crosby process." Perhaps you will say that the English artizan thinks of his fellow-men and objects to seeing the hand-hook makers thrown out of work. If so, perhaps he may be induced to look a little further, and remember the much more extensive class of fishermen who will be benefited by having cheap hooks. He may even look a little further, and observe that the supply of fish is really the object in view, and that any invention which enables us to catch fish more cheaply and plentifully than before is a lasting good to the whole population.

IX.

And now before concluding let me say in a few words how I think you may most surely advance the condition of your order. It is not by fighting against capital and against machinery, but by having them on your side. Do not lay aside *associations*, but direct their exertions to the most useful ends. It is not Unions which seem to me and to many others mistaken; it is the object which Unions aim at, and still more the policy they adopt to reach it.

I wish to see workmen becoming by degrees their own capitalists—sharers in all the profits and all the advantages which capital confers. You cannot do without capital. He must be a dreamer who tells you that you can, and he only plays upon words who tells you that labour is capital.

Labour alone will not suffice for raising a factory, or a house, nor even for cultivating an acre of ground. You must have a sum of money to buy the tools and materials, or at all events to maintain yourself whilst you are working. If not, why do you not dispense with employers altogether, and raise your own factories and works?

But when once you determine to have capital on your side I believe you can do it: the Hall in which we meet is evidence that you can do it. Save money, however little, and invest it in a co-operative society, and let it grow, and when you have a little sum, join with others in co-operative works. I believe that there are a multitude of different kinds of business requiring only a moderate amount of capital, which workmen will readily be able to carry on upon their own account when they set themselves seriously to think of it.

There are many branches of trade, however, in which such great capitals are required that you can hardly be able to undertake them safely without the aid of capitalists. In some trades again, especially the iron trade, there are great ups and downs in profits. For several years losses rather than profits may be the result, and then for several years large profits may be reached. As the wages of the operatives have to be raised or lowered accordingly, I see no way of avoiding interminable disputes but by the workmen themselves being admitted to receive a share of the profits under the Industrial Partnerships Act. The Partnerships scheme has been tried with success in Messrs. Briggs' collieries, and Messrs. Fox, Head & Co.'s Newport Iron Mills. I believe that many employers are well inclined to try it, and it only remains for the men to appreciate the advantages of becoming themselves capitalists in a small way.

If other modes of conciliating the claims of labour and capital fail, it is yet open to you to form Boards of Conciliation, as proposed by Mr. Mundella, and successfully carried out at Nottingham. In these Boards representatives of employers and employed may meet and come to a clear understanding of the points of difference. As the rate of wages is always a matter of bargain, and should be freely determined by the course of the market, I do not think that such Boards of Conciliation should have any legislative power; but they may nevertheless be of the greatest utility in bringing the two parties to the bargain nearer together, so that all unnecessary causes of misunderstanding may be removed.

X.

A word more in conclusion: I cannot but believe that all this agitation about the labour question shows that the larger part of the people are feeling their way to a condition far higher and better than they have hitherto occupied. But they do not hit at once upon the right way. They feel themselves suffering under *something*, and they call it the *tyranny of capital*, and they organise themselves in opposition to capital. But this tyranny is really the tyranny of a man's own stomach; you must eat every day, and as long as you have no accumulated wealth, no savings, you must find work every day. You cannot help yourselves, and are at the mercy of the capitalist, who alone can give you work. But all this is changed for the man who has even a moderate amount of savings. Not only does he disarm sickness or misfortune of half its terrors, but he may also, by co-operation, become his own employer; and then he will, I presume, cease to complain of the tyranny of capital. I hope for the working-men of this country more than they generally hope for themselves: that they may become in a great degree their own capitalists, and may be the builders of their own fortunes.

I have the honour of a very remote connection with the

name of Mr. Cobden, as I fill the office of the Cobden Lectureship, established at Owens College as a memorial of his services to the people of this country. I have been charged by Mr. Macdonald, of the Trades Unionists' Political Association, with holding doctrines unworthy of the name of Cobden; but I beg to challenge anyone here to give a proof that my opinions are at variance with the opinions of Mr. Cobden as regards the freedom of trade or the freedom of labour. And to show you what were his views of the mode by which the people may raise themselves, I will end by quoting a sentence or two from a speech of his delivered at Birmingham on the 13th of November, 1849, at a time when he was in the full career of usefulness, success, and popularity.

He said: "I wish to see the great mass of the working-classes of this country elevate themselves by increased temperance, frugality, and economy. I tell you, candidly, that no people were ever yet elevated except through their own advancing wealth, morality, and intelligence; and anyone who tells the working-men of this country that they may be raised in the social scale by any other process than that of reformation in themselves, is interested either in flattering or deceiving them."—*Speeches of Richard Cobden, Esq., M.P., on Peace, etc., delivered during* 1849, *revised by himself*, p. 171.

ON INDUSTRIAL PARTNERSHIPS.*

    I. Present Evils.
    II. Boards of Arbitration and Conciliation.
    III. Trades Union Commissioners' Report.
    IV. Messrs. Briggs' Industrial Partnership.
    V. Messrs. Fox, Head & Co.'s Partnership.
    VI. Summary of their Scheme.
    VII. Mr. Babbage's Proposal of the Partnership Principle.
    VIII. Advantages and Difficulties of the System.
    IX. True Principles of Co-operation.
    X. Circumstances Limiting its Application.
    XI. Probable Effects upon the Working-classes.
    XII. Concluding Remarks.

I.

It was with great pleasure that I undertook to prepare the present lecture, because I have become more and more convinced of the extreme importance of the Industrial Partnership principle to the peace and well-being of the kingdom. The seeming novelty of the proposition, that workmen should become sharers in their master's profits, causes many persons to stigmatise the idea as impracticable, unsound, and opposed to experience. But I believe that the unsoundness is all in the present state of things, and that experience is not against the novelty but in its favour.

For can any one truly say that experience is in favour of the present relations of capital and labour? Does not

* A lecture delivered under the auspices of the National Association for the Promotion of Social Science, April 5th, 1870.

every one feel that there is an evil at work which needs a remedy? Does not the constant occurrence of strikes, and the rise of vast and powerful organisations of workmen, show that there is some profound unfitness in the present customs of the country to the progress of affairs? Bacon tells us that it is not good to try experiments in states, and that "we should stand upon the ancient ways;" but he adds, "unless the necessity be urgent, or the utility evident,"—and with deep wisdom he points out that "Time is the greatest innovator; and if time alter all things to the worse, and wisdom and counsel shall not alter them to the better, what shall be the end?" * I believe that his words apply to the present state of things, and that time is altering the status of the workmen of this country. As a great middle-class of merchants and manufacturers has arisen and asserted their position in the state, so I conceive that all these combinations and arbitrations, and regulations, and other devices in the various trades, betoken an earnest though often a mistaken impulse in the working-classes towards something better and higher than they yet enjoy. It is true that the innovations of time are slow and scarce to be perceived. It is our misfortune that we cannot measure and estimate what is going on in the present moment, and only when an evil has been long endured can we see how obvious and how necessary was the remedy.

I confess that I cannot myself see the end to the troubles which arise out of the contest of capital and labour, without some decided change. To overcome or destroy unions, and achieve peace in this manner, is the desire of some masters. To me this seems neither desirable nor practicable. Association of some kind or other is alike the sign and means of civilisation. In proportion as we become more civilised, societies and unions will ever multiply. It is only by substituting one more useful and beneficial form of organisation that another can be dissolved, and I think it can be demonstrated that union between each master and his men is the real union which will be a blessing to all.

* Essay on Innovation.

II.

Some men of great experience think that Boards of Arbitration and Conciliation will solve the difficulty; and there is no doubt that such boards have prevented strikes and disagreements. Anyone will admit that conciliation is better than open strife; but it does not follow that what brings peace affords a sound and thorough settlement. I have never been able to persuade myself that arbitration by an elected board or single individual is a theoretically sound measure. It appears to me to countenance the erroneous idea, so generally prevailing, that prices and wages can be and ought to be the subject of regulation. It tends to remove all free competition, to substitute one single arbitrary power for the two rival powers which now strive in every trade. The Act of Parliament under which such councils are established certainly provides that there shall be no power to fix a uniform rate of prices or wages, so that the Legislature has formally, at least, maintained the principles of free labour.

But unless the councils arbitrate in the matter of wages and prices, they do not touch the chief point in dispute; and if they do not fix rates which will practically be respected and enforced by public opinion upon the whole trade, where is the use of their arbitration? The tendency of all such arrangements would surely be to destroy the freedom of individual action; and any such tendency is directly contrary to the undoubted truths of economical science, which we must unflinchingly uphold at the peril of unmeasured evils. I am perfectly willing to allow that there are many details of trade relating to the hours and conditions of labour, the safety, comfort, and welfare of the men, which are rightly the subject of regulation; and in respect to such matters I wish to see the vigilance and energy of the unions and councils increased rather than diminished, provided that they will learn to discriminate between what they can, and what they cannot, properly regulate. But I fear that a long time must pass before the fallacies of protection will be thoroughly eradicated from the minds of men. Many a sad experiment must be made, and many a disastrous failure incurred, before the men of a trade will see that they cannot ultimately find their exclusive benefit in the injury of others, and that the supreme law of the general welfare forbids them to do it if they could. I feel that Sir G. C. Lewis was right when he said that mankind must suffer before they have discovered the true tendencies of the protective theory of labour now enjoying popular favour.

I believe, then, that we may say of the present time and subject, again in the words of Bacon, that, " a froward retention of custom is as turbulent a thing as an innovation." Nay, more so: the turbulence is in the present state of things, and the innovation, I trust, will be its end. If the masters insist upon retaining their ancient customs; if they will shroud their profits in mystery, and treat their men as if they were another class of beings, whose interests were wholly separate and opposite; I see trouble in the future as in the past. But I trust they will accept the change which time is pressing on them. The sharing of profits is one of those apparently obvious inventions, at the simplicity of which men will wonder in an after-age. There was a time in England, not so long ago, when wages were the last new invention, the most turbulent innovation. It seems natural now that a man should be paid for what he does; but, to our Norman forefathers the matter did not present itself in this light. The Public Record Office could furnish many a proof, I dare say, of the presumption and turbulence of those Saxon serfs who asked for pay. Laborious historians can trace precisely how the Saxon slave became by degrees the free and wage-paid journeyman. We can almost put our finger on the year when the thin end of the wedge was first inserted, and can point to every step in its progress home. Not without bitter strife and suffering was so great a change effected. There is the thin end of some wedge, as I believe, in the present state of things, and it is our duty to endeavour to detect the direction in which it is tending. It is the part of wisdom not to think that things will always be as they have been, still less to think that the relations of society can be shaped according to our own narrow wishes and ideas. It is the work of economical and social science to endeavour to detect those arrangements which must ultimately prosper, because they are founded on the true principles of human nature. And if, as I believe, the artizan will ultimately become the sharer in the profits of the work he does, and the zealous friend of the capitalist, we cannot do a more important work than facilitating and hastening the change.

At present we see the working-men of a trade usually banded together, endeavouring to restrict the number who can share in the work, often resisting more or less openly any considerable improvement that will yield more results in proportion to labour; in short, studying in some degree, but perhaps unconsciously, "how not to do it," instead of giving their whole thoughts and efforts "how to do most work with least time, trouble, and expense." We find them again labouring under the impression that their employers are a grasping set of monopolists, who contribute but little to their work, but draw enormous profits from it. Every increase of wages they can secure is too often thought to be twice blessed; it is so much to their own advantage, it is so much from the profits of those who have no right to it. The ardent unionist looks to the raising of prices, the restriction of labour, the limitation of supply, for the improving of his own condition. He does not see that all these measures, though beneficial apparently to himself, are directly contrary to the good of the whole community, and that if others acted on the same principles it would simply amount to a general striving after scarcity and poverty.

The masters contribute to all these erroneous notions by surrounding their profits and their losses with profound secrecy, and, though the ultimate result is different, there is no doubt that their immediate profit does depend upon keeping wages down. Acting, as they usually do, in more or less concert with other employers, they countenance, if they do not originate, the idea that combination should be in a horizontal direction between employer and employer, between workman and workman.

And then, again, what motive is there under present circumstances for a workman to be zealous and skilful? If he be but moderately efficient and active, the union will support him if discharged, and will oppose him if he seeks for better wages than his companions. Unless, as I believe is very generally the case, real honesty and love of doing his work in a workmanlike manner stimulate him, he can really have no motive for doing more than the average amount of work. We know that unions often oppose piece-work, or any such arrangement as secures a reward proportional to energy. When I think of all these things, I am surprised that work is so well done as it is; there must be a strong power of energy and honesty behind.

The advocates of industrial partnerships wish to see honest labour meet with its due reward. They consider that combination should be in a perpendicular, and not in a horizontal, direction. The master is to combine with his men, to be their true leader, and after all the ordinary costs of wages, interest, and superintendence are provided for, the surplus is to be fairly divided among all who have contributed towards it. There is no reason whatever, except long-standing custom, why the capitalist should take all the risk and have all the excess of profits. Workmen generally cannot wait beyond the week's end for their wages, and thus they have been obliged to part with all interest in their products for an immediate payment; but theoretical soundness is in favour of a totally different arrangement. In every work there are a thousand opportunities where the workman can either benefit or injure the establishment; and could he really be made to feel his interests identical with those of his employers, there can be no doubt that the profits of the trade could be greatly increased in many cases.

III.

Here I would point out that the Report of the Trades Union Commissioners is not only erroneous as regards questions of theory relating to industrial partnerships, but is, in point of fact, positively opposed to their evidence. They say : *

"It must be remembered that, as regards Messrs. Briggs' system, the principle is to limit the profits of the employer, and to give the workman, over and above his wages, a share in the profits of the concern, without subjecting him to any liability for loss. It is, then, not unreasonable to suppose that many capitalists will prefer the chances of disputes with their workmen, and even run the risk of strikes and temporary loss, rather than voluntarily limit their profits to 10 per cent., or any other fixed amount."

These statements totally misrepresent the system which we are going to consider. The Messrs. Briggs, as we shall see, do not allow of any fixed limit to their profits. Instead of 10 per cent. being their maximum profit, it is rather a *minimum*, since the interests and energies of the workmen are enlisted in ensuring them this amount, which is a first charge upon all the profits of the establishment. It is true that any excess of profits above 10 per cent. is shared with the men; but considering that the men, by abstaining from all strikes, agitations, or loss of time, and by promoting in every way the success of the firm, have greatly diminished the risks, there is not the slightest reason to suppose that the average profits of the masters will be decreased. The men cannot earn any dividend without an equal amount going into the pockets of their masters. Again, I venture to assert that this arrangement is entirely sound in principle, and that the arbitration and conciliation so much recommended by the Commissioners, although a good makeshift, is entirely unsound in principle.

But fortunately the time is past when this question need be discussed as a matter of theory only; it is now a matter of experience. It has been put to the test in more than one instance, and under circumstances which will meet every objection. The results are of a most conclusive character.

IV.

Although the history of Messrs. Briggs' partnership may be known to many, I must briefly recount it, that all may

* "Eleventh and Final Report of the Trades Union Commissioners," p. xxviii.

know what experience proves. Until the middle of the year 1865, Messrs. Briggs, Son & Co., had worked the Whitwood and Methley Junction Collieries by an ordinary private partnership. During ten years previous to that date four long strikes had occurred, causing a loss of seventy-eight weeks of work, not to speak of many minor interruptions. It would be under the mark, I believe, to say that there was an average loss of one day's work in the week, both to masters and men. In addition to this was the cost incurred in the struggles with the men, in importing non-unionists, and guarding the men and works from outrage. The anxiety and painful feelings engendered must not be unthought of. There were the usual sad concomitants of such struggles—evictions of the unionists, attacks upon the non-unionists, police guards, threatening letters, and the like; the whole culminating in a serious riot, trials at the York assizes and heavy sentences— there was, in short, a small civil war, just such as has, I hope, been brought to a close at the Thorncliffe Collieries. And when I hear of armed bodies of men attacking quiet cottages, the inmates driven to the higher stories, while fire is applied below, and all the other incidents which we have read, I almost feel as if we were in the Middle Ages, and border raids were still going on. The signal-beacon alone is missing, and the buzzer has taken its place.

The pecuniary result of the civil war at Whitwood was that the proprietors barely secured 5 per cent. profit on the average of ten years, and they were so thoroughly disgusted and pained at their relations with their men that they were on the point of throwing up the business. Fortunately the Companies Act of 1862 allowed of their introducing a new arrangement, and in July, 1865, the decisive experiment was made. This system consisted mainly in an engagement to divide with their men all excess of nett profit over 10 per cent.; at the same time the men were allowed and encouraged to purchase small shares in the undertaking, without, however, acquiring any power to interfere in the management of the business. The result is easily told. The pecuniary result I will postpone to the moral and social results of the change.

K

Peace has reigned where there was strife. Steady, zealous work has become the unbroken rule. Strikes are known only by tradition. Hardly a day's work has been lost; mutual feelings of confidence and esteem between employers and employed have been thoroughly established. These are facts beyond doubt or denial. I have heard them from the lips of one of the employers, and also from one of the men, and as they have been published for some time and have never been contradicted, we may receive them as certainly true. There is also little doubt that the moral condition of the neighbourhood is distinctly improved; there is less drunkenness, less fighting, swearing, and gambling.

The pecuniary result may be briefly summed up. During the four complete years which have passed since the partnership was constituted, the capitalists have received dividends of 12, 13, 13½, and 13⅓ per cent. The proprietors must have felt that a very pleasant limit had been placed to their profits. An average profit of 13 per cent. earned amid peace and goodwill, compared with 5 per cent. earned out of contention and riot, present advantages which even a Royal Commission might be supposed to recognise. But it passes me to conceive how seven gentlemen of great eminence, with a Lord Chief Justice at their head, could so far overlook the facts brought before them as to say that the Messrs. Briggs voluntarily limited their profits to 10 per cent. At the same time the workmen received dividends equivalent to the excess beyond 10 per cent., namely, 2, 3, 3½, and 3⅓ per cent., so that the total nett profits of the business were 14, 16, 17, and 16⅔ per cent., or more than three times what they had been in previous years! Many workmen have thus received dividends of £5, the largest sums that they have probably ever received at one time. These dividends were of course increased by any accruing from shares held in the capital account of the business, and one man has thus received altogether £10 in a single payment.

It may perhaps be said that all these gratifying results are due to the exceptional energy, good tact, and business-like qualities of the proprietors. I have no doubt they do possess all these qualities; but if so, we are forced to the conclusion that the most able and conciliatory masters cannot, under the ordinary relations of capital and labour, prevent their works from becoming a constant exhibition of ill-will, conflict, and riot. The Whitwood Collieries seem to me to furnish all the requirements of a perfectly decisive experiment. The re-constitution of the partnership in 1865 is the only cause to which we can attribute the undoubted change which has followed.

But the Commissioners remarked that when they reported the plan had only been tested during a period of comparative prosperity in the coal trade. It might be answered that since they reported, the state of the trade has not been at all prosperous, and yet there is no apparent effect. But I can fortunately refer to a second independent experiment, which entirely negatives their remark.

V.

It happens that Messrs. Fox, Head & Co., of the Newport Iron Works, Middlesbrough, had up to the year 1866 suffered even more from strikes than the Messrs. Briggs. Their works had stood idle about one-fourth of the time since they had been opened, and at the close of the long strike o 1866, they determined to adopt a partnership scheme closely similar to that we have been considering. The differences are not of a material kind, but the importance of their case arises from the fact that the partnership was constituted just at the commencement of a period of intense depression in the trade. The collapse of 1866, and the cessation of railway works, have rendered it difficult for any ironmaker to make a profit. In their first two annual reports, Messrs. Fox, Head & Co. were obliged to declare to their men that there was no bonus to divide, and it might have been expected that such disappointment and discouragement would have ended the scheme. But the accounts were audited, and the result certified by eminent accountants, and they were apparently received with confidence by the men. In the third year of the scheme, which has just ended, the proprietors were enabled to distribute a bonus of $2\frac{1}{2}$ per cent. or 6d. in the pound, on all wages. They find too that there is at the present time much more confidence, and a much better state of feeling at the works than existed there a few years ago. The period fixed for the first scheme having elapsed, they have just reconstituted the partnership, with some slight changes, for a period of five years. In short, the experiment had succeeded at Middlesbrough, in the midst of the most untoward circumstances, just as it had succeeded at Whitwood in a prosperous state of trade. If it would fail at all, surely the first two bad years would have displayed the weakness. The members of both these firms will, I believe, deserve the gratitude of the country for the firmness with which they have cast aside the current prejudices, and have put to a decisive test a plan which had everything but experience in its favour.

VI.

I owe to the kindness of Messrs. Fox, Head & Co., a copy of the rules on which their work is conducted, and that we may understand precisely the nature of the scheme, I have prepared a summary of the rules.

(1.) The employers are to have the sole and undisputed control of the works and the business.

(2.) No employés are to belong to Trades Unions.

(3.) Employers similarly are not to belong to any association of employers.

(4.) All questions concerning wages and prices are to be decided at the discretion of the employers.

(5.) Wages will, however, be those generally accepted in the district, but during any trade dispute the old rate is to be retained.

(6.) Working partners are to receive salaries at customary rates, approved by accountants.

(7.) Rate of interest allowed to capitalists is to average 10 per cent. during the continuance of the scheme.

(8.) Amount charged annually for renewals and depreciations of the work and plant is not to exceed on an average 6 per cent. per annum upon the outlaid capital.

(9.) Cost of all necessary repairs are to be charged to the cost of manufacture.

(10.) Costs of manufacture are to include all law, banking, and other incidental charges.

(11.) To meet bad debts a fund is to be created by an annual charge of 1½ per cent. of the gross returns. Should this fund prove insufficient the excess shall be charged to cost of manufacture. Any balance of the fund at termination of partnership to be carried forward should the partnership be reconstituted; otherwise it shall revert to capitalists.

(12.) Surplus profits beyond all the charges and costs of manufacture are to be divided into two equal parts, one half to be distributed to all employés—that is, all who have received wages or salaries during the year—in proportion to the amount so received by them.

(13.) The employers to appoint public accountants to audit accounts and report the result.

(14.) The public accountants to decide all matters in dispute.

(15.) Employés' bonuses unclaimed during one month to be forfeited.

(16.) All employés to share proportionately to the time they have served, however short.

(17.) All dividends not claimed to be carried to the profit and loss account of the following year.

(18.) Any employé joining a Trades Union or legally convicted of injuring the works to forfeit dividend.

(19.) Persons performing work by contract to furnish lists of the wages paid to their assistants, who will receive the dividend direct from the employers; the latter, however, will not be responsible for the correctness of the returns, and will decide all disputes at their discretion.

(20.) Should the year's profits not meet all the charges, including 10 per cent. profit to capital, the deficiency is to be charged to the profit and loss account of the following year.

(21.) Exempts from the scheme a certain patent manufacture belonging to Messrs. Fox, Head & Co.

(22.) No employé to acquire any of the rights or liabilities of a partner, or to be in any way exempted from the laws relating to masters and workmen.

(23.) The scheme is to be considered a continuation of that of November, 1866.

(24.) Employés will be considered as assenting to the scheme by merely accepting or continuing in employment.

This scheme came into operation on the 5th of February last, and is to continue in operation for five years.

VII.

It does not seem to be so generally known as it ought to be that, as far as can be ascertained, the real author of the system I am advocating is Mr. Charles Babbage. Nearly forty years ago his admirable work on "The Economy of Manufactures" was published, and it is truly difficult to overrate the genius which it displays. I never look into that work without discovering that it contains the germ of some truth that has since been recognised, or of some truth that is likely to be recognised. No one can read Chapter XXVI. without seeing how entirely he anticipated the advantages which have accrued from this proposal. The chapter is entitled, "On a New System of Manufacturing," and I shall ask your permission to read considerable extracts from it.

"A most erroneous and unfortunate opinion," he commences, "prevails among workmen in many manufacturing countries, that their own interests and that of their employers are at variance. The consequences are, that valuable machinery is sometimes neglected and even privately injured—that new improvements, introduced by the masters, do not receive a fair trial—and that the talents and observations of the workmen are not directed to the improvement of the processes in which they are employed. . . .

"Convinced as I am, from my own observation, that the prosperity and success of the master-manufacturer is essential to the welfare of the workman, I am yet compelled to admit that this connection is, in many cases, too remote to be always understood by the latter; and whilst it is perfectly true that workmen, as a class, derive advantage from the prosperity of their employers, I do not think that each individual partakes of that advantage exactly in proportion to the extent to which he contributes towards it; nor do I perceive that the resulting advantage is as immediate as it might become under a different system.

"It would be of great importance if, in every large establishment, the mode of payment could be so arranged, that every person employed should derive advantage from the success of the whole; and that the profits of each individual should advance, as the factory itself produced profit, without the necessity of making any change in the wages."

Mr. Babbage then points out that the mode of paying for work in the Cornish mines, by which the miners receive a certain part of the value of the ore raised, fulfils to some extent the conditions of a better system. Admirable results have followed wherever this mode of payment was adopted.

"I shall now," he continues, "present the outline of a system which appears to me to be pregnant with the most important results, both to the class of workmen and to the country at large; and which, if acted upon, would, in my opinion, permanently raise the working-classes and greatly extend the manufacturing system.

"The general principles on which the proposed system is founded, are:

"(1.) *That a considerable part of the wages received by each person employed should depend on the profits made by the establishment;* and,

"(2.) *That every person connected with it should derive more advantage from applying any improvement he might discover to the factory in which he is employed, than he could by any other course.*"

Thinking that it would be difficult to prevail upon capitalists to try the new system, involving an apparent change in the division of profits, Mr. Babbage suggests that it should be tried by small companies of working-men. He describes a plan not greatly differing from that on which not a few co-operative companies have since been started, the general principle being that every one should be paid proportionately to the services he has rendered towards the success of the company.

He enumerates the following as among the principal results of such an arrangement:

"(1.) That every person engaged in it would have a *direct* interest in its prosperity; since the effect of any success, or falling off, would almost immediately produce a corresponding change in his own weekly receipts.

"(2.) Every person concerned in the factory would have an immediate interest in preventing any waste or mismanagement in all the departments.

"(3.) The talents of all connected with it would be strongly directed to its improvement in every department.

"(4.) None but workmen of high character and qualifications could obtain admission into such establishments; because, when any additional hands were required, it would be the common interest of all to admit only the most respectable and skilful; and it would be far less easy to impose upon a dozen workmen than upon a single proprietor of a factory."

The sixth advantage is perhaps the most important, namely, the total removal of all real or imaginary causes for combination.

"The workmen and capitalists," says Mr. Babbage, "would so shade into each other—would so *evidently* have a common interest, and their difficulties and distresses would be mutually so well understood, that, instead of combining to oppress one another, the only combination which could exist would be a most powerful union *between* both parties to overcome their common difficulties."

To the following remarks I would especially draw the attention of capitalists, since they clearly point out the mistakes into which the Trades Union Commissioners have fallen upon this point.

"One of the difficulties attending such a system is, that capitalists would at first fear to embark in it, imagining that the workmen would receive too large a share of the profits; and it is quite true that the workmen would have a larger share than at present: but, at the same time, it is presumed the effect of the whole system would be, that the total profits of the establishment being much increased, the smaller proportion allowed to capital under this system would yet be greater in actual amount than that which results to it from the larger share in the system now existing."

It would be impossible more clearly to anticipate the doubts which have been felt, and the solution of those doubts which has been given by actual experience. Mr. Babbage's remarks about the interference of the law of partnership are rendered inapplicable by the alteration of the law, and the difficulty he notices concerning the discharge of incompetent or ill-behaved workmen does not affect the scheme I am advocating, in which the absolute power of management resides in the hands of the proprietors.

VIII.

It only remains for us now to consider more minutely the source and nature of the advantages which have been found in practice to follow from the adoption of this principle; we must also distinguish as accurately as possible the conditions of its success, and the character of the trades to which it is most suited. The chief obstructions which will stand in the way of its adoption must not be unnoticed so far as time will allow.

It is alike the great advantage and the great difficulty of this scheme that it requires the disclosure of the amount of profit made by the capitalists. So long as the employer surrounds his business with mystery, and carefully conceals the profit he obtains, it is natural that the workman should feel distrust, and probably over-estimate the amount of the share which is taken from the produce of his work. Every demand for wages and every strike is made in the dark, and the point to which the master carries resistance is the only real test of the sincerity of his professions. The master says, "I am making no sufficient profits," and the "state of trade will not allow me to advance your wages." The workmen reply: "We are not allowed to know what your profits are, but so far as we can judge we think the state of trade would allow of an advance; and therefore we cannot depend upon your vague assurances; the only way in which we can arrive at the truth is to try how long you will suffer your business to stand still." There is no doubt that this is at least a plausible argument for combinations and strikes; arbitration may overcome the difficulty in some degree, because the real state of trade and profit can be made known to a single arbitrator, or even a limited board, more freely than to the public in general. But, as I have said, arbitration presupposes that there is combination and concert on both sides, and that all the trade are willing to make the conditions of wages and prices the subject of regulation. All this is directly contrary to the principles of free labour and free trade.

The only other alternative which I can see is for the

masters to dissolve the mystery surrounding their profits in some degree. There is not the slightest necessity to make known positive losses, and all that need be published is the amount of excess, if any, beyond a certain fixed minimum, the truth of the report and the accuracy of the accounts to be certified by auditors or accountants of high position. I confess I should have little hope of masters overcoming their strong prejudices against such a proceeding were it not for one circumstance. The extension of limited liability companies will tend to render trade much less secret; for where there are a score or more of shareholders, any mystery about the rate of profit is out of the question. No doubt limited companies are a little out of favour just at present, owing to reaction after their recent rash creation. But there is a great future for joint-stock enterprise in one form or another, and when there are many shareholders among the capitalists, I see no reason whatever why the partnership principle should not at once be adopted as regards the men. The first to bring this principle into operation should be large companies owning coal mines, iron works, or any other large factories employing many labourers. And as a joint-stock company can less depend upon vigilant superintendence of their business when the managers are not the actual capitalists, it is all the more necessary that they should give each man an interest in the result. I perfectly feel how slowly this principle must make its way among private employers, but there are, nevertheless, many large companies existing which might embrace the principle at once without the slightest difficulty. Not to do so will argue, I should think, the greatest blindness to their own interests, and to those of the country generally. It is but a few years since the Legislature upheld the prejudice that it was impossible to allow anyone to share profits without obliging him to share the risks. But in the Act of 1862 this prejudice was given up, and I do trust that any other prejudices which stand in the way of this great reform may shortly be dissolved, now that the law gives a full opportunity for the trial.

It may be said that no firm would long stand if they could

be obliged at intervals to reveal the state of their business; any temporary embarrassment would thus become known, and their credit would be gone. But no such revelation is at all necessary. The only fact which need be published is whether the profits exceed the fixed minimum. It would be absurd to suppose that any inference as to the credit and solvency of the firm could be drawn from such a fact. As regards all the particular transactions, debts, contracts, and other affairs of a firm, exactly the same secrecy can be maintained as at present. It is clearly to be understood, too, that the sharing of profits does not entail the right to control, in any degree, the affairs of the firm, or to demand an investigation of their accounts. The employés of an industrial partnership will partially resemble the immense number of persons who now hold small shares of insufficient value to give them any appreciable voice in the management of the companies, or to make it worth their while to spend time, trouble, or money in the matter. No small part of the capital of the country is thus owned by purely passive recipients of the profits procured for them by larger capitalists, or directors and managers of companies intrusted with the money. Workmen sharing profits will be in the same position, except that in their own work or in keeping an eye upon the work of others, they will possess, every hour and every minute, the means of contributing something to the profits they share.

IX.

When we come to think about the matter, it is plain that industrial partnerships are founded upon the surest principle of human nature—self-interest. There can, I think, be but four motives which can operate upon a workman.

(1.) Fear of dismissal.

(2.) Hope of getting higher wages or a better employment.

(3.) Goodwill to his employer, and desire to fulfil his bargain honestly.

(4.) Direct self-interest in the work.

The first of these, no doubt, is sufficient to prevent the workman being much below the average of efficiency, but it cannot do more. The second is a powerful incentive where an employment allows of many grades, and promotion is free and depends on merit. In many of the ordinary handicraft employments, however, both these motives are to a great extent relaxed by the regulations of the unions which favour the equal payment of all moderately efficient workmen, and yield a strong support to those who are in their opinion wrongfully dismissed. The third motive is really operative to a greater extent than we should suppose, but is not one that we can expect to trust to. The fourth motive—direct interest in the work done—is entirely excluded by the present mode of payment, which leaves all profit to the master. It is upon this motive that the partnership principle depends. So far, indeed, is the principle from being a new one, that it lies at the basis of all ordinary relations of trade and private enterprise. The very opponent of industrial partnerships argues upon the ground that the employer must have all the profit because it is requisite to compensate him for all the trouble and skill expended in management; in short, that he must have powerful self-interest in the matter. But it may be safely answered that the men have so many opportunities of benefiting the work of a large factory, and they have so many means of injuring it by strikes and contentions, that it is entirely to the interest of the employer to buy their exertions and goodwill with a share of profits.

Though I have spoken of this scheme as an innovation, it is only so as regards the larger branches of trade. All that is proposed is to extend to other trades what has long been found absolutely indispensable in special trades. In the whaling trade, in fishing, and in the Cornish mining system, as Mr. Babbage pointed out;* in American trading-ships, and some other instances noticed by Mr. Mill in his remarks upon the subject;† in the form of co-operation adopted in the Welsh

---

* "Economy of Manufactures," p. 259.

† "Principles of Political Economy." Book IV., chap. vii., sec. 5, 3rd ed., vol. II, p. 335.

slate quarries; in all cases where work is paid for by commission or by piece-work, the principle is really adopted at the present day. It is quite a common custom I believe, and is growing more common, for banks or firms of merchants to give bonuses to their clerks after a prosperous year; and managers, schoolmasters, and others holding responsible positions, usually have a considerable part of their remuneration dependent on the profits of the business they manage. The principle is nothing but that of *payment by results*, and, more or less directly, it is that which must govern all trade in a sound state of things. It is, no doubt, the total absence of any direct or apparent participation in results on the part of ordinary artizans which gives rise to much of the trouble we encounter at present.

The partnership scheme is, I believe, by far the truest form of co-operation. We have heard a great deal of co-operation lately, until we may well be tired of the name; but I agree with Mr. Briggs* in thinking that many of the institutions said to be co-operative really lack the fundamental principle, that those who work shall share. If a co-operative retail store employ shopmen, buyers, and managers, receiving fixed and usually low salaries, superintended by unpaid directors, I can only say that it embodies all the principles of dissolution; it has all the evils of a joint-stock company without many advantages. Such would also be the case with any manufacturing co-operative company which pays fixed wages and salaries. Such a company might probably be described as a loose aggregation of a number of persons of small means, none of whom have an adequate motive for care or energy. I do hope very much from co-operation in many forms, but the name of the thing will not be sufficient; the real interests of all employed must be enlisted, if co-operative societies are to prosper and grow. But industrial partnerships, such as those of the Messrs. Briggs, and Fox, Head & Co., have all the advantages and none of the evils of joint-stock co-operation. They are managed by two or three working partners,

---

* "Lecture upon Strikes and Lockouts," *Sheffield Daily Telegraph*, 10th March, 1870.

whose whole energies and interests are bound up in the success of their management, and who are at the same time unrestricted by any power of interference on the part of those employed or of shareholders. They can thus act with all the freedom, secrecy, and despatch of private enterprise; and yet they carry with them the interest and sympathy of all they govern. They have all the advantages of true leaders of their men. It is well understood that a successful military leader must be perfectly unfettered in judgment and supreme in executive power; and yet he must manage to earn the confidence and devotion of his men. It is to a position resembling this that the Messrs. Briggs seem to me to have raised themselves by the courageous adoption of a true principle, and I do believe that when their example is followed, our works and factories will become so many united and well-organised regiments of labourers. Good leaders will seek good men, and good men in return will seek and attach themselves to good leaders. We shall have an honourable rivalry between one firm and another, as to which shall get the best men and pay the best dividends.

X.

But it is evident that the partnership principle is not equally applicable to all trades. Those kinds of manufacture where the expenditure is to a large extent paid in wages and by time, and where a large number of men are employed in a manner not allowing of any rigid test or superintendence of their work, will derive most advantage from it. Where a large amount of fixed capital is required, so that the expenditure on wages is less considerable, the advantage will not be so marked, unless indeed the fixed capital be in the form of machines or other property which can be readily injured by careless use.

The adoption of the principle, again, is of less importance where the work is paid for by the piece or by contract, as, for instance, in the Welsh slate quarries. In this case, however, a special form of co-operation has already been employed for a length of time, and attention has been called to the good results by Professor Cairnes, in "Macmillan's Magazine," January, 1865. But even where payment is by quantity, the men might usually save a great deal were their interests enlisted in economy. Thus, in collieries, the hewing of the coal is paid by the weight got, nevertheless the value of the coal greatly depends upon the proportion of the large coal to the broken coal and slack, and also upon the careful picking of the coal from duff or rubbish. Again, the cost of the wooden props, by which the roof is supported in a colliery, is a considerable item in the expenditure, and a careful coal-hewer can extract and save more than a careless one.

The Messrs. Briggs show that the saving by care in their own works might easily be as follows : *

In getting the coal unbroken	£1500 a year.
In getting the coal clean	1500 ,,
In saving of props	300 ,,
Total saving	£3300 ,,

This is independent of savings derived from superior care of the workings and property of the colliery generally.

It would be obviously undesirable to adopt the partnership arrangement where the risks of the business are very great, and arise chiefly from speculative causes, so that the amount of profit depends almost entirely upon the judgment and energy of the principals. In such cases, doubtless, the men could not compensate their masters by superior care for the dividends they would receive; and as the risks would remain undiminished, the dividends would really be subtracted from the legitimate profits of the capitalist. No one supposes for a moment that the scheme could succeed under such circumstances. But it would be entirely wrong to suppose that the scheme cannot adapt itself to trades with varying risk. As the Messrs. Briggs point out, there is no particular reason for adopting ten more than twelve or fifteen per cent., or any other rate

* "Report on the Formation, Principle, and Operations of the System of Industrial Partnership, adopted by Henry Briggs, Son & Co., Wakefield."

of minimum profit that may seem fitting to the circumstances of the trade. That rate will ultimately be chosen in each trade which yields current interest in addition to compensation for risk, trouble, and all other unfavourable circumstances which are not allowed for in the depreciation fund, the bad debt fund, or the salaries of the working partners. The working classes perfectly acquiesce in the great differences of wages existing between different trades, and it is not to be supposed that any difficulty would be encountered in choosing for each trade that rate of profit which experience shows to be proper. The sharing of the excess of profit with the men will certainly prevent the masters from receiving in highly prosperous years so much as they otherwise might have done, but this will be compensated by the less chance of loss in other years, and by the fact that any deficiency below the minimum profit is to be made good out of the proceeds of subsequent years before any excess is to be distributed. The zeal of the employés to gain a dividend will thus insure the masters receiving their fair and necessary profits in addition to any excess which fortune or good management may bring. To sum up briefly the effect of the principle upon profits, I may say that I believe when the partnership principle is fully tested in various suitable trades, the effects will be as follows:

(1.) To diminish the risk of the business as arising from trade disputes and other circumstances in the control of the men.

(2.) To render the profits more steady from year to year.

(3.) To increase the average profit in some degree.

(4.) To increase the earnings of the men in a similar degree.

XI.

But there is an incidental advantage which would flow from such a scheme of which we cannot overestimate the value. As the Messrs. Briggs say, when their dividends were distributed, numbers of men left the pay office "richer men than they had ever been before. Many had a five-pound note in their possession for the first time, and some few had two."

"It is also a very satisfactory feature of the case," they say, "that the amount so distributed has been almost universally *well* spent: by some in the purchase of shares in the company; by others in paying an instalment towards the purchase of a plot of freehold land, whereon to build a cottage; while the purchases of articles of furniture for domestic comforts were very numerous." I believe it would be impossible to meet with facts more promising for the future welfare of the country than these. Here is the first insensible action of the lever by which millions may be ultimately raised above the chance of pauperism.

The one great defect of character which seems often to neutralise all the excellences of the British artizan is want of thrift and providence. His financial calculations are too often restricted to the week, and he esteems himself solvent if the wages of one pay-day will last until the next. No matter how brisk trade be, no matter what remission of taxes be made, or how vast become our exports and our imports, there will be no real improvement in the prospects of our population till this habit be overcome. Workmen too commonly look upon their wages as a life annuity; to save, they often think is mean and selfish; capitalists may do that; there is something freehanded and generous in spending when there is a chance; and it is a singular fact that Trades Unions seldom (and, so far as my knowledge goes, never) encourage saving by the institution of savings banks. So far as such societies provide for the sick and disabled, replace the lost tools, and promise superannuation allowances, there is everything to be said in their favour. But even then they do it on a footing of enforced equality; the levies, subscriptions, and benefits are the same for all, and there is not the least opportunity for any man to make himself better off than the majority. Not the least encouragement is given to accumulation, and it must be added that even the best-conducted societies do not accumulate what will enable them to meet their ultimate liabilities. By a constant accession of young members, and possibly by recourse to extra levies, the large societies now existing can no doubt last for many years to come, but no one who examines their accounts, or considers the evidence given before the Commission, can avoid seeing that they must either break in the end or throw a most unjust charge upon a future generation. They trust too much to the constant incomings of each week. And this is the great error of all the working-classes. Hence arises the distress at every temporary oscillation of trade; the early marriages; the crowds who need employment; the young who cannot go to school because they must add their pence to their parents' shillings; the necessity of medical charities; and, most sad of all, the crowding of the old into the wards of the workhouse. It is no doubt true to say that out of 20s. a week it is not easy to save. I admit it, but say that it must be done if things are to be better than they have been. In improvidence and in ignorance, the majority of the population are involved in a vicious circle. They are ignorant because their fathers were ignorant, and so will their children be ignorant to the end of time, unless the State interferes with a strong hand. They cannot be provident because their fathers were not so for many generations back, and, were there not a prospect of some change, I should look upon improvidence and pauperism as the lasting curse of the English people.

But though the cause may seem a slight one, I should anticipate the best results from workmen receiving part of their earnings in yearly dividends. It would insensibly teach them to look beyond the week; it would give an opportunity for making a fair beginning; and from the evidence we have, such does appear to be the result. There is no doubt that the very poorest classes of labourers are really unable to save any appreciable sum of money, but I believe that this is by no means the case with artizans. Receiving often £75 or £100 a year, they are really much better able to save than many clerks, shopmen, and others who would nevertheless be more provident. We ought by this time to give up the notion that one who wears a black coat is better off than one whose coat is rough and soiled with work. The poorer section of the working-classes, I have allowed, must still for some time be dependent and incapable of placing themselves beyond the reach of distress. But I am confident that the richer section of the working-classes may soon despise all notions of assistance and dependence. By the Post Office Life Assurance system they can provide for their widows and children in case of accident or early death; by deferred annuities they can insure comfort for old age and remove every risk of the workhouse; sick societies will insure them from the pressure of prolonged illness; and he who can further accumulate a sum in the Post Office or other savings banks can meet a period of bad trade, or can emigrate at will. It is only by accumulation and providence in some of these modes that he who depends upon his labour can be raised above the chances and almost inevitable vicissitudes of life. Weekly wages cannot be depended on; and it is only in becoming small capitalists that the working-classes will acquire the real independence from misfortune, which is their true and legitimate object.

XII.

Before concluding I may say that it is an unpleasant circumstance concerning discussions upon capital and labour, that the sympathies and antipathies of large numbers of men are involved in the question, and that it is hardly possible to discuss the subject without prejudice, or at least the imputation of prejudice. I am much inclined to fear that some who are the professed teachers of the science, and should view it as a matter of science in the most unbiassed manner, allow their sympathies to lead their judgment. It speaks much indeed for the character of English statesmen that the three greatest popular leaders of our time—Cobden, Bright, and Gladstone—have been the foremost to uphold the doctrines of free trade and free labour, whether they were popular or unpopular. The emphatic condemnation which Mr. Gladstone pronounced at Oldham, upon some of the more common objects and rules of Trades Unions stamped him, it seemed to me, as one of the most upright and fearless of ministers. It is the statesmen of England, rather than the political economists, who have upheld the inestimable principle of freedom in labour.

For my own part I do think that the principle of unionism, so far as relates to the regulation of wages, is fundamentally and entirely wrong, but I see no reason why I should therefore be supposed to have less sympathy with working-men. I believe that they are striving earnestly and honourably to raise their own condition, but that they take the wrong way to do it. From wrong they must ultimately come to right, and I have no doubt that they will achieve more than they look for. But this right road will not be in struggling vainly against capital, but in making capital their ally. If the masters do not take the initiative and adopt the partnership principle, the present evil state of affairs must be much prolonged; but I do not doubt that the hard, sharp line which now exists between capital and labour will ultimately vanish. Partnerships of industry are, no doubt, an innovation, having hitherto existed only in exceptional trades and rare experiments; but I assert confidently that *they are an innovation of which the utility is evident and the necessity urgent.* They are required, not by the restless desire of change, but as the natural sequel of great revolutions in our social condition. Our great factories and our great army of artizans have sprung up within one hundred years, and it is quite to be expected that so vast an innovation should lead to other innovations. The lives of ourselves and our fathers and our grandfathers have been passed in the midst of peaceful revolutions, such as society has not known before; and it is most legitimate and proper that the artizan should seek to work yet another revolution—in his own moral and material condition. Already the artizan is less below his wealthy employer than he is above the poor dependent labourer of former days; and I do believe that we only need to throw aside some old but groundless prejudices, in order to heal the discords of capital and labour, and to efface in some degree the line which now divides employer and employed.

DISCUSSION.

Thomas Hughes, Esq., Q.C., M.P., in the Chair.

The Chairman said he felt with the lecturer, that the time was come when the question no longer depended upon theory, but upon experience. This experience had been detailed to them. He had himself been connected with the experiments that had been tried, and had been an original shareholder in Briggs's Colliery. He had gone down to their first meeting. In the late summer of 1865 the company had been formed, and in the early autumn of 1866 the first annual meeting had been held, at which he was present, and saw the results of the first year's working. It was extremely interesting to see the effect produced by the working of the principle in so short a time. The state of things previously had been extremely serious; there had been constant disputes and social war between masters and men for many months, and the collieries had been kept at work under the supervision of the police. He could not say that all doubt had at once disappeared; there was some feeling of doubt among the men whether the scheme was not one for putting more money into the pockets of the employers. Every man who chose to take out a penny book, and to have his wages entered in it, was entitled to a share in the annual division; and though the number of men was about 1000, only about 100 of them had sufficient confidence in the scheme to take out these books. He believed the great effect was produced by the first annual meeting, when the 100 men all came out each with a considerable bonus: this was what had made the new plan popular with the men. Since then matters had gone on from better to best, and now every man and boy on the works took good care to take out his book and to have his wages regularly entered. The coal trade during the past two years had been, in general, very dull and bad; almost as depressed as the iron trade; nevertheless, in spite of that depression, the prosperity of these collieries had continued, and there had only been a difference between the two years of one-half per cent. in the terms. The lecturer had also anticipated some of the advantages of the industrial partnership system. He had referred to the prophecies of Mr. Babbage, one of which was, that the best workmen would be glad to work on a principle of the kind. This had been justified within the last few weeks. He had gone down a few weeks since to the Cleveland iron district as arbitrator between the masters and the men, on a question of the advance of wages. There he had found that the Messrs. Briggs had determined on starting a new experiment in the iron trade in that district. The senior partner had had great jute works in Dundee, and, being an enthusiast in the matter of industrial partnerships, had been very anxious to convert the works at Dundee into one, but had not been able to persuade his partners to do so, probably because Scotchmen were very hard to convince. He had therefore determined to give up his partnership and to come to the Cleveland district to start these ironworks. The chief secretary of the Trades Unions there had told him (Mr. Hughes) that since it was known that the experiment was to be tried, all the best workmen had said that they would come and work for him, while many (and some of these had saved as much as £200) had expressed a wish to invest capital in the undertaking. He had been offered a complete staff of workmen all teetotalers. Thus it was clear that the northern workmen appreciated this movement. He could also confirm the remarks of the lecturer on another point. When he was down there, some fourteen or fifteen men sat at one side opposite to fourteen or fifteen masters at the other, and the only factory in the district not represented was that of the Messrs. Fox, Head & Co., and from them they had a communication, stating that they had just divided a bonus for the past year and were perfectly contented. He might also mention as an instance of faith that was felt in the system of the Messrs. Briggs, that Mr. Briggs had had offers from many of the co-operative societies of capital for his new undertaking. The Halifax Society had applied for shares to the amount of £10,000. The lecturer had alluded to the Report of the Trades Union Commissioners. He (Mr. Hughes) was not responsible for that report, inasmuch as he, with another member, had been obliged to dissent from it, and had presented another Report to Her Majesty. He agreed with the lecturer in thinking that the principle of this scheme had not been understood or appreciated by the Commission, and thought the Report must have done harm in many places. He did not think the system had been appreciated either by masters or men, and he hoped this lecture would be extensively circulated, and would lead to a better understanding of the subject. He thought he need not say much on the subject of Trades Unions, as he saw that they were exceedingly well represented in the room, but he must say a few words in reference to one point, namely, as to the exclusive system of industrial partnerships. The Messrs. Briggs had, it was true, absolute power, but they were now by no means fearful of the admission to some share of power of the people who were working with them, and they had established a committee of men, who met to advise them, and who had suggested many valuable improvements. They had also given the workingmen the power of sending one director to the board, so that one of the five directors was now a working shareholder in the mine. He quite agreed with the lecturer that this system offered the best solution which had yet been arrived at of the great labour question. He quite felt that the system of arbitration was only a sort of stopgap, and could only bring about a truce, but never a satisfactory peace. To have arbitration it was necessary to have two hostile organisations. While the men were kept in ignorance of the details of the business, and could only form a guess at the amount of the master's profits, a permanent peace could not be hoped for, such as he thought would come about by the development of the industrial partnership system. Those that had tried it deserved well of their country. They had done more for the prosperity of England, and for its establishment on a firm basis, than many who had made more noise.

Mr. Hughes having to leave, Mr. Frederic Hill was called to the chair.

Mr. Pare said that he doubted whether the division of the

profits had been made in the most equitable manner. If the capitalist had, in the first instance, secured his 10 per cent. the workman ought to divide, not half, but the whole of the profits above that amount. It was not the workman's business to regulate production. Exchanges and monetary arrangements were at present in a perfect state of chaos, and we had panics regularly every ten years for want of a scientific system of the exchange of productions. The workmen could not be expected to bear any losses which accrued from production or exchange.

Mr. Dudley Baxter said the colliery trade was one very favourable for the trial of this experiment, because labour was so large an element in the work; and it was a great thing for men to be able to work in that way. But suppose they took the silk or cloth manufacture, or any that depended upon competition with others abroad, or upon other circumstances, and came to the time when for months together sales could not be made; how were they to do? Or suppose a coal-pit took fire, and the business was thus stopped, were the profits on capital to go on? Most likely this would put an end to the partnership, and the men would go elsewhere. The principle was applicable to some portions of industry, but could not be applied to all labour. One principle would be applicable to one branch, and another must be worked in another place, where the conditions of labour were different.

Mr. Lamport thought the great difficulty of applying the principle to a great variety of trades was, that it had never been tried. He had been largely engaged in the cotton trade, as well as in ship-building, and he ventured to say that at the present moment it would be impossible to apply this principle to these trades. It might, however, ultimately be so applied. In the cotton manufacture it would not be very difficult, perhaps, to calculate every week the amount of profit or loss by taking the market prices of raw cotton, and often yarn or cloth manufactured; but there was not one manufacturer in a hundred who chose to rest his chance of profit upon the difference between raw and manufactured material. They always speculated, and how was this point to be regulated? He apprehended there must be a division between the profits of the merchant and those of the manufacturer. There must, in fact, be a difference of profit in every business. In the cotton business you could not take a fair average on a term of less than ten years.

Mr. Applegarth believed that many of the good things detailed by the lecturer were not entirely attributable to the principle of industrial partnerships. All that could be said in its favour, could also be said of the Nottingham stocking weavers, both as regarded the establishment of peace and the material advantage of increased wages. The lecturer had spoken of the attempts of the unions to enforce a uniform rate of wages throughout the trade, but they never had attempted to do so. They fixed a minimum rate, and merely said a skilled workman should receive this, but they did not in any way prevent his obtaining more. The lecturer had prophesied the bankruptcy of the unions, but he (Mr. Applegarth) said they would not break. He admitted the ten years' existence of the Amalgamated Carpenters was not enough to justify this assertion; perhaps the twenty years of the Amalgamated Engineers was scarcely sufficient, but there was the society of the Ironfounders, which had existed for fifty-seven years upon the same principles, and he thought this experience was worth more than all the calculations of actuaries. He would ask the lecturer to point out where working-men were earning £100 a year. In the carpenters' trade, which was one of the most skilled in the country, the wages were 28s. per week, and he thought that not one man in five had fifty-two weeks' work in the year. This brought the amount under £72 a year. He admitted that their own vices and failings were accountable for many of the grievances from which they suffered. It had been said that a great difficulty arose from their want of knowledge; but where did the practical knowledge come from for conducting the industries of the country? All the skill in the building trade had come from the bench side, and the masters in this business had been working-men. Some years ago he had been much in favour of industrial partnerships, because he thought everything would be of value that would give the workman an insight into the difficulties of employers; but he was strongly of opinion that the plan would cut two ways, and he feared that it would content the working-men with their position, and in this way be mischievous. He believed it would apply to many branches but not to others; but he had a faith, moreover, that the time would come when large capitalists would conduct business in the country with a more true and proper regard to the interests of their workmen than had been the case.

Dr. Hodgson said they had had an honest as well as an intelligent man speaking to them, and telling them what he had seen, for the good of all classes in society. He agreed with the lecturer with respect to arbitration; it showed that there was something unsatisfactory in the state of things. Suppose that they were told that arbitration was an excellent mode of reconciling differences between husband and wife, would they consider that an evidence of the satisfactory nature of the marriage relations? There ought to be no more occasion for arbitration between employer and workman than between husband and wife. He had no idea that this principle of partnerships would supersede the principles of free trade and competition. As to the amount of the sum fixed as the first charge on the business, that was not a matter of equity or inequity; it was simply a matter of pure arrangement between the employers and the employed. There was no principle in the matter, just as there was no principle concerned in a working-man's having 30s. a day, or 30s. a week; it was a pure matter of arrangement dependent on the labour market.

Professor Jevons did not think there was much difference between himself and Mr. Applegarth as to the rate of wages; some workmen, such as the iron-puddlers, made much more than £100. As to the breaking of Trades Unions, he had said that they either do so, or place a burden upon posterity. If a colliery took fire, and the works came to an end, the loss could not be charged upon future profits. Certain allowances had to be made for risks of an extraordinary character, and this was one of them. In the company which Briggs was now organising he proposed to make 15 per cent. the minimum profit, a rate with which the men were perfectly satisfied, so that he in fact promised a return of 15 per cent. on the capital. No doubt this question was a more difficult one, and it would be only in the course of time that it would be worked out so that it might be extended to various trades. In the cotton trade there were great profits and great losses, and it was not fair to throw either entirely upon the workman. However, he saw no difficulty in spreading these over a series of years.

Mr. Frederic Hill, in asking the meeting to record a vote of thanks to the lecturer, took occasion to say that a friend of his some time since, who resided at Singapore, wanted a house built, and applied as advised to a Chinese, who made an agreement to do the work for a certain sum. He found out shortly that all the men employed had a share in the profits of the undertaking, and every man took care not only to do as much work as possible, but to see that his next neighbour did his work well also. On inquiry he found that this system is universal in China, and that every shopman there has a share in his master's profits, so that the Chinese had been before us in this matter of industrial partnerships, as well as in so many other matters.

MARRIED WOMEN IN FACTORIES.*

WHILE engaged in preparing a small treatise, "The State in its Relation to Labour," my attention has been strongly called anew to the importance of the question of the employment of married women in factories and workshops. The bearing of the question is, of course, instantly seen when it is considered that every mother so employed abandons her infants and young children for ten hours in the day to the care of other, usually careless hands. The subject has long been one of chronic controversy in the manufacturing districts, especially in Manchester, where it is every now and then debated in the newspapers and public societies. In the "Transactions of the Manchester Statistical Society," especially, will be found a series of papers on the several phases of the matter, by the late Dr. George Greaves, Mrs. M. A. Baines, Dr. Noble, Dr. Syson, Mr. T. R. Wilkinson, and others.

The Manchester Sanitary Association is ever registering and considering the infant mortality of the district. Almost every volume of the "Transactions of the Social Science Association" contains papers more or less directly bearing on the subject. The Reports of the Factory Inspectors, especially those of Mr. Baker, have recorded from time to time the most valuable facts, as well as the inferences and reflections of the Inspectors; and there are various other official publications to be presently mentioned, in which the question has been almost

* "Contemporary Review," January, 1882.

exhaustively treated. Yet nothing has been done, although it is impossible to stir the mass of records without discovering that the evils recorded are appalling in their nature. Can such things be in a Christian country? is the exclamation which rises to the lips in contemplating the mass of misery, and, especially, the infinite, irreparable wrong to helpless children, which is involved in the mother's employment at the mills.

It is a strange topic for reflection how the public, morbidly fixing their attention on some wretched murderer, or a score of dogs or rabbits sacrificed for the enduring interests of humanity, can calmly ignore the existence of evils which are so extensive that the imagination fails to grasp them clearly. It is a curious, and yet unquestionable fact, that a comparatively small and unimportant work is often undertaken with ardour, whereas a vastly greater and more urgent work of the same kind produces only languor. Thus Mr. George Smith succeeded in arousing intense sympathy for the small number of children brought up (often not brought up) in canal boats. The peculiar circumstances of the canal boats, and the definite manageable extent of the ideas involved, conduced to the success of the very proper movement which Mr. Smith carried out to the point of legislation. But infant mortality in general is, I fear, far too wide and vague an idea to rivet the attention of the public.* It is a question involving the whole of the lower-class population of the manufacturing districts. The actual excess of deaths is to be counted in tens of thousands. Briefly stated, the question concerns the mode of death of certainly 30,000 infants, and perhaps as many as 40,000 or even 50,000 which perish annually in this country through preventible causes. In no small number of cases the deaths are actually intentional infanticides, committed in a manner which defies the scrutiny of a coroner and jury. Thus the Registrar-General, in his Thirty-seventh Annual Report (p. xxiii.), refers ominously to the large number of infants suffocated in one town, and

* I prefer to adopt this explanation of the public apathy about this subject; but a correspondent maintains that "it is simply one of the phases of middle-class selfishness."

demands special inquiry, which, of course, has never been made.* In by far the largest number of cases, however, we may be glad to conclude that it is not real murder which we deal with, but a mixture of thoughtlessness and carelessness, varying in criminality from manslaughter up to mere misadventure and ignorance of an entirely innocent character. But in any case the facts are of the most serious nature, and must form suitable matter for reflection in the approaching Christmas season, round warm firesides and well-covered tables.

To form some preliminary idea of the amount of infant mortality with which we have to deal, we may turn to any of the recent annual reports of the Registrar-General, and we find a table giving the deaths of children under five years of age in the principal great towns. Thus, in the Forty-first Report, p. xxxvi., we find that the estimated numbers of children under five years of age in nineteen large towns add up to a little more than a million (1,023,896), while the number of deaths of such children was 85,250. The rate of mortality, however, varies extremely, being as comparatively low as 59·4 in 1000 in Portsmouth, rising to 65·8 in Brighton, 66·2 in Bristol, 73·2 in Newcastle, 74·8 in Wolverhampton, 78·6 in London, 82·9 in Leicester and Nottingham, and so on, until we reach gradually the higher amounts of 93·8 in Salford, 95·2 in Birmingham, 95·9 in Sheffield. The place of dishonour is occupied by Liverpool, with an infant mortality rising to a climax of 103·6 per 1000. In that great seaport the infants (under five years of age) are decimated annually! Now, if we assume that, with proper sanitary regulations, the infant mortality in towns ought not to exceed that of Norwich, which is on the average about 70 per 1000, we readily calculate that the excess of infant deaths in the other great towns in question amounts to 13,500 annually. But the question clearly depends upon the average of sanitation which we conceive possible. Portsmouth, which we should not at first expect to find

---

* On this subject see the paper on "The Destruction of Infants," by Mr. F. W. Lowndes, M.R.C.S.: Social Science Association, 1876, Report, p. 586.

very favourable to infant life, maintains an average as low as about 60 per 1000. The Registrar-General remarks that this low rate is probably owing in some measure to the presence of a large number of military and naval men, and dockyard artificers, representing several thousands of selected healthy lives. The dockyard affords employment to a large number of artisans, and there is not that inducement in Portsmouth for mothers to neglect their offspring which there is in the factory towns. I entertain, however, some doubt whether there is any reason for regarding Portsmouth as really exceptional; and if we take its rate as a standard, we find that the excess of the other great towns amounts to about 24,000, which, of course, does not include the excessive mortality of a multitude of smaller towns. Let it be observed that we have nothing to do here with the contrast between town and country. In a highly rural county, such as Dorsetshire or Wiltshire, the infant mortality does not usually exceed about 40 per 1000, and even sinks as low as 35.

I do not intend, in the present article, to enlarge upon the remarkable differences in regard to mortality which the great towns exhibit. Liverpool is especially anomalous, because, though standing at the head of the list, it has no great textile factories which would take women away from home. Renewed and very careful inquiry has, indeed, quite satisfied me as to the correctness of the explanation which I gave in 1870* of the excessive mortality of such towns as Liverpool and Salford. Until statists will constantly bear in mind the fact that the different towns and counties of England are to a great extent peopled by races of different characters, it will remain impossible to understand the profound sanitary discrepancies which they exhibit. It is not, however, to my purpose to dwell upon the influence of a mixture of population; it is only necessary

---

* "Journal of the Statistical Society," September, 1870, vol. xxxiii. pp. 323–326. Also reprinted in this volume as Appendix B to Opening Address as President of the Section of Economic Science and Statistics, British Association, 1870. See, however, the opposite opinion of Mr. T. R. Wilkinson, as expressed in his paper, "Observations on Infant Mortality and the Death-rate in Large Towns." Manchester Statistical Society, 1870–71, pp. 49–55.

to refer to the point as explaining anomalies which would otherwise seem to tend against the inferences to be drawn concerning other matters. In this article I prefer to direct the reader's attention to one of the existing social evils, which is unquestionably the cause of much of the infant mortality alluded to: I mean the employment of child-bearing women away from home. This is, beyond doubt, the most important question touching the relation of the State to labour which remains unsolved.

It has long, indeed, been one of the most frequent and urgent proposals of trade unionists that married women should be "taken out of the mills." The so-called labour advocates are often a great deal nearer the truth than the general public believe. But then, unfortunately, they give reasons for their opinions, and these reasons will not always bear examination. Thus, in favour of the summary exclusion of married women, it is argued that the market is overstocked, and that if married women were taken out, the operation would realise a great social and domestic benefit, whilst "much of the overplus labour would be reduced." This, however, is obviously bad political economy. We cannot possibly increase the welfare of the people by lessening labour, the source of wealth. No workers, too, are more to be admired than some married women, who, by indomitable industry and good management, maintain a family of children and a husband too. Where the husband is disabled by accident, illness, imprisonment, or otherwise, or has deserted his family, the wife cannot but be praised if she attempts to take his place and save the children from the Union. There will exist, again, many cases of married women without children, or whose children are past infancy, where the prohibition of employment would rest on no special grounds, and would be little short of tyrannous.

There is a reverse side of the question, which it is impossible to overlook. As pointed out by one of the factory inspectors,* no small number of women managing households and bringing up young children are, unfortunately, unmarried.

---

* Mr. Baker, Report, October, 1873, pp. 122-8.

Now, a law excluding married women from factories would obviously have the most disastrous effects upon these unhappy women, by banishing, in most cases, all hope of marriage. In too many cases it is the woman's power of earning wages which constitutes her hold upon the paramour. Beyond doubt, then, the exclusion of the class "married women," simply by that definition, cannot for a moment be contemplated. It is the class "child-bearing women," that legislation must deal with, if at all. Opinions will differ greatly, however, as to the extent, means, and purpose of the legislation required. The slightest form of interference would consist in excluding women from factories for a certain number of weeks before and after confinement. Mr. Mundella explained to the Factory Acts Commission of 1875 that in Glarus, and some other Swiss Cantons, a woman was obliged to remain at home for six weeks in all, fixing the time at her own discretion. There can be so little doubt as to the hygienic advantages of such a law, that the only question seems to be the possibility of enforcing the law. What is practicable in a small mountain district like Glarus, where everybody knows everybody else, might totally fail in an ocean of population like that of Lancashire or London. It will be generally agreed that the employer can hardly be made responsible for delicate inquiries into the condition of his female mill-hands. The Factory Act Commissioners bring forward, moreover, other serious difficulties; for instance, the danger of adding a new and very powerful motive for concealment of birth.

It appears pretty plain that if there is to be legislation concerning child-bearing women something more thorough is required. The women may be quite fit for work in one month; but what about the infant? The latter is pretty sure to be relegated to that scourge of infant life, the dirty fungus-bearing bottle. I do not think that it will be possible for the Legislature much longer to leave untouched the sad abuses which undoubtedly occur in the treatment of infants, especially in the manufacturing districts. The existence of such abuses is sufficiently indicated by the high rate of infant mortality already alluded to. More than ten years ago (May to July,

1870), a long controversy took place in *The Manches*. *Guardian* as to the existence and causes of this excessi mortality. It was evoked by a paper read by Mr. Baxend to the Literary and Philosophical Society of Manchest throwing doubt upon the facts; but it appeared to be co clusively shown by Dr. Arthur Ransome that there was enormous death-rate of very young children in Manchest and certain other towns. About the same time Sir W. Charley, Mr. Ernest Hart, Mr. George Hastings, and oth gentlemen formed an Infant Life Protection Society; and t subject was also brought before the House of Commons] the first-named gentleman. The Report of the Select Coɪ mittee on the Protection of Infant Life* contains startliɪ revelations, which have never received the attention th imperatively demand. The following passage from the Repo of the Committee (p. 4) contains a concise statement of wh they considered to be proved concerning infant mortality:

"The ordinary mortality among infant children under one year age is estimated at 15 or 16 per cent.; but the mere fact of their beiɪ hand-nursed, instead of being breast-nursed, will, unless great care taken, raise the death-rate, even in well-conducted 'homes,' to 40 p cent. and upwards. In the inferior class of houses, where the childɪ put out to nurse are, for the most part, illegitimate, the death-rate m: be 40 to 60 per cent. in the rural districts, and in the large towns, whe the sanitary conditions are more unfavourable, it mounts up to 70, ε or even 90 per cent. All the witnesses concur in this; and there a three or four circumstances which strongly confirm their gener opinion."

It is frequently implied or stated throughout the "Repoɪ Evidence, and Appendices," that the present treatment infants often amounts practically to infanticide. According the late Dr. Lankester, then coroner for Middlesex, illegitima children are "killed off" before they are one year old; aɪ the Committee calmly assume that not more than one in tc of such children ever lives to grow up. In a petition presentc to the Home Secretary by the British Medical Associatic

---

* Parliamentary Paper, No. 372, 20th July, 1871. Collected Seriɛ vol. vii. p. 607.

(Report, p. 237), it is asserted that no action of the police can discover the great amount of secret infanticide which is daily perpetrated in this metropolis and elsewhere. The same body asserts that "in manufacturing towns, where children are placed out by the day, a very large infant mortality exists, chiefly owing to the administration of insufficient or improper food and opiates, by the women in whose charge the children are placed."

And again, we have this important statement: "Those children who live, and reach adult life under such adverse circumstances, are physically and morally weak, and in most instances lapse into pauperism and crime."

After reading some of the facts contained in this grim Report, it is impossible not to concur in this remark of the Infant Life Protection Society, though it occurs to one to ask, what has become of the Society? "It is astounding to all those who know the facts connected with baby-farming that . . . the State has left this great mass of helpless infant life to suffer and die in the hands of persons too many of whom make of death a trade."

The question, however, referred to the Committee was merely that of the best means of preventing the destruction of the lives of *infants put out to nurse for hire by their parents*. By "put out to nurse," was taken to mean put out *for more than twenty-four hours at a time*. Thus the treatment of children generally was not expressly considered, and the recommendations of the Committee resulted in nothing more than a Bill for the registration of persons who take for hire two or more infants under one year of age to nurse *for a longer period than a day*. In the next session the Bill became law, under the title of "The Infant Life Protection Act, 1872" (35 & 36 Vict. c. 38). In addition to registration, the law requires every registered baby-farmer to send notice to the coroner of all deaths in the registered houses, so that inquests may be held in the absence of medical certificates satisfactory to the coroner.

We will presently consider the working of this Act.

Although the Report of this Committee contains the largest

collected body of facts, a good deal of information, very mu
indeed to the point, may be found in the Reports of t
Medical Officer to the Privy Council. It is needless for me
say how replete all these Reports are with sanitary research
of the highest importance; but the document most to (
purpose is a report, kindly pointed out to me by Dr. Mou
made by the late Dr. Henry J. Hunter on the excess
mortality of infants in some rural districts of Englan(
As, indeed, this report treats of agricultural districts,
might seem to have little bearing on our subject. I
the parts of the country examined by Dr. Hunter afford
an experiment of a most significant and conclusive cl
racter. A serious increase of infant mortality had be
observed in certain marshy agricultural districts, and the o
apparent antecedent was the bringing of the land un(
cultivation. As this change, however, might be expected
banish the malaria of the fens, it seemed, at first sight, 1
accountable that the infants died off the more rapidly as 1
climate became more healthy. A little inquiry, howev
showed that an influence far more fatal than malaria had co
into operation. The mothers had gained employment in :
field-gangs, and had left their infants to the care of the
women. That this was really the cause was established
the concurrent evidence of all witnesses examined by
reporter. The peculiar importance of this result is, that
here have the influence of married women's employment fr(
from the circumstances of town life.

The excessive mortality of Salford or Nottingham, we s
is not due alone to the bad sanitary condition of the cou
and streets, for like infant mortality makes its appearance
the most rural parts. We have, in fact, *a true and comp
induction, pointing to the employment of women away f(
their homes as the efficient cause of their children's decadence*

Dr. Hunter's Report is crammed with other informati
more instructive than pleasant. It is unfortunate that s

* Sixth Report of the Medical Officer of the Privy Council, 1
pp. 454–62 (Parl. Paper, 1864, No. [3,416], vol. xxviii).

valuable inquiries should be buried in scarce Blue Books, which are hardly accessible, except in the British Museum or a few other public libraries. After describing in a few touching sentences the history of many a young woman who finds herself a mother while she is yet really a child herself, he proceeds (p. 458):

"A worse degree of criminality is found in older mothers. After losing a child or two, they begin to view the subject as one for ingenuity and speculation. It is related that on the birth of a second or third bastard the neighbours will say: 'So-and-so has another baby; you'll see it won't live.' And this becomes a sort of joke, in which the mother will join; public opinion expressing no condemnation of her cruelty. A medical man is called to the wasting infant, because there is so much bother with registering. The mother says the child is dying, and won't touch food. When he offers food the child is ravenous, and fit to tear the spoon to pieces. On some of the few occasions on which the surgeon, in his disgust, has insisted on opening the body, the stomach and bowels have been found quite empty."

Dr. Hunter enters pretty fully into the natural history of "Godfrey," the compound of opium, treacle, and infusion of sassafras, to which many thousands, perhaps hundreds of thousands of infants have succumbed. This is so commonly demanded in many districts that it becomes the "leading article" at the shops. The shopkeepers, in the zeal of competition, sell "Godfrey" at cost price, as the best means of inveigling improvident mothers. One inconvenience of this excessive competition is, that different specimens of "Godfrey" vary much in strength, and a nurse who incautiously administers a new brand of the cordial is sometimes alarmed at the result. Thus, says Dr. Hunter (p. 459): "It has not unfrequently happened that a nurse has substituted her own 'Godfrey' for her client's" [query? her client's "Godfrey" for her own] "and, frightened at its effects, has summoned the surgeon, who finds half-a-dozen babies—some snoring, some squinting, all pallid and eye-sunken—lying about the room, all poisoned."

There are peculiar technical means, it seems, which surgeons use in such emergencies to bring the babies round, but I need not describe them. Suffice it for our purpose that Hunter asserts it to be the general opinion of medical practitioners

that "ablactation and narcotism" would be the true descrip
tion of the cause of more than half the infantile death
recorded, whatever may be the "advanced symptoms" returne
to the registrar.

Hardly less instructive is the previous Report of D
Greenhow on the infant mortality of certain manufacturin
districts.* It was elicited from a man working in a factory a
Birmingham, where many married women were employed, tha
ten out of every twelve children born to them died within
few months after birth. The man had been accustomed t
collect the money for the funeral expenses, and he ought t
know. In the course of Dr. Greenhow's further inquiries
was frequently found that two-thirds or three-fourths of th
children born to the women had died in infancy; and, "on th
other hand, it was remarkable how, in other instances, th
majority of the children were reared when the mothers di
not work in factories, or discontinued doing so whilst nursing
(p. 196).

The following passage (p. 192) is also very much to th
point, explaining how the system works:

"Women, being obliged to attend at the factory at an early hour, ar
always hurried in the morning, and may be seen on their way to tl
mills, hastening along the streets with their children only half-dresse
carrying the remainder of their clothes and their food for the day, to l
left with the person who has charge of the child during the mothei
absence; and this ofttimes on a cold winter's morning, in the midst (
sleet or snow. . . . Parents who thus intrust the management of the
infants so largely to strangers become more or less careless and indi
ferent about them; and, as many of the children die, the mothei
become familiarised with the fact, and speak of the deaths of the
children with a degree of nonchalance rarely met with amongst wome
who devote themselves mainly to the care of their offspring."

The complete concurrence of opinion as to the influence (
the mother's absence on the health of the infant is thu
explicitly summed up (p. 192):

"All the medical men who gave evidence on the subject of the prese1
inquiry, besides several clergymen, ladies who are accustomed to vis

---

* Fourth Report of the Medical Officer of the Privy Council, 186
pp. 187–196. Parl. Papers, 1862, No. 179, vol. xxii.

the poorer classes at their dwellings, Scripture-readers, relieving officers and other persons who have paid attention to the subject, unhesitatingly expressed an opinion that the system under which the mothers of young children are employed at factories and workshops, away from home, is a fruitful cause of infantile sickness and mortality."

Such, then, is the progress of civilisation produced by the advancing powers of science and machinery; two-thirds to three-fourths, or even as much as five-sixths, of the infants dying of neglect. On this point all the Official Reports concur so unanimously that they may well be described as "damnable iteration." *

It seems necessary, indeed, to mention that, according to the last issued Annual Report of the Registrar General for England (Forty-second Report, containing the abstracts for 1879), there has been a decrease of infant mortality in recent years, especially during the years 1876–79 when the rate per 1000 males, which had been 73 or 74, fell to an average of 67·0. This low rate, however, may be partly due to the unusual healthiness of the year 1879, when the rate was no more than 64. It is worthy of notice, too, that mortality was nearly as low in the years 1841–45, namely, 68·8, and then it rose rapidly to 77·4. There is some ground for suspecting that want of active employment in the mills may actually lead to saving of life in the aggregate. In any case, while the mortality of infants under one year of age continues to be as much as 50 or 60 per cent. higher in some towns than in others, we cannot possibly deny that there exists an immense amount of preventible evil.

Let us consider now the results which have flowed from the legislation promoted by the Committee on the Protection of Infant Life. With the kind assistance of Mr. Edward Herford†, who has so long and so ably filled the office of Her

---

* Mr. Newmarch said at the British Association in 1861 (Report, p. 202): "The rate of infant mortality was almost the best test of civilisation."

† Important evidence on the subject of Infant Mortality was given by Mr. Herford before the Committee. See the Questions, 1907 to 2155. See also the Report, p. iii.

Majesty's Coroner for Manchester, I have been able to acquire sufficient information.*

Mr. Herford himself believes that the Act is a dead letter. This opinion is entirely borne out by the statement of Mr. Malcolm Wood, the Chief Constable of Manchester, to the effect that there are actually no houses at all in that city registered under the Act. Mr. Michael Browne, the Coroner of Nottingham, has never heard of any application for a license under the Act in Nottingham or its neighbourhood. The Coroner of Birmingham believes that the same is the case in that great and model town, and he is of opinion that infantile mortality is enormously increased by bad nursing, feeding, and want of care on the part of the mother. The Chief Constable of one very large town, being asked for information touching Charley's Act, rather naïvely replied that he could not recollect having ever received any application for information about it before. On the other hand, from the Medical Officer of Health of Liverpool, I learn that there actually have been ten applications for registration, but only one of these was found to come under the clauses of the Act; and at present there are no houses at all on the register. At Bolton, also, the Act is a dead letter, though the Coroner, Mr. Rowland Taylor, says that he has never had a case before him of malpractices by nurses.

Some statements which Mr. Browne, of Nottingham, has added to his letter, are, however, so startling that I must quote them *in extenso.*† He says:

"You know we stand notoriously high as to infant mortality, and I attribute that in a great measure to the young women being employed

---

* It must be understood that no systematic or extensive inquiry has been made. I have no information for London or any other towns not mentioned above; but the answers obtained sufficiently inform us as to the state of the case.

† That Mr. Browne's opinions are far from being hastily formed is apparent from the fact that like opinions are expressed in his letter and tabular statement of the results of inquests on children found dead, as printed in the Fourth Report of the Privy Council, p. 192 : Parl. Paper, p. 176, 1862, vol. xxii.

in warehouses, factories, etc., and knowing little or nothing of the duties of wives and mothers, so that infants suffer sadly from neglect of every kind, and great numbers die from improper feeding. It is a very common practice for young mothers (married as well as single) to place their infants in the care of other women for the day, and I am constantly *lecturing* them on gross improprieties I find prevailing in such cases . . . Some years ago I held an inquest on a very young child, whose parents were earning from 50s. to 60s. a week, but who put out their infant to nurse, because, as the mother told me, she could not attend to it herself, having to be at work at the warehouse. The nurse very coolly admitted that she had (had) the care of eighteen children (five of them her own) and only one was living!"

I have not the least doubt that facts of this kind might be multiplied to almost any extent by adequate inquiry. In fact, inquiry is hardly needed; the state of the case is patent and admitted in the districts in question. The evidence taken before the Infant Life Protection Committee in all probability applies as strongly now, or nearly so, as it did ten years ago. In any case, it is a fact that the infants are "killed off" almost as fast now as they were ten or twelve years ago. As the last bit of iteration, I will give the following extract, culled from a Manchester newspaper,* purporting to come from a recent Report of Mr. Leigh, the Medical Officer of Health for Manchester. After informing us that in 1878-9 the deaths of children under five years of age in Manchester formed about 44 per cent. of the whole, while in other places the rate does not exceed 33 per cent., he goes on to say :

"The chief cause of a heavy infant mortality is the neglect which young children meet with in the lower stratum of society. In some cases the mother is employed in out-door labour, and the child receives no proper sustenance. It is left to the care of a girl too young even to take care of herself, and is exposed, with very scanty clothing, to the inclemency of the weather; or it is left in the care of some old woman, who quietens its cries for warmth and nourishment with repeated doses of laudanum, in the form of ' Godfrey's Cordial,' or some similar farrago; and at an early age dies from convulsions in one case, and from bronchitis or other lung affection in the other."

---

* They appear to print so few copies of reports in Manchester, that I have been unable to procure a copy of the Report in question.

As a remedy for this sad state of affairs, Dr. Ransome, Mr. T. C. Horsfall, and various members of the Manchester and Salford Sanitary Association, advocate the establishment of day nurseries, where the mothers, while going to the mills, may deposit their young children under good supervision. If nothing else be done to mitigate the fate of infants, such nurseries are simply indispensable; but surely they form a mere palliative, and if they came into general use would tend to increase the evil they are intended to mitigate. While such institutions remained few in number, and were personally inspected by members of the Sanitary Association, all would no doubt be done which care and medical science could suggest. Even under the most painstaking inspection, much is to be feared from the assembling of many infants daily in the same room, owing to the extraordinary facility with which infectious diseases are spread among the very young. The evidence given before the Committee above referred to seems to be conclusive on this point, and the following are the remarks of the Committee in their Report (p. vi.):

"As regards children in charitable institutions, it is clearly ascertained that the aggregation of them in crowded rooms is so fatal to infant life that it has become necessary to remove them into various Homes. It was so with the Foundling Hospital nearly a century ago. The same has been observed in the Home in Great Coram Street; so that now they are put out by twos and threes in other places. A similar system exists in France; for while the children were aggregated in foundling hospitals, it was found that from 70 to 80 per cent. died; and now that they are placed out singly with nurses, and properly inspected, the mortality has been reduced from 20 to 30 per cent."

It would appear, then, that frequently the only chance of saving infant life is the reverse of that intended by the Sanitary Association—namely, to isolate the children. But if such nurseries are to be of much good they must be hundreds in number, and they would then inevitably become the scenes of fearful abuses. The law provides no inspection or regulation for them of any kind, and institutions established for the protection and care of infants are, curiously enough, expressly exempted from the provisions of the Protection of Infant Life

Act. Inspection by volunteer members of committees may of course maintain good management in a few nurseries; but we learn, from plenty of cases, how little such management is to be depended upon where the patients are incapable of complaining.

Although the Infant Life Protection Act is clearly a dead letter, there is no evidence to show exactly how it has failed. It may, of course, be possible that the care-takers of infants, knowing that it is a penal offence to take charge of more than one infant, or in the case of twins two infants, at the same time, have discontinued the practice. In that case the Act has succeeded better than any other law I can think of, in entirely suppressing the evil against which it was directed. But it is much more likely that the women in question do not so much as know of the existence of the law in question. Whether we look to the number of married women employed in factories, or the excessive infant mortality as already estimated, there can be no doubt that the Act in question has not in the least touched the real evils under which infants fade away. Let it be clearly understood, too, that the Act referred to does not really apply to the question before us, because its clauses do not extend to persons who take infants under their care *for a part of the twenty-four hours only.* An old woman might have a score or two of infants, and dose them at her discretion; but providing that they were carried to their homes at night, there would be no infringement of the law. Both the Act and the inquiries of the Committee were directed against the evils of "baby-farming;" but whether baby-farming be suppressed or not, there remains the vastly more extensive evils connected with baby-nursing while the mother has gone to the mills. The Act, in short, though founded on the best possible intentions, has served as a mere cover for the apathy of the governing classes.

But we are on the horns of a dilemma; the infants die as it is, and they will probably die if nurseries are established. We want some more radical remedy, and the best remedy would perhaps be found in some law which would practically oblige the mother to remain at home as long as she has children below the school age. It is very desirable that women who have no such domestic duties should have the freest possible access to employment; but where infants and very young children are in the case, the *salus populi* leads to a totally different view. There are no duties which are more important in every respect than those which a mother is bound by with regard to her young children. The very beasts of the field tend and guard their whelps with instinctive affection. It is only human mothers which shut their infants up alone, or systematically neglect to give them nourishment.

It must be evident, too, that the facility with which a young married woman can now set her children aside, and go to earn good wages in the mills, forms the strongest possible incentive to improvident and wrongful marriages. There are many statements in the Reports of the factory inspectors to the effect that dissolute men allure capable young women into marriage with the idea that the wives can earn wages, and enable their husbands to idle away their time. Taking into account the practical infanticide which follows, it would be impossible to imagine a more unsound, or, it may be said, a more atrocious, state of affairs.

It seems impossible, then, not to concede that the employment of child-bearing women leads to great abuses; and when these abuses reach a certain point, they may become all that is needed to warrant legislation. As to the exact form which such legislation should take, inquiry, if not experiment, must guide us. The law of Switzerland and some foreign countries, even if it could be carried out in our populous towns, seems to be inadequate. Probably it would be well to impose restrictions and penalties upon the negligent treatment of infants, without waiting until the case ripens for the coroner's court. It ought to be a punishable offence to shut very young children up in a house alone, or otherwise to abandon them for any considerable length of time, except, of course, under the pressure of emergency. But I go so far as to advocate the *ultimate complete exclusion of mothers of children under the age of three years from factories and workshops.*

The objection which will naturally be made to this proposal is, that there are no means of carrying the law into effect. It is granted that any law which, like the Infant Life Protection Act, becomes entirely ineffective, is a reproach to legislation, and by first quieting agitation, and then discouraging further efforts, does far more harm than good. Some effective machinery, or attempt to devise such machinery, must be provided in any law on the subject. As in the case of all the other factory legislation, trial and experience must show how that machinery can be improved and rendered adequate to its purpose. The history of such legislation, in fact, already affords important hints. The failure of the Workshops Acts of 1867 shows that nothing can be trusted to local or municipal action in these matters. The powers of the law must be exercised, as in the case of the present Factories and Workshops Act, from Whitehall. Again, it is generally conceded by all who have paid the least attention to this matter, that the employers cannot be burdened with the duty of inquiring into the nature of a woman's home duties. The penalties must fall therefore directly upon the persons most immediately implicated.

Fully conscious how impossible it is to foresee difficulties or even absurdities in making suggestions of the sort, I nevertheless venture to suggest that a moderate pecuniary penalty should be imposed upon every able-bodied husband, or reputed husband, whose wife, having the charge of any child under three years of age, shall be found to be employed regularly in any factory or workshop under the Act.

Moreover, any person who systematically takes charge of the infants of any man, thus liable to penalty, should be liable to a like penalty, without respect to the question whether it appears to be done for profit or not. Of course, no penalty would be inflicted where the caretaking was only occasional, as when a wife is going to bring or take back work to be done at home. Only where factory books prove that a woman was regularly employed under the Factory Act, would it be desirable to prosecute. The employers, however, might be obliged to furnish evidence of the woman's attendance at the factory. Moreover, lists of the women fined, or otherwise known to have broken the law, might be sent to the employers of each town or district, by the factory inspectors, the employer being then finable if he engages a woman whose name appears in the list. A woman giving a false name or address should be more severely punished.

The conduct of the requisite inspection and prosecution cannot possibly be left to the ordinary police. All experience seems to show that, in our modern complicated society, there must be differentiation of functions—that is to say, a special duty must be performed by a special officer. As, however, the present factory inspectors and sub-inspectors are heavily weighted as it is, they cannot possibly undertake the proposed new duties, nor would the appointment of a large number of assistant inspectors of any kind or rank be readily acquiesced in. The disconnection which now exists between the Central Government in Whitehall and the several police authorities, renders any direct prosecution difficult or impossible. But I venture to suggest that it would not be unreasonable to require by law that every borough or district having its own police should be required to assign one, two, or even three police officers, as might be required, to carry out the provisions of the proposed law, acting under the directions of the factory inspectors. Already the police perform a good many special services, as in the inspection of weights and measures, sanitary inspection, supervision of ticket-of-leave men, and so forth. Now, I fancy that an active police officer would soon discover infractions in the law; for the carrying of infants along the public street to a nursing-house is a thing evident to anybody, and the officer would only need to follow the woman to the factory, and he would have at once all the evidence needed. Probably there would be little difficulty in obtaining evidence; for the operative classes would receive the law with gratitude rather than aversion, partly perhaps misled by fallacies already referred to, and partly convinced by the evil results which are now before their eyes. If so, their concurrence and assistance in carrying out the law might be looked for. As regards the interests of employers it must be obvious that whatever they might suffer from the lessened supply of labour during the first ten years would be amply repaid by the abundant supply of vigorous young mill-hands which would then begin to be available.

Although the complete exclusion of child-bearing women from factory employments is the object to be aimed at, the violence of the change might be mitigated for a time. Licenses might be given to particular large factories to employ such women on the condition that they establish on or close to their premises *crèches* under constant medical supervision, where the mothers might visit their infants at intervals during the day. This plan has been adopted by some of the wealthy and benevolent manufacturing firms in France, and is said to have produced most beneficial results.* But no such *crèche* should be allowed to exist except under direct Government inspection, and, in any case its existence should be regarded as a transitional measure.

Widows and deserted wives would need to be gently dealt with: if, having a numerous family, they ought to have poor-law relief, to be added to the small earnings which they can make by home employment. In the long-run it would pay for the State to employ them as nurses of their own children. Where there are only one or two infants, the mother might be allowed to deposit them for the day at a *crèche*, established for and restricted solely to such cases, or at employers' *crèches*, just mentioned.

It is impossible not to see that there are difficulties in the matter which can be resolved only by trial. How, for instance, would such prohibitive legislation act in the case of reputed married couples? But it cannot, of course, be expected that the necessary details of legislation can be foreseen by any single writer. Before anything is done in so formidable a matter, there must be a minute inquiry into the treatment of

* Transactions of the Manchester Statistical Society, 1868-9, p. 10.

young children by a Royal Commission. It is strange that such a formal inquiry has never yet been made, except with regard to the very restricted scope of Charley's Act. Older children have over and over again been taken under the view and care of the State. As a consequence, we have the Elementary Education Act, and the Factory and Workshop Act, by which ample care is taken of young persons from the age of five years upwards. Those who survive infancy are now pretty safe; they will have healthy schoolrooms and healthy workshops. But below the age of five years they are still, with slight exception, abandoned to the tender mercy of their mothers—or, rather, the old women armed with "Godfrey." The Factory Act Commissioners of 1876 dismissed this subject briefly, and declined to advocate any restrictive measures because they might in their opinion tend to promote infanticide. But I venture to think that the fearful rate of infantile mortality now existing in parts of the manufacturing districts, sufficiently approximates to infanticide to overbalance any evils to be expected from restrictive legislation.

The objection may no doubt be made, that the exclusion of child-bearing women from works in public factories would be a new and extreme case of interference with the natural liberty of the individual. Philosophers will urge that we are invading abstract rights, and breaking through the teachings of theory. Political economists might, no doubt, be found to protest likewise that the principles of political economy are dead against such interference with the freedom of contract. But I venture to maintain that all these supposed natural entities, principles, rules, theories, axioms, and the like, are at the best but presumptions or probabilities of good. There is, on the whole, a certain considerable probability that individuals will find out for themselves the best paths in life, and will be eventually the best citizens when left at liberty to choose their own course. But surely probability is rebutted or destroyed by contrary certainty. If we find that freedom to work in factories means the destruction of a comfortable home, and the death of ten out of twelve of the offspring, here is palpable evil which no theory can mitigate. What can be more against all principle, all right, nature, duty, law, or whatever else is thought to be most immutable and sacred, than that a mother should learn to hear "with nonchalance" that her infant had died at the nursing-house, while she herself was at the factory? The social system, like the human frame, may become so far diseased that the intervention of the physician is imperative.

Speaking of liberty and rights, it must be apparent, too, that the parties most seriously concerned in the matter are the infants. They have no means of raising a public agitation, or, if they venture to protest in their own manner, are soon stilled with "Godfrey." But surely if there is any right which is clearly founded in the natural fitness of things, it is the right of the infant to the mother's breast. She alone can save from virtual starvation and death. She alone can add inches to the stature, fulness to the muscles, and vigour to the mind. It is in the present state of things that rights and principles are most flagrantly cast aside. And the origin of all this evil is often some idle and dissolute young man, who marries or seduces a young girl, knowing that he can afterwards live upon her wages.

All sorts of objections were made, time after time, to the Factory Laws as they gradually rose, step by step, from their first small beginning in 1802. Now all classes recognise that these laws were absolutely necessary to guard the population against the dangers of a novel state of things, as to which evolution had not had time to work out its spontaneous cure. No doubt, in the course of generations, the manufacturing population would become fitted to its environment, but only through suffering and death illimitable. We can help evolution by the aid of its own highest and latest product—science. When all the teachings of medical and social science lead us to look upon the absence of the mother from home as the cause of the gravest possible evils, can we be warranted in standing passively by, allowing this evil to work itself out to the bitter end, by the process of natural selection? Something might perhaps be said in favour of the present apathetic mode of viewing this question if natural selection were really securing the survival of the fittest, so that only the weakly babes were killed off, and the strong ones well brought up. But it is much to be feared that no infants ever really recover from the test of virtual starvation to which they are so ruthlessly exposed. The vital powers are irreparably crippled, and the infant grows up a stunted, miserable specimen of humanity, the prey to every physical and moral evil.

When looked at from the right point of view, factory legislation confers or maintains, rather than destroys, rights and liberties. The Factory and Workshop Act of 1878 seems to be a mass of vexatious restrictions: in reality it is the Great Charter of the working-classes. It is one of the noblest products of legislative skill and patience. It sums up the experience and the positive experiments of eighty years in the alleviation of factory life; but there is no reason to look upon it as the ultimatum of such alleviative legislation. It affords, no doubt, a resting-place; but it affords also the best encouragement to proceed with several other measures of like nature. Of all these, I venture to hold that the question of married women's employment, in spite of its extent and its difficulties, should take precedence. The growing wealth of the kingdom, and the ever-advancing powers of machinery, allow that to be done now which might not have been done before. Nor could any years be more propitious for the purpose than the next five or six, which will in all probability comprise the prosperous part of the commercial cycle. The achievement of a well-designed Act upon the subject, though causing, no doubt, some trouble and distress for a few years, would be followed, a few years later, by almost incredible blessings to the people, and blessings to the realm. Many a home would be a home which cannot now be called by that sweet name. The wife, no longer a mere slattern factory hand, would become a true mother and a housekeeper; and round many a Christmas table troops of happy, chubby children would replace the "wizened little monkeys" of girls, and the "little old men" boys, who now form the miserable remnants of families.

NOTE.—During the last few weeks of his life my husband was much occupied with the question of infant mortality, as he had undertaken to prepare a paper on that subject for the meeting of the Social Science Association, held at Nottingham last September. That paper was never to be written, and the results of his many hours of labour were therefore lost. I can only say here that he had most carefully examined into the statistics of infant mortality in every town of every county throughout England and Wales, and that he told me that he thought from this exhaustive inquiry he should be able to give most convincing proof of the influence which the absence of the mother at work has upon the death-rate of the children, and of the urgent need which exists for legislation upon the subject.

H. A. J.

INAUGURAL ADDRESS

AS PRESIDENT OF THE MANCHESTER STATISTICAL SOCIETY
ON
THE WORK OF THE SOCIETY IN CONNECTION WITH THE QUESTIONS OF THE DAY.*

    I. Stagnation of Trade.
    II. Commercial Fluctuations.
    III. Pauperism, and the Means of decreasing it.
    IV. Medical and other Charities.

It has been suggested to me that I might suitably open the discussions of the present session of our society with some general remarks upon the subjects which might profitably come under our notice. One main object of a statistical society is simply to collect and publish information concerning the condition of the State or the people, and our transactions show that this object has not been neglected; but experience proves that our meetings afford an excellent opportunity for the discussion, in a perfectly unbiassed spirit, of questions of great and immediate public interest. With no foregone conclusions to support, and nothing to restrict the limits of fair and calm discussion, we meet here mutually ignorant, it may be, of the religious sect or public party to which one member or another may belong. From the author of the paper for

* Read November 10th, 1869.

the evening we receive statistical facts combined in a systematic or scientific form; and here, if anywhere, the truth is allowed to prevail from its own inherent strength. For the last thirty-six years the society has pursued an unobtrusive—probably too unobtrusive—a career; but a little inquiry would show that its career has been of great utility. On many subjects it has elicited opinions both new and true; it has either originated or given an impetus to the public discussion of various questions now bearing or likely to bear benefit to the State. And it has not altogether been unworthy of its position in a city and county which have heretofore been considered fertile in great and novel principles.

I.

We meet at a time when considerable stagnation of trade undoubtedly exists, and there are not wanting persons who endeavour to spread abroad the notion that free trade is a failure. We are told that the results of our present commercial policy must be inquired into, and that a system of reciprocity treaties must probably be substituted for a perfect free trade. Living though we still do in the metropolis and stronghold of free trade, we cannot be wholly indifferent to the existence of such notions, and it is worth while to consider what we ought to do. In upholding a spirit of perfect impartiality we cannot refuse to entertain the question if it be brought before us by any member who might happen to share those notions, and wish to support them by well arrayed facts. And if "a Manchester Manufacturer," or other anonymous agitator of this subject, trusts his own figures, and cares to submit them to a searching discussion, we would find an impartial body of critics here. But this is surely the most we need do. The burden of proof is upon those who agitate the question, and were we in this society, or were the country in Parliament, to start an inquiry into the subject, it would be yielding infinitely more weight to the facts hitherto adduced than belongs to them. Freedom of trade may be regarded as a fundamental axiom of political economy; and though even axioms may be mistaken, and different views concerning them must not be prohibited, yet we need not be frightened into questioning our own axioms. We may welcome *bonâ fide* investigation into the state of trade, and the causes of the present depression, but we can no more expect to have our opinions on free trade altered by such an investigation than the Mathematical Society would expect to have the axioms of Euclid disproved during the investigation of a complex problem. It would not be the principles of free trade that would be in question, but the political events, the great fluctuations in the supply of cotton or corn, and especially the reckless or even criminal proceedings of certain portions of the trading-classes which have disturbed the course of unrestricted industry.

There is something ludicrously illogical in the way in which "a Manchester Manufacturer" fixes upon a temporary depression of trade, easily accounted for by the most obvious causes, in order to discredit the great and permanent policy of the country. Such a writer trusts much to obliviousness. One would suppose, from the way he writes, that depression of trade and want of employment were wholly new experiences in this country, never heard of before the days of Peel. But a very slight reference to the records of past years would convince us that we should be grateful for the way in which the beneficent principles of free industry have mitigated the intensity of distress which has recurred at intervals of years under every financial *régime*. It would be tedious to remind you in any detail of the severe destitution and trouble of the years 1817–19, which occurred after the restrictive system had long been in operation, and before the idea of free trade was hardly broached. If it be objected that long wars had then enfeebled the industry of the country, I will mention instead the distress of the year 1826, which occurred at a time when the speculative energies of the kingdom had certainly not been dormant, and while hardly any important steps had yet been taken towards free trade. But I prefer to direct your attention to the years 1841–43, which bring us nearer to the present order of things, and show how wholly unconnected with the tariff is a certain temporary depression of industry. Let anyone take a volume of a Manchester newspaper for 1842, and in the early part of that year he will find in every page evidence of "the appalling and unparalleled distress" as it was called which then prevailed in the manufacturing districts of the West and North. In some places, especially Paisley, the population was said to be starving for want of employment, and the Government was implored to send food. The Government did not send food, but they did insist upon the repression of serious disturbances which arose among an almost desperate people. The bread riots, which occurred in this city in the latter part of 1842, can hardly have escaped the memory of all who are here.

This, let me remind you, took place when the tariff was still published in the form of a book, with an index to the very numerous articles contained therein; when the arrangements of Providence for the supply of food were improved by an ingenious sliding scale; when we attempted to repress the industry of neighbouring countries by an export duty on coal and certain other materials; and promoted our own manufactures by a general *ad valorem* import duty on manufactures of cotton, woollen, linen, iron, etc., varying from £5 to £30 per £100. It was the discontent and agitation arising during those gloomy years which finally determined the country in favour of free trade, and it is an extraordinary coincidence that the very year which has witnessed the removal of the last trace of protection in the small corn duty, just repealed by Mr. Lowe, should have brought an agitation, however limited and contemptible, for a reversal of that great work.

II.

For my part, when I consider how great are the causes which have lately concurred to derange our trade, I feel exceedingly thankful that we have so easily surmounted crises like those of the cotton famine, and the collapse of 1866. Our own transactions contain ample information to enable anyone to understand our present position, and the real causes of stagnation. I know no one who has expounded in so thorough, and, as it seems to me, so sound a manner the causes of commercial fluctuations as Mr. John Mills. His paper on Credit Cycles and the Origin of Commercial Panics shows in the clearest way that these recurrent periods of depression are not due to any artificial causes, nor can they be accounted for by the state and regulations of the currency; they have recurred under a *régime* of inconvertible paper currency, a *régime* of free issues of convertible paper, and a *régime* of regulated issues upon a metallic basis. I may add that in other countries similar panics have occurred where there was a purely metallic currency, and bank notes were unknown. They have also recurred, as I have already mentioned, under every form of tariff which has existed in this country during the present century, or even longer. Mr. Mills has proved that such fluctuations have a deeper cause which we can only describe as the *mental disposition* of the trading classes. As a fact, there is every ten years or thereabouts an excitement of hope and confidence leading to a profusion of speculative schemes, the incurring of a great mass of liabilities, the investment of a great amount of floating capital, and an intense temporary activity of trade. As we know too well, there follows inevitably a corresponding reaction, and we are now in the third year of what Mr. Mills has so well called the Post Panic Period. I trust that he will before long favour us with a continuation of his admirable paper, pointing out how completely the course of events is justifying his remarks.

There are at present signs of the dawn of commercial activity. The first slight blush of returning day is beginning to show itself. The promoters of companies are beginning again to put forth their proposals in an extremely diffident and deprecatory manner. As there are no unfortunate reminiscences attaching to deep sea cables, they are selected to lead off with, and I do not doubt that before two or three years are over we shall again have occasion to fear the excessive confidence and the occasional want of integrity of projectors. It is a very significant fact that the iron trade, after several years of depression, is now beginning to be active. If masters and men in that trade would only let it take its natural course there would soon be nothing to complain of; and it will be truly unfortunate if a premature advance of wages and prices—for such is thought by many to be the recent decision of the trade in South Staffordshire—should drive their better fortune from them. Prosperity is probably only a question of a short time, and the close connection which exists between the demand for iron and the amount of fixed investment about to be made, seems to render the price of iron the best commercial weather-glass.

What there may be in the trade of this district which is not adequately explained by the recent collapse may surely be due to the lingering effects of the cotton famine. This society has furnished the public, in Mr. E. Helm's Review of the Cotton Trade, during the years 1862–68, with probably the best arranged facts concerning the position of the cotton and some related branches of manufacture. His tables form quite a small hand-book of the subject, and no one can doubt that the disproportion which he proves between the manufacturing power and the supply of cotton is quite adequate to explain the state of things. And we must remember that the general depression of trade profits and employment unfortunately co-operates with the high price of the material at present to restrict the home and foreign demand for cotton goods. The cotton manufacture has thus been beset with every possible disadvantage, and it is absurd indeed to turn round and throw the whole blame upon that freedom of foreign commerce by which alone we can obtain a pound of cotton-wool.

One word upon reciprocity treaties. Those who harp upon this idea, because they have no other to offer, overlook the fact that every act of commerce is a treaty of reciprocity. We cannot import without we export to an equal value, and we cannot export without we import. When we broke down the barriers around our own shores we could not stimulate an inward without also stimulating an outward current. The current would doubtless be stronger were the barriers around other shores removed; but were it our habit to wait until other nations are ready to accompany our steps of progress, we should still be where we stood in 1819.

III.

I am glad to see that one result of the present depression of trade has been to direct attention to the enormous amount of pauperism existing in this country. The recent increase of the last few years indeed is fully accounted for by the temporary state of industry, and a few years of prosperity will doubtless restore things to what they were. But is there any time in the present century when we could look at the undoubted returns of our poor-law relief and say that they were not a matter of regret and anxiety? Can we say that we are in a sound social state when all our triumphs in science, in mechanical invention, in manufactures, and in trade leave us still with one million of the people in the state of hopeless misery and dependence.

It is true that the present generation is not responsible for the creation of so much wretchedness. Pauperism is the general resultant of all the bad and all the omitted legislation of the last five hundred years. We have enough to answer for without reproaching ourselves with the deficiencies of our forefathers. Our reproach must be that, enjoying a greater amount of wealth, and greater opportunities than ever before fell to the lot of any nation, we have not done more to correct the results of former neglect. But I apprehend that what we want is not so much desire to accomplish the work as unanimity concerning the mode to be adopted. As pauperism is the general resultant of all that is wrong in our social arrangements it cannot be destroyed by any single measure; it can only be reduced by such exertions as raise the intelligence and provident habits of the people. Material well-being has comparatively little effect, for, however high the wages of an artizan may be, they may be spent intemperately, and on the slightest reverse of fortune his family or himself may come to the workhouse. It is distressing to find that a population such as that surrounding this city, which, on the whole, perhaps, has as great a command of good food and all the comforts of life as any in the world, has nothing to fall back upon, no accumulated savings of consequence, and that they are, therefore, ever ready upon the least breath of adversity to come upon the public funds. No people can be really well off unless to their material prosperity be joined habits of providence and foresight, which will lead them to fortify themselves in the position they have once attained.

General education is, doubtless, the measure which most nearly approaches to a panacea for our present evils. If I do not say much on this subject it is not because I do not feel much, but because I do not know so much of the details of the subject as would warrant me in speaking of it to many members who are already fully and practically acquainted with it. I will only suggest that, as this Society has, from its first establishment, taken a leading part in those inquiries and discussions which have led to the present wholesome state of public opinion, it might now fitly give attention to the minutest details of the legislation required. Compulsory attendance at school we must have, and I wish some of our members would investigate the most efficient means of carrying out the future law.

Another obvious mode of cutting off the springs of pauperism is to repress drunkenness. Here, again, we meet a question on which public opinion has pronounced itself in a general sort of manner, but where the details are still entirely in doubt. I was very glad that our member, the Rev. Mr. Steinthal, brought the subject of the licensing laws before us in a paper which left nothing to be desired as regards perfect acquaintance with the details of legislation and recent public discussion on the subject. But I am very sorry that I cannot accept his conclusion that the Permissive Bill of the United Kingdom Alliance is the best measure to repress intemperance. It aims at the more or less complete prohibition of a traffic which cannot be entirely destroyed, and, as I for one think, ought not to be entirely destroyed. It does not aim, so far as I can see, at exactly the right object; and I cannot persuade myself that its object could be carried out in practice. No one can doubt that so powerful a society does great good by drawing attention to the evils which exist; but I wish that an equal support could be given to the exceedingly sensible and practicable measures advocated by the Licenses Amendment League of this city. What we want, as it seems to me, is a carefully regulated and limited traffic, controlled by a well-enforced law, administered by a body of magistrates or other men who will ignore altogether the interests of the publicans, and look steadily to the infinitely greater object of the public good.

Among minor measures for the decrease of pauperism I may mention those advocated by Mr. Barwick L. Baker, in a most valuable and practical paper read to the society last session. Vagrancy is one of the abuses certain to grow up under a poor-law unless it be administered with the utmost care; and I trust that the experience of Mr. Baker may meet with proper attention from the Poor-law Board. It is creditable to our society to draw forth practical information such as this paper contains.

Another important effort is now being made in this city to decrease pauperism—I mean the placing out of pauper children in the families of respectable artisans—one of our members, Mr. Charles Herford, being foremost in the undertaking. It is well known that those children who are brought up in the workhouse almost invariably return there sooner or later, and thus form a strictly hereditary class of paupers. There can be no more direct mode of cutting off a branch of the stream of pauperism than thus to arrest it in the period of childhood. The scheme, so far as it is yet carried out, acts admirably, judging from what I have heard and seen of it, and I trust Mr. Herford will shortly give us the result of his experience in the matter.

IV.

I now wish to advert to a subject which has not, I think, received the attention it deserves. I refer to the tendency of medical charities and the poor-law medical service to nourish the spirit of pauperism. Considerable indignation has been occasioned by the neglect of sick paupers which has occurred in some parishes, and there is a movement for a general and uniform improvement in the medical treatment of paupers.

Everyone must hold in the highest estimation men who, like the author of "Social Duties," devote the highest talents to a work of this kind; and few who have read this work could have failed to acquiesce in the humane views put forth. Yet I think we must take care lest in yielding to the impulses of humanity we do more harm than good. I fear we may make the Union hospital so easy of access, and so attractive, that it may lead half-way to the Poor-house itself. Whenever I see the admirable infirmary built at Withington by our member Mr. Worthington, and described in our Transactions, this is the thought which suggests itself. But I feel bound to go further, and call in question the policy of the whole of our medical charities, including all free public infirmaries, dispensaries, hospitals, and a large part of the vast amount of private charity. What I mean is, that the whole of these charities nourish in the poorest classes a contented sense of dependence on the richer classes for those ordinary requirements of life which they ought to be led to provide for themselves. Medical assistance is probably the least objectionable of all the forms of charity, but it nevertheless may be objectionable. There is nothing more sure than that a certain percentage of any population will be suffering at every moment from illness or disease. It is almost certain that every man, woman, and child will require some medical treatment, and no family is really in a solvent condition which is not prepared to meet the average expenditure for this purpose. Every hospital and free dispensary tends to relax the habits of providence, which ought to be most carefully cultivated, and which cannot be better urged than with regard to the contingency of sickness. *The Times* not long ago published some very remarkable and complete statistics, compiled by Mr. Hicks, showing that the annual revenue of the established charities of London alone amounted to more than two millions a year. I fear that not only is a large part of this wasted in the excessive costs of management, but that a further large portion really goes to undermine the most valuable qualities of self-reliance, and so form a bribe towards the habits of mendicancy and pauperism. About forty years ago it became apparent to the statesmen of that day that the Poor Laws, as then administered, were doing immense injury by allowing a distribution of public money in aid of wages, and encouraging every one to rely upon the public funds for subsistence. I fear we are in danger of falling into a similar mistake now by placing upon the ratepayers or upon charitable persons the whole cost of the medical service of the poorer classes. There is really no reason why such a state of things should exist, and many why it should not exist. At present the result of almost all charitable efforts is to make the poor look upon assistance as a right and natural thing in every contingency of life. If they merely want a little medicine there is a free dispensary; if they have a bad eye or ear, there are appropriate institutions; if anyone is in weak health he seeks a free order of admission to a Southport or a Buxton Hospital; and when the most natural possible crisis in a poor woman's life approaches, she looks forward to the aid of St. Mary's Hospital. Now, I ask, why should the poorer classes be thus encouraged and instructed to look to the wealthier classes for aid in some of the commonest requirements of life? If they were absolutely unable to provide for themselves the reason would be a strong and intelligible one, but I do not believe that the people are really in such a hopeless state of poverty. On the contrary, the wages of the greater part of the working-classes, and in these districts almost the whole, are probably capable, if wisely expended, of meeting the ordinary evils and contingencies of life, and were providence in small matters the rule, the most unhesitating aid might properly be given in the more unforeseen and severe accidents and cases of destitution.

But there is little use in bewailing an evil unless some mode of remedying it can be found. There is not much difficulty in discovering the only remedy applicable to medical charities. No one can seriously think of abolishing those charities; but why should not the working-classes be required to contribute towards institutions mainly established for their benefit. Self-supporting dispensaries exist in many places which afford all requisite aid to any person subscribing some such small amount as 1*d*. or 2*d*. each per week. I have heard that some of the London hospitals have considered the idea of adopting this system, and refusing aid in all minor cases but to their own subscribers. It would not be necessary to render the hospitals self-supporting. Endowments and public contributions would usually enable every hospital or dispensary to give back in medical aid several times the value of what is given in small contributions. The object would be not so much to raise money as to avoid undermining the prudent habits of the people. Non-contributors might still be relieved, but only on the payment of a fine; and, of course, cases of severe accident, illness, or destitution would still be relieved gratuitously as at present.

We cannot be supposed yet to have reached a point at which the public or private charity of one class towards another can be dispensed with, but I do think we ought to look towards such a state of things. True progress will tend to render every class self-reliant and independent. Self-help is the truest kind of help, and you confer the greatest benefit upon a person or a class of persons when you enable and induce them to do without your aid for the future. Money spent in the education of the young has this beneficent effect. Money spent in most other modes of charity has generally the opposite effect. Hence, I venture to look upon £1 spent in the education of the young as worth £50 spent in most other charitable uses.

I am hardly likely to overlook or underestimate the mistakes committed by Trades Unions, but can we deny that they embody the true spirit of self-help? So far as their funds are spent upon the relief of sickness, the support of those who are *bonâ fide* out of employment, or crippled by accident, they represent the truest form of providence, and they are already one of the bulwarks against the flood of pauperism. I do not despair of the time when these societies will understand the harmful and hopeless nature of their struggle against capital, and when that day comes, and working-men devote themselves to the accumulation of capital and the employment of it for their own benefit, a new and more hopeful order of things will not be far distant.

Having ventured to speak against the abuse of medical charities, I think I need not spare my remarks upon an innumerable multitude of other charities which have nothing to recommend them. I allude to the small doles of money and bread, coals and blankets, and other articles, which, in almost every parish in England, are given out chiefly through the hands of the clergy at intervals, according to the benevolent but mistaken intentions of testators. In Manchester I have seen the Cathedral entirely filled by an indiscriminate crowd of poor persons, each summoned to receive a blanket or coverlet. Every one, of course, must know that a certain amount of physical comfort may thus be caused; but what is this to the demoralising effect of such casual charity upon the energy and prudent habits of the recipients? I do not hesitate to say that such charities are an *unmitigated nuisance*, and that the money is not merely thrown away but used to do harm. It would accordingly be a most salutary measure to divert a considerable part of these misused funds to the promotion of education. Such funds are really public and not private funds, and when the State recognises in the Poor Law an indefeasible right of every person to maintenance under certain most necessary conditions, and spends a huge annual sum of money in consequence, it has a perfect right and duty to inquire into the application of other public funds which really go to swell the crowd of paupers.

The British Poor Law of 1832 is one of the wisest measures ever concerted by any government, and we of this generation hardly appreciate what it has saved us from. But I much fear lest any mistaken feelings of humanity should lead us to relax the rigour of its application, and to allow it in one way or other to be circumvented and counteracted. Should this be so, then, I say that British pauperism is simply a hopeless and permanent, and probably an increasing reproach to the civilisation of this country. Doubtless the state of things is somewhat better than it was before 1832; but, considering the nature of the reforms since effected, the amount of the wealth acquired, and the general amelioration in the other ranks of society, I venture to say that the improvement in the numbers and prospects of the poorest class who are or may become paupers, is really inconsiderable. And I shudder to think what might be the effect of any serious impediment to our future progress, such as a long-continued war, the competition of other nations, or a comparative failure of our own material resources.

OPENING ADDRESS

AS

PRESIDENT OF SECTION F (ECONOMIC SCIENCE AND STATISTICS)

OF THE

BRITISH ASSOCIATION FOR THE ADVANCEMENT OF SCIENCE,

At the Fortieth Meeting, at Liverpool, September, 1870.*

THE field of knowledge which we cultivate in this Section is so wide, that it would be impossible, in any introductory remarks, to notice more than a few of the important questions which claim our attention at the present time.

The name Statistics, in its true meaning, denotes all knowledge relating to the condition of the State or people. I am sorry to observe, indeed, that many persons now use the word *statistical* as if it were synonymous with *numerical*; but it is a mere accident of the information with which we deal, that it is often expressed in a numerical or tabular form. As other sciences progress, they become more a matter of quantity and number, and so does our science; but we must not suppose that the occurrence of numerical statements is the mark of statistical information.

In order, however, that any subject can be fitly discussed by a Section of this Association, it should be capable of scientific treatment. We must not only have facts, numerical

* Printed in the "Journal of the Statistical Society," September, 1870.

or otherwise, but those facts must be analysed, arranged, and explained by inductive or deductive processes, as nearly as possible identical with those which have led to undoubted success in other branches of science. I have always felt great gratification that the founders of this Association did not in any narrow spirit restrict its inquiries and discussions to the domain of physical science. The existence of this Section is a standing recognition of the truth that the condition of the people is governed by definite laws, however complicated and difficult of discovery they may be. It is no valid reproach against us that we cannot measure, and explain, and predict with the accuracy of a chemist or an astronomer. Difficult as may be the problems presented to the experimentalist in his investigation of Material Nature, they are easy compared with the problems of Human Nature, of which we must attempt the solution. I allow that our knowledge of the causes in action is seldom sure and accurate, so as to present the appearance of true science.

There is no one who occupies a less enviable position than the Political Economist. Cultivating the frontier regions between certain knowledge and conjecture, his efforts and advice are scorned and rejected on all hands. If he arrives at a sure law of human nature, and points out the evils which arise from its neglect, he is fallen upon by the large classes of people who think their own common-sense sufficient; he is charged with being too abstract in his speculations; with overlooking the windings of the human heart; with undervaluing the affections. However humane his motives, he is lucky if he escape being set down on all sides as a heartless misanthrope. Such was actually the fate of one of the most humane and excellent of men, the late Mr. Malthus. On the other hand, it is only the enlightened and wide-minded scientific men who treat the political economist with any cordiality. I much fear that, as physical philosophers become more and more successful, they tend to become like other conquerors, arrogant and selfish; they forget the absurd theories, the incredible errors, the long-enduring debates out of which their own knowledge has emerged, and look with scorn upon our economic science, our statistics, or our still more vague body of knowledge called social science, because we are still struggling to overcome difficulties far greater than ever they encountered. But, again, I regard the existence of this Section as a satisfactory recognition of the absolute necessity of doing our best to cultivate economic subjects in a scientific spirit.

The great and everlasting benefits which physical science has conferred upon the human race are on every side acknowledged; yet they are only the smaller half of what is wanted. It daily becomes more apparent that the highest successes in the scientific arts and manufactures are compatible with deep and almost hopeless poverty in the mass of the people. We subdue material nature; we spin and weave, and melt and forge with a minimum of labour and a maximum of result; but of what advantage is all this while human nature remains unsubdued, and a large part of the population are too ignorant, careless, improvident, or vicious to appreciate or accumulate the wealth which science brings. Chemistry cannot analyse the heart; it cannot show us how to temper the passions or mould the habits. The social sciences are the necessary complement to the physical sciences, for by their aid alone can the main body of the population be rendered honest, temperate, provident, and intelligent.

In this kingdom during the last thirty or forty years we have tried a mighty experiment, and to a great extent we have failed. The growth of the arts and manufactures, and the establishment of free trade have opened the widest means of employment and brought an accession of wealth previously unknown; the frequent remission of taxes has left the working classes in fuller enjoyment of their wages; the poor laws have been reformed and administered with care, and the emigration of millions might well have been expected to leave room for those that remain. Nevertheless within the last few years we have seen pauperism almost as prevalent as ever, and the slightest relapse of trade throws whole towns and classes of people into a state of destitution little short of famine. Such a melancholy fact is not to be charged to the political economist; it is rather a verification of his unheeded warnings; it is precisely what Malthus would have predicted of a population which, while supplied with easily earned wealth, is deprived of education and bribed by the mistaken benevolence of the richer classes into a neglect of the future. What can we expect while many still believe the proverb, that "Where God sends mouths, He sends food," and while a great many more still act upon it?

I am glad to say that, in spite of all opponents, we have an Education Act. Three centuries ago the State recognised the principle that no person should be allowed to perish for want of bread; for three centuries the State has allowed the people to perish for want of mind and knowledge. Let us hope much from this tardy recognition of the greatest social need, but let us not withdraw our attention from any other causes of evil which still exist in full force. I wish especially to point out that the wise precautions of the present poor law are to a great extent counteracted by the mistaken humanity of charitable people. Could we sum up the amount of aid which is, in one way or other, extended by the upper to the lower classes, it would be almost of incredible amount, and would probably far exceed the cost of poor law relief. But I am sorry to believe that however great the good thus done, the evil results are probably greater. Nothing so surely as indiscriminate charity tends to create and perpetuate a class living in hopeless poverty. It is well known that those towns where charitable institutions and charitable people most abound, are precisely those where the helpless poor are most numerous. It is even shown by Sir Charles Trevelyan, in a recent pamphlet, that the casual paupers have their London season and their country season, following the movements of those on whom they feed. Mr. Goschen and the poor law authorities have of late begun to perceive that all their care in the administration of relief is frustrated by the over-abundant charity of private persons, or religious societies. The same family often joins parish relief to the contributions of one or more lady visitors and missionaries. Not only improvidence but gross fraud is thus promoted, and cases are known to occur where visitors of the poor are duped into assisting those who are secretly in possession of sufficient means of livelihood.

Far worse, however, than private charity are the innumerable small charities established by the bequest of mistaken testators. Almost every parish church has its tables of benefactions holding up to everlasting gratitude those who have left a small patch of land, or an annual sum of money, to be devoted to pauperising the population of the parish throughout all time. Blankets, coals, loaves, or money are doled out once or twice a year, usually by the vicar and churchwardens. More or less these parish charities act as a decoy to keep the most helpless part of the population nominally within the fold of the Church. The Dissenters, where they are strong enough, retaliate by competing for the possession of the poor by their own missions, and thus the reproach of the Roman Catholic Church, that it fostered mendicancy, holds far too true of our present sects. With private charity no law can interfere, and we can do nothing but appeal to the discretion of individuals. With testamentary charities it is otherwise.

We are far yet from the time when so beneficial a measure will be possible, but I trust that we are rapidly approaching the time when the whole of these pernicious charities will be swept away. We have in this country carried respect to the wishes of past generations to an extent simply irrational. The laws of property are a purely human institution, and are just so far defensible as they conduce to the good of society. Yet we maintain them to the extent of wasting and misusing no inconsiderable fraction of the land and wealth of the country. It would be well worthy, I think, of Mr. Goschen's attention, whether all small parish charities might not be transferred to the care of the guardians of the poor, so as to be brought under the supervision of the Poor Law Board, and distributed in accordance with sound principle. I should refuse to see in all such public endowments any rights of private property, and the State which undertakes the ultimate support of the poor, is bound to prevent its own efforts to reduce pauperism from being frustrated, as they are at present.

And while speaking of charities, it is impossible to

avoid noticing the influence of medical charities. No one could for a moment propose to abolish hospitals and numerous institutions which are absolutely necessary for the relief of accidental suffering. But there is a great difference between severe accidental disease or injury and the ordinary illnesses which almost everyone will suffer from at various periods of his life. No working man is solvent unless he lay by so much of his wages as will meet the average amount of sickness falling to the lot of the man or his family. If it be not easy to determine this amount, there are, or may be, sick clubs which will average the inequalities of life. In so far as trades unions favour the formation of such clubs, they manifest that spirit of self-reliance which is the true remedy of pauperism.

But the wealthy classes are, with the best motives, doing all they can to counteract the healthy tendencies of the artisans. They are continually increasing the number and resources of the hospitals, which compete with each other in offering the freest possible medical aid to all who come. The claims of each hospital for public support are measured by the number of patients it has attracted, so that, without some general arrangement, a more sound system is impossible. Hospitals need not be self-supporting, and in cases of really severe and unforeseen suffering, they may give the most lavish aid; but I conceive that they should not relieve slight and ordinary disease without a contribution from those benefited. As children are expected to bring their school pence, though it be insufficient to support the school, and as Government has wisely refused to sanction the general establishment of free schools, so I think that every medical institution should receive small [periodical contributions from the persons benefited. Arrangements of the kind are far from uncommon, and there are many self-supporting dispensaries, but the competition of free medical charities has, to a great extent, broken them down.

The importance of the subject with which I am dealing can only be estimated by those who have studied the statistics of London charities, prepared by Mr. Hicks, and published in *The Times* of 11th February, 1869. It is much to be desired that Mr. Hicks, or some other statistician, would extend a like inquiry to all parts of the United Kingdom, and give us some notion of the amount of money expended in the free relief of the poor.

Closely connected with this subject is that of the poor law medical service. Admirable efforts are being made to improve the quality of the medical aid which all persons sufficiently poor can demand, and some unions have already erected hospitals almost perfect in their comfort and salubrity. It will be conceded by everyone, that those sick persons whose charge is undertaken by the public ought to be treated with care and humanity. Where medical aid is given at all, it ought to be good and sufficient. But the subject seems to me to be surrounded with difficulties, out of which I cannot find my way. The better we make the poor law medical service, the more we shall extend and deepen the conviction, already too prevalent, that the poor may make merry with their wages when well and strong, because other people will take care of them when sick and old. We thus tend to increase and perpetuate that want of self-reliance and providence which is the crowning defect of the poorer classes. In this and many other cases it seems as necessary as ever that our humane impulses should be guided by a stern regard to the real results of our actions.

I now turn to a subject which must come prominently before our Section : I mean the future financial policy of the kingdom. We are now at a most peculiar and happy epoch in our financial history. For thirty years or more a reform of the tariff has been in progress; and it is only a year since the last relic of the protective system was removed by Mr. Lowe's repeal of the small corn duty. One great scheme is thus worked out and completed. Henceforth, if duties are remitted it must be on a wholly different ground—as simple remission of revenue, not as the removal of protective duties which benefit some to the injury of others. It might well be thought difficult to overlook the difference between a tax for revenue purposes and one for protective purposes; and yet there are not a few who seem not to see the difference. We are still told that there is no such thing as free trade, and that we shall not have it until all custom-houses are swept away. This doctrine rests, however, upon a new interpretation of the expression "free trade," which is quietly substituted for the old meaning. Cobden, however much he might be in favour of direct taxation, took care to define exactly what he meant by free trade. He said:

"What is free trade? Not the pulling down of all custom-houses, as some of our opponents try to persuade the agricultural labourers. Our children, or their offspring, may be wise enough to dispense with custom-house duties; they may think it prudent and economical to raise revenue by direct taxation; we do not propose to do that.

"By free trade we mean the abolition of all protective duties.

"We do not want to touch duties simply for revenue, but we want to prevent certain parties from having a revenue which is to benefit themselves, but advantage none else; we seek the improvement of Her Majesty's revenue."

Let us, then, candidly acknowledge that in Cobden's sense free trade is actually achieved. Anyone the least acquainted with our revenue system, knows with what skill our tariff has been adjusted by Peel, Gladstone, and Lowe, so that the articles taxed should be of entirely foreign production, or else the customs duty should be exactly balanced by an excise duty. We have now a very large revenue of about forty millions, raised by customs or excise duty on a small number of articles, with the least possible interference with the trade of the country. A very large part, too, is raised upon spirituous liquors, the consumption of which we desire, on other grounds, to reduce rather than encourage.

For the future, then, the remission of customs duties will be grounded on other motives than it has often been in the past, and it becomes an open question whether there are not other branches of revenue far more deserving attention. It must not be supposed that foreign trade is to be encouraged before everything else. The internal trade and industry of the country are at least equally deserving of attention, and it may be that there are stamp duties, license duties, rates, or other taxes which, in proportion to the revenue they return, do far more injury than any customs duties now remaining. It is impossible, for instance, to defend the heavy stamp duty paid by the articled clerks of attorneys on their admission; and, if I went into detail, it would be easy to point out scores of cases where the attention of the Chancellor of the Exchequer is needed.

I may point to local taxation especially as a subject requiring attention even more than any branch of the general revenue. Until within the last few years the importance of the local rates was to a great extent overlooked, because there were no adequate accounts of their amount. The returns recently obtained by the Government are even now far from complete; but it becomes apparent that at least one-fourth part of the whole revenue of the kingdom is raised by these neglected rates and tolls. Their amount is more than equal to the whole of the customs duties, upon the reform of which we have been engaged for thirty years. Nevertheless we continue to allow those rates to be levied substantially according to an Act passed in the reign of Queen Elizabeth. The recent partial inquiry by a select committee has chiefly served to prove the extent and difficulty of the reform which is needed. Whole classes of property which were unrated three centuries ago are unrated now; and it will be a matter of great difficulty to redress in an equitable manner inequalities which have been so long tolerated. The subject is of the more importance because there is sure to be a continuous increase of local taxation. We may hope for a reduction of the general expenditure, and we shall expect rather to reduce than raise the weight of duties; but all the more immediate needs of society, boards of health, medical officers, public schools, reformatories, free libraries, highway boards, main drainage schemes, water supplies, purification of rivers, improved police, better poor law medical service—these, and a score of other costly reforms, must be supported mainly out of the local rates. Before the difficulties of the subject become even greater than they now are, I think that the principles and machinery of local taxation should receive thorough consideration. At present the complexity of the laws relating to poor rates is something quite appalling, and it is the herculean nature of the reform required which perhaps disinclines financial reformers from attacking it. Several most able members of the Statistical Society have, however, treated the subject, especially Mr. Frederick Purdy, Professor J. E. T. Rogers, and Mr. Dudley Baxter.

I am glad to be able to draw the attention of the Section to the fact that the Statistical Society of London have received from Mr. William Tayler, one of the members, the sum of fifty guineas, to be awarded by the society to the author of the best essay on the Local Taxation of the United Kingdom.

We have considerable opposition raised to customs and excise duties because they are indirect taxes; but the fact is, that direct taxation is practically impossible. Careful examination shows that it is difficult to draw any clear distinction between taxes in this respect. There are few or no direct taxes borne only by those who pay them. The incidence of the local rates, for instance, is an undecided question; but I do not doubt that they fall to a considerable extent indirectly. The incidence of the stamp duties is almost wholly indirect, but defies investigation. The income tax, no doubt, approaches closely to the character of a direct tax; but it has the insuperable inconvenience of being paid by the honest people and escaped by the rogues. I am inclined to look upon schemes of universal direct taxation as affording much scope for interesting speculation, but as being, in practice, simply impossible.

I have another point to urge. Is not the time come when the remission of taxes, whether of one kind or another, may properly cease to be a main object? The surplus revenue of future years will, doubtless, be more than sufficient to enable the Chancellor of the Exchequer to reform or abolish those small branches of internal revenue which occasion far more inconvenience and injury than they are worth. There will still, should war be happily avoided, remain a considerable surplus, and the question presses upon us, Shall this revenue be relinquished, or shall it be applied to the reduction of the national debt?

In considering this subject I may first point out that there probably exists no grievous pressure of taxation, and no considerable inequality as regards the several classes of the people. We are now able to estimate, with some approach to accuracy, the actual proportion of income which is paid by persons of different incomes. The accounts now published by Government, and the labours of several eminent statisticians, especially Professor Leone Levi and Mr. Dudley Baxter, permit us to make this calculation. The most recent addition to our information is contained in an elaborate paper read by Mr. Baxter before the Statistical Society in January, 1869, and since published in the form of a volume. Mr. Baxter has, with great industry and skill, collected a mass of information concerning the habits of persons in different classes of society, which he combines with the published accounts of the revenue, and with the statistics of income previously estimated by himself and Mr. Leone Levi. Both he and Professor Levi come to the conclusion that the working-classes, so long as they make a temperate use of spirituous liquors and tobacco, pay a distinctly less proportion of their income to the State, and even intemperance does not make their contribution proportionally greater than those of more wealthy persons.

It happens that, before I was aware of Mr. Baxter's elaborate inquiries, I undertook a similar inquiry on a much more limited scale, by investigating the taxes paid by average families spending £40, £85, and £500 a year. My conclusions, as might be expected, were not exactly coincident with those either of Mr. Baxter or Professor Levi, yet there was no great discrepancy. I conceive that families of the classes mentioned, consuming moderate quantities of tobacco and spirituous liquors, all pay about ten per cent. of their income in general or local taxation, allowance being made for the recent reduction of the sugar duty and the repeal of the corn duty.* But there is this distinction to be noticed, that the

* See Appendix A, p. 212.

taxation of the middle classes is mostly unavoidable, whereas at least half the taxation of the poorer classes depends upon the amount of tobacco and spirituous liquors which they consume. Families of artisans or labourers, abstaining from the use of these stimulants, are taxed very lightly, probably not paying more than 4 or 5 per cent. of their income. Now, while many men are total abstainers, and many are intemperate, I think we cannot regard the taxes upon stimulants as we do other taxes. The payment of the tax is voluntary, and is, I believe, paid without reluctance. The more we thus investigate the present incidence of taxation, the more it seems inexpedient to proceed further in the reduction of the customs and excise duties. The result would be to leave by far the larger mass of the people almost free from anything but local taxes, and to throw the whole cost of Government upon the wealthier classes, and especially those who have tangible property.

But I venture to raise another question: I doubt whether the remission of taxation does as much good at the present day as it would at a future time. There are comparatively few signs that the wages of the working-classes, even when sufficient, are saved and applied really to advance the condition of the recipients. All is expended in a higher scale of living, so that little permanent benefit results; and when bad trade comes again, there is as much distress as ever. It is only with the increase of education and temperance that the increase of wages will prove a solid advantage. Thus, when the really hurtful taxes are removed, it by no means follows that the further remission of taxes leads to the profitable expenditure of income. The money may be spent in a way far more profitable to the whole nation than it will be spent by those whose taxes are remitted.

I am glad, on this and many other accounts, that the propriety of reducing the national debt is beginning to be very generally recognised. The question was ably raised by Mr. Lambert during the recent session, and both in the House of Commons and in the newspaper press, many strong opinions were expressed in favour of reduction. In fact, there was almost a general feeling that Mr. Lowe's small measure of reduction was altogether inconsiderable compared with our opportunities and the greatness of the task before us. During every interval of peace we ought to clear off the charges incurred during the previous war, otherwise we commit the serious error of charging to capital that which should be borne by income. If a railway company needs periodically to renew its works, and charges all the cost to capital, it must eventually become insolvent; so if at intervals we require to maintain the safety and independence of this country or its possessions by war, and do it all by borrowed money, we throw the whole cost of our advantage upon posterity. If, indeed, one great war could free us from all future danger, we might capitalise the cost and leave it as a perpetual mortgage upon the property of the country; but if the effect of any war wears out, and we are liable to be involved in new wars at intervals, then we cannot fairly or safely go on adding perpetually to the mortgage upon the national property. The wars at the commencement of this century have secured for us fifty years or more of nearly unbroken peace, and yet at the end of this period of ever-advancing wealth, the great debt stands almost at the same figure as at the commencement. We enjoy the peace and leave our descendants to pay its cost.

If it be said that this country is now far wealthier and more able to endure the annual charge of the debt than ever before, I would point out that the expense of war is also greatly increased. If we consider the cost of the Abyssinian expedition, or the vast debts which other nations have lately or are now incurring, it is evident that we may have in a great war to incur hundreds of millions of debt, or else relinquish our prominent position. Let us hope that such calamities will be spared to us; but let us not suppose that we may avoid them by being negligent and unprepared. It is not many months since Mr. Lowe declared that we must maintain our system of taxation substantially as it is, in order to supply revenue adequate to possible emergencies. The wisdom of his view is already apparent; but I hold that he should have gone further, and strengthened our hands by a measure for the reduction of the debt worthy of his boldness and the surplus at his command. But the fact is that little can be done in such a matter by any minister unless he be supported by a strong public opinion.

The remarks which I most wished to make are now completed, and there only remain one or two minor topics to which I will more briefly allude.

The excessive mortality in great towns seems to demand more close attention than it has received. For many years Liverpool stood at or near the top of the list as regards mortality, but by strenuous efforts it has been rendered more healthy. Manchester, on the other hand, although often considered the best paved, best watered, and in some other respects the best managed town in the country, has lately taken a very high or even the highest place as regards mortality. In Salford, too, the death-rate has steadily grown in recent years. It would seem as if we were entirely at fault, and that all our officers of health, sanitary commissioners, and the improvements of science and civilisation, cannot prevent nearly twice as many people from dying as would die in a healthy and natural state of things.

Within the last few months attention has been drawn to this subject by a prolonged discussion in *The Manchester Guardian*. It was occasioned by Mr. Baxendell, who brought before the Manchester Literary and Philosophical Society certain statistics tending to show that the mortality of Manchester was not due to any peculiar excess in the rate of infantile mortality. It was an old opinion that in a manufacturing town like Manchester the children are neglected, while their mothers are employed at the mills; but Mr. Baxendell showed that the deaths of infants under five years actually bear a less proportion to the whole number of deaths than in any other of the large towns. This conclusion was somewhat severely criticised by the Medical Officer of Health for Salford, and by Dr. Ransome and Mr. Royston, of the Manchester Sanitary Association. The latter gentlemen pointed out that the true mode of computation is to compare the deaths of infants with the number of infants living, and the deaths of adults with the number of adults. But even when calculations are made in this manner it still turns out that the adult mortality of Manchester is as excessive as the infantile mortality. Manchester mothers are thus exonerated from the charge of neglect, but at the same time a most important and mysterious problem is left wholly unsolved.

Our perplexity must be increased when we consider that Liverpool and Manchester, though both very unhealthy towns are quite contrasted as regards situation and the kinds of employment they present. If we compare Liverpool with other seaports, such as Bristol, Hull, and London, it is found to exceed them all considerably in mortality. Bolton, Bury, Preston, Stockport and other towns have more women employed than Manchester, comparatively speaking, yet they are more healthy. The size of the town, again, is not the chief cause, for London, though many times more populous than any other town, is decidedly healthy. The sites of the towns do not give any better solution of the difficulty, London having probably as unhealthy a site as any of the other large towns.

I am surprised that more attention has not been drawn to the probable influence of a poor Irish population in raising the death-rate. It occurred to me that the great towns which are most unhealthy agree in containing a large proportion of Irish, and agree in nothing else which I can discover. To test this notion I have calculated, from the census returns of 1861, the ratio of the Irish-born adult population in all the larger towns of Great Britain.* It then becomes apparent at once that the unhealthy towns of Liverpool, Manchester, Salford, Glasgow, Dundee, etc. are all distinguished by possessing a large population of Irish, whereas the healthy towns of London, Birmingham, Bristol, Hull, Aberdeen, etc., have less than $7\frac{1}{2}$ per cent. of adult Irish residents. Sheffield is the only remarkable exception to this induction. It might seem that, in order to confirm this conclusion, I should show the death-rate in Dublin to be very high. On turning to the accounts of the Irish Registrar-General, we find the Dublin rate to be low; but then we find that the Dublin birth-rate is

---

* See Appendix B, p. 213.

even lower in proportion. In fact the registry system in Ireland gives results so much lower in every respect than those of Great Britain, that we must either conclude the state of population to be utterly different there from what it is here, or we must suppose the registration to be very incomplete. If after further investigation this suggestion should be found to explain the high and mysterious mortality of many towns, it will, I think, relieve us from some perplexity, give us more confidence in sanitary measures, and point out exactly where most attention is needed.

The next two or three years will be a time of great interest to statisticians on account of the approaching census of 1871. We shall soon possess data which will assist us in many investigations, and enable us surely to estimate many of the changes in progress.

There is only one suggestion concerning the census which it occurs to me to make, namely, that it ought to be taken in as nearly as possible a uniform manner in all the three parts of the United Kingdom. It need hardly be pointed out that the value of statistics almost entirely depends upon the accuracy and facility with which comparisons can be made between different groups of facts, and a very slight variation in the mode of making the enumerations of the census or tabulating the results, will lead to error, or else render comparison impossible.

Reasons, the force of which I cannot estimate, have led to the establishment of distinct registry offices in Edinburgh and Dublin. Not only are the ordinary reports concerning births, deaths, and marriages drawn up independently in the several offices for England, Scotland, and Ireland, but even the census is performed by the separate authorities in the three kingdoms. Consequently, we have really three censuses and three reports, and, at least in 1861, the tables were constructed to a great extent in different modes in these reports. Thus there is a total want of that unity and uniformity which, in a scientific point of view, is indispensable. If there is one thing more than another which demands perfect unity and centralisation, it is the work of the census and the Register Office; but if we cannot have one central office, let us hope that the several Registrar-Generals will co-operate so as to produce the nearest approach to uniformity in the census. The different territorial divisions and arrangements may require some modifications in the mode of enumeration, but except in this respect, there should be perfect identity.

I should like to direct your attention for a moment to the very copious and excellent statistical publications with which we are now furnished by Government. Owing partly to the prejudice against blue books, and partly, probably, to the ineffective mode of publication, the public generally are not aware that for the sum of eightpence any person can obtain the Statistical Abstract of the Board of Trade, containing an admirable selection from the principal statistics of the country during the preceding fifteen years. For a few shillings, again, may be had the "Miscellaneous Statistics" of the Board of Trade, furnishing a wonderful compilation of facts concerning three recent years, though I wish that this information could be brought more nearly up to the time of publication.

By degrees a considerable amount of system has been introduced into our parliamentary papers. They have always been sufficiently copious—rather too copious in fact; but until the last twenty years they consisted mainly of disconnected and accidental accounts, which were exceedingly troublesome to statisticians, and often of no use whatever. It is from regular annual publications, carried on in a uniform manner, that we derive the most useful information, that which is capable of comparison and digestion. The annual reports which have for some years been issued from various Government departments are the best source of statistics; and I may suggest that there are several public departments, for instance, the Mint, which do not yet give any regular annual reports.

I would especially point again to the last Report of the Inland Revenue Department as a model of what we might desire from other departments. In addition to the usual annual report, it contains an abstract of the previous Reports for ten years back, and, what is still more valuable, complete tables of all inland duties from their first establishment, some of the tables going back to the beginning of last century. We are thus provided with a complete history of the inland revenue. I cannot but believe that in many other departments there is much valuable information which might be furnished to the public in like manner at a very slight cost.

Under other circumstances I should have had something to say to you concerning international money. Just before the present unhappy war broke out, a Commission in Paris had reported in a manner greatly facilitating the adoption of an international money in the British Empire and in America; at the same time a conference was about to be held in Berlin, which would probably have resulted in some important measures as regards Prussia. Everything, in short, was favourable to the early adoption of a common money. But it need hardly be said, that all hope of such a great reform must be deferred until peace is once again firmly established.

Since this Association last met, the great experiment of transferring the telegraphs to Government control has been carried out. The result has been to some extent disappointing. The proprietors of the telegraphs, when negotiating with Government, discovered that their property was about twice as valuable as they had before considered it. The enormous profits which they made out of the sale, seem to me to throw immense difficulty in the way of any similar transfer in the future. It becomes, for instance, simply chimerical to suppose that the Government can purchase the railways, which are about two hundred and fifty times as valuable as the telegraphs, and which, if purchased in the same way, would cost considerably more than the whole national debt. The working of the telegraphic department, again, confirms the anticipation that we must not expect from it any such results as followed the establishment of the penny post. Many people already look forward to the time when the uniform cost of a telegram will be 6*d*., but I believe that they will be disappointed. They overlook the essential difference that a great number of letters may be conveyed almost as cheaply as one letter, whereas every telegram occupies the wires for a definite time, and requires to be delivered, generally speaking, by a special messenger. Thus, if we are to have the rapid delivery without which telegrams seem to me nearly valueless, the property and staff, and, of course, the expenses of the department, must expand nearly proportionally to the business. A reduction of the rate to 6d., by bringing a great increase of work, would greatly augment the expenses of the department, and inflict a loss upon the nation.

APPENDIX A.

Estimate of the proportion of expenditure paid as taxes, general or local, by average families of man and wife, with one child over 10 years of age, and one child under 10 years. The families are supposed to expend respectively the total amounts of £40, £85, and £500, and to represent the classes of labourers, artisans, and middle-class persons. The family expending £500 a-year is supposed to maintain three servants.

	Family spending per Annum.		
	£40.	£85.	£500.
	Per Cent.	Per Cent.	Per Cent.
Taxes on necessaries — Tea, sugar, coffee, fruit	1·0	1·1	0·6
Local taxes	2·5	2·4	1·9
Income tax, house and legacy duty .	—	—	3·4
Stimulants—Beer, spirits, wine, tobacco	5·5	4·1	1·8
Total per cent. of income .	9·0	7·6	7·7

In the above statement no allowance is made for many of the stamp, license, and minor customs duties, or the net revenue of the post office, so that six or seven millions of revenue remain unaccounted for. These duties fall mainly upon the wealthier classes, and if they could be apportioned, would probably raise the payments of the middle-class and artisans' families to 10 per cent., the labourer's payment remaining somewhat less than 10 per cent. No account is taken of intemperate consumption of spirituous liquors and tobacco. Many of the license duties are taken into account in calculating the effect of the customs duties, and an allowance of 20 per cent. is added to the duties on commodities to cover the interest charged by the dealers who advance the duties.

APPENDIX B.

ON THE CONNECTION BETWEEN THE IRISH POPULATION AND THE RATE OF MORTALITY IN TOWNS.

I have tested the suggestions made in the text in a variety of ways, and have, in almost every case, met with confirmatory evidence.

In calculating the percentage of Irish population in any town, I have taken the numbers only of the population of twenty years of age and upwards, for the obvious reason that if an Irish family live for a few years in England, they may have children registered as English born, although they live under the same sanitary conditions as their Irish parents.

The following statement compares the proportion of Irish population with the mortality in some of the principal towns:

	Proportion of Irish Population; Census of 1861.	Rate of Mortality per 1,000, on the Average of 1851-60.
Liverpool . . .	34·9	33·3
Manchester . .	20·6	31·6
Salford . . .	12·7	26·1
Newcastle . .	9·0	27·4
Bradford . . .	8·6	25·7
Leeds . . .	7·5	27·8
Birmingham . .	7·3	26·5
London . . .	5·7	23·6
Sheffield . . .	5·2	28·5

The high mortality of Liverpool and Manchester is here in striking conformity with the large Irish population, and more recent returns of the Salford mortality would also exhibit conformity. Sheffield is the only serious exception.

In another calculation, I took a list of the mortality of eighteen English towns in the year of the census of 1861. I separated the towns into three groups, according as the mortality was:

1. At the rate of 28 or more per 1,000.
2. Between the rates of 24 and 26.
3. At the rate of 24 or less.

The percentage of Irish population *in the aggregate* of each group, and the average mortality, were then found to be as follows:

	Percentage of Irish Population.	Average Mortality.
Towns of High Mortality: Liverpool, Manchester, Newcastle, Preston, and Bolton	21·9	29·8
Towns of Medium Mortality: Leicester, Ashton, Oldham, Blackburn, Sheffield, Leeds	7·0	26·0
Towns of Least Mortality: Bradford, Nottingham, Birmingham, Dudley, Stoke, Wolverhampton, Stourbridge	5·6	22·9

With the above we may compare London, which has an Irish population of 5·7 per cent., and a mortality of 23·6, on the average of the years 1851–60.

Observing in another list that Altrincham, Bakewell, and Warwick were districts of low mortality, the rate scarcely exceeding 20 in 1,000, I calculated the Irish percentage as follows:

	Per Cent.
Altrincham	6·0
Bakewell	2·2
Warwick	2·0

Or, aggregating the three towns together, we find the Irish population to be on the whole 2·2 per cent., or less than half the average proportion of Irish throughout England and Wales, which is 4·52 per cent.

These facts appeared to me to be almost of a conclusive character by themselves, but in extending the comparison to the Scotch towns, we meet with the strongest possible corroboration. The eight principal Scotch towns happen to fall apart into two very distinct groups, the particulars of which are shown in the following table:

	Proportion of Irish Population, Census of 1861.	Rate of Mortality per 1,000, on the Average of 1855-63.
Towns of Large Irish Population:		
Dundee	23·8	27·3
Glasgow	23·0	29·8
Greenock	22·0	31·1
Paisley	18·1	26·5
Towns of Small Irish Population:		
Edinburgh	7·4	24·7
Leith	6·6	22·6
Perth	6·4	24·9
Aberdeen	1·8	23·1

Forming averages of the above numbers, we have:

	Average Proportion of Irish Population.	Average Mortality.
Towns of large Irish population	21·7	28·7
,, small ,,	5·5	23·8

It may not be unworthy of remark that in the most unhealthy towns—Liverpool, Manchester, Salford, etc.—the Irish women are in excess of the men; whereas in the most healthy towns—such as Hull, Leith, and Aberdeen—the women are even fewer than the men. The following is the proportion of

Irish women to the whole number of women in the healthy places:

	Per Cent.
Leith	5·3
Aberdeen	1·5
Bakewell	1·4
Warwick	1·9
Altrincham	4·7

We should naturally turn to ascertain whether the mortality in Ireland at all bears out the apparent effect of Irish immigration in England. Taking the average of a few years of the returns of births and deaths in Dublin, I find that the rates are in both cases almost exactly the same, namely, 26·1 per 1,000. In one return the deaths were 33·6, while the births were only 24·7. As the birth-rate much exceeds the death-rate in England and other progressive countries, we must either regard the population of Ireland as being in a very abnormal state, or we must reject the returns as wholly unworthy of confidence.

The Editor of *The Statistical Journal* has often appended a note to the Irish returns, calling attention to their apparent untrustworthiness. Until we know to what extent the returns are defective, they are simply misleading and mischievous; but if they are at all approximate to the truth, they lend strong support to the supposition that English mortality is greatly influenced by Irish immigrants.

CRUELTY TO ANIMALS—A STUDY IN SOCIOLOGY.*

Some philosophers hold that whatever we feel in our conscience to be right, is right. Others assert that the course of action to be approved is evidently that which leads to the greatest balance of pleasure over pain. In casting up this credit and debit account, we may properly include not only the pleasures and pains of all mankind, but those of the lower animals, so far as they can be estimated and compared with human feelings. However these fundamental questions of moral science may be settled, it is curious to reflect how little the two standards of right do, as a matter of fact, correspond. In a great many instances which might be pointed out, public sentiment condemns and rigorously represses one particular form of hurtful action, while it condones or approves deeds of a parallel nature equally against the greatest-happiness principle. Prevailing moral sentiments seem to be founded on no nice appreciation of comparative evil and comparative good.

It has often struck me that the English people are under some misapprehensions about their national virtues. Long ago they abolished public lotteries, and a lottery wheel is now considered a wicked and demoralising thing, except in its rather ominous connection with the sale of works of art. But though lottery wheels are abolished, they tolerate the

* "Fortnightly Review," May, 1876, vol. xix., pp. 671–684.

existence of a betting system as demoralising as any lotteries which ever were held. It is true that there are laws against betting in public, which save the national conscience in some degree; but everyone is aware that the nation deliberately ignores the existence of betting rings among its own aristocratic governors, and does not make earnest efforts to suppress the practice.

The English feel their superior virtue, again, in the matter of slavery. They set the world the example of abolishing this odious thing; the very name of slavery cannot be endured in England. When it became known that certain South Sea Islanders were being kidnapped occasionally, and carried into some sort of slavery in Queensland, the Government took prompt and effectual measures against this abominable practice; but when it was stated that the Australian aborigines in the north of Queensland were being shot like kangaroos, or poisoned wholesale by strychnine, one solitary member of parliament went so far as to ask the Government whether this was true. The Government replied that they did not know, but would make inquiries, and nothing more has been heard of the matter to the present day. Accounts which I have heard of the proceedings in the border districts of Queensland are simply dreadful. These accounts may or may not be true,* and I should not like to vouch for them; but the point is that English society, though it runs wild about surrendering a fugitive slave, has never cared even to ascertain whether or not scores of the Australian natives are shot like kangaroos, or poisoned by strychnine, like the native dogs.

The most remarkable, however, of all such cases of dis-

---

* Since writing the above I have found that these statements are to a great extent confirmed in a work just published upon Queensland, called "The Queen of the Colonies." A squatter destroyed a whole tribe of blacks by giving them a bag of flour poisoned by strychnine. This crime is comparable with that of Thomasson. No attempt was made to punish him. Another case, in which two blacks were intentionally poisoned by strychnine, is also mentioned. The shooting and poisoning of natives are said to have ceased in the last few years; but ought we to be satisfied by vague and unsupported assertions in a matter of this kind?

proportionate moral sentiment is found in the case of cruelty to animals. In this respect, again, the English are pre-eminently a virtuous people. Less advanced or, it may be, degenerate nations still indulge in savage sports like bull-fighting. I remember that a kind of thrill of horror went through the newspapers when it was once reported that the Empress Eugénie had attended a bull-fight. Long ago the English abolished such a brutal practice as bull-baiting, which is now only a matter of history. It is pleasing to hear of the intelligence and success with which the police everywhere follow the tracks of cock-fighters. A party of men cannot meet on the most secluded moor in the country, but the force are down upon them before many "mains" have been fought. The praiseworthy efforts of the Society for the Prevention of Cruelty to animals are unceasing. A man ties crackers to the tail of a pigeon to make it fly better. He is marched before a magistrate and fined. An ingenious menagerie-keeper makes hyænas jump through a blazing ring. The bench denounce the gross cruelty, it having been given in evidence that hyænas are much afraid of fire; but they ultimately discharge the accused, on the ground that hyænas are not domesticated animals. Within the last few days a man has been fined for taming a horse by electricity. Again, it is thought a very cruel thing to bait rabbits or other animals in an enclosed space, and every now and then a beerhouse-keeper suffers under the Act against this cruel practice; but, curiously enough, if you only let the animals have a run in an open space before they are killed by the dogs, this is not cruel, being called *coursing* as contrasted to *baiting*. That is to say, if you let an animal endure the fear of death for a short time, and exhaust itself in vain efforts to escape, and then give it the actual pains of death, there is no cruelty.

But I need hardly go on at any great length to show that the sentiments of the public in respect of cruelty to animals are simply in a chaotic state. There is no approximation whatever to the utilitarian standard. An almost infinite amount of needless pain is inflicted upon the lower animals every day, and yet, because it is done in a familiar form, the inspectors of the Society pass it over, and indeed the laws take no cognisance of it. Sportsmen and ratcatchers ruthlessly leave wounded animals to die slowly and in torture. But if men tie crackers to the tails of pigeons, the fact of their conviction is telegraphed to every daily newspaper in the country, and appears under the sensational heading, "A New Phase of Cruelty."

By far the most irrational of moral sensations, however, is that excited by the revelations of vivisection. It is not too much to say that the public have almost unanimously been shocked by the details of experiments which the Society for the Abolition of Vivisection have taken care to make widely known. That a number of medical men should have met at Norwich, and coolly stood by to witness M. Magnan cut open the thighs of two dogs, and inject alcohol and absinthe therein, drove many people almost wild with indignation. When, in 1873, the authors of the "Handbook of the Physiological Laboratory" published their unlucky volume, and disclosed the secrets of the vivisection table, a part of the public seemed to become almost inarticulate with rage, that such things should be allowed in a Christian and an English country.

Words of sufficient strength seem to be wanting to express the feelings of anti-vivisectionists. Hellish, monstrous, abominable, horrid, horrible, devilish, diabolical, demoniacal, ghastly, sinful, wicked, detestable, villanous, atrocious, nameless, infamous —such are a few of the adjectives most commonly applied to the practice; and it seems difficult to suggest stronger ones. Yet, from the way in which the writers pile up the agony, they evidently think their language inadequate to the occasion. I noticed one letter, occupying half a column of small print, in a London evening paper, which might be described as one continuous yell of indignation from beginning to end. Mr. George Duckett, of the Society for the Abolition of Vivisection, probably gave a form to the suppressed feelings of many, when he described vivisection as hellish, horrid, and monstrous, as "an abomination imported from the Continent," and as "going hand in hand with Atheism."*

It is noticeable that not a few of the eminent men who have practised vivisection, or are immediately interested in its results, express almost equally strong feelings. Mr. Darwin, when asked what he would think of trying a painful experiment without anæsthetics, when it could be done as well with them, replied emphatically, "It deserves detestation and abhorrence." (Question 4,672.) Dr. Sharpey, referring to one of Majendie's experiments which he had witnessed in his youth, described it as "his famous, it might rather have been called infamous," experiment (Question 474). Other less eminent witnesses spoke almost in a similar tone of practices in which they were themselves deeply interested.

I hope that I should be one of the last to deny that it is hellish and infamous and detestable, and so forth, to inflict needless pain on the lower animals. But I wish to ask, If so, why does society, and English society especially, go on permitting the perpetration of hellish atrocities, on a most gigantic scale, in their very midst? Why does it allow practices of this hellish description to be fashionable amusements of the upper classes, patronised by royalty, purchased at vast cost, commented on by all the daily press, and by a number of special journals, as if these amusements were more important to humanity than all science and art put together? Can anybody deny that what is known as "sport," or as the "noble science," including hunting, coursing, deer-stalking, shooting, battue-shooting, pigeon-shooting, and angling, is from beginning to end, mere diversion founded on the needless sufferings of the lower animals? On what sociological or psychological grounds can we explain the fact that a comparatively small amount of pain inflicted for the lofty purpose of furthering science and relieving the ills of mortality should excite such intense feelings of disgust, while the infliction of almost infinitely greater amounts of pain in mere

* Report of the Royal Commission on Vivisection, p. 326.

trivial amusement seems to excite no corresponding feeling at all? Why is the country agitated with disgust at the report of a cock-fight, or a combat between a man and a dog, or the electrifying of a horse, while the newspapers send their special correspondents to India to describe the achievements of our future emperor in sticking pigs?

It might seem indispensable, in treating a question of this sort, to lay down some clear definition, showing what is cruelty and what is not; but any attempt to reconcile popular sentiments with a single definition of the term will utterly fail. To inflict pain for the pleasure of inflicting it, is unquestionable and malignant cruelty. To inflict pain negligently, and without any adequate motive, as when a butcher, habituated to the slaughtering of animals, pays little regard to the shortening of their last agonies, is also cruel. But it would not seem that the infliction of pain is always regarded as a necessary ingredient of cruelty. A large part of the public strongly condemns the practice of pigeon-shooting as a cruel and brutal amusement. But a bird when fairly shot dies instantaneously, without time to feel pain, and when the business is properly conducted no bird need be left in pain for more than a very brief time. But there can be no doubt whatever that, in shooting wild birds and rabbits, a large proportion of the animals are painfully wounded, and yet escape beyond the reach of the sportsman. Wyndham, in a remarkable speech which he made in favour of bull-baiting, asserted that in shooting there were ten birds wounded for one bird killed. I should think, or at least hope, that this is an immense exaggeration; in the absence of any data I will assume that, for ten birds or rabbits killed outright, there is only one painfully wounded. Now we can hardly suppose that the number of birds and rabbits shot annually in this kingdom is less than thirty millions, and we arrive at the fearful result that, to say the least, three million animals are painfully mangled yearly, partly to supply food, but mainly to afford amusement to the wealthy. Let us grant, for the sake of argument, that only half of these animals could be taken painlessly by nets. Then we must allow that a million and a half wounded animals suffer agonies for the mere diversion of our sporting classes. Strange to say, this enormous infliction of needless pain is seldom thought cruel. True sport is held to be a wholesome manly exercise. Pigeon-shooting is cruel, although the animals die speedily and certainly. Rabbit-shooting is not cruel, apparently because the poor wounded animals which escape die a lingering death out of sight.

It may be said that the sportsman does nothing more than the laws of nature authorise. He procures food by the most direct process, and kills animals in a rapid painless way. But this does not at all hold good of all sporting. From my own observation I can affirm that many sportsmen acquire a taste for the simple wanton destruction of life apart from all ulterior purposes. Provided an animal will only make a good moving target they want to shoot it. They will do this at sea, in woods, and inaccessible places where there is no possibility of recovering the animals, or of putting them out of pain if badly wounded. In Norway and Australia I have frequently seen the sporting instinct of the English develop itself in freedom, and I can only conclude that "sport" is synonymous with the love of the clever destruction of living things.

We should not speak of sportsmen as if they were all exactly alike, and I have no doubt that many of them would hate to leave an animal in pain when they could help it; but not so in every case. I have had narrated to me the proceedings of a highly aristocratic party, engaged in the fashionable amusement of battue-shooting. A wounded bird fell near to a group of country people, who were looking on at their superiors. The poor bird lay writhing in agony on the ground, and a bystander almost instinctively stepped forward to put it out of pain. He received such a rating from some of the aristocratic party for his impertinence as he has not forgotten to the present day, nor is likely to forget.

It does not seem possible to acquit women, especially women of distinction and fashion, of indirect participation in most extensive acts of cruelty. I do not lay so much weight as some do upon their attendance at pigeon-shooting matches.

Many a fine lady would turn sick at the notion of seeing a chicken slaughtered for her own table, who would sit by and compliment men on their skill in riddling pigeons and doves. There are fine distinctions in matters of this sort. But what I chiefly refer to is the irresistible tendency of women to ornament their hats and bonnets with the wings of birds. We speak of being "as happy as a bird;" yet all over the world a shocking destruction of the most happy and beautiful little creatures which exist is occasioned by the vanity of women, and especially by those who may pretend to be the most educated and sensitive. There are women who seem to become hysterical at the very name of vivisection. Has it occurred to them that by doing away with the use of birds' wings and feathers they would prevent the lingering, painful deaths, not simply of scores, or hundreds, or thousands, but of millions of sensitive animals? We should always remember that for each hundred birds shot, killed, and secured, there are ten, twenty, or perhaps more, which lie fatally wounded for hours or even days.

In connection with this subject of cruelty, I confess that a disagreeable truth is perpetually forced upon my mind, namely, that the amusements of the lower classes are readily denounced as cruel, while the sports of the squire and the aristocrat are held up as noble, though involving far more pain to animals. At one time there were local by-laws of manors, providing that no bull should be killed before it had been baited for the amusement of the people. But about the beginning of this century, when the manorial system had quite broken down, it was discovered that bull-baiting was a brutal and demoralising exhibition, and it was forthwith suppressed. Yet to the present day it is thought a fine thing to turn out a stag and chase it for hours in mortal agony, afterwards caging it up for another run. Some years ago I saw a revolting account in the papers of the way in which some Yorkshire squires had similarly conducted a beaver hunt, if I recollect aright. Yet when we come to think about it, I do not know that, except in being unusual, there is anything worse in such hunts than in ordinary fox-hunting—"the noble science," as it is called.

What, I should like to know, is there noble in it, except that many "noblemen" pursue it? A score or two of strong men, mounted on the fleetest horses, with a pack of highly-trained hounds, pursue one wretched little palpitating animal. It is true that Professor Newman, in his recent interesting article on Cruelty, endeavours to show very ingeniously that hunted animals do not suffer much, the physical exertion banishing the anguish of fear. Swift animals, he considers, are made to run. The real dread of death, he thinks, is felt when we sit in ambush and hear our enemies, as Idomeneus in Homer said, compassing our death. But surely the hunted fox must suffer this too when he gets into cover, and hears the dogs snuffing around him, or when he runs to earth and has to be dug out. I am told, too, that a hunted animal, supposing him to escape death, suffers very severely from cramp in the overstrained muscles. I see nothing in fox-hunting to render it otherwise than highly cruel, except that it is "noble." I fear, too, that the principal difference to be drawn between coursing and baiting, is that the latter is the form of sport most likely to fall within the means of the lower classes.

From these and many other instances, which will readily suggest themselves, we may learn that the popular notions of cruelty depend in a comparatively slight degree upon the real amount of pain inflicted. The attitude of mind of the inflicter, the circumstances of the infliction, the degree or way in which the pain is made manifest, and especially the frequency with which the act has been done in past times, or the social grade of those by whom it is usually done, are all taken into account.

Cruelty is, in fact, a highly complex notion, involving several distinct elements involved together in a most subtle manner. It is only by the aid of the new sciences of Sociology and Anthropology—with the guidance, in short, of Mr. Spencer or Mr. Tylor—that we can attempt to explain the apparent inconsistencies which meet us on every side in moral and social questions of this kind. But we may perhaps classify the elements of cruelty under four principal heads, as follows:

Firstly, the actual physical pain inflicted.

Secondly, the motive or purpose of inflicting the pain, or rather of performing the action which produces pain.

Thirdly, the degree in which the action in question is habitual and familiar.

Fourthly, the manner in which the pain is expressed and the circumstances of its infliction impressed upon the imagination.

We might call these elements of cruelty respectively, the *physical*, the *moral*, the *sociological*, and the *psychological elements*. Different acts of cruelty involve these elements in the most various proportions. When hyænas were made to jump through blazing hoops, this was at once pronounced to be gross cruelty, because it conflicted with our notions of what is habitual and recognised. When a man was prosecuted in Scotland for barbarously beating some sporting dogs in the process of training them, the sheriff held that this was not cruelty, because you could not have sporting dogs without training them. Here the element of habit comes in palpably. Sporting dogs are required for man's amusement, and the leaping hyænas were also employed to amuse visitors to the menagerie. What then is the difference, except in the familiarity of the amusement, unless indeed we remember that sporting dogs are chiefly wanted by the aristocratic classes?

The country is shocked now to hear that horses have been occasionally tamed by electricity in Yorkshire. Here the sociological element is again predominant. Horses may be tamed by any of the methods approved by our forefathers, though there is no proof that they are less painful; but the notion of using an electric shock for the purpose has given a moral shock to the country. In the same way we may explain the grotesqueness of the proposal made in that remarkable work, "The Unseen Universe," to punish criminals by the electric battery. You may starve a criminal, shut him up in a dark cell, or tear his back with the cat, but you must not do anything which conflicts so much with our notions of the proper and habitual as to call in the aid of science. It may be that electricity would give the most deterrent effect with the least permanent injury; but it would still be cruel on the sociological ground.

The psychological element in cruelty has regard to the degree in which the pain of the animal is made apparent to the spectator, and forced upon his imagination. There is a curious instance to this effect in the life of William Roscoe,[*] who tells us that in early life he spent many hours in strolling along the shore of the Mersey, or in fishing. But on one occasion, as he says in his own words, " I determined to become a sportsman; and having procured a gun, and found an unfortunate thrush perched on a branch of a tree, I brought him to the ground with fatal aim; but I was so horrified and disgusted with the agonies which I saw him endure in death, that I have never since repeated the experiment." William Roscoe, then, drew the line of cruelty between fish and fowl. The helpless flopping and struggling of the hooked fish did not impress upon him the sense of pain with sufficient acuteness to overpower the satisfaction of success. But the writhing of a tortured bird was an expression of suffering too strong to bear. I believe that much of the obloquy so wrongly cast upon Dr. Ferrier arose from his operating upon monkeys, whose grimaces, as described by him, approached too nearly to a human form. That this is so we may perhaps infer from the indignation expended upon the case of the unfortunate patient experimented on by an American medical man, as described in *The Spectator* of March 20th, 1875, and discussed in subsequent numbers. The woman was dying of a mortal disease, her brain was already exposed, she consented to the experiments, which were also painless. Yet the idea of sticking needles into her brain and exciting spasmodic movements and grimaces by electricity was held to be so cruel, although painless, that the operator left the country. Cruelty, then, does not necessarily involve the infliction of any appreciable pain; it may consist in the production of expressions which merely suggest ideas of pain. The psychological element of cruelty may, then, become so important as itself

[*] "The Life of William Roscoe," by his son, Henry Roscoe. 1833. Vol. i. p. 11.

to constitute cruelty almost entirely. It is not the knowledge, in a logical sort of way, that pain is needlessly and wantonly inflicted upon the lower animals which excites popular indignation, otherwise why does the sporting spirit meet with approval rather than disgust? Cruel actions, according to popular esteem, are simply those which bring the fact and intensity of pain too much before the imagination. It is something in the same way that we are more affected by hearing of one man killed half a mile off, than of ten thousand people perishing in an unknown part of China or South America.

The same perplexing difference of sentiments will be found to occur again as regards the rat-catching business. It is well known that there is a regular trade in live rats, which are caught in cage-traps, and then supplied at regular market prices to dog-fanciers, who want either to train young ratting dogs or to exhibit the powers of their pets. A great many people would call this traffic in rats a base, cruel thing; but this can hardly be on account of physical pain caused to the rats. They can suffer but little in the cage-traps, and a skilful ratting-dog disposes of a rat at a single toss. The same people who would denounce the cruelty of ratting never bestow a thought upon those dreadful serrated steel traps, actuated by a powerful spring, which catch the unhappy animal by any part of his body—head, trunk, legs, or tail—which happens to be within reach. Often must an animal caught in such a trap suffer for hours, and even for days, torments quite equal to those of the vivisection table without chloroform, the pangs of hunger being superadded. In these days of inventive progress it would be very easy to devise traps which would kill rats and mice instantaneously and with certainty. If the Society for the Prevention of Cruelty to Animals has offered prizes for the invention of such traps, or has taken any steps to reduce the immense amount of pain caused by the present traps, such efforts have not come to my knowledge.

Turning now to the Report of the Royal Commission on Vivisection, my own impression is very strong to the effect that no abuses of the practice of any importance have been proved. The rumours and hearsay evidence about the frequent private vivisections by students did not usually bear cross-examination, though in one town it is clear that a kind of small club of students had been experimenting. The story of the old horse kept for the purpose of practising operations in a veterinary school is also an unpleasant one (Questions 5,037–5,043). But if we allow that there was some cruelty in this single case, I do not think there is any need to expend much sentimental indignation upon it. The witness who made this case known was obliged to allow in his answers to other questions (5,052–5,054) that he had himself performed a far more painful operation on horses, namely, that of firing them without always taking the trouble to give them chloroform. The same witness denounced " the fearful cruelty " with which a particular dog had been treated by some students. Examination, however, showed (Questions 5,009–5,030) that the intention had been to kill the dog in the manner usually considered the least objectionable, namely, by the administration of prussic acid. The dose having perhaps been insufficient, the dog soon afterwards showed signs of life, and some students tried the effect of a little ammonia as an antidote. Having become partially sensible, it was promptly killed by a blow on the head. The dog probably suffered no pain, or as little as might be; and I see nothing so cruel in it as for a sportsman to shoot a bird, and then depart without taking the trouble to ascertain whether it is killed or only wounded.

A great deal of attention was given to the case of certain dogs which had been killed by strychnine in the presence of medical students, for the purpose of demonstrating the action of that fearful poison. As regards the physical pain caused, I see no grounds for complaint, while it is permitted for the squatters of Queensland to kill the native dogs in large numbers by strychnine. If the use of this poison is in itself cruel, then the Society for the Prevention of Cruelty should take means to prohibit its general use. It is on moral and psychological grounds, then, that the exhibition of the effects of the poison are to be objected to, if at all. But nobody denied that a medical man ought to learn the symptoms of strychnine poisoning, which might not only be met with in practice, but are very instructive in other respects. It was given in evidence by several high authorities that no one could adequately conceive the action of strychnine without witnessing it. So that the question really is whether medical students are to be prevented from gaining necessary knowledge in the most effective way, because it will harden and sear their moral natures to see an animal killed for the purpose.

It seems to me, speaking as one having no practical acquaintance with such matters, that if the exhibition of poisoned dogs is objectionable, then a great part of the clinical instruction of medical students is objectionable. Are students, for instance, to be allowed to study patients dying of hydrophobia or other dreadful diseases? To allow the general public heedlessly to see such painful sights would be disgusting, simply because it would be encouraging a morbid pleasure in the witnessing of pain. But it is a necessary part of the education of a medical man, not only to learn the nature of the diseases, but to harden his nerves, and to acquire the power of encountering the most dreadful cases of human suffering without losing his presence of mind. It is in clinical practice he acquires this power, and it seems to me out of the question, that after coolly scrutinising human suffering in all its worst phases, his moral nature will be destroyed by seeing the poisoning of a dog. No doubt it is a question admitting of discussion how far the constant witnessing of pain blunts the moral nature. But so far as I can judge of the medical men with whom I am acquainted, their moral natures have sustained no injuries. On the contrary, they are in general among the most humane of men, and all their affections and sympathies have been in no degree weakened by the painful scenes they constantly witness. Now, if this be so, I am quite unable to see how the exhibition, in a reasonable and necessary degree, of experiments upon the lower animals, conducted in as painless a way as the nature of the experiment allows, can have the dreadful moral consequences attributed to it by the anti-vivisectionists. As regards the physical element of cruelty, the student may well reflect that infinitely greater amounts of pain are daily inflicted, with the approval of the community, by the sportsman and the ratcatcher. As regards the moral element, he may feel assured that an able and experienced teacher would not exhibit useless experiments.

There is one thing which I much regret in this bitter discussion, namely, that questionable motives are imputed to those who practise vivisection for the purpose of research. Like most warm and intemperate partisans, anti-vivisectionists can see no good in those they pursue, and failing to convince people that experiments on animals are useless, they wish to make them out to be cruel on the second or moral ground, namely, that the experiments are performed merely for the purpose of gaining reputation or "notoriety," as they call it dyslogistically. They would have us believe that men like Dr. Ferrier or Dr. Michael Foster, although they may be discovering truths of some importance to suffering humanity, are not really doing it from humane motives. But can anything be more gratuitous and unfair? In the absence of any special reason, I altogether question our right to pry into private motives. If the experiments are well performed, and the results are, or are likely to be, in a fair proportion of cases, useful to mankind, I think that the private motives of the observer are not a matter for public animadversion. The law distinctly takes this view, allowing the fullest freedom of criticism upon an author's works, but treating remarks upon his moral character and private affairs in a very different way.

But assuming that we must discuss the question of motives, what can be more gratuitous than to question the pure intentions of vivisectors, while we leave physicists, chemists, geologists, and all other classes of discoverers, unchallenged? Can it be that a selfish love of notoriety is the spring of those exertions which have benefited mankind with all the progress of the sciences and arts? I have been astonished to see that one witness before the Commission, himself a scientific man of the highest standing, holds all original research to be selfish and demoralising. He said (Question 1,287), speaking of vivisection: "It is amenable to abuse when employed for the purpose of research; and I must say that, with regard to all absorbing studies, that is the besetting sin of them, and of original research, that they lift a man so entirely above the ordinary sphere of daily duty that they betray him into selfishness and unscrupulous neglect of duty." And again he says: "I mean to say that vivisection, in its application to research, may be somewhat more demoralising than other kinds of devotion to research; every kind of original research being a gratification of self, and liable to develop selfishness, which of course is the root of all unscrupulousness." Did ever a scientific man take so extraordinary a view of the moral aspects of the work in which he was engaged? I had previously been under the impression that, of all kinds of occupations, the labours of the scientific discoverer are least open to the charge of selfishness. The labours of the engineer, lawyer, banker, merchant, are not specially selfish, but they often result in the acquisition of so much riches that the individual may fairly aspire to the pleasure of shooting his own partridges, or even renting a grouse moor. But I should like to know how far the salary received by a professor of practical physiology, in respect of his skilful cutting up of dogs and cats, would go, after the payment of household expenses, towards the purchase of the privilege of slaughtering birds in the fashionable way. The vivisector, like most discoverers in pure science, must look for his reward in the pleasure of pursuing knowledge for its own sake, or for the sake of the millions of men who will in the future be benefited by his discoveries. Of course, I do not mean to say that the vivisector has clearly before his mind in each experiment the good of mankind generally. Men are usually driven to work for a great end by some instinctive tendency, some pleasure in the action itself, or some minor motive, just as the bee gathers a store of honey, not because he is conscious of its future utility, but because it is agreeable to gather it. We approve the industrious actions of the bee because they lead to a useful end; and it is quite sufficient defence of the vivisector's character that his labours are likely to result in the diminution of disease and suffering.

Moreover, suppose that the vivisector is consciously urged on by the love of reputation or fame, I have yet to learn that there is anything immoral or selfish in such love. Milton has described the love of fame as "that last infirmity of noble minds." To call it the love of notoriety is to use a question-begging epithet, assuming that vivisection is a cruel and morally bad practice. Notoriety is reputation gained by bad means, or those injurious to the community; fame is reputation gained by good means, or those beneficial to the community. There are not the slightest grounds upon which to attribute notoriety to the vivisector, while we attribute fame to the great statesman, orator, artist, engineer. And the desire of reputation, too, may be merely the desire of means towards an unselfish end. One who aspires to repeat the labours of a Harvey, a Jenner, or a Simpson, might well adopt the words which Tennyson has put into the mouth of Merlin:

> Fame with men,
> Being but ampler means to serve mankind,
> Should have small rest or pleasure in herself,
> But work as vassal to the larger love,
> That dwarfs the petty love of one to one.
> Use gave me Fame at first, and Fame again
> Increasing gave me Use. Lo, there my boon!
> What other? for men sought to prove me vile.
> * * * * *
> Right well I know that Fame is half disfame,
> Yet needs must work my work.

Looking to all the circumstances, we must conclude that this agitation against vivisection consists in a kind of sentimental frenzy, excited in persons of peculiar susceptibility by the minute descriptions of novel and sometimes painful operations described in books on practical physiology. The actual amount of pain inflicted cannot really be the ground of agitation, because, on any supposition, the physical pain needlessly inflicted by sportsmen, ratcatchers, and others, is infinitely greater. As I have already maintained, the moral element of cruelty is altogether wanting in vivisection—in all but a very few cases. It is merely the novelty of the thing to people's minds, the apparent villany and cool-bloodedness of cutting live animals, which excites the imagination. Sociology and psychology enable us perfectly to comprehend the frenzy of the Anti-Vivisection Society, but science and common sense will teach us to bear a slight wound to our sympathetic feelings that we may secure immeasurable blessings for future generations. Vaccination has already saved more lives than all the wars of Napoleon destroyed. Chloroform has prevented inconceivable amounts of pain. From the continued application of experiment to physiology we may look for other gifts such as these. "Where the pursuit of scientific truth and common compassion come into collision, it seems to me that the ends of civilisation, no less than of morality, require us to be guided by the latter or higher principle." So says Mr. Hutton, in his separate Report as member of the Commission; but the pursuit of scientific truth is the highest and most civilising and most compassionate work in which a man can engage. If he holds that we may not cause pain to a dog that we may save greater pain to a thousand human beings, then further argument would be useless. Mr. Hutton also seems to think that it is more justifiable to make experiments upon sheep, in a way likely to benefit other sheep, than if we experiment purely in the interest of man. We may injure one sensitive creature for the good of other creatures of the same rank, but not for the good of creatures of higher or, I suppose, lower rank. If this be his meaning, I can only allow that he possesses moral sentiments of a kind to which I am wholly a stranger.

I do not believe that there is any need for legislation in this matter at all. It is undesirable that students should privately practise vivisection, and it is most desirable that anæsthetics should be employed to the utmost possible extent; but after the attention of the public has been so strongly drawn to the subject, it is very unlikely that the slight abuses shown to have occurred will be repeated. The professors of practical physiology will have every reason to keep a watch, and they are more likely to be able to restrain their students than the police or the societies; but if prosecutions like that of M. Magnan are to be repeated, it will be necessary to protect vivisection by legislation, giving the duly qualified dissector a license to make experiments, somewhat as provided in Dr. Playfair's bill.

In view of the infinite benefits to mankind and the lower animals which we may confidently anticipate from this tardy application of true scientific method to the phenomena of life, it is altogether out of the question that we should attempt to repress or hinder vivisection. Legislation should be directed to legalising the practice on the part of those who are most likely to conduct it usefully, skilfully, and, as far as circumstances will allow, painlessly.

ON THE UNITED KINGDOM ALLIANCE AND ITS PROSPECTS OF SUCCESS.*

  I. Arguments against the probability of Success of the Alliance.
 II. Impossibility of predicting the Action of Ratepayers under the proposed Act.
III. Comparative Numbers of Electors required to pass the Permissive Bill and to put it in Action.
 IV. Action of a Prohibitory Liquor Law.
  V. Votes of the House of Commons on the Permissive Bill.
 VI. General Effects of the Action of the Alliance.
VII. Attitude of the Alliance towards other Bodies.
VIII. Its mistaken general Policy.
 IX. Practicable Measures for the Diminution of Intemperance.

I.

IN October last, the Bishop of Manchester delivered a speech at the Annual Meeting of the Church of England Temperance Society, in which he expressed his intention of voting in favour of the Permissive Prohibitory Liquor Bill, if it should ever reach the House of Lords. His Lordship, if he was correctly reported, told us that "no doubt the most effective remedy that was suggested at the present time, was the Permissive Bill;" but he went on to explain that we must not expect the Bill to become law "within any calculable time," and he added his opinion that, if it did become law,

* Read at the Manchester Statistical Society, March 8th, 1876.

it would certainly produce a chronic condition of tumult and anarchy.* It may well be questioned how a Bill, which is not to become law within any calculable time, and is then to occasion a chronic condition of tumult and anarchy, can be considered the most effective remedy for intemperance at the present time. An effective remedy surely means one that can be carried into effect, and will then effect its intended purpose.

The Bishop's speech brought strongly to my mind an argument against the policy and conduct of the United Kingdom Alliance, which for some years previously I had frequently considered. Before the Alliance can carry into effect their benevolent intentions, they must bring about three events, which seem to me substantially separate and independent. First, they must pass their Act; secondly, they must get localities to adopt it; thirdly, they must carry out the provisions of the law in those localities. Success in any one or two of these steps is useless and worse than useless without success in all three. But then the probabilities accumulate in a very serious manner against any course of action which thus involves several independent contingencies. This may be illustrated by an imaginary calculation. Taking a view of the case which many persons will think far too favourable to the Alliance, let us suppose that there is one chance in ten in favour of carrying the Permissive Bill during the next twenty years; supposing it carried, let us take one chance in five as the probability that it would be widely adopted by localities, after the interval of tumult and anarchy predicted by the Bishop. The Act being at last in force, let

* The following is a quotation from the Bishop's speech, as reported in *The Manchester Guardian*: "Supposing the Bill were passed, he looked with extreme apprehension at the chronic condition of tumult and anarchy which would be certain to prevail in attempting to carry it out in the large and populous communities. He could not conceive any state of things more terrible than possibly would ensue from the strife which would be engendered by that measure. He thought public opinion must ripen very much more fully than it had yet done before there was any chance of the Permissive Bill becoming an effective law; and he believed Sir Wilfrid Lawson felt that himself."

us take one chance in two as representing the probability that it will work satisfactorily, and suppress excessive drinking. If these events are independent and separate, we get the probability that they will all happen in succession in a manner favourable to the purposes of the Alliance, by multiplying together the separate probabilities. This gives us *one chance in a hundred as expressing the probability that the well-meaning supporters of the Permissive Bill will ever achieve in this way the desire of their hearts.*

This view of the matter, having been stated in a letter published by *The Manchester Examiner and Times* of October 28th, 1875, drew forth several able replies from members of the Alliance, among which the letters of the Rev. Mr. Steinthal and Mr. William Hoyle were the most formidable. Both of these gentlemen strike at the very root of my argument by asserting that the probabilities are not really independent of each other. "In England," as Mr. Steinthal says, "No measure can pass the Legislature which is not backed by public opinion, and the agitation which is being carried on throughout the United Kingdom in favour of the Permissive Bill is at one and the same time preparing the localities to try its beneficent provisions. . . . The Executive of the Alliance know that there are many places where the Bill would be immediately applied if it were to be passed next year." Mr. Hoyle says, nearly to the same effect, "It will be impossible for the Permissive Bill to pass the House of Commons, unless the country generally be educated upon the question, and the education which secures the passing of the Bill in the House will to a very general extent ensure its passing in the country."

While admitting that these members of the Alliance have selected the right mode of meeting my argument, I am still disposed to regard my view as substantially correct. It was not adopted by me on the spur of the moment, but had been maturely considered during several years.* I have, therefore,

---

* Since publishing the letter in *The Examiner and Times*, I have become acquainted with the publications of Mr. Joseph Livesey on the same subject. These are entitled: "Free and Friendly Remarks upon

sought this opportunity of giving a fuller answer to my critics than would be possible in a letter to a newspaper.

I do not pretend to say that the three events in question, the passing of the Permissive Bill, its adoption by localities, and its successful operation, are wholly and absolutely independent events; no doubt, in a majority of cases, those who vote for the Bill do so on the belief that it will be carried out, and then be successful; but so wide are the discrepancies, especially in legislation, between what man proposes and what he can effect, that I believe there is substantial independence.

The terms of the Permissive Bill appear to me to confess this independence, and even to take advantage of it. If the Bill cannot be passed before the people are educated to accept it, what is the use of making it permissive, and interposing the vote of local ratepayers? There are obvious objections to the partial application of such an Act, and one parish which maintains its public-houses will, to a great extent, defeat the benefits of prohibition in the neighbouring parishes. Why not then make the Bill a Compulsory Prohibitory Bill as it was in the early days of the Alliance? Because, as the Alliance very well knows, there would not be the slightest chance of passing such a Bill. There is a delightful uncertainty as to what would or would not happen after the passing of the Permissive Bill, and many contribute to the funds of the Alliance with the vague idea that they are promoting temperance, who do not really bring home to their minds what would be involved in the immediate suppression of the public-houses in their own borough or district.

II.

I will speak presently of the probability that the Permissive Bill, as at present drafted, ever will pass the House

the Permissive Bill, Temperance Legislation, and the Alliance;" Preston, 1862; and "True Temperance Teaching, showing the Errors of the Alliance and the Permissive Bill." London, Manchester, and Preston, 1873. (Heywood.)

I am glad to find that my opinions about the Alliance, although independently formed, are in accordance with those of one of the oldest and perhaps the most respected Temperance Reformer in the kingdom.

of Commons; but I deny that, if passed, we could in the least predict the action of the ratepayers. Nothing is more uncertain and inexplicable than popular votes, especially those in which the mass of the population have the predominating voice. Even after the poll is published, no one can surely tell why the electors so voted. No one will ever be able to show by what precise influences Mr. Gladstone's Government was driven from power in 1874. It may have been a genuine Conservative reaction, or disgust at the sudden dissolution, or the combination of the publicans, or more probably a union of these and other causes; but my point is that no one could have calculated upon the event. All that we can be sure of in popular votes is that we cannot estimate the motives in action, or the results to be expected. The Alliance say they have ascertained, by house to house inquiry, that in some places two-thirds or more of the ratepayers are willing to vote for prohibition. But I attach little importance to such inquiries. It is really less trouble to sign a voting paper or a petition than to refuse, when the person, if he knows what he is signing, must be aware that no practical result will follow the Act. In the case of Bristol, the publicans showed how readily they also could get signatures. It is one thing to sign papers which can have no effect—good or bad—during the present generation; it would be quite a different thing to sign such papers if the immediate result was to be the dreadful state of tumult and anarchy in the neighbourhood, so confidently expected by the Bishop of Manchester.

I am inclined to fear that on this point the Bishop is right. There is undoubtedly a substratum of English population always ready for riot, if any pretext can be found. And what better pretext could be given to them than the closing of their public-houses? The very number of the drunken is a main obstacle to sudden prohibition; it would be the easiest thing in the world for publicans to stir up such a tumult in boroughs or parishes adopting prohibition as would effectually deter the ratepayers of other parishes from voting for prohibition. Does the Bishop seriously believe that, if the application of the Act gave rise to tumult and anarchy, two-thirds of the ratepayers would be found willing to render the anarchy chronic by continuing to veto the sale of liquors in small quantities, while the more wealthy voters were for the most part consuming liquors with their accustomed freedom? The application of such a law would give too good a pretext for disorder, and I altogether deny that the inquiries of the Alliance give any ground for predicting the action of electors, in face of the various events which might happen. Moreover, the events which would follow the passing of the Bill would probably induce Parliament to repeal the Act with great expedition, as in the case of Colonel Wilson Patten's Sunday Closing Act. Various instances might be quoted in which too stringent measures for the repression of drinking have been followed by a disastrous reaction, and if we could, for the sake of argument, imagine the Permissive Bill carried, a reaction in public opinion and legislation would be almost certain to occur.

III.

In another respect there is a great difference between passing the Bill and putting it in action. The Alliance say that they must educate the country before they can pass the Act; but the Act is passed by a bare majority, elected by only a fraction of the whole ratepayers of the country. The application of the Act would require the vote of two-thirds of the ratepayers. The Alliance have in late years adopted what seems to me the fatal and most blamable policy of recommending their followers to vote only for Members of Parliament who will pledge themselves to support the Bill, irrespective of other social or political questions. It is evident, then, that if the Alliance had in rather more than half the constituencies of the United Kingdom a majority of loyal supporters, they could carry their Bill. It follows that one quarter of the whole number of electors, if disposed in a certain way among the constituencies, could certainly pass the Bill. We should have to allow, on the one hand, for the fact that the supporters of the Alliance are scattered in various proportions through all the constituencies of the kingdom, and, on the other, for the vast number of voters who do not go to the poll, and for those who, without approving of the Permissive Bill, vote on other grounds for supporters of it. No calculations on this subject could have the least pretensions to exactness; but, making the best judgment I can, I should say that, with one-quarter of the electors at their back, the Alliance could carry their Bill, and probably a less number would suffice. To carry the law into general operation, however, would require a majority of two-thirds in every parish or voting district. Now, two-thirds is two and two-thirds times as great as a quarter, and it comes to this, that the Alliance must educate the people between two and three times as much to put their law into action as to get it passed. This is one of the many grounds on which I would assert, in opposition to Mr. Steinthal and Mr. Hoyle, that the accumulation of probabilities is against the Alliance.

IV.

I decline to enter upon the question whether a prohibitory law, if really put in operation, would work successfully and diminish intemperance in a great degree. To adduce evidence for or against the probability of such a result would be quite impossible within the necessary limits imposed upon this paper. I take it for granted that anyone is justified in entertaining doubts upon the subject, and I think it is very favourable to the Alliance to assign one-half as the probability of prohibition suppressing drunkenness. The evidence derived from America or the colonies upon this subject is of the most conflicting character, and even if we allow that the closing of public-houses has been a blessing in one or two States of the Union, and in many rural parishes of England, it does not in the least follow that the same measure will be practicable and beneficial in great cities and among a population of very different nature. In countries where the people are educated up to the point of accepting prohibition by a very large majority, prohibition would probably work well; but I deny that the main body of the English people are anywhere near this point. There could be no objection to the Alliance educating people as much as they like or can; what I object to is the obstacles which they place in the way of more practicable measures, while they are striving after an object which cannot be carried out "in any calculable time."

v.

To judge of the probability that the House of Commons will pass the Permissive Bill, we must look at the results of the divisions which have taken place. They are as follows:

Votes on the Permissive Bill.

	Without pairs and tellers.		With pairs and tellers.	
	For.	Against.	For.	Against.
1864	35	292	40	297
1869	87	193	94	200
1870	90	121	115	146
1871	124	196	136	208
1872*	—	—	—	—
1873	81	321	90	330
1874	75	301	92	318
1875	86	371	94	379

Probably the fairest mode of measuring the preponderance of votes against the Bill is to calculate the ratio of all who voted against it to those who voted for it, which gives the following results:

Ratios of numbers of opponents to supporters.

1869	2·13	1873	3·67
1870	1·27	1874	3·46
1871	1·53	1875	4·03

The votes in the three last divisions, especially in the last of all, seem to me to show a strong desire on the part of a vast majority of the House of Commons to convince the Alliance of the hopelessness of its agitation. Up to, and perhaps including the year 1871, the prospects of ultimate success were flattering but deceptive; the supporters were continually rising in numbers, and their opponents were stationary or fluctuating. But in 1873, 74, and 75, we find

* In 1872 the Bill was talked out, and no division took place.

the supporters reduced to their earlier amount, being almost exactly the same in 1875 as in 1869, and in 1874 actually twelve less, while the opponents of the Bill have presented themselves in little less than double their former numbers.

If an unprejudiced statistician or meteorologist, accustomed to the examination of varying phenomena, were to examine these numbers, he would unquestionably conclude that the Alliance was a phenomenon which had passed its maximum, and was on the wane. For nearly twenty-three years the Alliance has always been making progress according to the statements of its own organs, and yet, between 1871 and 1873, we find its supporters in Parliament reduced by 30 per cent., and its opponents increased by 90 per cent. The last three divisions, and especially the last of all, evince a fixed determination on the part of the vast majority of the House not to pass the Bill, and not to allow any encouragement for the hope that it ever will be passed. Having regard to the hopeless and obstructive position of the Alliance, I may venture to express a hope that the next division will even more unequivocally show the opinion of the House upon the subject.

VI.

It may be said in favour of the Alliance that, even if its Bill never be passed, the efforts made to pass it enlist the interests of many persons in the temperance cause, and lead to the passing of minor restrictions on the liquor trade. The Alliance has, no doubt, made itself the head and front of the temperance bodies generally; it is a rallying point for all who are earnestly desirous of remedying the main cause of evil in the country. Members of Parliament and even Governments which will not actually vote for the Permissive Bill will yet, it may be urged, be induced to concede important measures against the publicans, and the publicans on their part will the more readily accept legislation in fear of the power of so formidable a body as the Alliance. But it is quite a question to my mind whether the agitation kept up by the Alliance does not act in just the opposite manner.

Surely, as regards the publicans, the action of the Alliance is most unfortunate. It teaches them to look upon all temperance reformers as utter enemies, and the struggle as one without quarter. The Alliance wish to suppress the trade of the publicans in a sudden and arbitrary manner, and they offer no compensation to those who have in many cases spent large sums in buildings and trade fixtures, in a business licensed by the Government. It is true that licenses are withdrawable on proof of delinquencies, and are only granted for a year; but there is the greatest possible difference between the mode in which licenses have hitherto been terminated and that in which the Alliance proposes to revoke them. Vested interests are, no doubt, a very great obstacle to all reforms, and any precedent which recognises their existence, and affords compensation, throws so much more weight upon future reformers. But I fear that sufficient precedents have already been created. The great sum paid to slave-owners in the British Colonies was quite a case in point. Military officers have been compensated to a very large amount for money invested in the purchase of commissions even beyond the terms of the regulations. Before the telegraph companies were suppressed they received two or three times the value of their property, the greater part being avowedly claimed for the goodwill of their business. Now, publicans may be good men or bad men, but at any rate they are men, and subjects of the Queen, and they have families to support, and can we suppose or expect that they will acquiesce in their own suppression and ruin? I must express very much doubt whether it would be right and just to suppress a trade in the way proposed by the Alliance without some provision for compensation. But if the ratepayers before voting for prohibition are aware that it will add sixpence or ninepence to the rates, I should like to know where they will get their majority of two-thirds. A rate of not more than a penny has proved in most places a sufficient bar to the adoption of that most inoffensive law—the Public Libraries Act. In the parish of Withington, where I reside, a bare majority of the ratepayers could never be got to vote for so necessary an expense as the lighting of the streets. This has lately been done under the authority of the Local Government Board; but I regret to say that the ratepayers still decline to incur the expense of mending the roads.

But whatever ratepayers may think about the Permissive Prohibitory Law, there is no doubt as to what publicans think. To them, if put into operation, it would be Domesday, and the result of the persistent agitation of the Alliance is to make the publicans band themselves together in opposition to all reforms. The publicans, like every other large body of men, include all kinds of characters, but I refuse to believe that they are wholly unreasonable and unwilling to acknowledge the evils which flow from their trade when badly regulated. If assured that license reform was not intended as a step towards their suppression and ruin, but that it would tend to the elimination of the less respectable members of the trade, I cannot believe that the publicans generally would oppose reform as bitterly as they do at present. The true mode of reforming the sale of liquor is to diminish competition, and to weed out the ill-conducted houses, until the value of the remaining licenses has been so far raised that their holders will not dare and will not have sufficient inducement to tolerate abuses.

VII.

The following are the terms in which the Alliance describes its attitude both towards the publicans and towards other schemes of licensing reform: "As the United Kingdom Alliance is constituted for the annihilation of the liquor traffic, and not for its sanction and regulation, your committee cannot, in loyalty to the trust imposed upon them, enter into any licensing scheme whatever; and they are bound, in self-defence and consistency, to look with coldness and even suspicion upon any proposals that favour the obnoxious policy of forcing licenses into communities in defiance of the people's wishes and petitions."* Thus the Alliance distinctly and expressly places itself in opposition not only to the publicans

* Nineteenth Report of the Executive Committee of the United Kingdom Alliance, 1870-71, p. 34.

as a body, but to all who propose in any way to sanction the sale of liquors.

The matter has been made all the worse by the recommendation to vote for no Member of Parliament who refuses to support the Bill. The adoption of such a policy must surely be considered as an act of desperation, but in any case, it cannot be sufficiently reprobated and repudiated by all who wish well to the progress of civilisation. Compromise is of the very essence of legislative change, and as society becomes more diverse and complicated, compromise becomes more and more indispensable. It is the only *modus vivendi*, as tastes and opinions gradually diverge. It need hardly be said that reforms of all kinds must be immensely retarded if the supporters of each measure insist upon getting their own scheme first through the House of Commons. Mr. Bright happily protested against trying to drive half-a-dozen omnibuses abreast through Temple Bar, but this is what it will come to if we have many bodies like the Alliance, each trying to have the road to itself. It is especially unfortunate when the first one is a heavy, impracticable machine, which can neither go forward nor be got out of the way. Yet such I believe the Permissive Prohibitory Bill to be, and the proceedings of the Alliance altogether strike me as the best possible example of *how not to do things* in legislation.

On these grounds I hold that the United Kingdom Alliance is the worst existing obstacle to temperance reform in the kingdom. It absorbs and expends the resources of the temperance army on a hopeless siege, and by proclaiming no quarter, it drives the enemy into fierce opposition to a man. The Alliance has already been in existence and active operation for twenty-two or nearly twenty-three years; it has had the most zealous leaders, and the most faithful followers; it has spent great sums of money, probably greater sums than any Association of the kind ever spent before, amounting to something like a quarter of a million sterling; its publications have been sown broadcast over the whole country; its petitions to Parliament have been numberless; and every Member of Parliament and every body of electors have been vexed by its persistent agitations.   Yet I venture to say that it is as far from its goal as ever.

VIII.

Before concluding I will go a step farther and assert that the whole policy and principles of action of such a body as the United Kingdom Alliance are mistaken and inexpedient. They set forth a definite scheme in a Bill, and demand this or nothing. The remarkable success of the Anti-Corn Law League has had, I believe, one evil effect. It has led many zealous people to believe that if they only band themselves together with sufficient determination, if they deliver enough speeches, scatter enough tracts, in short agitate with sufficient energy, they will ultimately carry public opinion with them. But we must not argue too readily from analogy in such cases. The Anti-Corn Law League aimed at an object which could unquestionably be effected by the mere passing of an Act. There was no permissive legislation in it. The actual results of the abolition of duty on corn were as well understood by economists and by all unprejudiced persons of moderate intelligence as any question in social science can be. The mass of the people were readily induced to join in a cry for cheap bread, even if they did not clearly understand how it was to be secured. The struggle was thus one of the mass of the people against a body of landlords taking a selfish and mistaken view of their own interests. The success of the League was substantially accomplished in five or seven years.

In the case of the United Kingdom Alliance everything is different. The real struggle would not begin until the Bill was passed; the mass of the people would in most cases be against the law, and the operation of the law, as I maintain, must be altogether a matter of uncertainty. When we know so many useful legislative changes which might be passed, and which would be sure to have a more or less favourable effect, it seems to me a most deplorable fact that twenty-two years should have been spent upon one impracticable Bill. So considerable are the chances against the success of any legislation, as could easily be proved by an examination of the statute book, that we should not spend a quarter of a century on any one law, unless, perhaps, we are perfectly assured of the success of that law when passed. It would not be difficult to point out certain definite principles which should guide a wise reforming legislator in the selection of the laws he should advocate. Solon, when asked whether he had given the Athenians the best laws he could devise, replied: "Ay, the best laws that they could receive." He has often been blamed, but the progress of Sociology is establishing his wisdom. We now know that laws are not good or bad with respect to any invariable standard, but in reference to the changing character of society and man. The successful reformer is one who sees for what legislative change the people are ripe, and concentrates the popular energy upon it. But the members of the Alliance are wrong at every point. They try to force upon the country a law for which it is certainly not ripe; they absorb forces which might be most usefully employed in immediate action upon a scheme which, if carried at all, must be a thing for the future. They allow that they must educate the people for the measure (this is admitted by Mr. Steinthal and Mr. Hoyle), but they confuse together the agitation and the education. It is one thing to educate people for a future change of legislation; it is another thing to ask them to pass the law next year, and in the meantime to look coldly upon all other projects of reform.

IX.

There is no use attempting, at the end of this paper, to discuss in detail the measures which will probably be passed by the general consent of the community as soon as the Permissive Bill is out of the way. Were that Bill a forlorn hope—the only measure by which we could hope to repress drunkenness—I should be among its warmest advocates; but, as a matter of fact, it stands in the way of some dozen reasonable and practicable proposals. The Sunday Closing Bill, if passed, would probably decrease drunkenness by a fourth or fifth part, without interfering in any appreciable degree with the due freedom or convenience of any person. The refusal of all new licenses to publicans or beer-shop keepers, so long as the number of the houses exceeds one to five hundred inhabitants, seems to me a very proper and workable measure. It was among the proposals of the National Union for the Suppression of Intemperance. The rule might have to be relaxed in the case of thinly populated districts, along the course of important highways, and in great centres of trade and traffic, and various details would have to be considered relating to the boundaries of districts, and the mode of estimating the population—whether, for instance, by the last census, or, as I should propose, by the number of houses on the rate books, counting five inhabitants for each house. But I see no considerable difficulty in applying such a maximum to strengthen the hands of the magistrates in their use of the licensing power.

Another measure which appears to me absolutely indispensable, and to admit of no delay, is the entire revocation of grocers' licenses. The granting of such licenses was no doubt a well-meant step; it was supposed that people would be drawn away from the public-house by the facility with which they could obtain liquors of better quality to consume at home. But I fear that for one who is drawn away from the public-house, twenty or fifty will ultimately be drawn to it. The mistake thus committed was only exceeded by that of the Beershops Act, another well-intended measure, which was to wean people from the use of strong liquors by the facility of getting weak ones. There is the most overwhelming evidence to show that free trade and competition in the liquor trade lead to disastrous results. It is difficult to imagine how anyone could ever have looked upon facilities for the distribution of liquors as a mode of diminishing intemperance. Competition in all other trades tends to the healthy development of the trade, and the consequent increase of the quantity sold. But in the case of liquors our object is to decrease, not to increase the sale, and we must therefore take the opposite course, and place obstacles in the way of the trade which will make liquors dearer and more troublesome to get. At present the only difficulty is to avoid buying them, so numerous are the shops at which they are pressed upon the customer. It is worthy of consideration whether there ought not to be an inflexible rule established that, where any kind of intoxicating liquor is sold, no other commodity shall be sold for consumption off the premises. I am inclined to think that the trade should be restricted to two classes of dealers—first, licensed victuallers and innkeepers selling mainly, if not exclusively, for consumption on the premises, and selling nothing else except the ordinary victuals for guests; and secondly, beer, wine, and spirit merchants, allowed to sell liquors in any quantity for consumption off the premises.

I may also suggest that the time has probably arrived when a further addition may safely be made to the duty on spirits. The last change was made in 1860, when the duty on British spirits and on rum was raised from 8s. to 10s. per gallon, and that on brandy was reduced from 15s. to 10s. 5d. per gallon. We should remember that since 1860 prices in general have been rising much, the wealth of the purchasers has been considerably increased, as indeed is sufficiently shown by the augmented consumption. With the increased efficiency and number of the police force there can be no fear of any serious increase of smuggling or illicit distilling. An addition of 2s. per gallon to the duty on spirits would produce a handsome sum for the Chancellor of the Exchequer, and would at the same time aid in repressing the worst form of drinking.

The proposals of the License Amendment League of Manchester for the regulation of the traffic also deserve the most careful consideration.

I mention these measures merely to show how many comparatively easy steps could be taken if the weight of temperance reformers were united to support them, instead of being wasted on the Permissive Bill. No doubt it will be plausibly answered that if free trade in liquors leads to drunkenness the proper step is to prohibit the sale of liquor, and it is inconsistent to advocate a regulated traffic instead. But the retort is easy, that the United Kingdom Alliance do not venture to be consistent and thorough-going. On their own principles they ought to adhere to the Maine Liquor Law with which they began, and agitate for real prohibition of the sale of liquor. As it is, they only venture to ask for the capricious action of separate parishes and boroughs in suppressing the public sale, while leaving all individuals free to get their own supplies of liquor by purchase elsewhere. I cannot avoid the conclusion, then, that nearly a quarter of a century of time and a quarter of a million of money have been wasted in advocating one of the worst devised measures which was ever brought before a legislature. The Permissive Bill, we are told, will not be passed in any calculable time; I venture to assert that it will never be passed at all.

EXPERIMENTAL LEGISLATION AND THE DRINK TRAFFIC.*

I.

"A FOOL, Mr. Edgeworth, is one who has never made an experiment." Such are, I believe, the exact words of a remark which Erasmus Darwin addressed to Richard Lovell Edgeworth. They deserve to become proverbial. They have the broad foundation of truth, and the trenchant disregard of accuracy in detail which mark an adage. Of course, the saying at once suggests the question : What is an experiment? In a certain way, all people, whether fools or wise men, are constantly making experiments. The education of the infant is thoroughly experimental from the very first, but in a haphazard and unconscious way. The child which overbalances itself in learning to walk is experimenting on the law of gravity. All successful action is successful experiment in the broadest sense of the term, and every mistake or failure is a negative experiment, which deters us from repetition. Our mental framework, too, is marvellously contrived, so as to go on ceaselessly registering on the tablets of the memory the favourable or unfavourable results of every kind of action. Charles Babbage proposed to make an automaton chess-player which should register mechanically the numbers of games lost and gained in consequence of every possible kind of move.

* "Contemporary Review," February, 1880, vol. xxxvii. pp. 177–192.

Thus, the longer the automaton went on playing games, the more experienced it would become by the accumulation of experimental results. Such a machine precisely represents the acquirement of experience by our nervous organisation.

But Erasmus Darwin doubtless meant by experiment something more than this unintentional heaping-up of experience. The part of wisdom is to learn to foresee the results of our actions, by making slight and harmless trials before we commit ourselves to an irrevocable line of conduct. We ought to feel our way, and try the ice before we venture on it to a dangerous extent. To make an experiment, in this more special sense, is to arrange certain known conditions, or, in other words, to put together certain causal agents, in order to ascertain their outcome or aggregate of effects. The experiment has knowledge alone for its immediate purpose; but he is truly happy, as the Latin poet said, who can discern the causes of things, for, these being known, we can proceed at once to safe and profitable applications.

It need hardly be said that it is to frequent and carefully-planned appeals to experiment in the physical sciences, that we owe almost the whole progress of the human race in the last three centuries. Even moral and intellectual triumphs may often be traced back to dependence on physical inventions, and to the incentive which they give towards general activity. Certainly, political and military success is almost entirely dependent on the experimental sciences. It is difficult to discover that, as regards courage, our soldiers in Afghanistan and Zululand and the Transvaal are any better than the men whose countries they invade. But it is the science of the rifle, the shell, and the mountain gun—science perfected by constant experimentation—which gives the poor savage and even the brave Boer no chance of ultimate success in resistance. To whom do we owe all this in its first beginning, but to the great experimentalist, the friar, Roger Bacon, of Oxford, our truest and greatest national glory, the smallest of whose merits is that he first mentions gunpowder; yet so little does the English nation yet appreciate the sources of its power and greatness that the writings of Roger Bacon lie, to a great extent, unprinted and unexplored. It is only among continental scholars that Roger Bacon is regarded as the miracle of his age and country.

No doubt it is to Francis Bacon, the Lord High Chancellor of England, that the world generally attributes the inauguration of the new inductive era of science. This is hardly the place to endeavour to decide whether the world has not made a great mistake. Professor Fowler, in his admirable critical edition of the "Novum Organum," has said about all that can be said in favour of Lord Bacon's scientific claims; yet I hold to the opinion, long since stoutly maintained by the late Professor De Morgan,* not to speak of Baron Liebig† and others, that Lord Bacon, though a truly clever man, was a mere dabbler in inductive science, the true methods of which he quite misapprehended. At best, he put into elegant and striking language an estimate of the tendency of science towards experimentalism, and a forecast of the results to be obtained. The regeneration of these last centuries is due to a long series of philosophers, from Copernicus, Galileo, Descartes, Newton, Leibnitz, down to Watt, Faraday, and Joule. Such men followed a procedure very different from that of Francis Bacon.

II.

Now we come to the point of our inquiry. Is the experimental method necessarily restricted to the world of physical science? Do we sufficiently apply to moral, social, and political matters those methods which have been proved so valuable in the hands of physical philosophers? Do our legislators, in short, appeal to experiment in a way which excepts them from the definition of Erasmus Darwin? English legislation, no

---

* "A Budget of Paradoxes," p. 49. Also his Memoir "On the Syllogism, No. IV., and on the Logic of Relations." "Cambridge Philosophical Transactions," 1860, vol. x. p. 2, foot-note. See also Todhunter's "Account of the Writings of Dr. William Whewell, with Selections from his Literary and Scientific Correspondence," vol. i. p. 227.

† Essay on Lord Bacon.

doubt, is usually preceded by a great amount of public discussion and parliamentary wrangling. Sometimes there is plenty of statistical inquiry—plenty, that is, if it were of the right sort, and conducted according to true scientific method. Neverthless, I venture to maintain that, as a general rule, Parliament ignores the one true method of appealing directly to experiment. Our Parliamentary Committees and Royal Commissions of Inquiry pile up blue-books full of information which is generally not to the point. The one bit of information, the actual trial of a new measure on a small scale, is not forthcoming, because Parliament, if it enacts a law at all, enacts it for the whole kingdom. It habitually makes a leap in the dark, because, I suppose, it is not consistent with the wisdom and dignity of Parliament to grope its way, and confess to the world at large that it is afraid of making mistakes. Now, I maintain that, in large classes of legislative affairs, there is really nothing to prevent our making direct experiments upon the living social organism. Not only is social experimentation a possible thing, but it is in every part of the kingdom, excepting the palace of St. Stephen's, the commonest thing possible, the universal mode of social progress. It would hardly be too much to say that social progress is social experimentation, and social experimentation is social progress. Changes effected by any important Act of Parliament are like earthquakes and cataclysms, which disturb the continuous course of social growth. They effect revolutionary rather than habitual changes. Sometimes they do much good; sometimes much harm; but in any case it is hardly possible to forecast the result of a considerable catastrophic change in the social organism. Therefore I hold unhesitatingly that, whenever it is possible, legislation should observe the order of nature, and proceed tentatively.

Social progress, I have said, is social experimentation. Every new heading that is inserted in the London Trades' Directory is claimed by those private individuals who have tried a new trade and found it to answer. The struggle for existence makes us all look out for chances of profit. We are all, perhaps, in some degree inventors, but some are more bold and successful than others. Now, every man who establishes a shop or factory or social institution of a novel kind is trying an experiment. If he hits an unsupplied need of his fellow-men the experiment *succeeds*; that is to say, it has something succeeding or following it—namely, repetition by himself and others. The word "success" is a most happy one, etymologically. To have success is to have a future—a future of imitators.

It is quite apparent that all the great novelties of recent times have been worked out in this tentative way. How, for instance, has our vast and marvellous railway system been developed? Did it spring forth perfect from the wise forethought of Parliament, as Minerva, fully armed and equipped, leaped from the head of Jupiter? On the contrary, did not our wise landowners and practical men oppose railways to the very utmost—until they discovered what a mistake they were making? There is no great blame to them. Who, indeed, could see in the rude tram-line of Benjamin Outram the germ which was to grow into the maze of lines and points and signals which we now pass through without surprise at Clapham Junction or at London Bridge? That most complex organisation, a great railway station, is entirely a product of frequent experiment. *Gradatim*—Step by Step—would be no unapt motto for any great industrial success. In such matters experiments are both intentional and unintentional. Of the former the public hears little, except when they result in some profitable patent. The preliminary trials are usually performed in secret, for obvious reasons, and the unsuccessful ones are left undescribed, and are quickly forgotten. As to unintentional experiments, they are too numerous. Every railway accident which happens is an experiment revealing some fault of design, some insufficiency in the materials, some contingency unprovided for. The accident is inquired into, and then the engineers set to work to plan improvements which shall prevent the like accident from happening in the future. If we had time to trace the history of the steam engine, of gas lighting, of electric telegraphs, of submarine cables, of electric lighting, or of any other great improvement, we should see, in like manner, that the wisdom of Parliament has had nothing to do with planning it. From the first to the last the rule of progress has been that of the ancient nursery rhyme—Try, try, try: And if at first you don't succeed, Try, try, try again.

To put the matter in the strongest light, let the reader consider what he would say about a proposal that Parliament should decide arbitrarily, by its own wisdom, concerning any great impending improvement: take, for instance, that of tramways and steam tramcars. It is quite conceivable that steam tramcars will eventually succeed so well as to replace horse conveyance to a great extent. All main highways will then, of course, be laid with tram-rails. But what should we think of the wisdom of Parliament if it undertook to settle the question once for all, and, after taking a score of Blue Books full of evidence, to decide either that there should be no steam tramcars, or that steam tramways should be immediately laid down between all the villages in the kingdom? The House of Lords did take the former course two sessions ago, and prohibited the use of steam on tramways, because it might frighten horses. In the next session they felt the folly of opposing the irresistible, and expressly allowed the *experimental use* of steam on tramways.

One of the points about the railway system which the Government of the last generation undertook to settle once for all, was the proper place for great railway stations in London. A committee, chiefly consisting of military men, decided that the railway stations should not be brought into the centre of London. Hence the position of the stations at Euston, King's Cross, Paddington, Waterloo, and Shoreditch. At great cost their decision has been entirely reversed.

It may perhaps be objected that these are matters of physical science and practical engineering, in which the supremacy of experiment has long been recognised. That is not wholly so; for the success of a system, like that of the railways or tramways, depends much upon social considerations. However that may be, there is no difficulty in showing that the same principles apply to purely social institutions. If anything, it is the social side of an enterprise which is usually most doubtful and most in need of experiment when it can be applied. To construct the Thames Tunnel was a novel and difficult work at the time, but not so difficult as to get the populace to use it. The *Great Eastern* steamship was another instance of a great mechanical success, which was, to some extent, a social and economical failure. Many like cases might be mentioned, such as the real ice-rinks lately invented.

How is it that any kind of purely social institution is usually established? Take the case of the Volunteer Force. This was commenced, not to speak of earlier movements, or the ancient Honourable Artillery Company, by a few isolated experiments, such as that of the Exeter Rifle Corps in 1852, and the Victoria Rifle Corps in 1853. These succeeded so well that when, in 1859, fears of invasion were afloat, the imitative process set in rapidly. Of course, wise practical people laughed at the mania for playing at soldiers, and most people clearly foresaw that, when once the volunteers had got tired of their new uniforms, the whole thing would collapse. But experience has decided very differently. The force, instead of declining, has gone on steadily growing and substantially improving, until a good military authority lately spoke of it as the only sound part of our military system. How much has the wisdom of Parliament had to do with the creation of this force? I believe that even now the Government and the military classes do not appreciate what the volunteer force has done for us, by removing all fear of safety at home and enabling the standing army to be freely sent abroad.

Take again the case of popular amusements. Would Parliament ever think of defining by Statute when and how people shall meet to amuse themselves, and what they shall do, and when they shall have had enough of it? Must not people find out by trial what pleases and what does not please? The late Mr. Serjeant Cox is said to have invented Penny Readings for the people, and they answered so well under his management that they were imitated in all parts of the kingdom, and eventually in many other parts of the world. Spelling-bees were, I believe, an American invention, and had a very lively but brief career. Many recent courses of popular scientific lectures arose out of the very successful experiment instituted by Professor Roscoe at Manchester.* Many attempts are just now being made to provide attractive and harmless amusements for the people, and this must, of course, be done in a tentative manner.

It is curious, indeed, to observe how evanescent many social inventions prove themselves to be; growth and change have been so rapid of late that there is constant need of new inventions. The Royal Institution in Albemarle Street was a notable invention of its time, chiefly due to Count Rumford, and its brilliant success led to early imitation in Liverpool, Manchester, Edinburgh, and perhaps elsewhere. But the provincial institutions have with difficulty maintained their *raison d'être*. After the Royal Institutions came a series of Mechanics' Institutions, which, as regards the mechanic element, were thoroughly unsuccessful, but proved themselves useful in the form of popular colleges or middle-class schools. Now, the great and genuine success of Owens College as a teaching body is leading to the creation of numerous local colleges of similar type. This is the age, again, of Free Public Libraries, the practicability and extreme usefulness of which were first established in Salford and Manchester. When once possessed of local habitations, such institutions will, it may be hoped, have long careers; but bricks and mortar are usually requisite to give perpetuity to a social experiment. When thus perpetuated, each kind of institution marks its own age with almost geologic certainty. From the times of the Saxons and the Normans we can trace a series of strata of institutions superposed in order of time. The ancient Colleges of Oxford and Cambridge, the mediæval Guilds surviving in the City Companies, the Grammar Schools of the Elizabethan age, the Almshouses of the Stuart period, the Commercial Institutions of Queen Anne's reign, and so on down to the Free Libraries and Recreation Palaces

---

* All the lectures delivered in the eleven annual series instituted by Professor Roscoe at Manchester have been reported and published by John Heywood, of Manchester and Paternoster Row. Most of the lectures may be had separately for one penny each.

of the present day. Even styles of architecture are evolved by successful innovation—that is, experiment followed by imitation, and this was never more apparent than in the imitation which has followed upon Sir Joseph Paxton's grand experiment at the Exhibition of 1851.*

Now, my contention is, that legislators ought, in many branches of legislation, to adopt confessedly this tentative procedure, which is the very method of social growth. Parliament must give up the pretension that it can enact the creation of certain social institutions to be carried on as specified in the "hereinafter contained" clauses. No doubt, by aid of an elaborate machinery of administration and a powerful body of police, Government can, to a certain extent, guide, or at any rate restrain, the conduct of its subjects. Even in this respect its powers are very limited, and a law which does not command the consent of the body of the people must soon be repealed or become inoperative. But as regards the creation of institutions, Parliament is almost powerless, except by consulting the needs of the time, and offering facilities for such institutions to grow up as experience shows to be successful. But an unfortunate confusion of ideas exists; and it seems to be supposed that because, for reasons of obvious convenience, the civil and criminal laws are, as a general rule, made uniform for the whole kingdom, therefore the legislative action of Parliament must always be uniform and definitive. When an important change is advocated, for instance, in the Licensing Laws, Parliament collects abundant information, which is usually inconclusive, and then proceeds to effect all over the kingdom some very costly and irrevocable change; a change which generally disappoints its own advocates. Take the case of the Sale of Beer Act of 1830, generally known as the Beershop Act. This is a salient example of bad legislation. Yet it was passed by the almost unanimous wisdom of Parliament, the division in the House of Commons on the second reading

* I do not remember to have seen the importance of this imitative tendency in social affairs described by any writer, except the French Engineer and Economist, Dupuit, who fully describes it in one of his remarkable memoirs, printed in the "Annales des Ponts et Chaussées."

showing 245 ayes and only 29 noes. The Act originated with Brougham, in the sense that he had in 1822 and 1823 brought in somewhat similar bills, which were partially adopted by the Government of 1830. The idea of the Act was to break down the monopoly of the brewers and publicans; to throw open the trade in beer on free-trade principles; and by offering abundance of wholesome, pure, weak beer, to draw away the working-classes from the ginshops. All seemed as plausible as it was undoubtedly well intended. Objections were of course made to the Bill, and many people predicted evil consequences; but all such sinister predictions were supposed to be spread about by the interested publicans and brewers. Nevertheless, the new Act was soon believed to be a mistake. Sydney Smith, though he had not many years before pleaded for liberty for the people to drink rum-and-water, or whatever else they liked (*Edinburgh Review*, 1819), quickly veered round, and gave a graphic account of the beastly state of drunkenness of the Sovereign People.*

It may be safely said that the Beershop Act realised all the evils expected from it, and few or none of the advantages.†
It is difficult to say anything in favour of the bar at the corner public-house, except that it is better than the dirty low little beershop, hiding itself away in some obscure recess of the streets. The first is at any rate under the gaze of the public and the control of the magistrates; the beershop, until within the last few years, was too likely to become the uncontrolled resort of the worst classes. Even now that the beershops are brought under the Licensing Magistrates many years must elapse before the evil wrought by the Act of 1830

---

* "The new Beer Bill has begun its operations. Everybody is drunk. Those who are not singing are sprawling. The Sovereign People are in a beastly state."

† "The Beershops are considered as most mischievous. . . . . Similar representations are made in East Kent. A magistrate expressed his opinion that no single measure ever caused so much mischief, in so short a time, in demoralising the labourers. The evidence of the High Constable of Ashford is very strong." "Extracts from the Information Received . . . as to the Administration and Operation of the Poor Laws." 8vo, 1833, p. 24.

can be thoroughly removed. This then is a striking instance of a leap in the dark, which ought never to have been committed by a prudent legislature. When the Sale of Beer Bill was under discussion the Chancellor of the Exchequer seemed to feel that it was a Bill which needed experimental trial; for when objection was made that the Act would not extend to Scotland, he urged that it might be better to try the Act in one part of the kingdom in the first instance, and then, if it were found to be beneficial, and to answer its intended objects, it might be extended to other parts.*

In more recent years the granting of grocers' licenses for the free sale of all kinds of spirituous liquors is likely to prove itself to be an equally disastrous leap in the dark. With the very best intentions, and on the most plausible theoretical grounds, Mr. Gladstone's Government greatly extended the free sale of wine and beer, so that now, in some popular watering-places, I have noticed that almost every third shop window is ornamented with a pyramid of beer bottles. Yet the late Government have only succeeded in making the grocer's shop the avenue to the publican's bar. No one can for a moment believe that the free sale of liquors for home use has in the least degree weakened the publican's hold on his customers. If I had on *à priori* grounds to plan out a scheme of liquor traffic, I should just reverse the existing law relating to Beer-shops and Grocers' Licenses. I would prohibit the "off" sale of liquor on any premises where other articles were sold; the purchaser desiring to buy wine, beer, or spirits for home use should be obliged to go to some one of a comparatively few well-marked shops dealing in those things alone. On the other hand, where liquor is sold for consumption on the premises, I should oblige the seller to furnish food and reasonable sitting accommodation. This would be nothing more than a return to the old law about Licensed Victuallers, which yet exists in the letter, though it has been allowed to fall into practical abeyance. The very reasonable law obliging publicans to afford general entertainment was sadly broken down by the

* "Hansard's Debates," 8th April, 1830, New Series, vol. xxiv. p. 26.

Beershops Act, which provided unlimited means for the drinking of beer, pure and simple, without food of any kind. But my contention is that we must not proceed in such matters on *à priori* grounds at all. We must try.

Perhaps it may be said that every new law is necessarily an experiment, and affords experience for its own improvement, and, if necessary, its abrogation. But there are two strong reasons why an Act which has been made general, and has come into general operation, can seldom serve as an experiment. Of course, a great many Acts of Parliament are experimentally found to be mistaken, for they never come into considerable operation at all, like the Acts to promote registration of titles, not to mention the Agricultural Holdings Act. Such cases prove little or nothing, except the weakness, and possibly the insincerity, of the Legislature. But if an Act comes largely into operation it is practically irrevocable. Parliament cannot say simply "as you were," and proceed to a new and more hopeful experiment. A social humpty-dumpty cannot be set up again just as it was before, even by the Queen's men. The vested interests created are usually too formidable to be put aside, and too expensive to be bought up. A good many years, say seven, or ten at the least, are needed to develop properly any important legislative experiment, so that the same generation of statesmen would not have more than three or four opportunities of experiment in the same subject during the longest political career. If we divide up the country, and try one experiment on one town or county, and another on another, there is a possibility of making an almost unlimited number of valid trials within ten or twenty years. But, apart from this consideration, a general legislative change is not a true experiment at all, because it affords no clear means of distinguishing its effects from the general resultant of social and industrial progress. Statistical facts are usually numerical or quantitative in character, so that, if many causal agencies are in operation at the same time, their effects are simply added together algebraically, and are inextricably merged into a general total. Thus, the total numbers receiving poor-law relief, or the numbers apprehended in the kingdom for drunkenness, are numerical results affected by the oscillations of trade, by the character of the seasons, the value of gold, etc., etc., as well as by the Acts of the Legislature. To make a valid experiment we must have a certain thing subject to certain constant conditions, and we must introduce a single definite change of condition, which will then be probably the cause of whatever phenomenon follows. It is possible, indeed, to experiment upon an object of varying conditions, provided we can find two objects which vary similarly; we then operate upon the one, and observe how it subsequently differs from the other. We need, in fact, what the chemists call a "blind experiment." Suppose, for instance, that an agricultural chemist or a scientific farmer wished to ascertain the effect of a new kind of manure; would it be rational for him to spread the manure over all his available land? Would it not then be doubtful whether the increase or decrease of yield were due to the manure or the character of the seasons? In this case his neighbours' crops might, to some extent, furnish the blind experiment, showing what had been the ordinary yield. But, of course, the obvious mode of procedure is to spread the new manure over a part only of each experimental field, so that the difference of the crops on the different patches brings out, in a most unquestionable way, the effect of the manure. Not only is the smaller experiment, in a logical point of view, far better than the larger one, but it is possible to try many concurrent small experiments upon a farm of moderate extent.

I maintain that, if our legislators are to act rationally, they will, as far as possible, imitate the agricultural chemist. The idea, for instance, of obliging, or even allowing, all the boroughs in the kingdom simultaneously to adopt the Gothenburg plan would be ridiculous and irrational. The cost and confusion which would arise from a sudden general trial must be very great; many years would elapse before the result was apparent. And that result would not be so clear as if the trial were restricted to some half-a-dozen towns. In the meantime it would be far better that other boroughs should be trying other experiments, giving us many strings to our bow, while some towns would actually do best for the country by going on as nearly as possible in their present course. Specific and differentiated experience is what we need, before making any further important change in the drink trade.

Not only is this the rational method of procedure, but it is practically the method to which we owe all the more successful legislative and administrative reforms of later years. Consider the Poor Law question. During the eighteenth century, Parliament made two or three leaps in the dark, by enacting laws such as Gilbert's Act, and very nearly ruined the kingdom by them. The great Poor Law Commission commenced its operations in the soundest way by collecting all available information about the treatment of the poor, whether at home or abroad. But, what is more to the point, since the new Poor Law was passed in 1834, the partially free action of Boards of Guardians, under the supervision of the Poor Law Commission and the Poor Law Board, has afforded a long series of experimental results. The reports of Mr. Edwin Chadwick and the late Sir George Shaw Lefevre are probably the best models of the true process of administrative reform to be anywhere found. In more recent years several very important experiments have been tried by different Boards of Guardians, such as the boarding out of pauper children, the suppression of vagrancy by the provision of separate vagrant cells and the hard-labour test, and the cutting down of outdoor relief. If the total abolition of outdoor relief is ever to be tried, it must be tried on the small scale first; it would be a far too severe and dangerous measure to force upon the whole country at a single blow. Much attention has lately been drawn to the so-called "Poor Law Experiment at Elberfeld," which was carefully described by the Rev. W. Walter Edwards, in an article in *The Contemporary Review* for July, 1878, vol. xxxii. pp. 675–693, bearing that precise title.

Even when an Act of Parliament is passed in general terms applying to the whole kingdom at once, it by no means follows that it will be equally put into operation everywhere. The discretion necessarily allowed to magistrates and other authorities often gives ample scope for instructive experiments.

Some years since the Howard Association called attention to what they expressly called "The Luton experiment," consisting in the extraordinary success with which the magistrates of Luton in Bedfordshire enforced the provisions of the "Prevention of Crime Act." The number of committals to gaol from Luton and its vicinity was reduced from 257 in 1869 to 66 in 1874. The only fault of the experiment consists in the possibility that the thieves and roughs migrated; but this difficulty would be less serious had the experiment been tried in larger towns.

What little insight we can gain into the operation of the Licensing Laws is mainly due to the considerable differences with which they have been administered in different places. Such is the latitude of discretion given by the law, that magistrates can often make very distinct experiments. A short time ago the magistrates of Glasgow intentionally and avowedly made the experiment of locking up in gaol all the drunkards brought before them. When I last heard about this experiment it was on the point of failing, because the gaols of Glasgow were all quite full, and still the drunkards were coming to the bar. In 1863 the Licensing Magistrates of Liverpool commenced a most interesting experiment, by declaring their intention to adopt "Free licensing"—that is, to grant licenses to any suitable persons who applied for them. The publicans' licenses were increased from 1,674 in 1862 to 1,940 in 1866. The system was abandoned in this last year, owing to a change in the constitution of the Bench. None of the magistrates who advocated the change, we are told, ever recanted, but some who supported the change to a restrictive policy have been disappointed with the results. The teaching of this real experiment has been carefully discussed by Mr. S. G. Rathbone, in a very able letter, published in *The Times* of the 12th of February, 1877, as also in his evidence before the Lords' Committee of Inquiry on Intemperance (Questions 259–384, etc). But, apart from his objections to the interpretation put upon the facts, the experiment was not continued sufficiently long, and the town in which it was tried is so unique in the annals of intemperance as to be ill-fitted for the purpose.

Much attention has been drawn recently to the merits of the so-called Gothenburg Scheme, the adoption of which has been so ably advocated by Mr. J. Chamberlain, M.P. Now, what is this advocacy but argument from a successful experiment? The municipal authorities of Gothenburg allowed a certain method of conducting the sale of liquor to be tried there, and the success was apparently so great that other Swedish towns are rapidly adopting the same plan. This is just the right procedure of trial and imitation. But if Mr. Chamberlain means that, because the plan succeeds in Gothenburg, therefore the municipal authorities of English towns ought at once to be obliged to purchase and administer the public-houses, he goes much too far. All we ought to do is to try the system in a limited number of towns. Anyone acquainted with the bright little Swedish seaport, and the orderly polished lower-class population of Sweden, will be in no hurry to draw analogies between their condition and that of our great, busy, turbulent Anglo-Irish towns. At any rate it is obvious that experiments ought to be made upon the most closely proximate cases which can be found, and if three or four such towns as Birmingham, Bristol, Bolton, and Newcastle-upon-Tyne could be induced to try the Gothenburg scheme, it would be an ample first experiment. Even between English towns the differences of magnitude, race, occupation, and local government are often so great that it is by no means certain that the same scheme will succeed equally in all. The differences in the intemperance rates in the several boroughs of England, to which I shall, perhaps, draw attention on a future occasion, are so extraordinary and profound that the Committee of the House of Lords were thoroughly bewildered on the subject. Under such circumstances it should not be assumed that uniform legislation must be the ultimate object of our efforts.

It is a most important question how far the proposals of the United Kingdom Alliance for the Suppression of the Liquor Traffic can be approved from the point of view here taken up. I venture to maintain that those proposals, so far as embodied in the Permissive Prohibitory Bill, now dropped, had all the possible evils of a great legislative leap in the dark, with few of the corresponding possible advantages. Four years ago, in a paper read to the Manchester Statistical Society, I gave reasons for believing that the long-continued and costly proceedings of the Alliance were simply thrown away, except so far as they might be a warning against similar unwise attempts at legislation. I showed that the Alliance were striving against triple improbabilities: firstly, the improbability (as manifested by the decreasing ratio of the ayes to the noes in the House of Commons' divisions) that Parliament would ever pass the Bill; secondly, the improbability that, if passed, the Permissive Act would be largely adopted by local authorities; thirdly, the improbability that, if adopted, it would succeed in lessening intemperance. According to the mathematical principle of the composition of probabilities by multiplication, the probability that any good would ever result from an agitation costing more than a quarter of a million pounds, and extending already beyond a quarter of a century in duration, was practically *nil*. The only effective answers given to my arguments were that of the Rev. Mr. Steinthal and one or two others, who held that the probabilities in question are not altogether independent, because Parliament could hardly be forced to pass the Bill unless there were extensive localities wishing to adopt it. There is a certain amount of truth in this objection, but it does not to any great degree strengthen the position of the Alliance. Their proposals in their original form seem to me to have the character of a vast experiment, so vast that it was intended to involve the extinction of the trade of publicans and liquor dealers generally in all parts of the country. Now, that is an experiment, because it is exceedingly doubtful whether the population would tolerate such an interference with their habits, when the meaning of the Act came home to them. The information which we can draw from Maine, or other places where prohibition of the traffic has existed, is most conflicting in itself, and remote in analogy. Accordingly, I should much like to see the prohibition of the public sale of liquor tried in several large English boroughs and districts, provided that the necessary Act for the purpose could be carried without stopping all other legislation on the subject.

Within the last twelve months Sir Wilfrid Lawson and his followers have had the excellent good sense to drop the Permissive Bill, and proceed, by way of Parliamentary resolution, in favour of "local option." I really do not know exactly what is meant by "local option." Perhaps the Alliance itself does not know; the wisest course would be not to know, that is, to leave a latitude of meaning. In any case they have changed their policy. For year after year, for nearly the average length of a generation, it was the eleven clauses and one schedule of the Permissive Prohibitory Liquor Bill, pure and simple. Now it is "local option." Even if "local option" mean option of prohibition, a resolution is a more tentative method of procedure than the precise clauses of the celebrated Bill. But if, as I fondly hope, "local option" will be interpreted to mean option for local authorities to regulate the liquor traffic in the way thought to be most suitable to the locality, including prohibition when clearly desired by the inhabitants, then the matter assumes a much more hopeful aspect. Not only will the resistance to such a proposal be far less than to the Permissive Bill, but there will be considerable probability that when passed some successful experiments will be carried out. In fact, this "local option" would just be the mode of giving a wide field for diverse experiments which I am advocating. The teetotalers would be at liberty to try their experiments, but they would not in the meantime stop the progress of many other experiments, some of which might, in the course of ten or fifteen years, offer a sound solution of this most difficult problem. Of course I am aware that this question of the drink traffic is to a considerable extent a political one. There is a good deal which I might say upon this topic, but it would not be suitable to the tenor of my theme. If the political condition of England be such that the social reform of the people is not the main purpose of our Government, then we must hope that there are brighter lands where the political position is very different.

The best way of dealing with the liquor trade would be to hand over the matter to the hands of a strong executive commission framed somewhat on the lines of the Poor Law Commission. This body should have the power of authorising schemes proposed by local authorities, and should supervise the working of such schemes, and collect minute information as to the results. They would work entirely through local authorities, whether the corporations of cities and boroughs, or the benches of Licensing Magistrates. Before allowing any very serious experiments, such as the abolition of the public sale, the local authority would have to present evidence that the mass of the inhabitants was in favour of such a measure, and the Commissioners would then probably assign a suitable district, and authorise police regulations suitable for the most advantageous trial of the experiment. This method would carry out to the fullest point the idea of a "local option." Free licensing might be tried in Liverpool, and such other boroughs as liked to venture on such a hazardous experiment. The Gothenburg scheme would be adopted by Birmingham and a few other towns. Manchester might prefer the slighter measure of a rigid restriction and supervision of the public-houses. It is to be hoped that Sunday closing and a lessening of the week-day hours would be voted by many local authorities, and the experiment of remodelling the trade, as suggested above, ought certainly to be tried. I should also much like to see some trial made of the important suggestion put forward by Dr. John Watts, at the last meeting of the Social Science Association. He suggests that in each town or district a limited number of licenses should be sold by public auction or tender. His purpose apparently is to limit the number of licenses, and yet to secure the profits of the monopoly to the community.

After the expiration of ten or fifteen years, Parliament would be in possession of a great amount of really practical information, but the probability is that it would not be found necessary to pass any great Act for the subsequent regulation of the traffic. The scheme which was found to work best would by degrees be imitated in the districts of corresponding circumstances, just as the Gothenburg scheme is being imitated in other Swedish towns. I do not think that in a matter of this sort the final law need be exactly uniform. In the Licensing Act of 1872, it was found undesirable to fix a uniform hour of closing public-houses all over the country. Owing to the difference of habits, the metropolitan area was allowed one hour later at night, and considerable latitude was left to the Licensing Magistrates to vary the hours of closing. Surely such matters approximate more in character to hackney cab regulations or matters of police, which have long been left to the borough authorities. It is only the political question looming behind the social or legislative question, which could warrant Parliament in deciding that people shall go to bed one hour earlier in the country than in London. But parliamentary experience concerning the Licensing Act of the late Cabinet, and the now defunct Permissive Bill, cannot encourage any party to press for a further great general measure of licensing reform. As to the present state of things, it could not be much worse nor more absurd. What with the great variety of kinds of licenses, the doubts and fears of the magistrates as to their power of withdrawing licenses or restraining extension of premises, the remissness—to use a mild expression—of the police in prosecuting the offences of publicans, and the universal facility of obtaining any amount of drink at the nearest grocer's shop—I say things really cannot be much worse than they are. Under the vigorous exertion of local option the state of affairs would undoubtedly improve in some parts of the country; the pressure of public opinion, of the proposed Commissioners, or, in the last resort, of Parliament, would eventually force the negligent localities to follow the example of the most successful "local option schemes."

Let it be understood that I do not for a moment suppose that there is much, if any, novelty in the proposals made above. In one place or another almost every suggestion, except, perhaps, that of a superintending Commission, has been made and discussed. The Lords' Committee have themselves recommended "that legislative facilities should be afforded for the local adoption of the Gothenburg and of Mr. Chamberlain's schemes, or of some modification of them." And the Lords have themselves recognised the value of social "experiments" in providing counter-attractions to the public-house. In their final Report, dated the 17th of March last, they remark (p. xliv.):

"These experiments are too recent, and, in spite of their rapid increase, too partial and limited to enable the Committee to pronounce with confidence on their ultimate success, or on the extent of the influence they may exercise in diminishing intemperance; but they desire to express their strong opinion that, if generally prosecuted and conducted with due regard for the wants and comforts of a population among whom education is gradually diffusing a taste for enjoyment far less coarse and gross than in the past, they are destined to have an important influence for good. It is obvious that the desire for recreation is felt by all classes alike."

What is this, however, but an express recognition by the House of Lords of the need of experimentation as regards the entertainment and recreation of the people? I fail to see how such experimentation either can or ought to be confined to philanthropists. If we look around and notice the vast new restaurants of London, the innumerable glittering railway bars in all parts of the country, the music halls of all ranks and kinds, the dancing and drinking saloons of some provincial towns—such as Nottingham—and the great enterprise with which such places of recreation as the Pomona and Bellevue Gardens at Manchester are conducted, we shall see that social experiments are not confined to the teetotalers. Indeed, it would not be difficult to prove that the nugatory Licensing Laws, as now administered, present the least possible obstacle to the publicans in pushing their experiments, while they do prevent social reformers from interfering, or from establishing counter-experiments on an equal footing. It is hardly too much to say that the Licensing Laws are laws to give a license to the publicans and grocers to do what they like to extend the sale of spirituous liquors.

Although the liquor traffic presents the widest and most important sphere for social experiment, there are many other matters to which it must be applied. Consideration in detail must show whether, in each case, the tentative method is or is not the proper method. But it is easy to name several other reforms which ought, in all probability, to be approached in the experimental manner. Thus peasant proprietorship ought certainly to be tried in Ireland, as it was intended to be tried under the Bright clauses of the Irish Land Act. I am familiar with most of the economic objections to peasant proprietorship in this kingdom, and I have read sufficient of the large literature of the subject to know that evidence in favour of and against such a tenure of land is exceedingly divergent and perplexing. The proper resource then is to *try the thing*—not by some vast revolution in the land-owning of Ireland, as proposed by the late Mr. Mill, a measure which, in the first place, would never pass Parliament, and, if it did, would cost an enormous sum of money, and probably result in failure—but by a small and progressive experiment. "Earth hunger" is a very potent passion, and I believe it is that from which the Irish people are really suffering. Bread and bacon are not the only good things an Irish peasant might aspire to; a place to call his own, a share of the air and sunlight of his native isle, and a land-bank in which to save up the strokes of his pick and spade, might work moral wonders. It is not safe to predict the action of human motive; but, at any rate, try it, although the trial cost as much as one or two first-rate ironclads, or a new triumph over a negro monarch. Surely the state of our Irish Poland is the worst possible injury to our prestige.

Much doubt exists, again, as to whether imprisonment is necessary to enforce the payment of small debts. If needless, it is certainly oppressive. But if the abolition of the power of imprisonment, on the part of County Court judges, would really destroy the credit of the poorer classes with their tradesmen, a general measure to that effect would be dangerous and difficult to retract. I do not see how the question can be decided, except by trying the effect in a certain number of County Court districts, and watching the results.

It would be well worth the trouble to try the effect upon a certain body of inhabitants of the most perfect sanitary regulation, somewhat in the manner foreshadowed by Dr. B. W. Richardson in his City of Hygeia. This I should like to see tried, as regards the middle classes, in some newly-built watering-place, with full and special powers of sanitary regulation to be granted it by Parliament, avowedly as an experiment. At the same time, a few large blocks of workmen's dwellings ought to be built and placed under experimental sanitary laws. I am convinced that legislation must by degrees be carried much further in this direction than is at present the case, but it ought to proceed tentatively.

One of the difficult questions of the present day is—How can London be supplied with water? There would be few engineering difficulties if it were allowable to separate the supply of pure water for drinking and cooking purposes from the much larger quantities required for other purposes. Will people drink the impure water? Who can decide such a question satisfactorily, except by experiment on a moderate scale? What could be more absurd than to spend millions upon procuring a separate supply of pure drinking water for the population of London, and then finding that the population would drink the impure water? Many other like matters must be referred to trial, but it is not the purpose of this article to present a catalogue of experimental reforms, or to follow the argument out into all the possible details.

I am well aware that social experiments must often be subjected to various difficulties, such as the migration of inhabitants, or even the intentional frustration of the experiment by interested parties. I have heard it said that the prohibition of liquor traffic could not be tried on a small scale, because the publicans would be sure to combine to send liquor into the area. If they did so, the fact could readily be put in evidence, and if they can defeat the teetotalers in detail, I am quite sure that they will defeat them upon any very great and general measure like the Permissive Bill. As to migration of inhabitants, it must be provided against either by suitably increasing the areas of experimental legislation, or else by collecting information as to the amount and probable effects of the migration. But the main point of my theme is to prove that we cannot really plan out social reforms upon theoretical grounds. General argument and information of all kinds may properly be employed in designing and choosing the best experiments, but specific experience on a limited scale and in closely proximate circumstances is the only sure guide in the complex questions of social science. Our method must be that of the supremely wise text: "Prove all things; hold fast that which is good."

ON THE ANALOGY BETWEEN

THE POST OFFICE, TELEGRAPHS, AND OTHER SYSTEMS OF CONVEYANCE OF THE UNITED KINGDOM,

AS REGARDS GOVERNMENT CONTROL.*

It has been freely suggested of late years, that great public advantage would arise from the purchase and re-organisation of the electric telegraphs and railways of the United Kingdom by the Government. So inestimable indeed, are the benefits which the Post Office, as reformed by Sir Rowland Hill, confers upon all classes of society, that there is a great tendency to desire the application of a similar reform and state organisation to other systems of conveyance. It is assumed, by most of those who discuss this subject, that there is a close similarity between the Post Office, telegraphs, and railways, and that what has answered so admirably in one case will be productive of similar results in other parallel cases. Without adopting any foregone conclusion, it is my desire in this short paper to inquire into the existence and grounds of this assumed analogy, and to make such a general comparison of the conditions and requirements of each branch of conveyance, as will enable us to judge securely of the expediency of state control in each case.

* Read at the Manchester Statistical Society, April 10th, 1867.

It is obvious that I cannot, in the time at my disposal, take more than a simple and restricted view of the subject. I cannot, on the one hand, consider all the difficulties that arise from the partial monopolies possessed by private companies at present, nor can I, on the other hand, take into account all the social or political results connected with an extension of Government management.

Much difference of opinion arises, even in a purely economical point of view, upon the question of the limits of State interference. My own strong opinion is that no abstract principle, and no absolute rule, can guide us in determining what kinds of industrial enterprise the State should undertake, and what it should not. State management and monopoly have most indisputable advantages; private commercial enterprise and responsibility have still more unquestionable advantages. The two are directly antagonistic. Nothing but experience and argument from experience can in most cases determine whether the community will be best served by its collective state action, or by trusting to private self-interest.

On the one hand, it is but too sure that some of the state manufacturing establishments, especially the dockyards, form the very types of incompetent and wasteful expenditure. They are the running sores of the country, draining away our financial power. It is evident too that the House of Commons is at present quite incapable of controlling the expenditure of the dockyards. And as these establishments are never subjected to the test of commercial solvency, as they do not furnish intelligible accounts of current expenditure and work done, much less favour us with any account or allowance for capital expenditure, we have no security whatever that the work is done cheaply. And the worst point is, that even if Government establishments of this kind are efficiently conducted when new and while the public attention is on them, we have no security that this state of things will continue.

To other Government establishments, however, the Post Office presents a singular and at first sight an unaccountable contrast. Instead of Mr. Dickens's picture of the Circumlocution Office, we are here presented with a body of secretaries and postmasters alive to every breath of public opinion or private complaint; officials laboriously correcting the blunders and returning the property of careless letter-writers; and clerks, sorters, and postmen working to their utmost that the public may be served expeditiously. No one ever charges the Post Office with lavish expenditure and inefficient performance of duties.

It seems then that the extremes of efficiency and inefficiency meet in the public service, and before we undertake any new branch of State industry, it becomes very important to ascertain whether it is of a kind likely to fall into the efficient or inefficient class of undertakings. Before we give our adhesion to systems of State telegraphs and State railways in this kingdom, we should closely inquire whether telegraphs and railways have more analogy to the Post Office or to the dockyards. This argument from analogy is freely used by everyone. It is the argument of the so-called Reformers, who urge that if we treat the telegraphs and the railways as Sir Rowland Hill treated the Post Office, reducing fares to a low and uniform rate, we shall reap the same gratifying results. But this will depend upon whether the analogy is correct—whether the telegraphs and railways resemble the Post Office in those conditions which render the latter highly successful in the hands of Government, and enable a low uniform rate to be adopted. To this point the following remarks are directed.

It seems to me that State management possesses advantages under the following conditions :

1. Where numberless wide-spread operations can only be efficiently connected, united, and co-ordinated, in a single, all extensive Government system.

2. Where the operations possess an invariable routine-like character.

3. Where they are performed under the public eye or for the service of individuals, who will immediately detect and expose any failure or laxity.

4. Where there is but little capital expenditure, so that each year's revenue and expense account shall represent,

with sufficient accuracy, the real commercial conditions of the department.

It is apparent that all these conditions are combined in the highest perfection in the Post Office. It is a vast co-ordinated system, such as no private capitalists could maintain, unless, indeed, they were in undisputed possession of the field by virtue of a Government monopoly. The forwarding of letters is a purely routine and equable operation. Not a letter can be mislaid but someone will become aware of it, and by the published tables of mail departures and arrivals the public is enabled accurately to check the performance of the system.

Its capital expenditure, too, is insignificant compared with its current expenditure. Like other Government departments, indeed, the Post Office does not favour us with any statement of the capital value of its buildings, fittings, etc. But in the Post Office accounts, we have a statement of the annual cost of buildings and repairs, together with rents, rates, taxes, fuel, and lights. In the last ten years (1856–65) the expense has varied from £39,730 in 1864 to £106,478 in 1859, and the average yearly expense has been £72,486, which bears a very inconsiderable ratio to £1,303,064, the average cost of the Post Office staff during the same years. Compared with £2,871,729, the average complete expenditure of the Post Office during the last ten years, the cost of the fixed property of the department is quite inconsiderable. This very favourable state of things is due to the fact that all the conveyances of the Post Office system are furnished by contract, while it is only the large central offices that are owned by Government.

Before proceeding to consider the other systems of conveyance, I must notice that the Post Office in reality is neither a commercial nor a philanthropic establishment, but simply one of the revenue departments of the Government. It very rightly insists, that no country post office shall be established unless the correspondence passing through it shall warrant the increased expense and it maintains a tariff which has no accordance whatever with the cost of conveyance. Books, newspapers, and even unsealed manuscripts, can be sent up to the weight of 4 oz. for a penny; whereas, if a sealed letter in the least exceeds ½ oz. it is charged 2*d*. It is obvious that the charges of the Post Office are for the most part a purely arbitrary system of taxes, designed to maintain the large net revenue of the Post Office, now amounting to a million and a half sterling.

It will thus be apparent that Sir Rowland Hill's scheme of postal tariff consisted in substituting one arbitrary system of charges for a system more arbitrary and onerous. This was effected by a sacrifice, at the time, of about one million sterling of revenue; but it must be distinctly remembered that it was net revenue only which was sacrificed, and not commercial loss which was incurred.

A telegraph system appears to me to possess the characteristics which favour unity and State management almost in as high a degree as the Post Office. If this be so, great advantages will undoubtedly be attained by the purchase of the telegraphs and their union, under the direction of the Post Office department.

It is obvious in the first place that the public will be able, and in fact obliged, constantly to test the efficiency of the proposed Government telegraphs, as they now test the efficiency of the Post Office. The least delay or inaccuracy in the transmission of messages will become known, and will be made the ground of complaint. The work, too, of receiving, transmitting, and delivering messages, is for the most part of an entirely routine nature, as in the case of the Post Office. The only exception to this consists perhaps in the special arrangements which will be needed for the transmission of intelligence and reports to the newspapers.

It is hardly necessary to point out, in the second place, that a single Government telegraph system will possess great advantages from its unity, economy, and comprehensive character. Instead of two or three companies with parallel conterminous wires, and different sets of costly city stations, we shall have a single set of stations; and the very same wires, when aggregated into one body, will admit of more convenient arrangements, and more economical employment. The greater the number of messages sent through a given office, the more regularly and economically may the work of transmission and delivery be performed in general.

Furthermore, great advantages will arise from an intimate connection between the telegraphs and the Post Office. In the country districts the telegraph office can readily be placed in the Post Office, and the postmaster can, for a moderate remuneration, be induced to act as telegraph clerk, just as small railway stations serve as telegraphic offices at present, the station-master or clerk being the operator. A great number of new offices could thus be opened, without any considerable expenses for rent or attendance. The Government, in short, could profitably extend its wires where any one of several competing companies would not be induced to go.

In all the larger towns the cost of special delivery may perhaps be removed by throwing the telegrams into the ordinary postal delivery. It is understood that a scheme for the junction of the telegraphic and postal system has been elaborated by the authorities of the Post Office, partly on the model of the Belgian service; and it has been asserted that the scheme would comprehend some sort of periodical deliveries. In the great business centres, at least, very frequent periodical deliveries could be made. For the services of a special messenger an extra charge might be imposed. Prepayment of all ordinary charges by stamps would greatly facilitate the whole of the arrangements; and it has been suggested that where there is no telegraph office, a prepaid telegram might be deposited in the nearest post office or letter box, and forwarded by the mail service to the nearest telegraph office, as is the practice in Belgium. It is evident that the number of telegrams will be increased, as the facility for their dispatch, by the united system of posts and telegraphs, is greater.

A low and perhaps uniform tariff would complete the advantages of such a system. It is supposed, indeed, that it would not be prudent at first to attempt a lower uniform rate than one shilling for 20 words; but it is difficult to see how a *uniform* rate of this amount can be enforced, when the

London District Telegraph Company for many years transmitted messages for sixpence, or even fourpence.

The question here arises, how far the telegraphs resemble the Post Office in the financial principles which should govern the tariff. The trouble of writing a telegraphic message of 20 words is so slight, that the trouble of conveying it to a telegraph office and the cost of transmission form the only impediments to a greatly increased use of this means of communication. The trouble of despatching a message will undoubtedly be much decreased in most localities by the Government scheme, and if the charge were also decreased, we might expect an increase of communications almost comparable with that of the Post Office under similar circumstances. Even a shilling rate is prohibitory to all but commercial and necessary communications, the post office being a sufficient resource, where the urgency is not immediate. Accordingly it is found that a reduction of charges increases the use of the telegraphs very much. In the Paris telegraphs a reduction of the charge from one franc to half a franc has multiplied the business *tenfold*.

The experience gained too, in the reduction of the telegraphic rates in Belgium, on the 1st of December, 1865, is very important as to this point. When in 1865 the uniform rate was 1 franc for 20 words, the number of internal messages was 332,721, producing (with the double charge on the telegrams exceeding 20 words) 345,289 francs. In 1866, the number of internal messages was 692,536, or more than twice as many, producing 407,532 francs, the increase of receipts being 18 per cent. It is true that the working expenses were considerably increased at the same time, so that the net profits of the whole establishment fell from 204,940 francs to 122,112 francs. This loss of net revenue is partly attributed to the extension of the telegraphs to the remote villages. And it is probable that in future years the net profits will be to some extent recovered.

But it must be allowed that the working expense of the

electric telegraph is its weak point. The London District Telegraph Company have not succeeded in paying dividends, although their low charges brought plenty of business. The French lines are worked at a considerable loss to the Government. Belgium is a country of very small area, which decreases the expense of the telegraphs, and yet the reduction of rate has caused a sacrifice of net revenue only partially made up by the higher profits upon international messages in transit.

It is quite apparent that the telegraphs are less favourably situated than the Post Office as regards the cost of transmission. Two letters are as easily carried and delivered at one house as a single letter, and it is certain that the expenses of the Post Office do not increase in anything like the same ratio as the work it performs. Thus while the total postal revenue has increased from £3,035,954, in 1856, to £4,423,608, in 1865, or by 46 per cent., representing a great increase of work done, the total cost of the service has risen only from £2,438,732, in 1856, to £2,941,086 in 1865, or by 21 per cent. In the case of the telegraphs, however, two messages with delivery by special messenger cause just twice the trouble of one message. The Post Office, by periodical deliveries, may reduce the cost of delivery on its own principles, but it cannot apply these principles to the actual operations of telegraphy; it cannot send a hundred messages at the same cost, and in the same time as one, like it can send one hundred letters in a bag almost as easily as one letter. It is true that the rapidity of transmission of messages through a wire can be greatly increased by the use of Bain's telegraph, or any of the numerous instruments in which the signals are made by a perforated slip of paper, or a set of type prepared beforehand. But these inventions economise the wires only, not the labour of the operators, since it takes as much time and labour to set up the message in type or perforated paper as to transmit it direct by the common instrument. Economy is to be found, rather, in some simple rapid instrument of direct transmission, like the Acoustic telegraph, than in any elaborate mechanical method of signalling. There is no reason, as far as we can see at present, to suppose that a Government department will realise any extraordinary economy in the actual business of transmission. The number of instruments and the number of operators must be increased in something like the same proportion as the messages. And as every mile of wire, too, costs a definite sum to construct and maintain in repair, it follows that, strictly speaking, the cost of transmission of each message consists of a certain uniform terminal cost, with a second small charge for wires and electricity, proportional to the distance.

It will be apparent, from these considerations, that we must not rashly apply to the telegraphs the principles so admirably set forth by Sir Rowland Hill, in his celebrated pamphlet on the Post Office. When the financial conditions of the telegraphs are in many points so different from those of the Post Office, we cannot possibly look for any reduction of charges to such an extent as he proposed in the case of the Post Office. Whatever reduction may be found possible will arise rather from adventitious points in the scheme—the economy in office accommodation, the aid of the Post Office in delivery, and so forth.

Under these circumstances it would doubtless be prudent not to attempt any great reduction of charges at first, and if we might eventually hope for a sixpenny rate for 20 words, it is certainly the lowest that we have any grounds at present for anticipating. And though uniformity of charge is very convenient, it must be understood that it is founded on convenience only, and it seems to me quite open to question whether complete uniformity is expedient in the case of the telegraphs.

So far, we have, on the whole, found the telegraph highly suitable for Government organisation. The only further requisite condition is that, as in the Post Office, no great amount of property should be placed in the care of Government officials. If experience is to be our guide, it must be allowed that any large Government property will be mismanaged, and that no proper commercial accounts will be rendered of the amount due to interest, repairs, and depreciation of such property. It is desirable that a Government department should not require a capital account at all, which may be either from the capital stock being inconsiderable in amount, or from its being out of the hands and care of Government officials. Now, this condition can fortunately be observed in the telegraph system. The total fixed capital of the telegraph companies at present existing is of but small amount. I find the paid up capital of the five companies concerned to be as follows:

Electric and International	£1,084,925
British and Irish Magnetic	621,456
United Kingdom	143,755
Private Telegraph Company	95,822
London District Company	53,700
Total paid-up capital	£1,999,658

The above statement includes, I believe, all the actual working public telegraphs within the United Kingdom, except those which the London, Brighton, and South Coast, and the South Eastern Railway Companies maintain for public use upon their lines. With the value of these I am not acquainted.

Omitting the Private Telegraph Company, as it is not likely to be included in the Government purchase, and having regard to the premium which the shares of the Electric and International Company obtain in the market, and the greater or less depreciation of other companies' shares, I conceive that the complete purchase money of the existing telegraphs would not much exceed two and a half millions sterling.

To allow for the improvement of the present telegraphs, and their extension to many villages, which do not at present possess a telegraph station, an equal sum of two and a half millions will probably be ample allowance for the present. The total capital cost of the telegraphs will, indeed, exceed many times the value of the property actually in the hands of the Post Office, but then we must remember that the latter is but a very small part of the capital by which the business of the Post Office is carried on. The railways, steamboats, mail coaches, and an indefinite number of hired vehicles, form the apparatus of the postal conveyance, which is all furnished by contract, at a total cost, in 1865, of £1,516,142. The property concerned in the service of the Post Office is, in fact, gigantic, but it is happily removed from the care and ownership of Government. Now, this condition, fortunately, can be observed in the Government telegraphs.

The construction and maintenance of telegraph wires and instruments is most peculiarly suitable for performance by contract. The staff who construct and repair the wires and instruments, are quite distinct from those who use them, and there need be no direct communication or unity of organisation between the two. Just as a railway company engages to furnish the Post Office with a mail train at the required hour each day, so it will be easy for a contractor to furnish and maintain a wire between any two given points. And it is obvious that the cost of a wire or instrument, and even the charge for the supply of electricity, can be so easily determined and are so little liable to variation that scarcely any opportunity will arise for fraud or mismanagement.

There is a company already existing, called the Telegraph Construction and Maintenance Company, which is chiefly engaged in laying submarine telegraphs, a work of far more hazardous character, but which it has carried on successfully and profitably. And it is certain that if it were thought desirable, some body of capitalists would be found ready to construct, hold, and maintain in repair the whole apparatus required in the Government telegraph service, at fixed moderate charges. Thus would be preserved in completeness those conditions under which the Post Office has worked with such pre-eminent success.

It can hardly be doubted then that if the electric telegraphs of this kingdom were purchased by the Government, and placed in the hands of a branch of the Post Office department, to be managed in partial union with the letter post, and under the same conditions of efficiency and economy, very gratifying results would be attained, and no loss incurred. But, inasmuch as the analogy of the telegraphs and Post Office fails in a very important point, that of the expense of transmission, we should guard against exaggerated expectations, and should not press for any such reduction of rates as would land us in a financial loss, not justified by any economical principles.

It might fairly be hoped that the Post Office department would be able to extend its wires to a multitude of post towns and villages which have not offered sufficient inducements to the present telegraph companies. The number of telegraph stations in the United Kingdom in 1865 was 1,882, whereas there were in that year 3,454 money order offices, and as many as 16,246 receptacles for letters, under the care of the Post Office. The number of private telegraphic messages in 1865 was 4,650,231, which bears but a small ratio (1 in 155) to the number of letters in that year, viz., 720,467,007. It is stated that in Belgium the telegrams are 1 in 73 of the letters, and in Switzerland 1 in 69. This disproportion is the less to be wondered at when we consider, that the telegraphs are only available in this country to those who dwell in large towns or near railway stations. No less than 89 towns of more than 2,000 inhabitants are said to be without telegraph offices, and among these Cricklade has 37,000 inhabitants, Gateshead 33,000, Oldbury 16,000, Pembroke 15,000, Dukinfield 15,000. I find that in the whole of the United Kingdom there is on an average one telegraph station to 16,500 persons; whereas there is stated to be one for every 15,000 in Belgium, and one for every 10,000 in Switzerland. It is well known that in the United States especially, the use of the electric telegraph is much more general than in this country. These facts seem to show that the policy of the existing companies has not led to that extensive use of the telegraph in which we ought to have been foremost. These companies are satisfied if they can pay a good dividend on a limited amount of capital, which they avoid increasing to any considerable extent. They have ceased to compete one against another, but are able to prevent any attempts to bring new capital into the field. Under these circumstances it cannot be doubted that the Government should immediately carry out the scheme which we have been considering for the purchase and reorganisation of the telegraphs.

Some persons might possibly be opposed to this extension

of Government interference and patronage, as being not so much in itself undesirable, as likely to lead to a greater and more hazardous enterprise—the purchase and reorganisation of the railways.

It is well known that opinions have been freely expressed and discussed in favour of extending Government management to the whole railway property of the United Kingdom. I should not like to say that this should never be done, and there are doubtless anomalies and hardships in the present state of our railway system, which demand legislative remedy. But, after studying Mr. Galt's work on railway reform and attending to much that has been current on the subject, I am yet inclined to think that the actual working of our railways by a Government department is altogether out of the question, while our English Government service remains what it is.

The advantages which might be derived from a single united administration of all the railways are doubtless somewhat analogous to those we derive from the Post Office, but in most other respects the analogy fails completely and fatally. Railway traffic cannot be managed by pure routine like that of the mails. It is fluctuating and uncertain, dependent upon the seasons of the year, the demands of the locality, or events of an accidental character. Incessant watchfulness, alacrity, and freedom from official routine are required on the part of a traffic manager, who shall always be ready to meet the public wants.

The moment we consider the vast capital concerned in railways, and the intricacy of the mechanism and arrangements required to conduct the traffic, we must see the danger of management by a department of the English Government. The paid-up capital of the railways of the United Kingdom, including the outstanding debenture loans, amounted in 1865 to £455,478,143; whereas the current working expenses of the year were only £17,149,073, or $3\frac{3}{4}$ per cent. of the capital cost. More than half the receipts, or 52 per cent., go to pay a very moderate dividend of about $4\frac{1}{2}$ per cent. (4·46 per cent. in 1865) on the enormous capital involved. The railways are altogether contrary in condition then to the Post Office, where the capital expense was quite inconsiderable compared with the current expense. And I think I am justified in saying, that until the English Government returns reliable accounts of the commercial results of the dockyards, and other manufacturing establishments, and shows that they are economically conducted, it cannot be entrusted with the vast and various property of the railways.

It has been suggested indeed, that a Government department would conduct the traffic of the railways by contract; but I am unable to see how this could be safely done. The care of the permanent way might perhaps be thus provided for, though not so easily as in the case of telegraph wires. But the other branches of railway service are so numerous and so dependent upon each other, that they must be under one administration. As to the proposal to break the railways up into sections, and commit each to the management of a contractor, it seems to me to destroy in great part the advantages of unity of management, and to sacrifice much that is admirable in the present organisation of our great companies. I am far from regarding our present railway system as perfect; but its conditions and requirements seem to me so entirely contrary to those of the Post Office, that I must regard most of the arguments hitherto adduced in favour of State management as misleading.

I may add that should a Government system of telegraphs prove successful, and should the public desire to extend state management still further, there is a most important and profitable field for its employment in the conveyance of parcels and light goods. Prussia possesses a complete system of parcel posts, and the Scandinavian kingdoms, Switzerland, and possibly other continental countries, have something of the sort. In this country the railways collect, convey, and often deliver parcels for high and arbitrary charges; a number of parcels companies compete with the railways and with each other. An almost infinite number of local carriers circulate through the suburban and country roads, in an entirely unorganised manner. The want of organisation is remedied to a slight extent by the practice of passing parcels from one carrier to another, in a haphazard sort of way, but at each step the parcel incurs a new, uncertain, and generally large charge. A vast loss of efficiency is incurred on the one hand by the parallel deliveries of a number of companies in each town, and on the other hand by the disconnected services of the private carriers. A Government system of conveyance, formed on the model of the Post Office, collecting, conveying, and distributing parcels and light goods, by one united and all-extensive system, at fixed and well-known charges, and carrying out this work by contract with the railways and with the owners of the carriers' carts in all parts of town and country, would confer vast benefits on the community, and at the same time contribute a handsome addition to the revenue. It would tend to introduce immense economy and efficiency into the retail trade of the kingdom, bringing the remotest country resident into communication with the best city shops. It would lighten the work of the Post Office, by taking off the less profitable and more weighty book parcels; and it would, in many ways, form the natural complement to our telegraph, postal, and money-order system. But a scheme of this sort is of course entirely prospective; and it seems to me sufficient at present for the Government and Parliament to consider whether the reasons brought forward by various individuals and public bodies throughout the country in favour of a Government system of telegraph communications are not sufficient to warrant an immediate execution of the plan.

POSTSCRIPT.

11th June, 1867.

In the original paper as read before the Society, a scheme for a Government Parcel Post was more fully considered and advocated, but as there seemed no immediate prospect of such a scheme being discussed, the part of the paper containing it was abbreviated before printing. It now appears, however, that the Railway Commissioners in their Report, which has lately been published (dated 7th May), propose that the Railways should combine by aid of the Clearing House to form a consolidated system of parcel conveyance. Sir Rowland Hill on the other hand, in his separate Report, advocates a small parcel post at a uniform rate, to be conducted by the present machinery of the Post Office, such as had, it appears, been proposed by Mr. E. J. Page in his evidence. It appears to me more plain than ever that however great the advantages of such minor schemes, they should be considered only as preliminary to a general organisation for the conveyance of light goods (say up to 100 lb.) throughout the United Kingdom; in fact to a system of Parcel Posts almost co-extensive with the present Letter Post. I believe that it is almost impossible at present to conceive the advantages that would flow from the cheapness, ease, and certainty of transmission attainable in such a system.

THE POST OFFICE TELEGRAPHS AND THEIR FINANCIAL RESULTS.*

There is no need to describe the course of events which led, in February, 1870, to the actual transfer of the telegraphs to the postal department, and to their reorganisation and extension, at the cost of the public. The public are practically aware of the fact that they have, in every money-order office, a conveniently situated telegraph office, whence they may, at the cost of a shilling, send a message to any town or almost any village in the United Kingdom. The messages appear to be generally delivered with speed and regularity, and most people are satisfied, so far as I can gather.

Under the fostering care of a Government department, the traffic has indeed grown enormously, the number of ordinary messages sent in a year being now about 20,000,000, instead of 6,000,000, as it was just before the transfer. The intelligence transmitted for the newspaper press has been multiplied more than a hundredfold, from 2,000,000 to 22,000,000 of words. According to a statement which went the round of the newspapers, the number of offices has been increased from about 2,000 to little short of 5,600. The telegraph lines now extend over 24,000 miles, with 108,000 miles of wire, compared with 5,600 miles of line, with 49,000 miles of wire, and the average price of a telegram has been reduced from 2s. 2d. to 1s. 2d. The number of telegraphic instruments has been

* "Fortnightly Review," December, 1875, vol. xviii. pp. 826-835.

increased, it is said, in the extraordinary proportion of 11,600 worked by the Post Office, against 1,900 possessed by all the companies. I do not know who first put afloat these numbers, but I find from Mr. Scudamore's Official Report (p. 73) that in reality the telegraph companies had, in 1865, 16,066¼ miles of line, 77,440½ miles of wire, and, in 1868, 6,196 instruments, numbers which compare very differently with those of the Post Office.

Nevertheless, it will be agreed that the practical working of the department is now satisfactory, and but for the statements of certain gentlemen recently commissioned by the Treasury to report upon its financial position, it might have seemed that the results of the transfer afforded matter only for congratulation. This Report, however, shows that the working expenses of the department have steadily advanced, until they form 96⅔ per cent. of the income, leaving scarcely anything to pay the interest on the large sum of about £10,000,000 sterling sunk in the system, or to meet contingent expenses and liabilities. When we observe the steady way in which the working expenses have advanced in proportion, being rather more than 57 per cent. in the fourteen months ending 31st March, 1871, 78¾ per cent. in 1871-2, 89½ in 1872-3, and 91½ per cent. in 1873-4, it becomes impossible to hope that the telegraphs will ever pay their real expenses under the present tariff and regulations.

I have no hesitation in saying that in a financial point of view the purchase of the telegraphs has been a blunder, and that it was brought before Parliament and the country upon representations which have proved in many particulars contrary to fact. I need hardly say that the capital cost of the present telegraphs has been at least four times what was estimated. In his first Report (p. 37), Mr. Scudamore distinctly and confidently asserted that the whole of the property and rights of every description of the companies might be purchased for a sum within £2,400,000. Between two and three times as much has been paid, and there are yet contingent claims of unknown amounts to be met. This discrepancy, however, is nothing to that regarding the cost of reorganising the system. Mr. Scudamore estimated the cost of all the required extensions at £100,000, and, though this sum seemed absurdly small, he elaborately explained before the Select Committee (Q. 1922) that it would be ample to cover the whole cost of the transfer and extensions. We now know, not exactly what the real cost has been, but that it may be roundly stated at several millions, instead of £100,000. In a paper on the subject of the telegraphs, read to the Statistical Society of Manchester, in April, 1867, I estimated the cost of the transfer and reorganisation of the telegraph system, apart from the purchase-money, at £2,500,000; and thus, without pretending to any special knowledge on the subject, I was at least twenty-five times more correct than the Government officer charged with the business.

We were promised a net annual revenue of from £200,000 to £360,000, and were told that we might rely upon this "with almost entire certainty" (Q. 1900*), even with the moderate traffic of 11,000,000 telegrams. At the same time it was plausibly asserted that, as the business increased, the expenses would increase in a much lower ratio (Q. 1867, 2441). I have calculated that, in order to verify Mr. Scudamore's predictions, we ought now to have a *net* revenue from the telegraphs of £600,000, instead of such a trifle as £36,725 in the year ending 31st March, 1875. When we inquire into the particulars of the present great expenditure, like inconsistency between predictions and results is met with. It was not unreasonable to expect that the one centralised staff of officers and engineers required by the Post Office would be less numerous and costly than the aggregate of the four or more separate staffs maintained by the companies. Accordingly, Mr. Scudamore asserted over and over again that this would be the case. He says (Report, p. 38) : "In their case the average expense is swelled by the costs of a divided management, by the rent of many separate establishments, by the maintenance of a staff of engineers, inspectors, and

---

* These numbers refer to the questions in the evidence taken before the Select Committee on the Electric Telegraphs Bill, 1868.

superior officers for each of four companies, whereas one such staff would suffice under a united management." Similar statements were made in various stages of his examination before the Select Committee (Q. 2152, etc.), and we were even told that, in the higher grade of clerks, the rates of salary under the Post Office would be lower than in the companies (QQ. 3296—3298). Compare such statements with those in p. 8 of the Treasury Commissioners' Report, where we are informed, "That the salaries of all the officials of the telegraph companies were very largely raised after their entry into the Government service," and that, in fact, "much higher rates are paid by Government for the subordinate work of the Civil Service than are given by private employers for similar duties." Nor does the amalgamation seem to have effected any economy at all; for we are told, on the same authority, "That the staff at present employed for the supervision of the Consolidated Service in the secretary's office, the engineer-in-chief's office, the divisional engineer's offices, and the account branch is comparatively greatly in excess of that considered necessary under the divided management of the telegraph companies." In regard to the account branch, I may point to Mr. Scudamore's assertion (Q. 2438), that the previously existing staff of the Post Office could, with a trifling additional expense of £1,000 a year or so, undertake all the accounts of the telegraphs. After calculating that the companies must spend at least £12,000 a year on accounts, he says: "I will undertake to say, without the slightest fear, that the accounts will not cost us £1,000 in addition to what we already spend for accounts." Again, he says emphatically: "£1,000, I am confident, is an extremely liberal estimate for that." Now we are told on the best authority that the staff of the account branch of the telegraph department is in excess comparatively of that of the aggregate of the old companies, that is, I presume, in excess *comparatively* to the traffic conducted.

It ought not to be forgotten that throughout the preliminary reports and the proceedings before the Select Committee, it was distinctly stated and promised that the

Post Office would not require or even desire a statutory monopoly of telegraphic business. Mr. Scudamore, in fact, said distinctly: (*Q.* 294) "I never should wish for that protection." Nevertheless, no sooner had the business advanced a step than a clause prohibiting all competition in inland telegraphic business was at once inserted in the Act of Parliament.

Various pleas have been put forward in defence of the department, the most plausible, perhaps, being the assertion that the results are exactly comparable to those of the Post Office after the penny postal reform. Nothing, however, can be more opposed to facts. It is true that the great reduction of postal charges caused a loss of net revenue of £1,159,000, and that twenty-four years elapsed before the same net revenue was again realised. This fact alone ought to be a caution to those who are so frequently and rashly asserting that low charges pay best. But there is this great difference between the postal and telegraph reforms—that the postal net revenue was never less than half a million, and, still more, that it immediately began to recover, so that by the year 1847 it had nearly reached a million. To put this matter in the clearest light, I have compared the net revenue of the Telegraph Department with that of the Post Office, during corresponding years before and after the penny postal reform. The results are in the following table :

	Net Revenue and Profit.	
	Post Office.	Telegraphs.
First year before reform	£1,659,087	—
First year after ,,	500,789	£303,456
Second ,, ,,	561,249	159,834
Third ,, ,,	600,641	103,120
Fourth ,, ,,	640,217	90,033
Fifth ,, ,,	719,957	36,725

There cannot be a greater contrast than between the rapid progress of the postal net revenue and the alarming decrease in the telegraph net revenue. This comparison entirely bears out the statement of the Treasury Commissioners that "The Telegraph Branch is not in the position of the Postal Department, after the introduction of the Penny Postage." It reminds one, too, of the remark of Adam Smith, that the Post Office was the only kind of business that Government had always managed with success.

The explanation of this difference, I believe, is that which I gave in my paper, published by the Manchester Statistical Society, on the Analogy between the Post Office, Telegraph, and other means of Communication, namely, that the Post Office stands in an entirely unique position as regards the great increase in traffic which can be carried on with a small increase of cost. Sir Rowland Hill's reform was sound and successful, because he really did show that an immensely increased business could be done at a uniform charge of one penny. A postman, to put the principle as briefly as possible, can carry a hundred letters as easily as one, and a ton of mailbags can be transmitted by railway almost as easily as a single bag. But it is totally the reverse with the telegraphs, in which each message has to be individually received by a clerk, transmitted, retransmitted, written out, and finally delivered by a special messenger. In this case every increase of traffic involves an increase of expense in nearly the same ratio as regards many items.

From the fallacy of imagining that we can do with the telegraphs or railways just what we have done with the Post Office has arisen all this miscalculation. Whatever we may think of the bargains which the postal authorities made with the telegraph companies, or of the manner in which they expended the Savings Bank money without authority, they doubtless believed that all would be justified when they could show a large net revenue. Mr. Scudamore stated his opinion to the Select Committee that (Q. 2252) "the estimated net revenue will cover any capital that can possibly be wanted.' I can well remember, too, that the newspaper press generally urged him on to a vigorous and fearless policy, on the ground that the telegraphs would be sure to pay if they were only brought to every man's door, and the charges made low enough.

It is curious to reflect what would have been the consequence, if, as many people wished, a uniform sixpenny rate had been adopted instead of a shilling rate. Some of the Select Committee seemed to be in favour of such a rate, and Mr. Scudamore almost committed himself to it, saying (Q. 2105), "I am very much of opinion that a sixpenny rate will eventually pay very well," and (Q. 2508, see also QQ. 2541–2546), "I should be very much surprised if we did not come to a sixpenny rate in a few years." One member of the Select Committee actually argued that the telegraphs would produce a larger net revenue at sixpence than at a shilling, on the ground that daily newspapers paid better now at a penny than formerly at sixpence. He appears to have entirely overlooked the fact that newspapers look somewhat to the revenue from advertisements, and that in many cases they would continue to pay handsomely if the printed sheets were given away.

The blunders into which so many have fallen about low telegraphic charges are the less excusable, because there was abundant evidence to show what would be the results. The United Kingdom Telegraph Company had introduced a uniform shilling rate between all the principal large towns, which give the most remunerative traffic, and had found it impossible to make a fair profit. The London District Company had tried sixpenny and fourpenny rates, and could not pay their working expenses. Mr. Grimston, the Chairman of the Electric and International Telegraph Company, wrote a review of the scheme of Messrs. Chadwick and Scudamore, in which he showed various strong reasons for believing that it could not pay. Subsequently, in a very able pamphlet, entitled "Government and the Telegraphs, a Statement of the Case of the Electric and International Telegraph Company," he stated these arguments at greater length, and showed what seem to me conclusive reasons for believing that, in the State telegraphs of Belgium and Switzerland, low charges had never really paid the working expenses, the international telegrams at a higher charge being the real source of profit. These warnings were well known to Mr. Scudamore, to the Select Committee, and to all concerned in the business, and Mr.

Scudamore attempted to show their groundlessness. Yet they have been verified. I ought to add that one member of the Select Committee, namely, Mr. Goschen, appeared to be fully aware of the real financial characteristics of the scheme brought before them; he evidently foresaw the results of the negotiations, and was in a minority of one in protesting against some of the principal resolutions of the Committee.

I come now to inquire what must be done under the circumstances. I regret to observe a great tendency in the public and the newspaper press to treat the matter lightly, on the ground that a quarter of a million is nothing to the English Government, and that we get the value back in convenience. Assuming, for the present, that the loss is only a quarter of a million, which I much doubt, I may observe that the money might be spent better than in paying for needless telegrams. Spent, for instance, upon scientific investigation, and the higher education of the people, it would return results incomparably more important, and would place this country at the head of the civilisation and intelligence of the world. But whether or not money should be spent in other ways, I hold that it is bad in principle to incur a loss upon work which can be so readily made to pay its own expenses. If the country thinks little of a quarter of a million annually, it is because its finances have been regulated on sound principles, and our position would have been very different had we many affairs on hand like that of the Telegraph Department.

Many would be quite ready to argue, with Mr. Edwin Chadwick, that there is really no loss at all, because everyone who sends a telegram probably saves more in time and convenience than the cost of the message. But if this be so, then I ask, Why should other people be taxed to pay for this profit and convenience? If it is so great an advantage to be able to send a message at any moment, why cannot the sender pay the real working expenses of the work, just as we pay the full cost of loaves and legs of mutton? We must pay ultimately in one way or another, and I see no particular reason why we should be taxed to promote the sending of messages, rather than a hundred other useful things. No doubt many of the telegrams produce great profit to the senders; then why should they not pay a small part of the profit to cover the expenses? On the other hand, a large part of the increased traffic on the Government wires consists of complimentary messages, or other trifling matters, which we can have no sufficient motive for promoting. Men have been known to telegraph for a clean pocket-handkerchief. I may even venture to doubt whether the immense quantity of press telegrams now sent through the wires, at a great loss to the department, is really requisite. This traffic is a hundred times as great as it was eight or ten years ago, and, of course, if one newspaper largely employs the telegraph, others must do so in self-defence. But would not much of the matter be just as useful if sent by post? Whether this be so or not, others must decide; but I entirely object on principle to the Government subsidising the newspaper press, as it practically does at present. The ruinously low press tariff was one of the worst features of the Post Office scheme.

The question still remains, What is to be done? Many people will deprecate any retrograde movement, as it is called, on the ground that all will come right of itself. But the public should disabuse themselves of this notion. The Treasury Commissioners, after a full inquiry, say: "The conclusion from these figures cannot be avoided, that, unless some check is put on the expenditure, or some means devised for augmenting the receipts, the management of the telegraphs will become a permanent charge on the finances of the country" (p. 11). My own opinion is, that the telegraphs ought to be not merely paying the bare interest on the debt, but laying up a sinking fund for the redemption of that debt, or for meeting increased cost of maintenance. A very large sum of money has been spent by the Post Office during the last seven years on new posts and wires, which require renewing every fifteen years, on an average, so that this cost must be re-incurred after eight years more. Is the Post Office providing for this cost out of present revenue, or is it leaving the matter till the evil time comes? Remembering that, according to the Treasury Commissioners, even the stationery required by the Telegraph

Branch was under-estimated, year after year, to the extent of one half, it would require a great deal to convince me that the department is even paying its expenses, not to speak of contingent charges in the way of pensions, the railway claims, extraordinary damage from snowstorms, and the ultimate redemption of capital. Mr. Scudamore formerly thought it desirable and probable, that the telegraph revenue would repay the capital cost in a term of years (Report, p. 148). My own impression is that, if we could have a real commercial audit of the accounts of the department, the present loss would be found to be more nearly half a million than a quarter of a million annually, including the interest on capital.

Some people, I feel sure, will urge the Government to reduce the tariff yet further. "Not pay at a shilling?" they will say; "then charge sixpence, and there will soon be traffic enough to pay." I quite agree that, at half the present charge, we should have a vast increase of messages; and I think it likely that the department would have to provide for fifty millions of messages a year instead of twenty millions. But if we could at all judge of the future progress of the working expenses by their past progress, the financial result of a sixpenny rate would be to give us a deficiency of a million and a quarter, instead of a quarter of a million. In all probability the deficiency would be not less than a million pounds annually.

According to the experience of the Electric and International Company, indeed, a double business (increased by 105 per cent.) was transacted, with an addition to the working expenses of only 33 per cent., and Mr. Scudamore assumed that the same would be the case in the Government service. "As a matter of course," he said (Q. 1888), "the average cost of a message decreases with the increasing number." This, unfortunately, has not proved true with Government officials, for an increase of traffic of 81 per cent., between 1871 and 1874, involved an advance in the current working expenses, apart from the expenditure of capital, of 110 per cent. Under such circumstances, the department might as reasonably expect to retrieve their position by lowering the charges, as a tradesman might expect to make money by selling cheaper than he buys. The case will appear all the more hopeless when we consider that the working expenses have advanced even since the introduction of the wonderful invention of duplex telegraphy, by which the carrying power of many of the wires has been doubled at a stroke, with very little cost.

The Treasury Commission make several suggestions as to the mode in which the revenue of the department could be raised to an adequate point. The inclusion of addresses in the twenty words, a tariff of 6d. for ten words, and a tariff of 1d. per word, are successively suggested. Of these the third seems to me oppressively and needlessly high; the second would probably cause more loss than gain, and still more hopelessly damage the revenue of the department. The first is surely the true course. It is found that at present the address of the sender consists, on the average, of four words, whereas two or three would be sufficient. The address of the receiver occupies, on the average, eight words. No less than fourteen words are required for the private service instructions of the operators, and with seventeen, the average number of words in a message, the total number of words transmitted for each shilling, on an average, is forty-three. At present, a person having very little to say is tempted to word his message fully, and fill it out, so as to make nearly twenty words, the charge being no greater. If the addresses were included in the twenty words, they would be abbreviated, say nine or ten words in all, leaving ten or eleven words for the message. This number of words would be sufficient for a considerable proportion of telegrams, when properly condensed, and the needless filling out would be checked for the most part. The average number of words transmitted for each shilling message would probably be reduced by ten words, or nearly twenty-five per cent., and the cost of transmission thus, in some degree, lessened. At the same time, the surcharge upon longer messages, whether charged at the rate of 3d. for five extra words, as at present, or $\frac{1}{2}d$. per extra word, as I should propose, would produce a distinct addition to the receipts. It is quite doubtful, however, whether these changes would make a good balance-sheet without a considerable addition to the newspaper tariff.

It has been quite recently stated that the Post Office Department is disposed to adopt the suggestion of a sixpenny rate for short messages. On the whole it might be desirable to try the experiment, for the purpose of convincing the public, once for all, that high profits do not always attend low prices. Nothing but a complete breakdown will make people discriminate between the financial conditions of letter-carrying and those of telegraphy. Yet it ought to be pretty obvious that a considerable part of the cost of a telegram will be nearly the same whether the message be long or short. The clerk's time in receiving the message, the service instructions sent by wire, the cost of stationery, the porter's time in delivering the message, and some other items, will be much the same in any case. If, then, the public pay only sixpence instead of one shilling for each ordinary message, it is exceedingly unlikely that the difference will be saved in the diminished cost of transmitting twenty-five per cent. less words.

In the letter branch of the Post Office the economical conditions of the work are entirely different. A large part of the expenses of the department remains nearly unchanged while the traffic increases, and only a small part is actually proportional to the number of letters carried. Thus a reduction of charges in the Post Office often leads to such an increase of traffic that the net revenue, even at the lessened rate, is ultimately increased. But this happy result can only be achieved in the absence of any serious increase of working expenses. Now, in the telegraph branch a growth of traffic, as we have seen, and as experience proves, leads to a great increase of working expenses, and it follows almost inevitably that any reduction of the minimum charge for a message will cause a further deficit in the telegraph accounts.

The financial failure of the Telegraph Department must be deeply regretted, because it puts an almost insuperable obstacle in the way of any further extension of government industry in the present generation. The proposal that the Government should purchase the whole railways of the kingdom was, indeed, never a practicable or even a sensible one, as I have endeavoured to show in a paper published in the Owens College Essays. The notion that an experienced official could be appointed to negotiate the purchase of the railway property and then reorganise it in the style of the Telegraph Department, is simply humorous. But to one who has looked through the documents respecting this telegraph business, the conviction must come home that such an operation can hardly be repeated, even on a small scale. When we remember how profits running for ten years only were bought at twenty years' purchase; how the owners of a rotten cable since relaid, received more than the whole money they had spent upon it; and how the extension of the telegraph lines, when purchased, cost considerably more than the whole of what had previously been spent by the companies on the invention and introduction of the system, we must see that a series of disastrous precedents has been established.

One of the greatest needs of the country at present is a Government system of parcel conveyance, which would relieve the Post Office of the larger books and other unremunerative heavy traffic, and at the same time organise into one system the great number of carrying companies, parcel delivery companies, and country carriers which now exist. At present the waste of power in the delivery of parcels at consumers' houses is extremely and absurdly great, and the charges made are in many cases exorbitantly high. A well organised system of parcel posts would produce benefits quite comparable with those of the penny postal reform, and would immensely improve the methods now employed in retail trade, and the distribution of goods to consumers. But if we must first buy up the rights and profits of all at present engaged in the conveyance of parcels, in the style of the telegraph purchase, the scheme becomes impracticable.

The accounts of the Telegraph Department unfortunately demonstrate what was before to be feared, namely, that a Government department cannot compete in economy with an ordinary commercial firm subject to competition. The work done is indeed great, and fairly accomplished on the whole, and some people regard the achievements of the department as marvellous. They forget, however, that it has been accomplished by the lavish and almost unlimited expenditure of the national money, and that many wonders might be done in the same way. If the English people like to spend their public revenue upon cheap telegrams, of course they can do so, though there may be two opinions about the wisdom of the expenditure. But in any case it is not wise for us to forget the extreme discrepancies between what was promised and what has been achieved by the telegraph department.

POSTAL NOTES, MONEY ORDERS, AND BANK CHEQUES.*

THERE can be little doubt as to the need felt by the public for more convenient means of remitting small sums of money by post. The increase of correspondence between different parts of the country is constantly multiplying the number of small debts, debts which cannot be paid by passing coin from hand to hand. The practice is rapidly growing up of buying supplies of draperies, teas, books, and numberless other commodities from well-known firms, situated in a few of the larger towns. Only a well arranged system of parcel posts, as pointed out in the article "A State Parcel Post," in *The Contemporary Review* (January, 1879, vol. xxxiv. p. 209), is needed to develop this mode of traffic immensely. But even with the present vexatious charges on small goods traffic, the number of parcels distributed must be very large, and each parcel, as a general rule, necessitates a postal payment. The facility of railway travelling, again, leads people to reside further from their friends than in former days, and multitudes of domestic servants, workmen away from home in search of work, commercial travellers and tourists, require either to receive or remit small sums of money.

The Postal Money Order System is older than is generally supposed, having existed in one form or other since 1792. In its present form, however, the system dates only from the year

* "Contemporary Review," July, 1880, vol. xxxviii. pp. 150-161.

1859, and extensions and improvements are frequently announced. In safety and eventual certainty of acquittance, money orders leave little to be desired. The payer has only to walk to the nearest Money Order Office; wait five or ten minutes while other customers are being served; fill up a small application form; decide, after mature deliberation with the postmaster, and reference to a private official list, upon the Money Order Office most convenient to the payee; than wait until the order is duly filled up, counterfoiled, stamped, etc.; and finally hand over his money, and his work is done, with the exception of enclosing the order in the properly addressed letter. The payee, too, may be sure of getting his money, if all goes well. He need only walk to the Money Order Office named, sign the order, give the name of the remitter, and then the postmaster, if satisfied that all is right, and if furnished with the indispensable advice note from the remitting office, will presently hand over the cash. But sometimes the advice note has not arrived, and the applicant must call again; not uncommonly the payer, with the kindest intentions, has made the order payable at a distant office, imagining, for instance, that Hampstead Road Post Office must be very convenient to a resident of Hampstead. The payee must then make a tour in search of the required office—unless indeed he or his friend happens to have a banking account, when all goes smoothly in a moment, and the banker instantly relieves him of further labour in obtaining the seven shillings and sixpence, or other small sum, which the Postmaster-General holds for his benefit. But, seriously speaking, time is too valuable to allow us to deal with many money orders. Business men must long ago have demanded a complete reform of the system, were it not that the bankers came to the rescue of the department, by agreeing to collect the orders, and the Post Office people soon discovered that the banker was the safest and easiest medium of collection.

Within the last six or seven years, however, an interesting attempt has been made to replace money orders by bankers' cheques. There used to be a tradition that it was illegal to draw a cheque for less than twenty shillings; and many people still have an uneasy feeling about drawing a cheque on Lombard Street for half-a-guinea. But the Cheque Bank, established by the late Mr. James Hertz, has helped to change all this. Not only do people now draw very small cheques in their own cheque-books, but, if they happen not to possess that luxury, they walk into a neighbouring stationer's or draper's shop and ask for a Cheque Bank cheque, which is simply filled up and handed over in exchange for the money without more ado. This cheque may be posted to almost any part of the habitable world, and will be worth its inscribed value, for which most bankers, hotel-keepers, and other business people will cash it, irrespective of advice notes and localities. About six years ago, when preparing my book on "Money," for the International Scientific Series, I inquired minutely into the working of Mr. Hertz's scheme, which seemed to form the downward completion of the banking system, and after six years of subsequent experience, I see no reason to alter the opinions I then expressed about the new kind of bank. The Cheque Bank has met with but one real check, and that is the penny stamp duty, in respect of which the bank must already have earned a large revenue for the Government, while the Money Order system has occasionally been losing revenue.

The Post Office authorities, not unnaturally moved by this state of things, have now produced a scheme for the issue of Postal Notes, which, if successful, are no doubt intended to supersede money orders and Cheque Bank cheques as well. The Bill now in Parliament for establishing this scheme bears the names of the present Postmaster-General Professor Fawcett, and of Lord Frederick Cavendish. The rather startling draft regulations which accompany the Bill purport to be the orders of the Right Honourable Henry Fawcett. But it must surely be understood that this eminent economist is not responsible for the details of the scheme, except in a purely official capacity. The Bill, though altered in details, is not now put forward for the first time, and it is due either to the late Postmaster-General, Lord John Manners, or else to that vague entity "The Department." But whatever be its origin this Bill is an interesting document, and its clauses imperatively demand consideration.

The idea of the system is to issue orders for fixed integral sums, rising by steps from one shilling as a minimum, to half-a-crown, five shillings, seven shillings and sixpence, ten shillings, twelve shillings and sixpence, seventeen shillings and sixpence, to a maximum of one pound. A person wanting to remit, say nineteen shillings, must therefore apply for the next lower note, namely, seventeen shillings and sixpence, together with a shilling note, and then add six penny stamps, and enclose the whole to the payee. These notes will be issued, apparently, with a blank space for the name of the payee, and another for the name of the office where they are to be paid. In this condition the order may be handed about like a piece of paper money, and will have, so far as I can understand the Bill and regulations, absolute currency. Like a coin, it will be *primâ facie* the property of its holder, and its *bonâ fide* owner will be unaffected by the previous history of the note. Any holder, however, may fill up one or both blanks, and it then becomes payable only to a particular person and (or) at the particular office named. It would appear, however, that if the payee thus named in the order signs the receipt at the back, the note again becomes practically payable to bearer, like an endorsed cheque to order. Clause 8 of the regulations provides that if the note bears a signature purporting to be the signature of the payee, "it shall not be necessary to prove that the receipt was signed by or under the authority of the payee." There are elaborate provisions for the crossing of these Post Office cheques, both generally and specially, and it would seem that even though the name of a distant Money Order Office be inserted in the blank, a banker may, under Clause 10, safely cash a note. The regulations point distinctly to a desire of the department to withdraw their notes from circulation as much as possible, through the banking system of the kingdom.

The currency of these notes is somewhat restricted by Clause 11 of the regulations, which provides that when more than three months old notes will only be paid after deduction of a new commission equal to the original poundage, and a like further commission for every subsequent period of three months, or part of such period. Payment may under the next clause be refused in case a note bears signs of tampering or fraud. Then follows the important provision, that "a postmaster may refuse or delay the payment of a postal order, but shall immediately report such delay or refusal, with his reasons for it, to the Postmaster-General." As, however, this report seems to be intended for the private satisfaction of the Department, and there is no clause requiring the postmaster or the Postmaster-General to give reasons to the holder of the note, this regulation makes the notes convertible into coin *at the will and convenience of the Department.* There is no act of bankruptcy nor breach of engagement in refusing payment. The local postmaster has simply to give as his reason for suspending payment that he has no funds, and the Department will doubtless regard his reason as a very good one.

Perhaps the most extraordinary clause of the regulations is No. 16, which provides that, if a note be once paid by any officer of the Post Office, both the Postmaster-General and all his officers shall be discharged from all further liability in respect of that order, "notwithstanding any forgery, fraud, mistake, or loss which may have been committed, or have occurred, in reference to such order, or to the procuring thereof, or to obtaining the payment thereof, and notwithstanding any disregard of these regulations, and notwithstanding anything whatsoever." Thus is Professor Fawcett, by his own mere fiat—for this clause occurs only in the regulations which purport to be the act of the Postmaster-General—made to shelve the whole common and statute law of the realm in his own favour. Even his own regulations, laid down in the same fiat, are not to be binding on this potentate, who is to be free from all question "notwithstanding anything whatsoever." These words are indeed a stroke of departmental genius. Red tape is potent for binding the outside public; but within the Department no bonds of law or equity are to be recognised in case of error, "notwithstanding anything whatsoever."

I came to the study of this scheme much prejudiced in its favour, because it might be the means of breaking down the absurd objection of the English people to the use of one pound notes. A well-regulated issue of such notes would conduce to everybody's convenience, and might give a substantial addition to the revenue, with absolute immunity from financial risk. But then such a currency must be issued on the principle of the Bank Charter Acts, and under strictly defined statutory conditions. It must be absolutely convertible at the will of the *bonâ fide* holder, and must not be issued for such trifling amounts as one shilling or two shillings and sixpence. In Norway and Sweden, notes of about five shillings in value form a perfectly successful and convenient currency, but as a first experiment it would not be wise to advocate the issue of anything less than a ten shilling note. Even a one pound note currency with token gold half-sovereigns would meet all real needs. But after considering the details of this Post Office scheme, it presents itself as a currency "leap in the dark."

In the first place, it is quite doubtful whether the postal notes will really fulfil their ostensible purpose of enabling postal remittances to be made easily and safely. The case will be provided for, no doubt, if the notes can be purchased in bundles and kept in the cash-box, and if, again, they can be got rid of, when superabundant, in paying cab fares, small bills, etc. Few visits to the Post Office would then be needed, the notes being current. But what about safety? Almost every postal remittance on this system will contain not only paper money payable to bearer at any Money Order Office, but also postage stamps to make up the odd pence. An ingenious letter-carrier will probably soon learn how to detect the enclosure of postal notes, and even if he destroy the notes themselves, a fair average day's wages might at any time be made out of the stamps, by a systematic operator. Nor is any method of reading enclosures indispensable; for many newspaper offices, large shops, booksellers, and others, habitually receive so many small remittances, that a bold and sagacious post office servant might trust to the theory of probabilities, and prey judiciously on the correspondence of a few favourite firms. The Department appears to have entirely overlooked the circumstances which give such security to bankers' cheques, especially Cheque Bank cheques, namely, that they are made out for odd sums, are seldom or never in the company of postage stamps, are returned for verification and payment within a few days, and, when crossed, are only payable through a bank, that is, through the hands of a perfectly well-known and responsible customer. If the postal notes are to be promptly returned for payment, they may prove even more troublesome than money orders; if they are to circulate as a small paper currency, they can give little security against peculation, especially considering the stamps which will usually accompany them. *The Statist*, indeed, in an able article on this scheme, in the issue of June 5th, which should be read in connection with an equally able article in the same journal for March 13th, seems to take for granted that these postal notes, with the accompanying stamps, will need to be remitted in a registered letter. But if so, the aggregate trouble and cost of the operation will be almost greater than in the case of the present money orders, and the *raison d'être* of these new notes disappears altogether.

The fundamental objection to be made to this scheme is, no doubt, as pointed out by *The Economist, Statist*, and several other important authorities, that it enables the Post Office Department to create a considerable circulation of paper currency, without providing any corresponding guarantees as regards a metallic reserve. It is a Bank Charter Act for St. Martin's-le-Grand, *minus* the sound principles embodied by Peel in that great Act. There is something humorous in the idea of a sound and sensible economist like Professor Fawcett being made by his Department, as the first step in his official life, to throw over all the nice considerations which belong to the theory of currency. In the lecture-hall at Cambridge, the examination-rooms at Burlington Gardens, or around the board of the Political Economy Club, a score of abstruse questions would arise about the raising of prices, the drain of gold, the seasonal fluctuations of a small paper currency, the proper limits of government industry, and so forth. But, as Postmaster-General, the Professor ignores all theory, and disclaims all liability, "notwithstanding anything whatsoever." Though hardly responsible for the details of a scheme framed while he was yet merely a professor, he will become responsible for them if he advocates the passage of the Bill through Parliament, or if he allows the scheme to crop up again in a subsequent session.

The worst point of the Bill is that it provides no regulations for the custody or disposal of the large sum of money which will be paid into the Department, if the public takes a fancy to the notes. It is quite impossible to estimate, by any reference to theory or fact, how large the balance will be. In all probability it will not be less than two or three millions sterling, and quite likely double that. If the orders should prove to be popular in the capacity of paper money, the circulation might possibly amount to twenty millions. No ordinary person, indeed, can pretend to understand how the Post Office people can manage to keep a cash reserve at each of nearly six thousand Money Order Offices. Markets, fairs, races, currents of tourists, fluctuations of trade must cause great and often unexpected variations of demand, and it is financially absurd and impossible, and against all the principles of banking, to divide a cash reserve into six thousand fragments! Nor, indeed, is there any provision for the regulation of a metallic reserve, or any reserve at all. The Department would, no doubt, like to have a few millions at their unfettered disposal; but surely a Post Office Bank Charter Act, devoid of any mention of a cash reserve, and with careful provisions for suspending payment whenever convenient, is a monstrous anomaly, and, I may almost say, an insult to the financial common sense of the country.

I suppose we ought to feel indebted to the postal authorities for condescending to give us the pretty full details contained in the present Bill and Draft Regulations. The earliest form of the scheme, as embodied in the Bill of June, 1877, consisted in simply suspending, as regards the Post Office, all laws restricting the issue of promissory notes payable to bearer—a simple *carte blanche* to the Department to embark in the issue of paper money. In each subsequent edition of the Bill they have condescended to be more and more explicit. Now the Draft Regulations give us all we can want to know, subject to this difficulty, that these regulations may be revoked and altered, within the limits of the Act, by the mere fiat of the Postmaster-General, subject to the consent of the Treasury and the somewhat illusory check of being laid before Parliament within fourteen days after it assembles. I feel sure that I express the opinion of every sound economist when I say that, if we are to have an unlimited circulation of one pound notes and small fractional currency, that currency must be issued under conditions clearly and inflexibly defined by statute. An examination of this Bill, however, will show that it is for the most part an enabling Bill; the restrictions, such as they are, are mostly contained in the regulations, and are revocable by Government without further appeal to Parliament. In fact, the second clause* of

---

* As it seems indispensable that the country should know upon what basis its future fractional currency is to be issued, I reprint here the 2nd clause of the 11 & 12 Vict. c. 88. It is well worthy of inquiry how far the 16th article of the Draft Regulations can be reconciled with the Act on which it purports to be based:

"And be it enacted, that it shall be lawful for the Postmaster-General, with the consent of the Commissioners of Her Majesty's Treasury, at any time hereafter, to make any regulations or restrictions relating to money orders, either heretofore granted or issued, or to be hereafter granted or issued, and to the payment thereof, and to the persons by or to whom the same shall be paid, and to the times at which, and the mode in which the same shall be paid, as the said Postmaster-General, with such consent as aforesaid, shall see fit, and from time to time, with such consent as aforesaid, to alter or repeal any such regulations or restrictions, and make and establish any new or other regulations or restrictions in lieu thereof; and that all such regulations and restrictions shall be binding and conclusive, as well upon the persons to whom such money orders have been, or shall be granted or issued, and the payees thereof, and all the persons interested or claiming under them, and all other persons whomsoever, as upon all officers of the Post Office; and all such regulations and restrictions shall have the same force and effect in all respects as if the same had been and were contained in and enacted by this Act; and that no action, suit, or other proceeding at law

the Post Office Money Order Act, 1848 (11 & 12 Vict. c. 88), which is embodied in the new Bill, appears to me to enable the Treasury to suspend payment altogether whenever they feel inclined so to do, right of action being barred, "Any law, statute, or usage to the contrary in anywise notwithstanding" (!)

The proposals of this Bill assume a still more ominous aspect when we consider them in connection with the kindred new Savings Bank Bill. This latter Bill, among other matters, is intended to raise the limit of deposits to be made in any one year in a Post Office Savings Bank from £30 to £100, and the total allowable deposit, apart from interest, from £150 to £250. The two Bills taken together disclose a settled design on the part of the Post Office to become a vast banking corporation, and to enter into direct competition with the bankers of the United Kingdom. It is impossible not to agree with the protest issued by the managers of the ten principal banks of Manchester, that such changes would involve a complete change in the *raison d'être* of the Post Office Monetary Department. The Post Office Savings Banks, as the Manchester bankers correctly remark, were intended to act as eleemosynary institutions—as, in fact, public schools of thrift. By the whole conditions of the original scheme they were designed to induce labourers, nursemaids, children, and other people of very small means to begin saving their odd shillings and half-crowns, and to a certain extent they have fulfilled that purpose. The Post Office was in this respect a *deus ex*

---

or in equity shall be brought, instituted, or commenced in any court, or before any Judge or Justice, or otherwise howsoever, against the Postmaster-General, or against any officer of the Post Office, or against any other person whomsoever, for or by reason or in consequence of the making of any such regulations or restrictions, or of any compliance therewith, or otherwise in relation to any such regulations or restrictions, or for or by reason or in consequence of the payment of any such money orders being refused or delayed by or on account of any accidental neglect, omission, or mistake, by or on the part of any officer of the Post Office, or for any other cause whatsoever, without fraud or wilful misbehaviour on the part of any such officer of the Post Office, any law, statute, or usage to the contrary in anywise notwithstanding."

machinâ—it was Jupiter called from above to help a thriftless residuum out of the mire of pauperism. The present limits of the deposits are quite sufficient to meet all the needs of this class. To allow a person to deposit as much as £100 in a year in a State Bank is to step over the line into a totally different class of operations. The matter is made all the worse by the fact that financially the constitution of the Post Office Savings Bank is bad and indefensible. As Mr. William Langton has abundantly shown, to receive a deposit to be paid at call, and then invest it in Government funds of variable value, always throws risk on the Government. A preponderance of withdrawals is always made while the funds are depressed, and an increase of deposits will usually coincide with a high price to be paid by the Department. Thus has already arisen a large deficit on the investments of the old Savings Banks to the extent of nearly four millions, a deficit which Mr. Gladstone is now very properly proposing to pay off by a terminable annuity. The Post Office Banks have hitherto avoided a like deficit by offering only 2½ per cent. interest, and keeping the amount invested moderate. But it by no means follows that what has hitherto answered fairly well on a small scale, will always answer as well on the bolder scale now proposed. Already the savings of the people, held on a radically false basis by Government, amount to about three-quarters of a hundred millions. With the enlarged limits proposed for the Savings Banks, and probably additional investments on account of the postal note deposits, we shall soon reach a hundred millions, or one-eighth part of the whole National Debt. Should any serious crisis ever occur, such as a great naval war (and how can we expect to be always free from danger ?), withdrawals would unquestionably take place, and the Government would be obliged to make forced sales of its own securities, running down its own credit, and incurring a deficit at the very time when it most needed resources. No doubt in such circumstances the Government would be obliged to raise a large loan in the open market, but this would really mean that when compelled to redeem its promises the Government would have to fall back upon those very bankers with whom it had been competing on most unfair conditions in easier times. The Post Office monetary schemes are essentially fair weather schemes, but they must founder, like *The Eurydice* and *The Atalanta*, in case of squalls and rough weather.

If the English Government is really fitted to do banking business, why does it not begin with its own accounts? Why leave the National Debt, the Dividends, the Revenue payments, and a variety of large public and semi-public accounts in the hands of the Bank of England, aided by a banking organisation generally? The fact of course is that not only from the time of Adam Smith, but from a much earlier date, it has always been recognised that a Government is not really a suitable body to enter upon the business of banking. It is with regret that we must see in this year 1880 the names of so great a financier as Mr. Gladstone, and so sound an economist as Professor Fawcett, given to schemes which are radically vicious and opposed to the teachings of economic science and economic experience.

Did space admit I might go on to show that the conditions which the Post Office demand as essential to the success of their monetary operations are tainted by a kind of political immorality. Every common carrier and every banker is responsible under complicated statutes and the common law for every act of negligence, and for not a few accidents involving no negligence. But the Post Office, though it enters into competition with the industry of the country, sets itself above the law. Even a registered letter, if lost, stolen, or destroyed by its own servants, throws no responsibility on the department, except as regards the tardy and absurdly small concession of £2, provided certain regulations be carefully observed. Now, the same department coolly proposes to issue an unlimited paper currency and to do a large part of the banking business of the country under like considerations of irresponsibility. Professor Fawcett, Lord John Manners, or whatever other deserving politician happens to hold the place of Postmaster-General, is to conduct a vast monetary business, and yet to be the final arbiter in all his own transactions with the British public, irrespective of the Law Courts.

Nor, if we investigate the matter, will it appear that there is any real need for these schemes, except to magnify the influence of "The Department" which propounds them. If the banking system of this kingdom were in a rudimentary state, like that of the Fiji Islands, there might be some reason why the Government should try to educate its subjects up to the banking stage of civilisation. But if anyone will take the trouble to look through the Banking Almanack, and to study some accounts of the bankers' clearing-house system, he will appreciate the degree in which the country needs to be taught banking. The Post Office, great as its system may be, is mere child's play compared with the wonderful organisation which settles transactions to the extent of one hundred millions per week in Lombard Street without the use of a single coin. The very remarkable statistics drawn up by Mr. Newmarch, and printed in the Banking Almanack for this year, go to show that the system of Branch Banks is being extended in a wonderful way, and bids fair to distance even in number the increase of money order offices. According to these statistics, the number of Branch Banks, as distinguished from separate Banks, or Head Offices, was in 1866, 1,226; in 1872, 1,386; in 1878, 1,801. The increase in the former interval was at the rate of about 13 per cent., and in the latter 30 per cent. ! The number of money order offices was in 1866, 3,454; in 1872, 4,300; in 1878, 5,719, and though the rate of increase is considerable, being in the first interval $24\frac{1}{2}$ per cent., and in the second 33 per cent., it does not manifest the same tendency to progressive advance which we notice in the branch banking system. There can be little doubt that the bankers of England and Scotland, if not interfered with, will, in the next ten or fifteen years, establish banking offices in every nook and cranny of the kingdom where there is any business at all to be done, and their competition will result in offering facilities for small savings and small payments which must altogether distance the operations of any Government Department.* An impartial review of the whole question can only lead us to the conclusion that the bankers are right in crying out to the Government, "Let us alone!" It is a new phase of the old economic adage—*laissez faire—laissez passer;* the only novelty in the matter is, that the cry is now addressed to a great Minister and an eminent economist, the latter of whom has advocated in his writings what the former has, to a great extent, carried into effect.

But to return to our more immediate topic of Postal Notes, I will now point out that it is only government interference which prevents bankers from organising a system of small payments by cheques, far more perfect, safe, and convenient than anything the Post Office can do. The Cheque Bank has already done more than the department; it has done a large business in small payments, with almost complete freedom from fraud, and has paid at the same time a large revenue to Government through the penny cheque stamp. But this penny tax, though quite inconsiderable in larger payments, becomes intolerably oppressive in the case of payments under a pound or two pounds. The Post Office probably loses on the smaller transactions of the money order system, and what revenue it does seem to gain is gained on the larger orders, at least so *The Statist* holds. For my part, I cannot see how we can be sure there is any gain at all, because the business is conducted

---

* In his speech on the Savings Bank Bill (June 18th), Mr. Gladstone is reported to have said : " If they had in this country a banking system so largely developed that it went into every town and considerable parish, he certainly should be very doubtful indeed as to the desirability of raising the upper limit of £200. . . . The Post Office Savings Banks for the three kingdoms were already beyond 6,000, and were rising at the rate of 300 banks a year ; but the other banks, notwithstanding the excellent development which they had undergone, hardly reached 2,000, banks and branches taken together."

There must be some mistake here; for Mr. Newmarch's figures show the total number of banks and branch offices in the United Kingdom to be 3,554, or 78 per cent. more than Mr. Gladstone is reported to have said. Moreover, the branches, as shown above, are being multiplied in an advancing ratio of multiplication ! Clearly, according to Mr. Gladstone's own admission, he ought to relinquish the part of the Bill raising the limit of deposits.

by the same persons and in the same premises as the general post business, and we can by no means be sure that each of the functions of a postmaster is separately paid in a degree adequate to its trouble. Nevertheless, the Cheque Bank, according to its last report, now about pays its way, in addition to paying a considerable revenue to the Crown.

There is needed but one change to set the whole matter right, and that is to reduce the stamp duty on small cheques, say those under £5 or £3, to one halfpenny. The penny stamp duty on receipts, as everyone knows, is not required in the case of receipts for less than £2, for the obvious reason that it would be absurdly oppressive in the case of small receipts. But exactly the same reason holds good for reducing the tax if not abolishing it in the case of small drafts. There need be no practical difficulty in doing this; for an Act of Parliament of little more than one clause might enact that any cheque form of any banker, bearing upon its face a printed and also an indelible perforated notice that it can only be drawn for a sum of (say) £5 or under, may be impressed at the Stamp Offices with a halfpenny stamp, and shall then be deemed duly stamped, all previous Acts notwithstanding, in the same way as if it had, according to the Stamp Act of 1870, been impressed with a penny stamp. Such a change in the law would create no monopoly for the Cheque Bank; for if the success of this bank became considerable, competitors would soon spring up, and there would be nothing to prevent any bank from supplying its customers with halfpenny cheques for small drafts. No doubt, the Cheque Bank, in urging the reduction of the penny stamp duty, does so from a weak, because an interested position, but it is possible for other persons to advocate the same measure from a purely public and disinterested point of view.

In the use of such small cheques there is nothing economically unsound. The experience of the Cheque Bank has shown that their cheques do not circulate for any considerable length of time. Being drawn for odd sums, needing endorsement and being all crossed, it is not likely they should circulate. They are exceedingly safe for postal transmission; no post office thief could possibly venture to negotiate cheques, which are, I believe, regularly treated as "duffer," or dangerous stuff. It is, indeed, a serious question for bankers, how they are to meet the trouble arising from any great multiplication of small cheques. But in any case I do not see how they are to avoid these small transactions, even if they desire it. Cheque Bank cheques are, I imagine, less troublesome than postal money orders, which bankers already collect in large numbers for their customers. As to the proposed small shilling and half-crown notes, it seems to me that they will give infinite trouble to bankers, who must not only sort and count them like the smallest fractional currency, but must examine the dates, to ensure that they are not running beyond the three months' interval of free currency. The Post Office clearly intend, if possible, to oblige the bankers to receive these small notes, judging from the regulations about crossing. If, indeed, the bankers unanimously refuse to receive such notes, the scheme must, I think, fall to the ground, even though Parliament should sanction it.

The general conclusion, then, to which I am forced to come is, that this scheme of postal notes is a mistaken one, which should never have been allowed to come forth under Mr. Fawcett's name. It is neither fish nor flesh; neither a well regulated paper currency, nor a safe system of banking payments. It is the scheme of a tenacious and aggressive *bureau* to underbid the Cheque Bank, and by setting at nought all the customary risks of monetary transactions, to secure the disposal of large funds, while throwing much of the trouble and cost upon the banking community. In the conveyance of parcels and small goods the Post Office has yet much to do, as I have taken trouble to prove; but in the direction of banking, it has already reached a limit which it cannot be safely allowed to pass.

POSTSCRIPT.

Since the above was in type, it has been stated that the Government will propose to amend the Bill by restricting the currency of the postal notes to one month. This will mar the beauty and success of the scheme. It will be indispensable in a subsequent Session of Parliament to enlarge the interval of currency to three months, if not the twelve months originally proposed by the department. Several homely proverbs occur to one: "Give an inch, take an ell"—"Get the thin end of the wedge in first." In regard to the Post Office Savings Bank deposits, the wedge is just now being driven home a little. The promoter of the Postal Telegraph Department disclaimed all idea of a statutory monopoly of telegraphic business, saying, "I never should wish for that protection." There is now an action pending in the Law Courts by which the department will bring the telephone companies well under control. Ministries come and Ministries go; the Department remains.—19th June, 1880.

A STATE PARCEL POST.*

At a season of the year when many persons are anxious about their Christmas hampers and their New Year's gifts, it is appropriate to consider whether our social arrangements for the conveyance of such-like small goods are as well devised as they might be. We all now feel how much we owe to Sir Rowland Hill for that daily pile of letters which brightens the breakfast table more than does the silver urn, and sweetens it more than the untaxed sugar basin. In these kinds of matters great effects follow from small causes, and a few pence more to pay, a few yards further to walk, or a few hours longer to wait, constantly decide whether or not it is worth while to send this little present, to order that little comfort, or exchange this parcel of library books. The amenities of life depend greatly upon the receipt of a due succession of little things, each appearing at the right moment. Wealth itself is but matter in its right place—happily disposed in quality and time and space. Hence it is possible that among the most insidious methods of social reform might be found a well organised State Parcel Post. That at least is the impression which leads me now to investigate the subject.

It may be said, indeed, that in a sense we already possess a State Parcel Post, because the Post Office authorities place no restriction upon what may be enclosed in a letter, provided that it be not injurious to other letters or dangerous in nature.

* "Contemporary Review," January, 1879, vol. xxxiv. pp. 209-229.

An inland letter is limited to 18 inches in length, 9 inches in width, and 6 inches in depth, and this space may be packed with cast-iron or platinum if you like, and yet transmitted by post, so far as the regulations in the British Postal Guide show. But except for very small light things, few people use the privilege, because the letter rate for large letters is 1d. per oz., which makes 1s. 4d. per lb., a prohibitory charge upon articles of any considerable weight. If I recollect aright, it was allowable some years since to forward parcels at the book rate of postage, which is only 4d. per lb., but trouble arose between the Post Office and the railway companies, so that this comparatively moderate charge is now rigidly restricted to literary matter.

A number of writers have from time to time pointed out the very great advantages which would arise from a general, well arranged, and cheap parcel post. It is stated on the best authority,* that such a post formed part of the scheme which Sir Rowland Hill submitted to the public, and Mr. Lewins, in his interesting account of "Her Majesty's Mails" (p. 247), points out what an unspeakable boon this suggestion of the father of the penny post would be when properly carried out. I regret that I have not been able to discover any explicit statement of such a scheme in the original pamphlets of Sir Rowland Hill, which are among the most cherished contents of my library. The proposal must, then, be given in other documents which I have not seen.

In subsequent years the Society of Arts took up the idea, and appointed a committee, which in 1858 published an elaborate and careful report upon the subject. They recommended that parcels should be conveyed by the Post Office at a moderate uniform tariff of charges, irrespective of distance. That scheme, we are told, was carefully considered by the postal authorities; and in still later years, as we may infer from Mr. E. J. Page's Evidence before the Railway Commission of 1865, the Post Office has entertained the idea.

---

* Royal Commission on Railways, 1865. Minutes of Evidence, Question 15,010.

Again, that veteran social reformer, Mr. Edwin Chadwick, advocated a parcel post delivery, in connection with railway reform, and a cheap telegraphic post. His paper was read at the Belfast meeting of the Social Science Association, and is printed in the Journal of the Society of Arts for October, 1867 (vol. xv. p. 720). The subject was unfortunately mixed with the, to my mind, visionary proposal to purchase the whole railways of the kingdom, and, naturally enough, nothing practical has resulted from the discussions in that direction. My own study of the subject commenced about the same year, when I prepared for the Manchester Statistical Society a paper " On the Analogy between the Post Office, Telegraphs, and other systems of conveyance of the United Kingdom, as regards Government control." After investigating in a somewhat general manner the conditions under which industrial functions can be properly undertaken by the State, I came strongly to the conclusion that a parcel post is most suitable for State management. But this part of the paper was, at the suggestion of the Society, very much abbreviated before being printed, so as to allow the arguments in favour of a Government telegraph system to be more fully developed.

In 1867, the Royal Commission on Railways published their Report, in which they strongly advocated the establishment of a parcel post. They remarked (p. lxiii.) that railway companies are not bound to carry parcels, nor is there in the railway Acts of Parliament any tariff for parcels, limiting the charges for collection and delivery. The public is, therefore, at their mercy. They consider that a separate tariff should be laid down and published to govern the conveyance as distinguished from the collection and delivery of parcels, so as to enable the rates of charge to be kept down by the free action of individuals acting as carriers by railway. Then they add:

"It is, however, apparent that the parcel service, so far as interchange is concerned, can never be efficiently performed for the public until railway companies co-operate through the Clearing-house to improve their arrangements for parcel traffic. Looking at the extent to which the railway system has now reached, we consider that the time has arrived when railway companies should combine to devise some rapid and efficient system for the delivery of parcels. We do not feel called upon to suggest the precise manner in which this may bo carried into effect; but the employment of a uniform system of adhesive labels for parcels, somewhat similar to that now in use on some of the northern lines for the conveyance of newspapers, is one of the most obvious methods for facilitating payment and accounting.

"If the railway companies do not combine voluntarily it may be necessary at some future time for Parliament to interfere to make the obligation to carry parcels compulsory, at a rate to be prescribed by law."

Sir Rowland Hill, who was a member of this commission, prepared a separate Report, in which he advocated the carrying out of his original idea, saying (p. cxvii.):

"It appears highly desirable that, as fast as railways become national property, provision should be made in the leases for giving effect to these views; and in the meantime, fully believing that the plan would prove beneficial to railway interests as well as to the public, it is hoped that arrangements for the purpose may be made (as suggested by Mr. Edward Page) for attaining the same end with the concurrence of existing companies."*

It would be hardly possible to over-estimate the advantages which would be derived by the community from an all-extensive, well organised, and moderately cheap parcel post. People may say that it is already possible to send a hamper or parcel from any one place to any other place in the kingdom for charges which, all things considered, are not very heavy. But this is not enough; the cost, after all, is only one element of the question in cases of this kind. Trouble, worry, uncertainty, risk, are influences which always affect traffic in a

* The only response, so far as I am aware, which has been made by the railway companies to the kind advice and somewhat feeble overtures of the Commissioners, has been a recent general increase on the already oppressive railway rates for parcels. In November, 1867, the imposition of this arbitrary tax created some indignation among tradesmen who were most likely to feel its immediate effects, and the Birmingham Chamber of Commerce convened a kind of representative indignation meeting. But I am not aware that their expostulations have had any effect, and I fear that even the Four Hundred, with Mr. Chamberlain, at their head, cannot shake a board of directors, with the Acts of Parliament in their favour. Thus, while the railway companies never cease to assail us with protests against the railway passenger duty, which at

degree insufficiently estimated. The Post Office authorities find that every new receptacle for letters which they set up increases correspondence by a certain amount; the trouble of going a hundred yards to post his letter stops many a letter-writer. So there are endless numbers of parcels which we should send and receive, if we knew that for a small calculable charge we could deposit them in a neighbouring shop, or hand them over to a cart passing daily at a fixed hour, with a feeling of certainty that such parcels would be dropped at the right doors in any part of the kingdom, almost with the celerity of the Post Office. The parcel traffic which might ultimately be created is such as one can only faintly conceive at present. Profound and always beneficial changes would be gradually produced in our social system. The Parcel Post would be discovered to be truly a method of social reform. Let us try to form some idea of the advantages to be expected from it.

In the first place, dealers and shopkeepers in every part of the kingdom would obtain their supplies of goods from the wholesale houses cheaply and promptly. Ordered by letter, goods might be returned within forty-eight hours; by telegraph the order might be executed, if necessary, in twenty-four hours. Thus the stock in hand might be kept down to the lowest point, and the largest profit might be earned upon the least investment of capital, with the least inconvenience to the consumer. In the second place, a vast increase would take place in the goods distributed directly to consumers in all parts of

the worst is five per cent. of the gross revenue, they coolly add to their duty upon all the small traffic of the country, which duty may be variously estimated at from 100 to 300, 400, or 500 per cent. upon the fair cost of conveyance. It is only the supineness of the public which could allow so gross an anomaly to exist. Much as we may admire the general efficiency and usefulness of the English railway system, taking it as a whole, it seems difficult to understand how sensible practical men like the directors can expect to have every vestige of state taxation upon *them* remitted, while they are to retain almost unlimited power to tax *us*—the people—at their discretion. If the railway duty is to be remitted at all, it must necessarily be in the manner of a *quid pro quo*, in part compensation, for instance, for the acquisition of the right of parcel conveyance.

the country by large retail or even wholesale houses. Already it is quite common to obtain tea by parcel from some well-known large tea-dealer, calicoes and linens from a large draper, seeds and garden requisites from the London, Edinburgh, or Reading seedsmen; small-wares here, ironmongery there, biscuits and cakes somewhere else. To cultivate their distant customers, those large houses often promise to send the parcel *carriage paid*, but they carefully specify "to any railway station in the United Kingdom." They are too well acquainted with the cost and uncertainties of delivery to take that burden on themselves. And as regards the railway charges, they seldom pay the extortionate tariff given further on, but, if in a large enough way, have a special contract with some railway.

For this mode of retail trade there is an immense future, only retarded by the want of the parcel post. By degrees all the more ordinary household supplies might be obtained in parcels direct from the ports or places of production. In many branches of trade the expenses of the middleman might be saved almost entirely. Weekly or even daily parcels of butter, bread, cakes, Devonshire cream, and all kinds of delicacies might be looked for. The rich would especially profit, as they usually manage to do. The vineries, hot-houses, and gardens of their country houses would be brought, as it were, close to their town houses. Already the railway traffic managers have displayed their usual cleverness by offering specially low terms for parcels of vegetables, game, etc., thus regularly transmitted to a rich man's house. Even a daily bottle of milk, hermetically sealed according to the new American invention, and thus perfectly preserved from fever germs, might be sent from the country to the town house at a cost distinctly below the prices of Belgravian dairies.

Literature would benefit immensely. The most remote country house might be as well supplied with Mudie's books as are the members of the London Book Society, or the dwellers near a Smith's bookstall. The utility of lending libraries, such as the London Library, the London Institution, the several music lending libraries, etc., would be developed to the utmost. Magazines, weekly papers, provincial papers, would more or less experience an increase of circulation;

although it is true that the means of distribution by railway or post are in many cases highly perfected already.

Then, again, there is an immense variety of now unconsidered trifles which would assume a new importance when we had but to wish, as it were, and the parcel was come or gone. The new toy for some child, the bundle of old clothes for a poor distant dependent, the basket of game for the hospital, the wedding present, the Christmas hamper, the New Year's gift—these would be multiplied almost like Christmas cards, to the great increase of trade, and the constant delectation of the receivers. The circulation and utilisation of things in general would be quickened.

It may be said indeed, that there is at present no lack of carriers and parcel companies; and this is quite true in a sense. If anything there are too many, and the result is that they can only be supported by high and repeated charges. Let us consider what are the existing means for the conveyance and distribution of small goods. In the first place, almost all the railway companies receive parcels at their stations, which they convey either by passenger or goods trains to any other of their stations. In the great towns each company has its own service of delivery vans which, within certain limits of distance, deliver the parcels free of further charge. When the consignee lives beyond a certain distance, the parcel is often handed over to some local carrier, who makes a new charge for delivery, at his own discretion; or else the railway company send their van on a special journey, and charge an extravagant price for the favour conferred, not extravagant perhaps in regard to the cost incurred in sending a cart with a single small parcel, but extravagant in proportion to the service performed. The railway companies also have arrangements for the exchange of parcel traffic at through rates, and an infinite number of small debits and credits thus arise, which have to be liquidated through the Clearing-house. So oppressive did these innumerable minute accounts become, that the companies adopted a few years ago a summary mode of dividing any receipts at a station which do not amount to five shillings in a month.

Secondly, there exists a considerable number of parcel conveyance companies which organise systems of distribution on a more or less extensive scale. As examples of these may be mentioned the Globe Parcel Express, Crouch's Universal Parcel Conveyance, Mann's Parcel Despatch, Sutton and Co. These companies are in some degree analogous to the excellent American Express Companies. Some of them undertake to convey parcels to almost any spot on the habitable globe; but they must depend upon local conveyances for performing the contract. In the United Kingdom, they, of course, make use of the railways for conveyance over long distances. At one time the railway companies, if I recollect aright, waged a war of extermination against them, claiming a right to charge each parcel sent by a parcel express at the parcel rates, although they might be packed in bulk. But the courts of law did not uphold this extravagant demand of the railways, and the express companies seem to carry on a flourishing business.

In the third place there is a number of local parcel delivery companies, each of which owns many vans and horses, but restricts its operations within the area of a town or other populous district. As examples of such may be mentioned the London Parcels Delivery Company, Carter, Paterson & Co., Sutton & Co.'s London System, etc. These companies serve the whole metropolitan area. Other large towns generally have similar companies on a proportionate scale. Liverpool, Glasgow, and Edinburgh especially have extensive systems of distribution.

Lastly, there is an almost infinite number of small disconnected carriers, who serve particular villages and lines of road. They are usually men who own one, two, or at most only a few carts and horses, who travel daily into some country town, and put up at a favourite public-house. This house serves as a depôt for parcels and messages left for them, and the carrier calls at various places on and off his usual route, whether to pick up or deliver small goods, according to instructions. Their charges are very various, and governed by no rule; except in London, the only law on the subject seems to be to the effect that the charge must be *reasonable,* whatever that may mean. But they seldom charge less than 4*d*. or 6*d*. for any parcel. The men are usually illiterate and slow in all their proceedings. Their number is often very great. In the London Directory for 1876 there are specified about 216 such carriers; in Glasgow, some years ago, there were 147, and many large towns would each have 100 or more local carriers.

All this mass of conveyances, be it remembered, is in addition to the vast number of private delivery carts employed by tradesmen. Great establishments, such as Shoolbred's, Marshall and Snellgrove's, Whiteley's, Maple's, Burton's, etc., etc., have each their own parcel delivery company, so to say. Some houses even have two deliveries a day in the metropolitan districts. The immense cost of such delivery staffs would be, to a great extent, saved by a parcel post; but it is, of course, not to be supposed that the ordinary tradespeople's delivery of meat, vegetables, etc., would be much affected.

At first sight this mass of carrying arrangements seems to be chaotic, but necessity is the mother of invention, and necessity has obliged these disconnected and often antagonistic bodies to work together to a certain extent. When one carrier gets to the end of his tether he assumes a right to hand on his parcel to any other carrier he likes, who "pays out" the charges already incurred, adds his own charge at discretion, and recovers the sum-total from the helpless consignee. Whether this practice is legal, in the absence of any distinct prior contract, I am not able to say; but it is, at any rate, sanctioned by force of habit and necessity. The larger parcel companies, of course, have arrangements with each other, and they often undertake to deliver goods in distant towns at the lowest rates, passing the parcels on from one to another.

One result of this multiplicity of carriers is that it is usually impossible to ascertain what the conveyance of a parcel will cost. For traffic between the large towns, indeed, there are definite tariffs published by the express companies, but these documents are not easily to be obtained. Between Manchester and London, for instance, a parcel under 1 lb. may (or lately might) be sent by mail train for 4*d*.; under 12 lbs., for 2*s*. From Glasgow to London the rate was 8*d*. under 1 lb.; 2*s*. 6*d*. under 12 lbs. But these charges include delivery only within town limits, which limits are drawn at the discretion and convenience of the deliverers. The multitudes who now dwell in suburban parts are almost entirely at the mercy of the carriers, who will either send their carts specially, and make a large extra charge, or hand the parcel over to local carriers, who impose their own new toll. Not long since a book, weighing less than 2 lbs., was presented at my house at Hampstead with a demand for 1s. for delivery. It appeared to come out of Fleet Street, but, wherever it came from, might have reached me by post from any part of the United Kingdom for 7d. or 8d. On refusing to pay an apparently extortionate charge without explanation, the book was promptly carried off, and I have never seen it since. With the railway companies the case is almost worse; not only do they, as we shall see, maintain an extortionate general tariff, but they have narrow limits of free delivery, and can charge anything they like for delivery beyond those limits. When living in the suburbs of Manchester in a very populous district only four miles from the centre of the town, I often had experience of this fact. In one case a book package weighing ½ oz. less than 3 lbs., and *carriage paid by the sender*, was charged 1s. 2d. for delivery by the railway company. About the same time another book, weighing a little *over* 3 lbs., was received by post, carriage paid, for 1s. 0½d., this being the whole charge, and delivery being far more rapid than by parcel van. On another occasion a parcel of seven copies of a book, weighing in all 5½ lbs., although *carriage paid* to the extent of 1s. 6d. at London, was charged 1s. 2d. for delivery at Manchester, in all 2s. 8d.; whereas, had the books been made up into two or more parcels at London and sent by post, they would have reached me for a total cost of 1s. 10d. The climax, however, was reached in the case of a parcel of forty copies of a book, which were received by railway at such a cost that each copy might have been made up into a separate parcel, and despatched by post to forty different addresses in all parts of the United Kingdom for about the same aggregate cost. Nor can the consignee protect himself against such extreme charges. The consignor knows and cares nothing about the delivery charges, and in the usual course sends the parcels to the nearest receiving offices. Instructions which I have repeatedly given to consignors are usually disregarded, and any attempt to recover the overcharge would be regarded as absurd.

Of course the cases which I have quoted are only specimens of what must be happening daily with hundreds of thousands or even millions of parcels. A sixpence or a shilling may be a trifle in itself, but multiply it by millions, and the matter becomes one of national importance. All large sums are made up of little units, and the history of the Post Office before Sir Rowland Hill's reform shows how small oppressive overcharges strangle traffic.

Let us now look at the charges which are made by the principal railway companies for conveyance and delivery within the usual limits. These are by no means uniform, and each company usually has exceptional rates for certain districts. The following table, however, which is an extract from the tables of the London and North Western Railway, contains a uniform tariff which has been recently adopted by the principal companies—such as the North Western, Midland, Great Northern—carrying to the north of London. It will therefore serve as a good specimen:

With few exceptions, the Scale of Charges (exclusive of Booking Fee) to or from Stations on the London and North Western Railway is as under:

For Distances of	Miles	And not exceeding	1 lb.		2 lbs.		3 lbs.		3 lbs. to 7 lbs.		Above 7 lbs. and not exceeding	Above.		Per lb.
		Miles.	s.	d.	s.	d.	s.	d.	s.	d.	lbs.	s. d.	lbs.	d.
	1	30	0	6	0	6	0	6	0	6	24	0 6	24	0¼
Above...	30	50	0	6	0	6	0	6	0	8	16	0 8	16	0½
,, ...	50	100	0	6	0	6	0	8	0	10	16	1 0	16	0¾
,, ...	100	150	0	6	0	9	1	0	1	3	15	1 3	15	1
,, ...	150	200	0	8	1	0	1	3	1	6	14	1 6	14	1¼
,, ...	200	250	0	9	1	0	1	6	1	9	16	2 0	16	1½
,, ...	250	300	0	9	1	0	1	6	1	9	16	2 4	16	1¾
,, ...	300	400	0	9	1	0	1	6	2	0	15	2 6	15	2
,, ...	400	500	1	0	1	3	1	9	2	6	18	3 0	18	2
,, ...	500	600	1	3	1	6	2	0	2	9	16	3 0	16	2¼
		Above 600	1	6	1	9	2	3	3	0	16	3 4	16	2½

A Special Scale is in operation in the districts of Lancashire and Yorkshire, and to the lines south of the Thames.

This tariff is wonderfully constructed. As regards the columns towards the right hand, I give the puzzle up altogether. It passes my understanding why the limit of weight should be made to vary at different distances from 14 lbs. to 15 lbs., 16 lbs., and 18 lbs. I have studied inductive logic; but no logic seems likely to disclose reason or method here. As regards weights under 7 lbs. there is at least the appearance of reason, and that reason is the exacting the utmost that the unfortunate owner of the parcel can be induced to pay. It is true that for small distances the charge, *exclusive of booking fee*, is not altogether immoderate. For 6*d.* a 7 lb. parcel may be sent 30 miles, a 2 lb. parcel 100 miles, and so on; this no doubt is designed to prevent competition by road carriers; but at larger distances, when horse conveyance is out of the question, the public is made to smart. A 1 lb. parcel transmitted 500 to 600 miles costs 1*s.* 3*d.*, exclusive of booking fee; by post the book rate is 4*d.* per lb., or barely more than the fourth part. The postal rate for a letter weighing above 12 oz. is 1*d.* for every ounce. The parcel rate then is only a penny less than the postal rate of a letter! What is most extraordinary about this tariff is the importance attributed to distance. I suppose a 1 lb. parcel sent from London to Glasgow may be put into the van at Euston, and never stirred until it reaches Glasgow; yet the mere transit costs the sender 6*d.* more than for short distances. Now we must suppose that 6*d.* covers all the terminal charges, and costs of collection and delivery, for this is all that the companies ask for short distance parcels, exclusive of booking fees, whatever they may be. Hence at least 6*d.* goes for the cost of traction, wear and tear of van, interest on capital, etc.; but a ton consists of 2240 lb., and a ton weight of 1 lb. parcels would be no great load for a van. Thus the tolls collected on merely carrying that ton load for 400 or 500 miles would be £56, and including collection and delivery it would be £112. A ton load of third-class passengers would yield only £25 all told.

These very excessive charges apply, it is true, only to the smallest parcels; on examining the other columns it will be found that the higher weights are charged at much lower rates, possibly to underbid competition by road, canal, or steamboat. But taking it as a whole this tariff may be described as devoid of all method. It seems to be a purely arbitrary series of numbers, evolved perhaps from the brains of railway magnates arranging a compromise at some conference of the northern directors.

To show, however, how the parcel charges compare with the various other charges made by the railway companies, I have constructed the following table from authentic data furnished by the railway time tables, the reports of railway commissions, etc. The table refers to no railway in particular, and the data were selected almost at random.

	d.
Small parcels	200
Medium	100
Large	40
Newspaper parcels	100
Passengers' excess luggage	66
Commercial travellers' luggage	33
First class passenger fare	175
Second class passenger fare	125
Third class passenger fare	75
Live poultry	100
Watercress	33
Milk	12
High class goods	32
Medium goods	13
Low class goods	4
Coal traffic, lowest rate	1¾

This is an extraordinary table, and shows what latitude the traffic managers allow themselves in taxing or assisting various trades. Like protectionist statesmen, they think the traffic cannot go on unless their vigilance eases or multiplies the burden. Our ancient system of duties, and bounties, and drawbacks, is faithfully reproduced in our railway tariffs, with their classes, and exceptions, and exemptions, and special rates, and endless minute distinctions.

An examination of the table will render it quite evident that the railway companies have deliberately treated the small parcel traffic as a close monopoly which they can tax with any charge they like. No excuse for such excessive charges can possibly be given. It may be explained, indeed, that the newspaper parcels, being a regular daily uniform traffic, can be more easily provided for; but how are we to apply the same explanation to commercial travellers' luggage? For the charge stated, many of the companies allow a commercial traveller to bring as many heavy packages as he likes, and to take them in and out of the trains as many times in the day as he likes, without extra charge. Several porters are sometimes needed to manipulate this luggage, and the train is occasionally detained thereby. But though the companies urge that they do this to promote trade in their districts, why cannot they promote the trade in small parcels also? If properly developed, this traffic would include an immense mass of orders for small tradesmen, and the vast loss of labour and money involved in the commercial traveller system might be partially avoided by the copious use of sample packages. Really it sometimes strikes me as very questionable how far a small body of directors, sitting at Euston Square or Paddington, should be allowed to constitute themselves the judges of the way in which the commerce and the traffic of the country are to go on. They can promote this form of traffic, oppress another, extinguish a third, in a way which Parliament itself would not venture to do.

But let us now turn to another side of this subject, and attempt to decide whether the conveyance of parcels is a kind of industry which is likely to be well and economically conducted by a Government department. As I have pointed out in two previous publications,* we must not assume that a Government department will manage every kind of industry as badly as the Admiralty manage the boilers of their ironclads, nor, on the other hand, as apparently well as the Post

* Transactions of the Manchester Statistical Society, April, 1867, pp. 89-104: On the Analogy between the Post Office, Telegraphs, and other Systems of Conveyance of the United Kingdom, as regards Government Control.—Essays and Addresses by Professors and Lecturers of Owens College, Manchester, 1874 (Macmillan), pp. 465-505: The Railways and the State.

Office manages the distribution of letters. The presumption is always against a State department; but in any particular kind of work there may be special conditions which render the unity and monopoly of Government control desirable and profitable. On this point I will take the liberty of quoting from my paper published by the Manchester Statistical Society, p. 91 :

"Before we give our adhesion to systems of State telegraphs and State railways in this kingdom, we should closely inquire whether telegraphs and railways have more analogy to the Post Office or to the Dockyards. This argument from analogy is freely used by everyone. It is the argument of the so-called reformers, who urge that if we treat the telegraphs and the railways as Sir Rowland Hill treated the Post Office, reducing fares to a low and uniform rate, we shall reap the same gratifying results. But this will depend upon whether the analogy is correct—whether the telegraphs and railways resemble the Post Office in those conditions which render the latter highly successful in the hands of Government, and enable a low uniform rate to be adopted. To this point the following remarks are directed :

"It seems to me that State management possesses advantages under the following conditions :

"1. Where numberless wide-spread operations can only be efficiently connected, united, and co-ordinated, in a single, all-extensive government system.

"2. Where the operations possess an invariable routine-like character.

"3. Where they are performed under the public eye, or for the service of individuals, who will immediately detect and expose any failure or laxity.

"4. Where there is but little capital expenditure, so that each year's revenue and expense account shall represent, with sufficient accuracy, the real commercial conditions of the department."

There can be no doubt, I think, that in all the four points specified above parcel traffic is highly suited to State management. It is conducted at present, as we have seen, by almost numberless disconnected or antagonistic companies and private carriers, who, though not particularly inefficient each in his own sphere, are highly wasteful and inefficient as a system. The operations of the parcel post, again, would be almost as routine-like as those of the Post Office. There would be none of the delicate scientific and technical questions involved in the building of ironclads or the construction of torpedoes. There would be nothing more occult in the carrying of a parcel than in the stamping and sorting and delivery of letters. There would certainly be some variations of traffic to be provided against, especially about Christmas time; but it would not be comparatively worse than the pressure of Christmas cards or valentines upon the Post Office. If necessary, it might be met by a temporary increase of charges during Christmas week. In respect of the third point, the parcel post is as favourably situated as the letter post. Nobody knows nor cares what is done with the boilers of H.M.'s ship *Pinafore* when cruising in Turkish waters; but everybody would know and care, each in his own case, if Mudie's parcel of novels was unpunctual, or the new dress gone astray, or the pot of Devonshire cream gone bad, or the author's life-long labour—his cherished manuscript—irretrievably lost. The officials of the Dead and Missing Parcel Department would need strong nerves and placid dispositions to stand the constant stream of indignation which would fall upon them. There could be no undetected laxity in the parcel department.

In respect, however, of the fourth point of State management there might be room for more doubt. The immense success of the Post Office is much dependent upon the fact that, in respect of letters, the Postmaster-General has little capital expenditure under his charge. The railway companies fortunately own and manage all the more elaborate instruments of carriage, and do the work of the Post Office by contract. The whole of the horse conveyance of the mails is also done by contract, or at least ought so to be done. All the minor post offices, too, are placed in private premises. Only the large buildings at St. Martin's-le-Grand, and the principal offices in the London districts and some of the larger provincial towns, are actually owned by the Government for postal purposes. Beyond this property they only own the letter bags, the stamps, the pillar boxes, and so forth—property in value quite inconsiderable. With the telegraph branch it is different; whether wisely or otherwise (and I incline to think otherwise), the Post Office actually own the posts and wires, instruments, and other fixed plant of the telegraphs. They construct and repair them; and, still worse, they find it necessary to call in the aid of the Royal Engineers to do this efficiently and economically. I have little doubt that all this work ought to have been put out to contract. But, however this may be, the difficulty would not much press in the case of the parcel post; for it would require no extensive and complicated series of scientific instruments for its conduct. The railway companies would of course do the long-distance conveyance; the collection and distribution would, equally of course, be done by hired carts; and, beyond a few weighing machines, porters' trucks, packing cases, and the like simple appliances, it is difficult to see what fixed capital the Parcel Department need own. Receiving and distributing offices would be needed, often on a rather large scale; but they might be leased or built, as was found most economical. Thus I feel sure that, in respect of capital expenditure, the parcel post would be far more favourably situated than the Telegraph Department, and would be closely analogous to the letter post.

Then, again, the parcel monopoly would in no appreciable degree interfere with the progress of invention, as the telegraph monopoly appears to do. In spite of Mr. W. H. Preece's vigorous attempt to show the opposite,* it is to be feared that the birthplace of the electric telegraph has ceased to be the foremost in the race of electrical inventions. Some half-dozen capital inventions, such as duplex and quadruplex telegraphy; the telephone, the carbon telephone, etc., have been made since the Government took the telegraphs. How many of them have been made on English soil? The telephone is, I believe, quite in familiar use in the United States: where is it yet made practically useful in England? The chill of red tape and circumlocution has fallen upon the zeal of invention, a zeal which fears nothing so much as the inertia of bureaucracy, and the cool indifference of My Lords of the

---

* British Association: Dublin Meeting. Journal of the Society of Arts, August 23rd, 1878, vol. xxvi. p. 862. See also p. 890.

Treasury. If ever future historians of a more advanced age inquire into the rise of a new civilisation in the nineteenth century, they will wonder at nothing so much as the treatment of inventors by the English Government. It is as bad and senseless in its way as the imprisonment of Roger Bacon, or the condemnation of Galileo. Neglect, contumely, confiscation, are the fate of the English inventor at the hands of the English Government.

I hold, therefore, that the conveyance of small goods is a kind of business which a Government department would carry on with a maximum of advantage and a minimum of financial risk or interference with the progress of science and industry. In some respects it would have been better to leave the work to the care of a combination of railway companies; but I fear they could never be induced to make the system complete. The whole movement of parcels up to 30 lbs. or 50 lbs. weight should therefore be carried on by a Government organisation closely analogous to that of the letter post, but yet distinct from it; parallel and co-operating when desirable, but not interfering or hampering the more rapid distribution of letters. This department would acquire the parcel business of the railway companies, and would also buy up the good-will of the parcel express companies. It would utilise the whole of the carriers' stock of carts, horses, offices, etc., by employing them on remunerative contracts; it would thus organise, rather than replace, the existing means of conveyance, but by introducing system where there was no system would much increase the efficiency of the present means. Instead of a multitude of carts traversing long distances often to deliver single parcels, each cart would serve one group of houses, to which it would proceed direct from the delivery office with a good load. When the traffic was properly developed, almost every house would have a daily parcel, or even several, and these would be delivered with a speed to which there is nothing comparable now except that of the penny post. As the shopkeepers would deliver almost exclusively through the parcel post, the streets would be freed from their multitude of vans, and customers would eventually be saved the enormous cost which some establishments must bear in maintaining a large staff of delivery carts. The consumers must, of course, bear all such expenses in the long run. As to the employés of the present companies, they would be "taken over" as part of the concerns, and would do doubt have their salaries advanced at once, as in the case of the telegraph companies.

One of the most important and difficult points to determine in connection with the scheme which I am advocating is the selection of a tariff for the future parcel system. The principles on which such a tariff must be founded require careful investigation. As we have seen, Mr. Edward J. Page, of the Post Office, adopts the idea of a uniform parcel rate, as it had been previously upheld by the Society of Arts; he would make the charge independent of distance, and vary it only with the weight of the parcel. The convenience of such a tariff, if it can be adopted, is obvious. With a pair of scales we can infallibly ascertain the weight of the parcel we are sending, and then calculate the fare to be paid. If distance enters, we have to ascertain also the position and distance of the place to which we are consigning the parcel. For this purpose we must consult tables which will seldom be at hand. The greater number of persons will be reduced to simply asking the receiving clerk what is to be paid; not only delay, but uncertainty and opportunity for fraud thus arise—all the disadvantages, in short, against which the fixed tariff of the Post Office insures us. There can be no doubt then about the excellence of a uniform charge irrespective of distance, if it can be adopted.

But on careful examination it will be found that Mr. Page's proposal must be intended by him to apply only to very small parcels, or else it betrays an imperfect comprehension of the subject with which he is dealing. I imagine he must have chosen a uniform tariff on the ground that it answers very well in the Post Office, and therefore must answer well with parcels. By such reasoning as this, one might infer that because a minute dose of prussic acid soothes and benefits the stomach, therefore a good large dose will be still more beneficial.

Mr. Page, like many another hasty theorist, forgets that a whole mail-bag full of letters only makes a moderate parcel. Taking letters at an average of half an ounce each, there are 32 to the pound, or 960 in a 30 lb. parcel. Thus the element of weight enters into parcel traffic, say from a hundred to a thousand times as much as into letter traffic. Sir Rowland Hill's admirable scheme of a uniform postal charge was based upon the carefully demonstrated fact that the mere transit cost of a letter to a distant place did not exceed that to a near place by more than 1–36th part of a penny. There was no coin sufficiently small to represent the difference of cost due to distance, and therefore he was enabled to embrace the uniform charge system. But a little calculation shows how different is the case with parcels.

The mileage rates charged by the railway companies upon goods vary exceedingly, and in the most casual manner. The minimum is usually about $1d.$ per ton per mile, and the maximum is somewhere about $7d.$ Now, $1d.$ per ton per mile is equal to $4\cdot 464d.$ per 100 lbs. per 100 miles, so that, if we were to assume only a medium charge of $3d.$ per ton per mile, a 100 lb. parcel transmitted 500 miles would cost, merely for transit, about $5s.\ 7d.$ The idea of charging this sum for the carriage of a 100 lb. package for a few miles would be prohibitory and absurd. But the rates from which I have been calculating are only those for ordinary goods by goods trains. For parcel traffic we should require either special rapid parcel trains, or else accommodation in passenger trains, which must be costly. Looking to the table given above, we can scarcely expect the railway companies to accept less than $25d.$ per 100 lbs. per 100 miles ($5\cdot 6d.$ per ton per mile)—that is, about a quarter of what they now charge for parcels. At this rate the cost of transmitting the following weights 500 miles, without any terminal charges, is worthy of notice:

		s.	d.
Parcel of 100 lbs.	. . . .	10	5
,, 10 lbs.	. . . .	1	0½
,, 1 lb.	. . . .	0	1¼
Letter of ½ oz.	. . . .	0	·04

It is evident that the analogy between the parcel and the letter post breaks down altogether. Even for a 1 lb. parcel the effect of distance is appreciable; for a 10 lb. parcel it could not be overlooked; for a 100 lb. parcel it would constitute almost the whole of the charge. We are thus reduced to three alternatives in case of adopting a uniform charge. Either (1) we must restrict the weight of parcels, so as to make the parcel post hardly more useful for sending goods than the present letter post; or (2) we must impose so high a charge as would be intolerably oppressive as regards small distances; or (3) we must impose so low a charge that the ordinary goods charges of the railway companies for long distances would be underbid by the parcel post. The result of the third alternative would evidently be that all goods would, as far as possible, be broken down into parcels, and transmitted at the cost of the State. This result would be quite intolerable.

All these alternatives, then, being inadmissible, it follows that a tariff irrespective of distance is impracticable, and we must revert to a mileage rate. The charge should consist of two components: (1) a fixed terminal charge of, say, $2d.$, to cover the costs of booking, delivery, etc.; (2) a mileage charge determined by the compound proportion of weight and distance. A very important point, however, would consist in fixing rightly the minimum charge for very light parcels. Now, parcel companies have been started to work at a minimum of $1d.$; at one time there was a Penny Parcel Company in London, and similar companies have been established in Glasgow and elsewhere. I learn that the Glasgow Tramway Company now convey and deliver newspaper parcels up to 3 lbs. weight for $1d.$ each, but other parcels up to 7 lbs. are charged $2d.$ as a minimum. I do not happen to know of the present existence of any company working with common parcels so low as $1d.$ even for short distances. But even if so low a rate were practicable in particular districts, it could not possibly be recommended for adoption in a general parcel system. The lowest rate which is practically existent in England at present is $3d.$ or $4d.$, and it would not be wise to attempt at first a lower rate than 3*d*. Taking a mileage rate of 5·6*d*. per ton per mile, or 25*d*. per 100 lbs. per 100 miles; adding terminal charges in each case to the amount of 2*d*.; and then raising the result to the next higher integral number of pennies, we obtain the following standard tariff: *

Under lbs.	50 Miles. s. d.	100 Miles. s. d.	200 Miles. s. d.	400 Miles. s. d.	600 Miles. s. d.
5	0 3	0 4	0 5	0 7	0 10
10	0 4	0 5	0 7	1 0	1 5
15	0 4	0 6	0 10	1 5	2 1
20	0 5	0 7	1 0	1 10	2 8
30	0 6	0 10	1 5	2 8	3 11
50	0 9	1 3	2 3	4 4	6 5
100	1 3	2 3	4 4	8 6	12 8

I give the charges up to 100 lbs. weight without implying that the parcel post should necessarily carry up to that weight.

I do not believe that there would be any serious difficulty in working such a tariff as this. The urban and suburban traffic, a very large part of the whole traffic, would fall entirely within the fifty mile limit, and the matter of distance need hardly be considered. I should propose to determine the charges for longer distances by reference to *tariff maps*, as was formerly the practice in the French post offices, when letters were charged at a distance rate. Minute differences are of no account in a general system of conveyance, so that we can readily substitute the distance as the crow flies for the actual distance travelled by road or rail. In the French post office the distances seem to have been measured by compasses applied to official maps; but a little device would save all trouble of measuring.

I would have tariff maps issued by the postal authorities, somewhat like the cheap useful map prefixed to Bradshaw's Guide, but rather larger and fuller, and showing places,

* After calculating this tariff, I find that it nearly corresponds with one which existed four years ago on the former Bristol and Exeter Railway, which charged 3*s*. for carrying 112 lbs. over a maximum of 100 miles. But I should propose the scale only as a first cautious one, and with the hope that slight reductions might be made after the system was in full working order.

instead of railways or other features. Upon the face of this map should be printed light-coloured concentric distance circles, with their centre upon any town or village for which the map was to indicate the tariff. All places within any one zone would have the same tariff as regards the central place; and it is possible that the tariff for the zone might be printed in colours actually within the space to which it applies. Such maps could be produced for every town and village in the country without extra cost; because, with a properly invented press, the colour stone or block could be shifted so as to print its centre over any spot, and the required number of copies would be printed off for the service of that particular place before shifting the circles for the next place.

In the establishment of a State parcel post a multitude of details would of course have to be considered, for the discussion of which there is no space and no need here. For instance, would the parcels be all registered and delivered only for receipts? I am inclined to think that this would be indispensable to prevent pilfering; but it is probable that the labour might be greatly facilitated by the use of some kind of numbered stamp, with perforated coupons. One part of the ticket being affixed to the parcel, serving also perhaps as an address label, the counterfoils might be used as receipts, or filed to save the trouble of booking. I have often amused myself with planning the details of such a scheme of ticket registration, to replace the cumbrous method of books and waybills; but it would be needless to suggest details here. I am sure that some such system will one day be adopted, and become as important and world-wide as the use of stamps and railway tickets. In some parts of Scotland it is already the practice to have duplicate penny and half-penny labels, one of which is pasted on any parcel sent to the left luggage office of any railway terminus, while the counterfoil is retained by the owner; thus when leaving town in the evening by train he can identify his parcel. The use of stamps on newspaper parcels is now quite general, and at least one company, the Bristol and Exeter, extended the use of stamps to their parcel traffic generally. The Glasgow Tramway Company too have adopted the parcel stamp with numbered coupon, to serve as a waybill, and to be torn off by the person delivering the parcel. An easy development of this system would soon replace the cumbrous booking method.

Any person seriously proposing the establishment of a general parcel post might no doubt be expected to produce some estimate of its probable cost. Much minute information, however, only to be obtained by the power of Parliament, would be needed to form a reliable estimate. I am encouraged indeed, to attempt some calculations by the fact that, in the case of the telegraphs, I was, in respect to one important item, twenty-five times more correct than Mr. Scudamore, with all his information,* though, of course, neither I nor any other reasonable person could have imagined beforehand how much he would have agreed to pay the telegraph companies for their rights. But in this case of parcel traffic, we have none of the accurate information which existed concerning the telegraph companies and their capitals and dividends. We have, of course, the official accounts of railway traffic, but the Act of Parliament under which these are collected allowed, or rather prescribed, a form of account in which the receipts from parcel traffic are merged with those from excess luggage, carriages, horses, and dogs! Nor are these items distinguished in any of the reports issued by the companies to their shareholders which I possess. Taking, however, Mr. Giffen's summary tables of railway traffic for 1876, we find that the totals of these items are given as follow :

England and Wales	£2,076,490
Scotland	237,115
Ireland	104,452
United Kingdom	£2,418,057

This sum represents the total gross receipts from such traffic, and as the working and capital expenses can hardly

* Transactions of the Manchester Statistical Society, 1867, p. 98. "Fortnightly Review," vol. xviii. N.S. p. 827.

be assigned in the case of such adventitious sources of revenue, it would no doubt be difficult for the railway companies to assign with any precision the net receipts from parcel traffic. Much information would have to be called forth by Parliamentary authority before it would be possible to frame any estimates of the sums of money involved in establishing a general parcel system. But there is the less need to produce any financial estimates at the outset, because I hold that if the tariff be rightly and cautiously framed, there must be a large margin of economy in the working of the department, which would insure a revenue sufficient to bear all probable charges. The business, as I have pointed out, is analogous to the letter post rather than the telegraph system; there is not the same risk of loss as there was in introducing the uniform shilling telegram, or the uniform sixpenny telegram, as sanguine people wished. The waste of horse-power, of men's time, and of railway carrying power is so immense under the present chaotic arrangements, that to the community as a whole there must be great profit, in reducing that chaos to systematic organisation. So far as I can venture to form any estimate of the financial magnitude of the proposed department, I should say that it will certainly not cost more than three or four times as much as the Postal Telegraph Department. This is no slight sum, indeed, but those who wince at it must remember that it is only about the *twentieth part* of what would be involved in the state purchase of the whole railway system. This favourite proposal I venture to regard as simply visionary, for reasons already given in the Owens College Essays; the advantages would be doubtful, the cost and risks enormous. But in buying up the parcel branch of traffic the cost and risk would be comparatively small, the advantages and profits immense and almost certain.

Practical men will no doubt have more belief in a parcel post when they learn that it is what has been long carried into effect in Prussia, as well as Switzerland, Denmark, and probably other Continental countries. It seems desirable that the details of these postal systems should be ascertained by our consular agencies, and described in their usual reports. But I am glad to be able to give the following minute account of the Government Parcel Post at Berlin, which I have translated from an interesting article on the postal service of Berlin, published in the Berne periodical called *L'Union Postale*, and reprinted in the *Bulletin de Statistique et de Législation Comparée* of the French Ministry of Finance, a copy of which I have the honour to receive from the Ministry.

"All the ordinary parcels (*colis*) destined for Berlin and its suburbs are sent to the parcel office (*bureau des colis*) which is situated in the Arrondissement N, or North, and which is charged with delivering the parcels directly to the houses of the consignees, provided that the latter inhabit the city proper, or one of the suburbs of Gesundbrunnen or Moabit. To give an idea of the importance of this service, and of the resources which it requires, it is sufficient to remark that during the year 1876, it has handled 3,003,131 parcels, and that the reduction of the charge to 50 pfennigs (about 6*d*.) per parcel, up to 5 kilogrammes (11 lbs.), independently of distance, has necessarily had the effect of increasing the traffic from day to day. And there has been appropriated to this service a whole series of contiguous buildings, in which are engaged 72 employés and 214 subordinate agents, without counting 19 boys employed to call over the parcels.

"Two special offices, installed in a separate building, are reserved for parcels addressed to persons or authorities (of which the number is actually 375) who have given instructions that their parcels should not be delivered at their residences; their exists another similar office for parcels destined for the garrison of Berlin. All the other parcels are transported to the residences by distributing vans, and are delivered to the consignees in return for the regulation porterage charge. The places in which the porters deposit and sort the packages are 75 metres (246 feet) long, and 11·60 metres (38 feet) wide, and are divided into 72 compartments. By well-considered organisation of the service, and an intelligent division of labour, it has been found possible to commence each distribution one hour after the arrival of the last consignment which is to form part of it.

"The deliveries take place, during the winter, three times each day (at 8, 12, and 3 o'clock), and in summer four times (at 8, 12, 3, and 5 o'clock); on Sundays the service is reduced to the two earlier deliveries. The number of carts (*voitures*) employed for each delivery is varied according to need; at present there are 62 employed in the first delivery, 36 in the second, 27 in the third, and 25 in the fourth. But during the winter months, when the traffic is very considerable, the first delivery requires 72 carts, without speaking of numerous hired carts which are required during Christmastide.

"As to parcels intended for the suburbs of Berlin (always with the exception of the suburbs Gesundbrunnen and Moabit), the parcel office forwards them by special waggons in care of its agents, to the local post offices respectively charged with their delivery."

Here is an interesting picture of an extensive and successful Government Parcel Post, doing a large business of three million parcels a year. Being unaware whether the charge of 6d. for parcels under 11 lbs. applies to Berlin only, or to conveyance over longer distances, it is not possible to judge of its pressure; but it is a higher minimum charge than we should think of proposing for a British parcel post.

In some parts of Scandinavia, also, there is a well-arranged Government Parcel Post, and Mr. J. E. H. Skinner tells us that in Denmark parcels not exceeding 200 lbs. in weight can be forwarded through the feld-post at a charge of 1d. per lb. for sixteen miles. This charge is far above what we should contemplate in this country; but it applies mostly to road conveyance.

Bad as are our arrangements for the distribution of small goods within the kingdom, the case is still far worse as regards transmission to foreign countries. Even between such great and comparatively near capitals as London and Paris, or London and Brussels, the smallest parcel, of less than 1 lb., cannot be sent for less than 2s. or 2s. 2d. Nevertheless, the postal convention enables us to send book matter weighing less than 2 lbs. for 1d. per 2 oz. Thus a book parcel just under 1 lb. will go as far as Rome for 8d., whereas a parcel of any other kind, of the same weight, will cost three times as much to Paris. Such are the anomalies which our apathy allows to exist. As regards the United States, it is worse still. A year or two ago I heedlessly undertook to send a book weighing under 2½ lbs. to New York, being under the impression that I could post it thither. But at the post office my book parcel was promptly rejected as exceeding the limit of weight. I then took it to two different American mail packet offices, each of which asked 7s. or 8s. for transmitting this small package. With this extraordinary demand I was obliged to comply, as I knew no cheaper mode of transmission. Now, the original value of the book in England was 10*s*. 6*d*.

In the case of small parcels conveyed by steamboat, the mileage cost must be an almost incalculably small fraction. In fact, about 1*d*. per lb. would be ample for the mere freight to America; adding, say 4*d*., for collection and delivery on each side, my book should have been transmitted for about a shilling; or *about one-eighth part* of what it cost. In fact, all this kind of traffic, when not superintended by the State, is treated as a close monopoly, to the great injury of the public, and in the long run, I am convinced, to the detriment of the carrying companies themselves.

There is plainly, then, a world of improvement to be effected in this, as in many other directions. But where is the Rowland Hill to effect it? Few have, like him, the happiness of looking back on a great social reform accomplished by his single-handed energy. Men of the younger generation have little idea of the manner in which he had to fight step by step against the bureaucracy of the Post Office. That department, which now congratulates and eulogises itself upon its wonderful achievements, should never forget that these inestimable improvements were forced upon it, as it were, at the point of the sword. I may have some future opportunity of pointing out how obstructive is the Post Office, or, at least, the Treasury, in refusing to extend the benefits of the Berne Postal Union to the whole world, as the English Government alone might do it. But one thing is enough at a time. It is with the infinite blindness, and selfishness, and obstructiveness of the railway companies in the matter of small goods that we have here to deal. I can scarcely comprehend why they should combine to suppress and strangle this one branch of traffic, when they so ably develop other branches. When it is a question of collecting and conveying milk, or fish, or cockles, or watercresses, nothing can be more effective, and in general economical, than their arrangements. As to the manner in which the railways distribute the morning London newspapers over the length and breadth of the land, nothing can be more wonderful or more satisfactory. But in the matter of small goods conveyance I have shown that blindness, monopoly, waste of labour, chaotic want of system yet prevail. So, though parcels may seem a petty matter, I yet hold that there is in this direction a really great work of social reform to be achieved. There is no reason why we should be separated as we are, either in Britain or in Greater Britain. When we learn to utilise properly our wonderful railway system, and to take advantage of the recent enormous progress of steam navigation, there is no reason why we should not make the whole world kin. Friendship, literature, science, art, civilisation in all its phases, are promoted by nothing so surely as the interchange of ideas and of goods. A universal parcel post would be the harbinger of universal free trade.

THE RAILWAYS AND THE STATE.*

A LITTLE experience is worth much argument; a few facts are better than any theory; the Government manages the Post Office with success; by a great reduction of charges it has created a vast business, and earns a satisfactory revenue; the Government has purchased and successfully reorganised the telegraphs, and is making them pay; therefore the Government ought to buy the railways, and we should then have railway fares reduced to a third of their present amounts, trains very regular, and accidents few or none. Such are, briefly stated, the reflections which have led many persons to join in an agitation, lately increasing, to induce the Government to undertake the gigantic task of acquiring, reorganising, and even working the whole system of railway conveyance in this kingdom. Although many other reasons, of more or less weight, are given for the change advocated, I believe that the main argument, consciously or unconsciously relied upon, is, that *because* the State Post Office and State telegraphs succeed, *therefore* State railways would succeed.

The argument from the Post Office is, in fact, continually appealed to. In his article upon the subject in *The Contemporary Review* of July last, Mr. Arthur Arnold says: " I regard the work of the railways as only a magnified postal system; the carriage of men and women, of boxes and bales,

* " Essays and Addresses, by Professors and Lecturers of Owens College, Manchester," 1874.

differs only in degree from that of letters and packets: as to the business of the State, it is evidently as lawful to do one as to do the other" (p. 248). He says again: "I conceive it possible that some day passengers and goods may travel by railway, as letters and parcels do by post, at one uniform rate —the same whether they be going thirty miles or three hundred" (p. 254). Mr. Galt, in the preface to his prolix work upon "Railway Reform," published in 1865, describes the results of Sir Rowland Hill's postal scheme, and then asserts distinctly: "The same principles applied with equal force to the conveyance of passengers and goods by railway, as to the conveyance of letters by mail-coach" (p. xviii.). In his recent paper, printed in *The Fortnightly Review* for November, he repeats the same notions: "No better illustration could be given of the result that might be anticipated from a reduction in passenger-fares than what our experience affords us during the last thirty years by the reform of our Post Office, and the reductions effected in custom and excise duties. The cases are in every respect analogous" (p. 576).

Exactly similar ideas pervade the paper of Mr. Biddulph Martin, read before the Statistical Society in June last, as well as the speeches of his supporters in the important discussion which followed. Even so profound and experienced a statistician as the president, Dr. Farr, was misled, as I think, into asserting that "the railway system may, like the Post Office, put every station in easy communication with every other station; and some future Rowland Hill may persuade Parliament to do for fares on the State railways what it has done for the postage of letters."

I need hardly stay to demonstrate that facts are valueless unless connected and explained by a correct theory; that analogies are very dangerous grounds of inference, unless carefully founded on similar conditions; and that experience misleads if it be misinterpreted. It is the party advocating State management who indulge in argument, theory, and speculation; and it is my purpose in this Essay to show that their arguments are unsound, their theories false, and their speculations chimerical. They misinterpret experience, they assume some doubtful facts, and they overlook other unquestionable ones; they advocate a measure which is fortunately so nearly impracticable, that there is no appreciable chance of its being carried out, but which, if it really were undertaken, would probably land us in great financial loss and much embarrassment.

All reasoning, no doubt, consists in arguing from case to case: we have experience of one trial, and we infer that what happens in this case will happen in similar cases. But, before drawing any such inference, we must carefully assure ourselves that the cases really are similar. If in regard to State control the railways are similar in economic and mechanical conditions to the Post Office, we may expect them to be successfully managed by a Government department; but if, as I believe, they lie under totally different conditions, the inference would be false, and we must look to quite different experience to teach us the probable result.

In a paper read before the Manchester Statistical Society in April, 1867, as also in evidence given before the Select Committee of the House of Commons on the Electric Telegraphs Bill, in 1868, I advocated the purchase of the telegraphs, on the ground that there was substantial similarity of conditions between the telegraphs and the Post Office. There appear to be four principal conditions under which State management of any branch of industry is successful:

1. The work must be of an invariable and routine-like nature, so as to be performed according to fixed rules.

2. It must be performed under the public eye, or for the service of individuals, who will immediately detect and expose any failure or laxity.

3. There must be very little capital expenditure, so that each year's revenue and expense account shall represent, with approximate accuracy, the real commercial success of the undertaking.

4. The operations must be of such a kind, that their union under one all-extensive Government monopoly will lead to great advantage and economy.

I need hardly point out in detail that these conditions are

almost perfectly fulfilled in the postal system. The public often seem to look upon the Post Office as a prodigy of administrative skill; they imagine that the officers conducting such a department must be endowed with almost superhuman powers to produce such wonderful results. Many of those officials are doubtless men of great ability and energy; nevertheless, it would be more correct to say that the great public services and the satisfactory net revenue of the Post Office are due, not to them, but to the nature of postal communication. As Adam Smith said, "the Post Office is perhaps the only mercantile project which has been successfully managed by every sort of Government." In spite of the defects inherent in all Government management, the Post Office yields a revenue, because the economy arising from a single systematic monopoly is enormously great in this special case.

I must draw attention to one point of postal administration which is entirely overlooked by the advocates of State railways, namely, that the Post Office department has always avoided owning any extensive property. They own the buildings at St. Martin's-le-Grand and the principal offices in some other large towns; but in all the smaller towns and villages they hire accommodation, or merely pay for it in the general remuneration given to the postmasters. For the rapid and regular conveyance of the mails the Post-Office is entirely dependent upon the much-abused railway system, without which, indeed, the post, as we now have it, would be impossible. Not even the horses and vehicles employed in the local collection and distribution of bags are the property of Government, being furnished, I believe, entirely by contract. From the latest report of the Postmaster-General, we learn that the total expenditure of the Postal and Money Order Department in 1872 was £3,685,000, of which £1,682,000 was paid in salaries, wages, and pensions; £928,000 for conveyance by mail-packets and private vessels; £619,000 for conveyance by railways; £145,000 for conveyance by hired coaches, carts, and omnibuses; while only £164,000 was expended upon buildings in the possession of the Post

Office, and upon the taxes, fuel, lights, etc., required in those buildings. The last item, too, was unusually large during the year 1872, owing to an exceptional expenditure of £48,000 on new buildings. On the average of the fifteen years, 1858–1872, the whole expenditure on buildings, repairs, and other requisites has not exceeded £120,000 per annum, in addition to £22,000 or £23,000 a year for mail-bags. Much of the recent expenditure on buildings must be charged, too, on the money order and savings bank business of the department.

The state of things is somewhat different in the Telegraph Department; for though telegraphic work is favourably situated as regards the first, second, and fourth conditions, it involves a considerable amount of capital expenditure. The cost of the telegraphs in the possession of the Postmaster-General already amounts to nine or ten millions, and it will probably have to be increased from time to time. The working of this department will, no doubt, afford us valuable experience in the course of ten years for judging as to the practicability of State interference in other branches of communication; but I hold that the few years yet elapsed since the purchase are insufficient to enable us to estimate the real results. A profuse expenditure of capital is still going on, and large claims against the department are still outstanding. If we must draw inferences, they will, in my opinion, be of an unfavourable character. We learn that in effecting a compulsory purchase even from four or five comparatively weak companies, a premium of about 100 per cent. must be paid by the public. Great indignation has been expressed at the prices which railway companies have to pay in the purchase of land; but equally bad cases might be found in the telegraph bargains. If the reports in the newspapers are to be trusted, the Isle of Man Telegraph Company received £16,106 for their business and property, which allowed a distribution of £11,774 to shareholders, who had paid up £5,000: so poor, however, had been the previous prospects of the company, that the shares might have been bought some years before at 5s. per £20 share, or less than the 160th part of what was obtained from Government. Generally speaking, the holders of telegraph shares received twice as much as the commercial value at which their shares had been previously rated.

In February, 1868, after the telegraph shares had somewhat risen, Mr. Scudamore estimated, in his official report upon the projected purchase, that the property and business of the telegraph companies would cost, at the most, three millions, and, adding £100,000 for the intended extensions, he named £3,100,000 as the required capital of the Department at the outset. In April, 1867, before the shares had risen, I had estimated the purchase-money as not likely much to exceed two and a half millions, to which I added an equal sum for the extension of the property. The actual cost of the scheme as yet cannot be stated at less than three times Mr. Scudamore's estimate, or nearly twice my own.

If we overlook the gigantic blunders made by the Department in conducting the purchase, and pay regard merely to the subsequent financial management of the telegraphs, we find little to give us confidence. Twice has the department defied the Treasury and the House of Commons by spending money without authority—the first time to the extent of £610,000, the second time to that of £893,000; these great sums being drawn from the general balances in the hands of the department, involving a distinct breach of trust as regards the Savings Bank balance. I need hardly mention the details of these extraordinary transactions, which will be familiar to many of my readers. The public seem to have condoned these irregularities with a facility which it is difficult to account for or to acquiesce in. The newspapers said that, if we are to have State telegraphs, we must find bold energetic officers, who will manage them with independence for the good of the public, and will not allow slight difficulties to hamper them. To put forward such a plea is to condemn State control altogether. If the circumlocution inherent in the relations of the Government offices, and the slowness of action of parliamentary Government be such, that the officers of an industrial department cannot successfully carry it on without defying all superior authorities and breaking the laws under which they hold funds, this is the strongest possible objection to State industry. Such difficulties never arose in the postal work, because, as I have said, the capital expenditure is there quite inconsiderable, and the current expenditure very regular in amount, so as to be easily estimated and controlled. Now, if out of a total not yet amounting to ten millions, a Government Department has managed to spend a million and a half without authority, what may we expect if a few energetic officials hold in their hands a property, of which the very lowest valuation is six hundred millions sterling, and a far more probable valuation a thousand millions? The Treasury does not even undertake to manage its own national debt, the work of which is placed in the hands of the Bank of England. I tremble to think what might be the financial results if a property exceeding the national debt in nominal value, and requiring in every part of it constant repairs, renewals, and extensions, were in the hands of a Parliamentary Minister, who might find some day that he had been illegally and ignorantly signing away great sums of money at the bidding of his subordinates.

Coming now to the subject of railways, it must be allowed that railway communication presents some conditions favourable to State control. The larger part of the traffic can be carried on according to a prearranged and published time-table, so that the public, whether in travelling or transmitting goods, will have apparently as good means as in the Post Office of scrutinising the efficiency of the department and exposing any laxity. The union of all railways in one complete system would allow of much economy in superintendence, in the use of the rolling-stock, the avoidance of competing trains, and so forth. The public would be saved from that most annoying circumstance, the missing of a train when passing from the lines of one company to those of another. It is commonly said, too, that enormous advantages will arise to the country when the rates of passenger and goods traffic are arranged with regard to the interests of the people rather than the interests of the shareholders. The elaborate system of classified rates for goods might be done away with, and all goods carried at two or three simple rates, little above the cost of carriage. I shall have to discuss various proposals which have been made, and will now only remark that the success of the Post Office is due to principles of management often exactly the reverse of those which it is supposed that the Government would apply to the railways. Mr. Galt and others strongly object to one kind of goods being charged differently to other kinds, when the cost of conveyance cannot be very different; but the Post Office charges a penny for the lightest letter, while it conveys two ounces of printed matter for a halfpenny. The very different postal rates for books, newspapers, letters, and cards form, in fact, a tariff carefully classified so as to produce a net revenue; and unless the somewhat high rates on sealed letters were maintained this revenue would soon melt away. The Post Office does not pretend to frame its tariff from regard to the cost of the services performed.

When we look more closely into the question of railway management we find all analogy to the Post Office vanishing. Not only is the capital of vast amount, being in 1871 of a total value of £552,682,000, but this capital is represented by property of the most various and complicated nature. There is not only the permanent way, with all its bridges, viaducts, tunnels, embankments, and other works, but thousands of station-buildings of all sizes, warehouses, sheds, repairing-shops, factories, offices, wharves, docks, etc. etc. The locomotive department has the charge of about 10,500 engines, needing constant care and repairs; the rolling-stock department owns about 23,000 passenger carriages, at least 276,000 waggons of various kinds, and other vehicles, making a grand total of more than 312,000, exclusive of locomotives. The railways of the United Kingdom undoubtedly form the most elaborate and extensive system of industrial property existing, and it is strange to reflect that the whole of this vast system has been produced in the last forty years by the genius of British engineers and the enterprise of British men of business. It is especially to be remarked that the property of a railway company forms a connected whole, and in order to secure safety and efficiency every department and every man must work harmoniously with every other.

Now, if we want to know how Government officers would manage such a property, we should look, not to the Post Office, which owns no property of any consequence, but to the Admiralty, which holds the dockyards and maintains a large fleet, or to the department of Public Works. Unless these departments are foully slandered, they are not remarkable for economical management. The waste and jobbery which goes on in them is one of the stock subjects of indignant oratory when Members of Parliament meet their constituents. Mr. Mellor, M.P., a member of the committee which was lately inquiring into the mode in which Government stores were purchased and sold, declined to disclose any facts known to him in that capacity, but cited some cases previously made public. Not long ago, for instance, ten or twelve tons of soldiers' buttons, which had never been taken from their wrappers, were sold as old metal. In the sale of old ships the purchaser has in numerous cases received considerably more for stores on board of the vessel returned than the amount of his purchase-money. Thus *The Medway* of 1,768 tons was sold at Bermuda for £2,180, but the Government repaid the lucky purchaser £4,211 for spare stores; in short, they gave away the remainder of the ship, with £2,041 in addition. Many similar stories, showing the utter want of economy in some Government departments, have, from time to time, been current, and they probably represent a very small fraction of what there might be to tell.

Let us now turn to consider the actual proposals made concerning a reorganisation of the railway system. There are two principal schemes put forward, as follows:

1. The State shall purchase the whole of the railways, and shall undertake all new works and extensions, but shall commit the working of the traffic to contracting companies, who shall lease the lines in large blocks, and manage the traffic under the superintendence of the Railway Minister.

2. The State shall not only purchase the entire aggregate

of railway property, but shall itself work the traffic, in the same manner as the telegraphs are now worked under the Postmaster-General.

It is remarkable that not one of the witnesses examined before the Railway Commission, intimately acquainted as they most of them were with railway traffic, would undertake to recommend the second scheme, though several of them held that great advantages would arise from the plan of leasing the lines in groups. It is especially worthy of notice that an elaborate scheme of the first kind was put forward by Mr. Frederic Hill, of the Post Office Department, in his evidence before the Railway Commission, and it was carefully considered and advocated by his brother Sir Rowland Hill, in his separate report as a member of that Commission. Mr. Frederic Hill has further stated his views in a paper communicated to the meeting of the Social Science Association at Newcastle-upon-Tyne, when they were fully discussed. The details of the scheme are too elaborate to be described here, and must be sought in the Reports of the Commission and of the Social Science Association (p. 450). Although there is much that is valuable in the proposals of these gentlemen, few have been found to concur in their principal suggestions, and the other members of the Commission declined to accept them. What chiefly strikes me in their opinions is the very distinct way in which Sir Rowland Hill and his brother, both possessing the most intimate acquaintance with the working of the postal system, decline to recommend that the Government should itself manage the traffic. Sir Rowland says: "I do not mean to recommend that any Government Board should take upon itself, in the gross, the duty now performed by railway directors. For the direct management of the lines I propose to provide by leasing them out, in convenient groups, to companies, partnerships, or individuals, as the case may be." Mr. Frederic Hill unequivocally asserts, "that it is expedient that the State should purchase the railways, but that it is not expedient that it should undertake their management." While entirely accepting their opinion against Government management, I fail to perceive how their own scheme could be carried out. It involves all the difficulties attaching to the acquisition, ownership, and extension of the vast railway property, and would, at the best, only secure a portion of the advantages arising from the more thorough-going schemes. I am, therefore, inclined to acquiesce in the opinion of Mr. Martin, who remarked that the leasing scheme appeared to be "an ingeniously contrived mixture of the disadvantages of both systems, without a single redeeming advantage."

It is difficult to see how these leasing companies would differ from the present great railway companies, except that, having sold their property to the State at a profit, they would continue to work the traffic in comparative freedom from responsibility as regards the safety of travelling, or its financial results. Let it be especially remarked, too, that such a proposal runs directly contrary to all experience derived from the Post Office, which, as already stated, confines itself to the conduct of the traffic, while depending upon contractors, especially upon railway companies and steamboat owners, for the use of all fixed property. Nevertheless, it is seriously proposed that in the case of the railways the State should purchase, construct, own, and repair the fixed property, but should leave individuals to compete for the conduct of the traffic. Perhaps the best-established empirical generalisation in political economy—Mr. Mill's opinions to the contrary notwithstanding—is, that the State is the worst of landlords; and it is now seriously proposed to make it the landlord of the whole railway system. It would surely be a much more sensible suggestion that the Government should be the leaseholder, and while leaving the permanent way and other fixed property in the hands of the present companies, under contracts to maintain and repair them as required, should confine its own work to carrying on the traffic in a manner analogous to the postal system. Even to this arrangement, however, there are insuperable objections, especially the fatal division of authority and responsibility which it would produce. Unity of management is the prime condition of efficiency and safety in so complicated a system as that of railway conveyance.

I proceed to discuss in more detail the objections to the second scheme, that the Government should both purchase and work the railways. I dismiss, as of no account, some of the evils attributed to it, as, for instance, the great patronage and political influence which it would place in the hands of the Cabinet. My objections are, that it would realise very few of the prodigious advantages anticipated from it, and that it would probably be a disastrous financial operation. It is impossible that I should find space in this Essay to explain fully the objections arising against the scheme; I must confine myself chiefly to showing that the great advantages expected to accrue from it are illusory, founded on false analogies, and generally inconsistent *inter se*. Government is to give us low fares, better carriages, punctual trains, universal through booking; it is to carry workmen daily to and from their work at nominal charges, to convey goods at cost price, to distribute the mails free of cost, to do away with all the differential charges which enable some companies to earn a fair dividend, while it is at the same time to reap a net revenue from railway traffic, over and above the present average dividends and interest on loans, and in due time to pay off the National Debt.

Assuming for the moment that the notion of the English Government purchasing and working the whole of the railways is conceivable, my picture of the results would be very different. In the first instance the Government would pay from 50 to 100 per cent. more than the property is commercially worth; the economy arising from unity and centralisation of management would be more than counterbalanced by the want of economy in the purchase, use, and sale of stores; the Government must either manage vast factories for making and repairing engines, carriages, and all the complicated machinery of the permanent way, or it must be continually buying by contract and selling waste stores again, with the pecuniary advantages familiar to us in the case of the Admiralty Department. In planning extensions it must stir up all kinds of local interests and intense agitation and competition, and all the struggles of the Committee-rooms would be repeated in another and perhaps a more corrupt form. In adjusting claims for compensation, whether for lands taken for extensions, for patent rights appropriated, or for personal injuries suffered, great difficulties would arise; the probability is, judging from experience in like matters before, that the landowners would get as exorbitant prices as ever, while the patentees and the unmoneyed persons would go the wall. The Post Office *never* pays compensation, even for the loss of registered letters, and the Telegraph Department is following the same principle in disclaiming all pecuniary liability for negligence or accident in the performance of its work. The public, though it could not enforce private claims, would expect all sorts of remissions of charges, just as it is now urging upon the Telegraph Department the reduction of charges to 6d. per message. The Railway Minister would be the rival in importance of the Chancellor of the Exchequer, and it would be impossible for him to bring forward a budget showing a satisfactory surplus without raising clamours for the remission of railway taxation, as it would be called. In the complication of the accounts the railway budget would far surpass that of the ordinary revenue and expenditure, and would deal with larger sums of money. Unless these accounts were kept in a manner very different from those of any Government Departments yet known, difficult questions about capital and current expenditure would creep in, and doubts would arise as to the real financial position of the greatest property ever put under the management of a single man. Royal Commissions and Select Committees would sit from time to time to endeavour to seek out the truth, but unless their success was much greater than that of similar bodies which have inquired into other branches of the public accounts and expenditure, they would not save the financial condition of the railways from falling into confusion. No English Government Department has ever yet, I believe, furnished a real balance sheet, showing the actual commercial results of a year's work, with allowance for capital invested, unless it be the Post Office, which, as I have said, has little or no capital expenditure to account for.

Such would be the character of the results to be expected from State purchase of the railways, judging by experience from the other branches of administration most closely analogous. It is, of course, impossible to say exactly in what degree each particular evil would manifest itself, and there would, no doubt, be some considerable national advantages to partially counterbalance the evils. What I wish more especially to show in the remainder of this Essay is, however, that the great advantages expected from Government management are of a chimerical character. The argument that men and women and trunks can be posted about like letters, is akin to that which leads a man every now and then to jump off his own house-top, because, as it is a mere question of degree, he ought, with suitable apparatus, to be able to fly like the birds.

One of the principal advantages to be gained from the State purchase of railways, in Mr. Galt's opinion, is a great reduction of fares, perhaps to a third of their present amounts. As this reduction would lead to a great increase of traffic, probably three times that at present existing, the trains would be much better filled; he even holds that, with the economical arrangements which a Government Department would adopt, this threefold traffic might be conducted with an *absolutely smaller* number of trains than run at present. The only point admitting of serious controversy in this scheme concerns the average number of passengers now carried in a train. An interesting discussion arose several years since in *The Times* upon train weights, and it was shown by Mr. B. Haughton, of the engineering staff of the London and North-Western Railway, that for every ton of passengers carried in a train there are twenty tons of dead and non-paying weight; even in the goods traffic the train weighs more than twice what it conveys. The question thus raised is partly one of mechanics, partly of traffic management. If safe and durable carriages of less weight could be constructed, a great saving would doubtless arise; but I see no reason whatever to suppose that a single Government office would be likely to effect improvements in mechanical construction which all the competing, dividend-earning companies, with their talented engineers, have been unable to effect.

There only remains, then, the question of filling the present trains much more full of passengers. The average number at present carried in a train is no doubt remarkably small. In 1865 Mr. Galt stated that the average number of passengers carried by each train was 71, or, including season-ticket holders, probably about 74. Excluding, however, the summer excursion traffic, he thought that the real average of the ordinary traffic was not more than 50 per train, and the chief ground of all his plans was the suggestion that, instead of 50, an average of 150 passengers might easily be carried in each train, without any appreciable extra cost.

The advocates of low fares seem entirely to forget that a train must be provided to accommodate the maximum, rather than the minimum, number of passengers. Passenger traffic is a most fluctuating and uncertain thing; the state of the weather, the season of the year, the days of the week, the occurrence of markets, fairs, races, public meetings, holidays, excursions, and events of all kinds, affect the numbers who travel by any train, and it is not within the powers of human wisdom so to vary the capacity of the trains from day to day that there shall always be sufficient accommodation, and little to spare. The difficulty is much increased by the necessity of consulting the comfort of passengers by providing three classes of carriages, distinct compartments for smokers and non-smokers, and especially *through-carriages* between important towns. A train thus contains, say, from five to twelve different kinds of passengers requiring distinct accommodation, and any passengers reasonably complain if they cannot find room in the kind of carriage for which they have paid, or if they have another class of fellow-passengers thrust upon them.

If it were the custom of railway companies to aim at filling their trains, the passengers would have to be almost indiscriminately mingled together; smokers and non-smokers would have to come to terms, through-carriages would have to be abolished, and, in fact, all that renders railway travelling tolerable would have to be relinquished. Moreover, when any accidental circumstance gave rise to a pressure of traffic, many passengers would inevitably be left behind at wayside stations. Now, men and women and children are not like goods, which can be laid aside for a few hours, or a day or two, until the pressure is over. They are greatly irritated and inconvenienced when delayed a few hours, and in the case of long prearranged journeys, or business engagements, detention from the want of train accommodation would be simply intolerable. In the case of omnibus traffic the vehicles can often be filled, because the distances are small, and the passengers left behind have the alternatives of waiting a few minutes for the next omnibus, or taking a cab, or, if it comes to the worst, walking. Omnibus trains running short distances, such as those on the Metropolitan Railways, can be filled pretty well on the same system, and it is not uncommon to have to wait for the next train. Reasonable complaints are made at present concerning the unpunctuality of travelling, and occasional detention from the failure of correspondence between trains; but this is nothing to what would happen if any attempt were made to fill carriages, on an average, say three-quarters full. Cheapness of travelling is not the chief benefit of railway conveyance; we gain still more from its rapidity, safety, certainty, regularity, frequency, and comfort. Millions of journeys are made in Metropolitan Railway trains, in spite of the bad air, at a cost of $4d.$ or $6d.$ or $8d.$, instead of by omnibus for $2d.$ or $3d.$ or $4d.$, simply to save time and trouble.

In order to reduce fares in any great degree, without incurring bankruptcy, every kind of retrograde measure would have to be adopted. In place of frequent half-filled rapid trains, a small number of large, slow, crowded trains, stopping at many stations, would have to be adopted, as on many Continental railways. Frequent changes at junctions would have to be made by those travelling to great distances, and the loss in time, trouble, and temper would more than balance any gain in money. Cheapness is not everything.

One of the wildest suggestions which has been made is to the effect that uniform fares for journeys of every length should be adopted. A gentleman proposed, I believe at a meeting of the Social Science Association, that passengers should be carried any distance at the nominal cost of 1*s*. first class, 6*d*. second class, and 3*d*. third class. He calculated that with a moderate increase of traffic this plan would produce a net increase of revenue of several millions yearly. Why not go a little further and carry passengers, like letters, for a penny stamp? Many people appear to have got a notion that there is some magical efficacy in low uniform rates, so that they are sure to produce a great net revenue. I can imagine no grounds for the notion except the great success of Sir Rowland Hill's penny postage. I believe it is the false argument from analogy again, that, because the Post Office pays with low uniform rates, therefore telegraphs and railways must pay under similar regulations. It would be interesting to learn how many persons, who in the present day admire and discuss the results of Sir Rowland Hill's reform, have ever taken the trouble to look into the original pamphlet in which he demonstrated the practicability of a uniform penny rate. They would there discover that his scheme was founded upon a most careful and scientific investigation into the cost of collecting, conveying, and distributing letters. He showed that even when the mails were carried by coach the average cost of conveying a letter from London to Edinburgh was only a 36th part of a penny. He concludes:* "If, therefore, the charge for postage be made proportionate to the whole expense incurred in the receipt, transit, and delivery of the letter, and in the collection of its postage, it must be made uniformly the same from every post town to every other post town in the United Kingdom, unless it can be shown how we are to collect so small a sum as the 36th part of a penny." He advocated a uniform rate mainly on the ground that it was more nearly proportional to *cost price* than any other which could be levied, the costs of collection, sorting, delivery, superintendence, etc., being by far the most important items, and being the same whatever was the distance between the points of receipt and delivery. The same considerations apply, but in a somewhat

---

* "Post Office Reform; its Importance and Practicability." By Rowland Hill. London, 1837, p. 19.

less degree, to telegraphy. It requires but little, if any, more time to send a message a longer than a shorter distance. The terminal charges for collection, the time of the operator, and that of the delivering messenger still form a large part of the whole cost; but the varying extent of the wires employed, and the number of times the message has to be re-transmitted, create some difference between the cost of different telegrams.

In railway conveyance totally different conditions exist. The larger part of the cost of conveyance is proportional to the distance travelled, arising from the consumption of fuel, the wear and tear of the rolling stock and permanent way, the wages of the engine-drivers, stokers, guards, and other persons whose time is occupied, together with the interest upon the capital invested in the property which is employed. It is only the terminal cost of station accommodation, clerks, porters, superintendence, etc., which are the same for a long and a short journey, and even these would not be the same if the passenger on a long journey had to change carriages often, requiring additional station accommodation, re-booking, assistance of porters, etc. It is quite absurd, then, to apply to railway passengers, each weighing perhaps, on an average, five thousand times as much as a letter, any arguments founded on Post Office economy.

Schemes of uniform charges are almost equally impracticable, whether the uniformity is to extend over the whole kingdom, or only over defined distances. In the former case the uniform rate must either be so high as to constitute a huge tax on locomotion over short distances, or so low as to form a great premium on long journeys, producing a vast financial loss, which would have to be borne by the people through general taxation. If the charge is to be uniform only between limits, one charge for distances under ten miles, another for all distances under fifty miles, and so on, the absurdity of the proposal is much less obvious, but the practical difficulties would be found to be insuperable. Arbitrary boundaries would have to be drawn round every large town, on passing which the fare would become much greater.

Barriers, far worse than any toll-bars, would be thus erected between town and country, and between one district and another.

One very plausible argument in favour of the transfer of the railways to the State is the profit which, it is represented, may be made out of the employment of public credit. The Chancellor of the Exchequer can borrow money at about $3\frac{1}{4}$ per cent. per annum, whereas a railway company cannot borrow under 4 per cent., and the average return to railway investments is about $4\frac{1}{2}$ per cent. It seems, then, that by borrowing money at $3\frac{1}{4}$, and employing it in a business which, even when badly managed, pays $4\frac{1}{2}$, there would be a clear profit of $1\frac{1}{4}$, which, upon a property of the value of five hundred millions, would give a clear revenue of six millions and a quarter annually. Nothing, however, could be more fallacious and unsound in every respect than such suggestions.

The good credit of the English Treasury merely means that all engagements will be paid. Railway companies are obliged to borrow on higher terms, because it is not sure that they will be able to declare dividends or pay interest on debentures when due, as many people have found to their cost. Now, if a Government Department undertakes to manage the railways they are bound to pay dividends, but unless they manage better than the companies they are likely to incur losses in some part of the business, which losses must be borne by the general revenue. The apparent net revenue of six millions and a quarter represents approximately the amount of loss to be expected. If the State manages the railways just with the same degree of skill and success as the companies, there would then be no gain or loss; if better, there would be gain accruing, not from good credit, but from good management; if worse, there would be certain loss. Thus, in theory, the use of the public credit proves to be a pure fallacy, and, if it were not so, there would be no reason why the Treasury should not proceed to invest money in many kinds of industrial enterprises besides railways and telegraphs.

When we come to look into the details of the financial

operations by which the transfer would have to be effected, it will be found that loss is almost certain to every body of persons except the shareholders. It is not to be supposed that any shareholder will consent to have his income reduced by the sale of his property. Thus, a person holding £10,000 in railway debenture stock, or good preference shares, paying say 4½ per cent., or £450, will require at the least such an amount of Consols as will pay the same annual income, namely, £15,000, which, at the present market price, would be worth £13,800. The operation must really involve a great loss to the State, because it gives a certain income instead of a somewhat precarious one. As a matter of fact, it can hardly be seriously supposed that railway property could be purchased at its present market value. All the ordinary stockholders would claim compensation for prospective gains, and during the discussion of the project there would be an enormous rise in the value of the shares. During the recent abortive agitation for the purchase of the Irish railways, the market price of the shares in one company rose from 8 to 37, and in other cases the rise was from 13¼ to 37½, from 33 to 84, from 46 to 65, from 66 to 93, from 99 to 112, and so on.

Now, the railway shareholders of the United Kingdom are almost co-extensive with the wealthy and influential classes. Those Members of Parliament who are not actually railway directors are probably, with few exceptions, shareholders, and it cannot be expected that they would consent to any sacrifice of their legitimate interests. The actual value of such a property as the whole railway system is a matter of speculation, but whoever suffers in the transfer, we may be sure that it will not be the shareholders or debenture-holders. If we may at all judge from experience furnished by the transfer of the telegraphs, everyone interested in railway property should agitate for its purchase by the State as the surest mode of increasing his own fortune.

There is yet another fallacy committed by the advocates of State purchase. They assume that because the Government have borrowed several hundred millions of money at 3¼ per cent., therefore they can borrow six hundred or a thousand millions more at the same rate. Such an assumption is totally unwarranted, and is opposed to the undoubted laws of supply and demand. Because there is a certain demand for Consols at 92 to the amount of seven or eight hundred millions, it follows almost inevitably that there would not be a demand for double the amount at the same price. There are a certain number of investors who prefer or require perfect security. To a great extent these investors are artificially created by the laws which oblige trustees and many public institutions to invest their property in the funds. There is another portion of the funds temporarily held by bankers, insurance companies, or other companies or persons having a floating balance of money. Other large portions are held by private individuals having a traditional attachment to the Three per Cents., or whose property has always been thus invested, and has descended to them in that shape. Now, it cannot be supposed that if another National Debt, equal to that already existing, were created, it could be absorbed by the same classes of investors. The ordinary railway shareholder is a more enterprising person than the Government annuitant. He would no sooner receive his share of the New Consols, equal in capital value to double the market value of his old shares, by paying the same or rather more annual income, than he would begin to think of getting 5 per cent. for his money instead of $3\frac{1}{4}$. He would seek for home or foreign investments of somewhat the same degree of risk and profit as his old shares, and unless the funds had already fallen considerably, he would assist their downward course by selling out. The old fundholders, unless they had foreseen the course of events, and sold out in good time, would thus suffer a serious depreciation of the market value of their property, whenever they had to sell it, and it would at the same time be quite out of the question to admit any right to compensation on their part, as this would establish a right to compensation on any future occasion when the Government might need loans, and thus lower the funds. State purchase would then, as it seems to me, resolve itself into an enormous job, by which shareholders would make their fortunes at the expense of fundholders, and of operatives and other un-moneyed persons.

Coming now to perhaps the most important point of the whole discussion, I must remind the reader of the fact stated above, that the Government will gain or lose by the railways, according as it manages them better or worse than the present companies. There are a few so undoubted advantages in unity of organisation, that, if not counterbalanced by the general laxity and want of economy in the care of Government property, a profit of some millions annually would thence arise. But in order that any such profit should continue to exist, the Government must work the railways at the rates which will pay best. It must make the railways a revenue department, like the Post Office, which takes care not to render its services at cost price. But the very writers who advocate State purchase, and tempt the public with glowing pictures of the profits to be thence derived, not to speak of the ultimate redemption of the National Debt, also tempt the public by promising a reduction of fares to a third of their present amounts. Now, these things are quite incompatible. If fares were much reduced, either the public must put up with very great inconvenience and discomfort in travelling, or else all net revenue must be sacrificed, and travellers must even travel to some extent at the cost of those who stay at home. We are told that there would be a great increase of traffic, and that, therefore, there would be a great increase of profits; but this argument is a complete *non-sequitur*, arising probably from false analogy to the Post Office business. In these days of high prices the butcher or coal dealer who should sell his goods below cost price would doubtless have an enormous business, so long as his capital held out. The railways would be in exactly the same position, except that they could carry on the process indefinitely by supplying the deficit out of the general revenue. Few people seem ever to reflect that postal communication stands in a very peculiar financial position, so that to argue from it to other kinds of business is to commit the logical fallacy of inferring from the special to the general. Its chief peculiarity is, that an increase of work done will not occasion a proportionate increase of cost. If twice the number of letters are collected and delivered, the labour of stamping and sorting is nearly twice as great, but almost all the other expenses increase in a very minor degree. The mails are of so small a weight in general, that the cost of conveyance is but little, if at all greater: this is true, at least of the letters, though not so strictly true of the newspapers and books, which form by far the least profitable part of the postal traffic. Finally, the cost of distribution is by no means proportional to the number, because the additional letters will often be delivered at houses which the postman would in any case have visited, and it can hardly be said to be more laborious to deliver ten letters than one. When additional letters are delivered at houses previously receiving none, these houses will usually lie within the circuit of the postman, so that his labour and time in making the distribution will not be much increased. The more, too, correspondence increases, the more obvious this source of economy becomes. If every house in the kingdom received a letter every day, and there were no heavy books or other matter to load the men unduly, then as regards the mere distribution, apart from sorting, the very same postman could deliver twice as many letters with hardly any increase of cost.

In the case of the railway passenger traffic, almost everything is different. Unless the comfort and certainty of conveyance are to be reduced, double the number of passengers must have nearly double the number of carriages, locomotives, engine-drivers, guards, etc. The station accommodation must be much increased, and more porters, clerks, and servants generally must be employed. It may sometimes happen that double accommodation more than doubles the cost, because in large towns and other confined positions very costly engineering works may be required to give additional space. No doubt, when a line of rails is but little used, it may be made to do double the work, and thus pay nearly double profit. Many of the chief lines in the kingdom, however, are already so overburdened with traffic, that expensive precautions must be taken to insure safety and efficiency, and an increase in that traffic involves a constant increase both of capital and current expenditure. This is the main difficulty in railway economy at the present time, and it will continue to be so.

Now, the railway reformers declaim at the same time against the extravagant expenditure of capital by the present companies and the high rates of charges. They do not seem to see that a reduction of charges would necessitate a further great expenditure of capital. It requires the utmost skill and care in the present traffic-managers to meet the strain upon the carrying powers of their lines occasioned by the progressive natural increase of traffic, and, if all the railways were managed by a few great officials in London, they would indeed require supernatural skill to carry, say a double or treble weight of persons and goods upon the same lines with equal speed and general efficiency. Yet this is what the railway reformers really contemplate and promise.

The general conclusion at which I arrive concerning the schemes of Government purchase is, that they are absolutely impracticable, and that the time, labour, print, and paper spent upon the discussion are wasted. Before I bring this Essay to a close, however, I wish briefly to examine the grounds upon which objections are raised to our present system. I feel sure that those objections are to a great extent erroneous, and that in many points the schemes put forward would greatly aggravate such evils as are at present existing.

There can be no doubt, for instance, that the punctuality of the passenger service has in the last two or three years been gradually growing less satisfactory, and much attention has been drawn to an apparent excess of railway accidents. I should like to see complete and accurate statistics of these accidents, and compare them with the amounts of traffic, before attaching so much importance to them as has of late been attributed to them by the newspapers. But taking, for the sake of argument, the worst view of matters—to what are such unfavourable results due? There is absolutely no evidence that railway management is becoming more lax; on the contrary, it is well known that the block system, and improved methods of signalling, are being gradually applied to all the lines of the kingdom; that the main trunk lines are in some cases being doubled; that stations and other necessary works are being extended at great cost; that the wages of railway servants are in many cases being raised and hours shortened; the tendency at least is always in the direction of improvement. How, then, do the results become worse? Simply, as I think, because the ever-growing traffic is overtaking the capacity of the lines and works. The effect is felt during these years, partly owing to the general activity of trade, which increases all branches of traffic, and places money in the pockets of the people, enabling them to spend more freely in travelling, and partly owing to the introduction of third-class carriages into nearly all trains, which measure has amounted to a substantial reduction of fares and extension of accommodation. The simple fact is, that many parts of the railway system are already worked beyond their safe capacity. There are not a few stations where three hundred trains, or more, pass in the twenty-four hours. When waiting for a short time at some of the great junctions, such as those of Crewe, Chester, Willesden, etc., I have often wondered at the system of management by which trains are successfully loaded and despatched every few minutes, and traffic of the most complicated description is regulated almost without a hitch. But, if traffic continuously increases, there must also be a continuous increase of station accommodation, sidings, spare lines of rails, and other means of avoiding the interference of one train with others. It unfortunately happens that the reconstruction of great stations is a most costly work. The public would not be satisfied with stations outside of the towns, and the new stations are for the most part situated in the very centres of trade and city traffic, where land is enormously expensive. The London and North-Western have recently spent half a million in the enlargement of the Lime Street Station at Liverpool, and before long they will have to spend nearly as much in a thorough reconstruction of the Victoria Station at Manchester. In both towns other large and central stations are in course of construction. Of the vast expenditure upon the numerous large metropolitan stations it is hardly necessary to speak. Allowing that the cost of travelling is somewhat higher in this country than on the Continent, I hold that for what we pay we get, as a general rule, services unparalleled in excellence.

The conclusive mode of deciding, as it seems to me, whether railways are badly and oppressively managed in this country will be to inquire whether, as a matter of fact, people are deterred from travelling by railways on account of the cost and danger. Every institution must be tried by its results, and if our railways are so much worse conducted than those of other countries, the proof ought to be found in the smallness of the traffic. I do not find that any of the writers who complain about our railways have taken the trouble to ascertain the comparative numbers of railway travellers in different countries. In the time which is at my disposal for the preparation of this Essay, I have not been able to discover the number of railway passengers on the much-praised railway system of Belgium, but so far as we can judge from France the advantage is vastly on our side. I find that in 1869 there were 111,164,284 separate journeys on the French railways, which, compared with a population of about thirty-eight millions, shows that each person on an average travelled not quite three times. Now, in the United Kingdom the number of railway passengers in 1867 was 287,807,904, which compared with 30,335,000, the estimated population for that year, shows that every inhabitant of the United Kingdom travelled on the average almost nine and a half times, or more than three times as often as an inhabitant of France. The use of the railways, too, seems to be very rapidly advancing in this country; for in 1870 every inhabitant of the United Kingdom travelled on the average 10·8 times by railway, and in 1871, not less than 11·8 times. Moreover, in these calculations no account is taken of the unknown number of journeys of the holders of season and periodical tickets. Estimate it how we will, the state of the passenger traffic in this country is very satisfactory.

People are fond of pointing to the Post Office as an example of the benefits of Government administration directed solely to the promotion of the public good; but between 1858 and 1870, the total number of letters delivered in the United Kingdom rose only from 545 millions to 863 millions, or by less than 59 per cent., whereas the number of railway passengers sprung up from 139 millions in 1858 to 336 millions, an increase of 141 per cent., being considerably more than twice the rate of increase of letters. If later returns were taken the results of comparison would be still more striking, owing to the recent great increase of third-class passengers. The Postmaster-General, too, lately discovered that he had been greatly over-estimating the numbers of letters delivered, the number for 1871 being stated now at 870 millions, instead of 915 millions as in the previous report. This vast error of 45 millions of letters, one of the largest errors I have ever heard of, does not increase our confidence in the Post Office statistics, and we are not informed how many years are affected by similar errors. The result of comparison must be in any case to show that these much-abused railway companies, acting only, as it is said, for the benefit of their shareholders, have yet developed business far more than the much-praised Post Office.

Taking all circumstances into account, there can be no doubt that England and Wales are better supplied with railways than any other country in the world. The comparison is complicated by the fact that countries differ very much in the density of population, and, as truly remarked by Mr. Dudley Baxter, it is absurd to suppose that the mountainous and thinly populated districts of Wales, Scotland, and the North of England, and Ireland, could be as closely reticulated by railways as the small, flat, densely-peopled kingdom of Belgium. Now the comparison of the area, population, and length of railways in the principal States of Europe gives the following results:

	Population per square mile.	Square miles of area to each linear mile of railway.
Belgium	451	6
England and Wales	389	5
Netherlands	291	13
United Kingdom	265	8
Italy	237	27
Prussia	180	19
Ireland	169	15
France	150	19

We find, then, that England and Wales are better supplied with railways in the proportion of 6 to 5 when compared with Belgium, although their population is less dense in the ratio of 389 to 451. Combining these two ratios, we discover that the length of railways here exceeds by 39 per cent. that in the best supplied Continental kingdom, regard being had both to population and area. This comparison is with respect to length only; if we looked to the comparative costs of the railway systems, which more nearly measure the difficulties encountered and the accommodation offered, the contrast would be far more striking. English railways cost about two and a half times as much per mile as those of the small kingdom of Belgium.

One of the chief complaints raised against the present state of railway conveyance refers to the high rates charged both for passengers and goods on British railways. Mr. Galt stated in 1866 that a person could travel 100 miles in a first-class carriage in Belgium for 6s. 6d., in Prussia for 13s., while in the United Kingdom it would cost 18s. 9d. The Royal Commission upon Railways carefully investigated this subject, and their conclusions only partially bear out Mr. Galt's statements. They found that the average rates of charge in the principal European countries are as in the following table, the numbers denoting in pennies, and fractions of a penny, the cost of travelling an English mile:

	England.	France.	Prussia.	Austria.	Belgium.
First Class	2·11	1·73	1·57	1·87	1·23
Second ,,	1·51	1·30	1·17	1·41	·93
Third ,,	·92	·95	·80	·94	·62

There can thus be no doubt that the fares are higher here than in any Continental country, and compared with Belgium the excess is considerable. But the Commissioners point out that, before we come to any safe conclusion, other circumstances must be taken into account. It is not usual to have to pay anything for luggage on British railways, whereas such charges are frequent and heavy on Continental railways. Considerable reductions are here made upon return and season tickets, which are seldom allowed abroad. It is also to be noted that the low first-class rates are often found to be delusive, as long journeys must almost of necessity be made in express trains for which the rates are higher.

We should also take into account the much greater average speed of English trains, and the much better accommodation (always excepting refreshments) offered in the English railway stations. Third-class passengers can now travel in express trains at fifty miles an hour for less than a penny a mile. In the comfort of the carriages, however, the foreign railways are before us.

Before we could really decide whether the cost of travelling in this country is excessive, we should have to compare the general cost of living here and elsewhere. If railway fares are high, it is also easy to show, indeed it is a common complaint, that the wages of operatives are high, that prices of provisions are high, that the cost of land especially is high. Except possibly in the case of the unfortunate agricultural labourers, all classes in this country are more highly paid and live at a higher rate than in other European countries, and under those circumstances it is quite to be expected that travelling should be somewhat more costly. Now, if the advocates of State purchase wanted thoroughly to establish their case, they ought to show that in spite of the higher cost of things in England, the English Government manages to carry out other branches of administration at a lower expense than other nations. But if inquiry were made into the cost at which we maintain a soldier or a sailor, it would be found that our Government pays a great deal more than any other European State. The profuse and uneconomical expenditure upon our army and fleet is a perennial source of discontent, expressed both in and out of Parliament. Some of this excess may be explained as due to exceptional circumstances in our position, but much is due to the essentially higher rates of salaries, wages, and prices in this country. Thus the late Colonel Sykes, in comparing the extent and expenditure of the English and French navies in 1865, pointed out* the greatly higher

* "Journal of the Statistical Society" for March, 1866, vol. xxix. p. 61.

rates of pay and allowances to officers and men, and the greater cost of provisions and clothing in the English navy. Yet the same Government, which is always wasting money on its army and navy, is to work miracles of economical management in the vastly more extensive, complicated, and delicate system of railway conveyance!

I must say, in conclusion, that I am perfectly aware of many evils and abuses existing in our present railway system. The charges for the conveyance of goods appear to be excessive in many cases, and it is remarkable that the goods traffic has not increased in anything like the same ratio as the passenger or the mineral traffic. There can be no doubt, too, that the arbitrary manner in which companies impose high rates where they have got the traffic safe, and lower them where traffic is to be attracted, gives rise to great grievance. It certainly seems to be quite intolerable that an almost irresponsible board of directors should be able to tax a town or a district after a fashion upon which the Chancellor of the Exchequer could never venture. The rates for the carriage of parcels, too, are very excessive and arbitrary; the whole of the arrangements, indeed, for the transmission of small goods in England are in a chaotic and utterly absurd state. It is in this direction, I believe, that the next important measure of Government management ought to turn.

I do not for a moment wish to assert that any railway company has acquired such right to a monopoly that it may go on indefinitely charging the public at unreasonable rates, nor do I think it right that a company should be allowed to make excessive profits from some portions of its lines to counterbalance the loss upon other portions. My argument is to the effect that the present companies do on the whole render better services to the public than those of any other railway system which can be brought into comparison with ours, and at charges which are, when all circumstances are taken into account, as low or lower than those elsewhere existing, as proved by the great numbers who do travel by railway. But in whatever points exceptions to this favourable state of things can be shown to exist, Parliament ought to apply strong remedies. The appointment of Railway Commissioners by the recent Act is a step in the right direction. If their powers are found to be insufficient to enable them to control the companies and prevent them from inflicting injustice, then their powers must be increased until they can carry out efficiently the purposes for which they were appointed. It is by applying ourselves to devise and create a judicious system of control and reform in details, and not by chimerical schemes of Government purchase, that we may really hope to improve and cheapen railway communication in the United Kingdom.

THE END.

CHARLES DICKENS AND EVANS, CRYSTAL PALACE PRESS.

www.ingramcontent.com/pod-product-compliance
Lightning Source LLC
Chambersburg PA
CBHW032022220426
43664CB00006B/334